Social Trends in American Life

Social Trends in American Life

Findings from the General Social Survey since 1972

Edited by Peter V. Marsden

PRINCETON UNIVERSITY PRESS

Princeton and Oxford

Copyright © 2012 by Princeton University Press
Published by Princeton University Press, 41 William Street, Princeton, New Jersey 08540
In the United Kingdom: Princeton University Press, 6 Oxford Street, Woodstock,
Oxfordshire OX20 1TW

press.princeton.edu

Library of Congress Cataloging-in-Publication Data

Social trends in American life : findings from the General Social Survey since 1972 / edited by
Peter V. Marsden.
     p. cm.
  Includes bibliographical references and index.
  ISBN 978-0-691-13331-7 (hbk. : alk. paper) — ISBN 978-0-691-15590-6 (pbk. : alk. paper)
1. Public opinion—United States. 2. Social surveys—United States. 3. United States—Social
conditions.   I. Marsden, Peter V.
  HN90.P8S63 2012
  303.3'8–dc23   2012018841

British Library Cataloging-in-Publication Data is available

This book has been composed in Minion and Myriad

Printed on acid-free paper. ∞

Printed in the United States of America

10 9 8 7 6 5 4 3 2 1

To James A. Davis

Contents

Preface and Acknowledgments

In the fall of 1971, James A. Davis requested National Science Foundation support for a project titled "Twenty-some Questions: A National Data Program for Sociology." The idea was to assemble survey data covering a wide range of sociological topics for a representative sample of the U.S. adult population and distribute them immediately and cheaply to all interested researchers. Davis's proposal suggested specifically that some 20 questions—on such topics as race relations, happiness, and trust in people—be added to an ongoing "omnibus" survey that already measured basic sociodemographic characteristics such as sex, race, and education. In retrospect, his proposal seems very modest.

That proposal led to the initial (1972) round of the General Social Survey (GSS). As actually implemented, it contained many more than the 20 questions of interest to social scientists that Davis had argued for, together with items from other projects about fluoridation of water supplies, dental care, national health care, hobbies and extracurricular activities for children, and playing musical instruments. The GSS became a stand-alone survey a year later.

Among signature features of that first GSS were its broad topical diversity and its commitment to timely and widespread dissemination of data— the latter a quite novel concept at the time, commonplace though it has become in the Internet age. Among the project's principal goals was advancing research and teaching in the social sciences by making high-quality social survey data accessible to students; as a 1973 Dartmouth College senior, I was an early beneficiary of this. It also sought to allow researchers to easily replicate, reexamine, and check each other's findings by making primary data available to all. Davis envisioned a program of repeated surveys, stressing standardized survey procedures—especially regular representative sampling of the U.S. adult population and administering particular items "in unchanged form each time"—in order to measure time trends.

Since then, the GSS has grown into a large and very widely used database— not only in its home discipline of sociology, but across the social sciences. Thousands of published research articles and books draw on its data, now comprising survey responses by more than 55,000 independently drawn Americans. Hundreds of thousands of students annually use the GSS while learning statistical methods or preparing research papers and projects. From time to time, topical modules question respondents in greater depth about particular subjects, and the range of subjects itself has grown to include such topics as sexual behavior, gay marriage, immigration attitudes, and contemporary racial stereotypes, among many others. Beginning in the mid-1980s, collaboration between the GSS and similar projects conducted elsewhere in the world developed the International Social Survey Programme, which facilitates internationally comparative survey research.

The essays in this book highlight the GSS's value as a resource for studying U.S. social change as reflected by attitude and behavior trends that now extend over more than three decades. At least one of the contributing authors of each chapter has long experience and deep familiarity with the GSS project, either as a principal investigator or as a member of its Board of Overseers. Several of them have previously published trend analyses based on the GSS that cover shorter time spans, as many other social scientists have. This book is distinctive, however, in presenting a set of trend analyses covering a range of topics that—taken together—sketch broad contours of recent U.S. change in phenomena including intergroup attitudes, political orientations, religious beliefs and behaviors, social connectedness, and subjective well-being. The value of the GSS database grows with each additional round, which not only portrays the state of social life in U.S. society at a particular point in time, but additionally adds to a growing archive of prospectively collected information tracking change in the views of ordinary Americans.

* * * * *

This book would not have been possible without the sustained support and dedication of numerous individuals and institutions needed to develop and maintain a program of ongoing survey data collection to monitor the state of U.S. society. Many agencies and foundations have provided the necessary financial resources for the National Data Program for the Social Sciences over the years. The most substantial and enduring funding comes from a series of awards made by the Sociology Program at the National Science Foundation—the most recent of which is cooperative agreement SES-0824618—that support collecting and disseminating GSS data. These awards fund the collection of the "replicating core" items on which the trend analyses in this book center and much additional GSS content. Of course, any opinions, findings, and conclusions or recommendations expressed in this material are those of the authors and do not necessarily reflect the views of the National Science Foundation.

Above and beyond financial support is the often-underappreciated intellectual and technical expertise required by a data collection and dissemination project that extends over decades. More individuals than I could hope to name here have contributed to the GSS in these ways, but it would not be what it is without the unmatched and unmatchable commitment of Director Tom W. Smith, whose encyclopedic knowledge of the project and seemingly limitless energy are legendary. Among many other contributors, I want to acknowledge over 80 social scientists who have given crucial guidance to the project as members of the GSS Board of Overseers and its predecessor bodies.

Like many collected works, this one took a good deal longer to assemble than first anticipated. I appreciate the efforts of its 23 authors as their chapters developed, and the patience that some of them displayed. As well, I am grateful for nudges at critical junctures from Duane Alwin, Mark Chaves, and Tom Smith. Mary Ellen Marsden, Eric Schwartz, Tom Smith, and Sameer Srivastava made helpful comments on drafts of the book's introductory chapter.

The initial concept for this book developed in discussions with Tim Sullivan while he was the sociology editor at Princeton University Press. I am gratified to have remained in touch with Tim as he has moved to Basic Books and most recently Harvard Business Review Press. Eric Schwartz at Princeton took up where Tim left off with remarkable dexterity, mixing patience, prompt and pointed advice, and efficiency, as circumstances required. And Janie Chan's professionalism and positive spirit have made even the routine parts of putting the book into final form a genuine pleasure. Dmitri Karetnikov was responsible for developing final versions of the many figures that appear in these pages, improving many of them in the process, and Kathleen Cioffi supervised the final production process. Joseph Dahm copyedited the manuscript, and David Luljak prepared the index.

At Harvard, Lauren Dye was responsible for managing and checking reference lists, among other details. Wendy Erselius aided me in obtaining source materials for the introductory chapter, handled much correspondence with authors and the press during the late stages of the project, protected vital blocks of time on my calendar, and periodically reminded me that "working on the book" too should receive some priority on my agenda. Jennifer Shephard provided expert and timely aid in the design of some figures. Harvard

University offers a rich and unique setting in which to pursue academic work, supporting completion of this project by providing office space, staff support, computing equipment, and remarkable colleagues.

* * * * *

Concluding his 1971 proposal, Davis wrote, "You have to start somewhere." His vision stimulated an extensive and dynamic data collection program that remains vibrant some 40 years later. Perhaps it is unusual to dedicate a book to one of its contributors, but we do that here to recognize Davis's mark on modern social science.

Peter V. Marsden
Harvard University
December 2011

Contributors

Duane F. Alwin, *Pennsylvania State University*

Shawna Anderson, *Duke University*

Lawrence D. Bobo, *Harvard University*

Karen E. Campbell, *Vanderbilt University*

Camille Z. Charles, *University of Pennsylvania*

Mark Chaves, *Duke University*

James A. Davis, *NORC and University of Chicago*

Glenn Firebaugh, *Pennsylvania State University*

Andrew Greeley, *NORC and University of Arizona*

Jennifer A. Heerwig, *New York University*

Michael Hout, *University of California, Berkeley*

Jana L. Jasinski, *University of Central Florida*

Arne L. Kalleberg, *University of North Carolina at Chapel Hill*

Maria Krysan, *University of Illinois at Chicago*

Drew Noble Lanier, *University of Central Florida*

Jeff Manza, *New York University*

Peter V. Marsden, *Harvard University*

Brian J. McCabe, *Georgetown University*

Julianna Pacheco, *University of Iowa*

Alicia D. Simmons, *Colgate University*

Tom W. Smith, *NORC and University of Chicago*

Sameer B. Srivastava, *Harvard University*

Laura Tach, *Cornell University*

James D. Wright, *University of Central Florida*

Social Trends in American Life

1

Introduction and Overview

Peter V. Marsden

This book reports on social trends among U.S. adults between the early 1970s and the first decade of the 21st century. Its chapters cover social and political phenomena arrayed across a wide spectrum. Some investigate and interpret changes in salient sociopolitical attitudes—regarding tolerance for free speech, black/white relationships, women's roles, politics and government, and crime and its punishment. Others ask whether confidence in major American institutions fell, or if connections to religious groups or other persons waned. Still others study shifts in how adults assessed their well-being as economic, political, and social conditions in U.S. society underwent sometimes-dramatic change.

The 12 studies that follow rest on survey data assembled by the General Social Survey (GSS) project since 1972. The GSS regularly questions representative samples of U.S. adults about their social, political, and economic attitudes, values, self-assessments, and behaviors. As well, it collects extensive background information about demographic and social characteristics that predict differences among Americans. This now-substantial data archive facilitates studies of social trends by ensuring that both measurements and samples are comparable over time. It supports studies of aggregate change, subgroup differences at particular points in time, and variation in trends across important subsets of U.S. adults.[1]

Thousands of social science studies draw on the GSS surveys, examining point-in-time variations among Americans, patterned change over time, or both. Many investigate specific but quite diverse subjects; examples include abortion rights (Hout 1999), participation in the arts (DiMaggio 1996), conceptions of mental illness (Phelan, Link, Stueve, and Pescosolido 2000), and work orientations such as organizational commitment (Marsden, Kalleberg, and Cook, 1993). A few more comprehensive studies compare and contrast trends across multiple topical areas. Smith (1990) inventoried hundreds of trends measured by the GSS and other repeated surveys conducted between World War II and the late 1980s, finding that "liberal" movements outnumbered "conservative" ones during that period, but also that liberalization began to wane after the mid-1970s. Davis (1992) examined 42 trends on diverse topics tracked by the GSS, suggesting that the later 1980s saw a "liberal rebound." Mitchell (1996) reported trends in numerous GSS survey items over two decades (1974–1994), with attention to differences between men and women, blacks and whites, older and younger adults, and the more and less educated. DiMaggio, Evans, and Bryson (1996) asked whether polarization— that is, disagreement surrounding social issues—grew over time, concluding in general that it did not (increased contention over abortion rights was an exception). Indeed, they reported that between-group differences in many social attitudes shrunk during the late 20th century.

Taken together, the chapters here offer some of the depth of single-topic studies together with the breadth of omnibus studies like Smith (1990), Davis (1992), and DiMaggio et al. (1996). The authors situate the trends they describe within—and interpret their findings with reference to—traditions of social science scholarship in their subject areas. Their topics cover much of the range of phenomena the GSS project tracks.

This introductory chapter first provides context for the studies that follow, drawing on prior research about change in the U.S. social, political, and economic landscape since the 1970s. Next comes an overview of this book's content, including some remarks about related GSS-based trend studies on other topics. I close by briefly calling attention to the variety of approaches and explanations that the authors use when offering accounts for the patterns of change they report. No compact statement about factors that underlie recent U.S. social change emerges. The extent and direction of trends differ considerably, both within and across topical areas—as is perhaps to be anticipated for such diverse phenomena.

A Changing U.S. Social Environment

Economic, demographic, political, and cultural conditions provide a backdrop for the changes in attitudes and behaviors discussed here. Previous studies portray change in those conditions as revealed by comparisons of

U.S. Census Bureau data over time (e.g., Farley 1996; Farley and Haaga 2005; Fischer and Hout 2006) or by integrating across a variety of archival sources that record developments and events during this period (e.g., Patterson 2005; Wilentz 2008).

In the early 1970s, the United States was emerging from the tumult of the 1960s: the upheavals of the civil rights movement, the optimism and interventionist impulses of Great Society initiatives, and the divisiveness and disillusionment surrounding the Vietnam War (Phillips-Fein 2011). The Watergate scandal and the first oil crisis took place just as the GSS began to follow the attitudes and behaviors of American adults.

Marked changes in the U.S. economy described by Levy (1998) were under way in the early 1970s and continued thereafter. The high productivity increases that fueled rising incomes and standards of living after World War II slowed, as did real wage growth. The poverty rate fell slightly, from 14.3% in 1969 to 10.1% by 1999 (Danziger and Gottschalk 2005, p. 55). Technological change and the onset of international competition, among other factors, contributed to deindustrialization and a loss of manufacturing jobs; employment in services and (later) information industries grew. Many newly created positions placed a premium on higher education—what Levy terms a "skill bias"; wages of well-educated workers rose much more rapidly than did those of others (Danziger and Gottschalk 2005, pp. 64–65). Many other new jobs were poorly paid, lacking health care, pension, and other workplace-linked benefits (Kalleberg 2011). Growing skill differentiation was one element behind a rapid rise in income inequality: Levy (1998, p. 199) reports that the share of income received by the top 5% of U.S. families rose from 15.6% in 1969 to 20.3% by 1996.

Among the most notable economic changes was the rising number of women engaged in paid employment. By 1994, over 75% of women aged 25–54 were in the labor force, compared to just 50% in 1970. During the same period, labor force participation among prime-working-age men dropped by 4 percentage points (Spain and Bianchi 1996, p. 82). The number of two-earner families therefore rose, allowing family incomes to grow despite stagnant wage levels (especially among men) during much of the period. A substantial gender gap in earnings narrowed somewhat during the 1980s, but women's average pay remained substantially beneath men's. Danziger and Gottschalk (2005, p. 67) report that this disparity remained relatively stable after 1993.

U.S. demography, family structures, and living arrangements underwent dramatic change. Birth rates fell from over 3 children per woman at the height of the baby boom years to under 2 by the mid-1980s (Fischer and Hout 2006, p. 66). Falling mortality rates accompanied lower fertility: life expectancy at birth continued its century-long rise, reaching well over 70 by 1988 (Treas and Torrecilha 1995). Together, these changes in vital rates raised the proportion of people in older age brackets and the median age in the U.S. population (Treas and Torrecilha 1995; Fischer and Hout 2006, pp. 63–66).

The same period saw notable changes in family structures and living arrangements. Among the most crucial of these were delays in the age of first marriage and rising rates of divorce (Lichter and Qian 2005). Cohabitation, childbearing outside of marriage, and childlessness rose somewhat (Spain and Bianchi 1996). These changes meant that people were married for less of their lives, leading one analyst to argue marriage became "deinstitutionalized" in the United States (Cherlin 2004). Variety in family structures grew as the number of "traditional" families composed of two married adults with children dropped. Many more adults, especially the elderly, lived alone (Fischer and Hout 2006).

A new wave of immigration commenced while these demographic shifts were under way. The percentage of foreign-born persons within the U.S. population grew from about 4% in 1970 to 11% in 2000 (Kritz and Gurak 2005, p. 269). The new immigrants came largely from Latin America and Asia—over a third of them from Mexico alone—rather than Europe and were typically younger than the native born. Their arrival added notably to U.S ethnic and cultural diversity: Hispanic Americans made up 13% of the U.S. population in 2000, slightly more than blacks (12%). Only 69% of Americans then had European origins, a substantial drop from 88% European in the early 20th century (Fischer and Hout 2006, pp. 25, 36).

Residential trends under way throughout the 1900s continued: population shifted away from the Northeast and Midwest toward the southern and western U.S. (Farley 1996), and suburban places grew. Differences between urban and suburban dwellers generally widened, while regional and rural–urban differences diminished (Fischer and Hout 2006).

One additional—and vital—20th-century sociodemographic trend was a broad expansion in education (Fischer and Hout 2006). Of those turning 21 in 1970, about 85% completed high school degrees; roughly 25% earned college degrees. On average, they completed over 13 years of schooling. These figures represented striking increases over even midcentury educational attainment levels, but they rose little further for cohorts maturing after 1970.

Political historians generally characterize this era as conservative (Wilentz 2008; Phillips-Fein 2011). Between 1969 and 2009, Republicans held the presidency for all but 12 years. Divided government was common, however: Democrats usually controlled Congress. Domestic initiatives were few by comparison with the 1960s, as politicians emphasized limiting rather than expanding government. While few social programs of the 1960s ended, economic policy favored free markets as a means toward economic growth, stressing tax reductions, deregulation, and reduced outlays for social welfare (Levy 1998; Patterson 2005).

Extensive technological changes during this period greatly expanded opportunities for Americans to contact one another (Fischer 2011). A national interstate highway network was completed, and airline travel grew. Access to telephone service broadened, and the cost of long-distance communication fell very notably. Later, the introduction and subsequent rapid development of new communication modes—cellular telephones, text messaging, electronic mail, and other Internet-mediated interaction—vastly altered the ways in which Americans interact with one another and obtain information.[2]

Much has been written of cultural shifts that took place during this period. A "minority rights revolution" (Skrentny 2002) led to broad diffusion and acceptance of principles of equal opportunity and nondiscrimination. With impetus from the civil rights movement that sought equal rights for African Americans, rights advocates soon extended their efforts to other groups including women, ethnic minorities, gays and lesbians, and the disabled.

Some authors wrote of falling civic engagement, loss of community, and a growing "sense of civic malaise" (Putnam 2000, p. 25). Others observed increasing individualism, worrying that aspects of it might be destructive (Bellah, Madsen, Sullivan, Swidler, and Tipton 1985). Still others (Hunter 1991) contended that cultural conflicts became reconfigured as debates between the distinct moral worldviews held by orthodox and progressive partisans. "Social issues," many of them made salient by changes in family structure and formation—e.g., abortion rights, artistic expression, divorce, homosexuality, pornography, school curricula—served as foci for these controversies. Patterson (2005) opines that media attention amplified the volume of these "culture wars" and that liberal positions came to predominate in many of them—although conservative participants articulated their stances vigorously.

The GSS survey data examined in the studies that follow were assembled while these societal changes were unfolding. Those studies trace shifts in how typical American adults viewed some of these phenomena and in how they assessed their lives in light of them. They often indicate that broad statements about social change during this period should be qualified and contextualized.

Changing Attitudes, Connectivity, and Well-Being

The coverage of the GSS is indeed "general." By measuring numerous broadly conceived "social indicators," it facilitates "social reporting" about societal conditions and how they change over periods of time (Land 1983). The GSS's attitudinal and behavioral measures touch on many spheres of life, including work, family, politics, religion, and social life, among others.

The three parts of this book discuss trends in social and political phenomena, social connectedness, and individual well-being, respectively. Chapters in the first part examine changing orientations toward key realms of sociopolitical life, centering attention on survey questions that contrast liberal and conservative conceptions of desirable social states—e.g., greater or lesser tolerance for free expression, a racially integrated society versus one partitioned along racial lines, or more and less punitive stances toward criminals. The second part analyzes changes in individual–society attachments at different levels—expressed confidence in major social institutions, links with and participation in religious groups, and informal socializing with other persons. The four studies in the final part examine over-time change and stability in subjective well-being—happiness, job and financial security—and in verbal ability.

Liberal and Conservative Movements in Sociopolitical Attitudes

Each of the first five chapters asks whether American adults grew more liberal or conservative in some way during this period. What it means to be "liberal" or "conservative" must be defined before engaging that question. This is not straightforward: Smith's overview study of social and political trends distinguished eight forms of liberalism regarding domestic matters (Smith 1990, p. 480): a "reformist" orientation supporting change in the status quo, a "democratic" impulse toward expanded electoral rights, a "libertarian" stance favoring civil liberties, an "interventionist" position endorsing government regulation, "centralist" advocacy of federal standard setting, a "humanitarian" disposition toward social welfare and caring for the disadvantaged, an "egalitarian" inclination toward equal opportunity and (sometimes) results, and "permissive" tolerance of nontraditional lifestyles and practices.[3]

These distinctions are important because people may be liberal in some domains and simultaneously hold conservative or moderate views in others, as intraparty struggles over political platforms exemplify. Trends in different aspects of liberalism can and do differ. GSS evidence presented in this part reveals relatively steady upward movements in libertarian, some egalitarian, and permissive views. Americans are predominately moderate in some other senses, especially regarding the role of government.

In chapter 2, James A. Davis extends his research on tolerance for nonconformity into the 2000s, following up on one of the very first articles based on the GSS (Davis 1975). Drawing on Stouffer's (1955) conceptualization, chapter 2 defines tolerance as the willingness to accord First Amendment–guaranteed rights of free expression to groups espousing unpopular views (e.g., atheists or racists) or lifestyles (homosexuals). Anchored on Stouffer's McCarthy-era baseline reading, it documents a steady rise in tolerance into the 2000s, but suggests that this may be decelerating. Davis concludes that generally liberal outlooks, not sentiments toward particular "target" groups, underlie rising tolerance. He attributes much growth in tolerance to the replacement of older, less educated cohorts by more recent ones. Because two principal drivers of higher tolerance—education and generally liberal outlooks—have stopped rising, Davis conjectures that tolerance may soon reach a plateau.

Chapter 3, by Lawrence Bobo, Camille Charles, Maria Krysan, and Alicia Simmons, depicts "the real record on racial attitudes" using a wide lens. Recounting results of mid-20th-century surveys as well as trends in GSS data, they show that formal principles of equal treatment (e.g., in schools and employment) came to be widely endorsed. They caution against concluding that U.S. society became "postracial," however. For example, in the 2000s white Americans remain more apt to attribute negative traits to blacks than to whites, reluctant to support interventions to redress persistent black–white inequality, and highly resistant to "special favors" for blacks. Overall, Bobo and colleagues document rising egalitarianism and dramatic change in some basic assumptions governing black–white relationships, together with little or no growth in reformist and interventionist orientations about racial matters. They highlight numerous "enduring frictions and conflicts that continue to make race such a fraught terrain."

Several previous GSS-based studies (e.g., Brooks and Bolzendahl 2004) revealed increasing acceptance of nontraditional gender roles. Karen Campbell and I build upon and extend these findings in chapter 4. Adults became less predisposed toward a "separate spheres" conception holding that women should specialize in caring for children and households while men predominate in the more public arenas of employment and politics. Most growth in acceptance of broadened women's roles took place by the mid-1990s, however, mirroring trends in women's labor force participation and their representation in political office (see also Cotter, Hermsen, and Vanneman 2011). We then illustrate the regional convergence noted by Fischer and Hout (2006), showing that southerners continue to espouse more traditional views about gender, but less so over time.

Apart from greater endorsement of free expression, support for equal treatment by race, and acceptance of a widened scope for women's roles, GSS evidence documents rising tolerance in related domains. In 1990, 40% of adults said they would object if a close relative were to marry a Hispanic American; this fell to 18% in 2004, and to 13% by 2010. The respective percentages questioning a marriage to an Asian American are very similar.[4] Loftus (2001) reports that beginning around 1990, fewer U.S. adults regarded homosexuality as "always wrong." Agreement that "homosexuals should have the right to marry" rose from an estimated 12% in 1988 to 35% by 2004, reaching 47% by 2010. Permissive dispositions toward premarital sex grew slowly after 1972, remaining relatively stable after 1980 (Harding and Jencks 2003).[5]

Greater tolerance for social equality in these respects did not extend to support for government action that would reduce economic inequality, however. Between 1978 and 2010, the fraction of GSS respondents strongly endorsing the proposition that "government ought to reduce the income differences between rich and poor" remained steady at roughly a fifth. A similarly stable but slightly smaller fraction felt strongly that government "should do everything possible to improve the standard of living of all poor Americans."[6]

Jeff Manza, Jennifer Heerwig, and Brian McCabe shift attention to changing orientations toward politics and government in chapter 5. They ask whether conservatism in political affiliations, national spending priorities, and social issue stances grew between 1972 and 2006, in keeping with Wilentz's (2008) label for the period, the "Age of Reagan." Some trends certainly accord with this image: Discernably more adults described themselves as "conservative" and identified as Republicans. Moreover, conservatives became much more apt to identify as Republicans, and gaps between Republicans and Democrats on some social issues widened, signaling limited rises in some forms of polarization (DiMaggio et al. 1996). Other findings are at odds with claims of a rising conservative tide, however. For example, in most years more adults described themselves as "moderate" than as either liberal or conservative, calling to mind Hunter's (1991, p. 43) caveat that "most Americans occupy a vast middle ground." Public opinion favored spending increases rather than reductions in many domestic arenas, though here as elsewhere Americans were reticent to call for greater government intervention. The overall portrait of political attitude trends that Manza and colleagues present is decidedly qualified and mixed.

Closing this part of the book is James Wright, Jana Jasinski, and Drew Lanier's study of trends in one social issue area, crime and how it should be punished. Calls for "law and order" were common in the 1960s; Smith (1990) found conservative opinion movements in this area, unlike most others. Chapter 6 here asks whether and how crime-related sentiments changed after a general decline in official U.S. crime rates began around 1994. Several attitudes regarding crime became more moderate thereafter: fear of victimization, preferences for increased spending on crime control, and dispositions to punish crimes more severely (including using the death penalty) all fell. Wright and colleagues argue that attitudes and behaviors about crime and punishment reflect moral stances and pragmatic considerations—including personal security—rather than more general political attitudes.

Trends in Confidence and Connections
The three trend analyses in the second part of the book bear on debates over whether Americans grew apart from their society and one another during the decades following the 1970s, as suggested in several prominent works asserting that some form of U.S. decline is under way (Patterson 2005). Social scientists gave special attention to Putnam's (2000) claim that the stock of "social capital" had been depleted. Among the numerous facets of social capital are interpersonal trust, institutional confidence, civic engagement through group memberships and/or political participation, and informal social contacts among persons. GSS data provided a key source of evidence for both Putnam's (1995, 2000) original work and subsequent research about his thesis. Paxton (1999) studied trends in social capital between 1975 and 1994, finding lower interpersonal trust, but no general drop in associational memberships or institutional confidence. R. V. Robinson and Jackson (2001) reported reduced trust levels among generations born after the 1940s.

In chapter 7 here, Tom W. Smith presents a detailed analysis of trends in confidence in 13 major institutional sectors. Confidence moved downward in most (the military is an exception), but Smith's discussion reveals substantial and important variations on this theme. For most sectors, reductions were both slight and irregular: only confidence in the press and television fell steadily. Smith interprets changes in confidence in light of sector-specific historical events: for example, confidence in political institutions shifts depending on the political party controlling the presidency or Congress, while confidence in economic institutions rises and falls over business cycles. He also highlights a "cohort-reversal" pattern that contributes to uneven confidence trends: adults born in and near the baby boom years appear least trustful of most institutions, while those in both earlier and more recent generations display more confidence.

U.S. society has long been differentiated along religious lines. Repeated surveys like the GSS are vital to studying religious affiliations and behaviors, since U.S. government data sources include no information about them. In Chapter 8, Mark Chaves and Shawna Anderson examine change in the religious indicators tracked by the GSS. Many core beliefs and behaviors remained stable between the 1970s and the 2000s, but the authors also detect several important though gradual shifts. Non-Christians and religiously unaffiliated persons became more numerous (see also Hout and Fischer 2002) and the fraction of Protestants waned, so religious diversity rose. More conservative Protestant denominations grew at the expense of "mainline" groups. Chaves and Anderson point to some indications that U.S. religiosity, though it is still high by international standards, dropped: lower religious participation, reduced belief in biblical inerrancy, and appreciably less confidence in religious leaders. Especially notable—and suggestive of some heightening in religiously based attitude polarization (DiMaggio et al. 1996)—is the closer coupling between religious involvement and both political and religious conservatism during this period.

In chapter 9, Sameer Srivastava and I turn to trends in informal social connectedness. In recent controversy and debate over this subject, some studies report contraction in social networks (McPherson, Smith-Lovin, and Brashears 2006), contrasting with others that indicate stability (Fischer 2011). Our analyses find that the frequency of socializing with relatives, friends, and neighbors changed modestly, but in different directions. Neighboring exhibits the clearest drop, balanced to an extent by recent upward movements in seeing relatives and friends. Overall, Srivastava and I conclude that no general network shrinkage appears to be under way. Socializing trends may reflect some restructuring of interpersonal networks, however, as other social changes proceed—including rising electronically mediated interaction and residential dispersion.

Stability and Change in Social Indicators

Some roots of sustained programs of repeated social measurement like the GSS lie in efforts to develop and measure social indicators. Proponents aspire toward a more comprehensive portrait of societal conditions than important economic indicators like unemployment rates yield. Some advocates saw social indicators as diagnostic criteria that could aid program assessment or guide social policy; others regarded them as more general tools for the ongoing monitoring of social change (Sheldon and Moore 1968). Many official statistics (e.g., crime, mortality, and morbidity rates) were proposed as social indicators. Others suggested perceptual measures to track self-assessed well-being or quality of life (Andrews 1974). Those promoting research programs for measuring social indicators stressed that they should collect data regularly and comparably in order to detect change.

All studies in this book report on social indicators in the broader sense of the term. Those in its final part examine trends—and some notable non-trends—in subjective social indicators. Two chapters focus on self-reported happiness, which—despite extensive economic and demographic change—has remained relatively steady since the 1970s. Another examines trends in perceived economic and employment security, while the fourth analyzes change in adult vocabulary knowledge.

Between 1972 and 2006, general happiness levels among American adults remained quite steady, though a minor drop can be detected. In chapter 10, Glenn Firebaugh and Laura Tach try to account for this stability, given the growth in real family incomes and standards of living that occurred during the era. Several factors—better health, being married, greater education, and higher income—make people happier at any given point in time. Firebaugh and Tach assert, though, that assessments of well-being in societies like the contemporary United States reflect not only absolute levels of living but also comparisons of one's income to that typical in a reference group of peers. Their analysis finds higher happiness among adults whose family incomes are higher than average for their age group at the time, implying that happiness rises only when income increases more rapidly than average.

Michael Hout and Andrew Greeley connect happiness with trends in religion. Chapter 11 draws on meaning-and-belonging theory to deduce that a religious affiliation heightens happiness through participation in collective religious rituals. Attendance and engagement appear key: a merely nominal religious affiliation makes people little happier. Notably, two religious foundations of happiness—affiliation with organized religious groups and attendance at services—have fallen, as Chaves and Anderson's chapter shows (see also Hout and Fischer 2002). Softened religious engagement, then, may contribute to the slight downturn in general happiness. In fact, Hout and Greeley report steady happiness among those who participate frequently in religious services, but falling levels among those who are less involved.

Next, Arne Kalleberg and I consider subjective well-being at work—both perceived security and job satisfaction. Kalleberg (2009) asserts that recent changes in U.S. economic organization made employment more precarious. Here, we find that jobs are viewed as less secure than in past decades, after we adjust for cyclical variations in unemployment (see Schmidt 1999). Insecurity appears to have grown fastest among the upper socioeconomic groups that historically have been least at risk of job loss. In keeping with happiness trends, though, job satisfaction remained very stable between the 1970s and 2000s. Gains in satisfaction during the course of employment countered lower satisfaction among cohorts of young workers entering the labor force. Present-day workers regard their jobs as less secure, but dissatisfaction need not follow if they regard precarity as a to-be-expected condition of employment.

Sectoral shifts toward a postindustrial economy centered on services and information make verbal skills more important to individuals and society alike. In chapter 13, Duane Alwin and Julianna Pacheco examine trends in adults' performance on a 10-item vocabulary battery administered within the GSS. Measured ability remained relatively steady over time. This stability reflects the confluence of two offsetting trends: lower baseline vocabulary knowledge among adults in post–World War II birth cohorts counterbalances achievement gains attributable to their greater schooling. The intricate analysis here assesses two explanations for apparent cohort-related drops in verbal knowledge—that the GSS vocabulary test became more difficult because its words grew obsolete and that the drops reflect population aging rather than cohort-related differences. Alwin and Pacheco conclude that little evidence supports either account and suggest that vocabulary declines in postwar cohorts reflect their family and school experiences as well as the selective survival of higher-ability adults.

A Note on Accounts for Change

The main object of the analyses here is to present and interpret over-time trends in the phenomena the GSS tracks, but many authors also offer accounts for the patterns of change they report. An accounting framework widely used among social scientists recognizes three distinct sources of change: period-related factors that affect everyone in a population at once, cohort-related ones reflecting generation-specific conditions that induce change via cohort succession, and age-linked change over the life course. Age-related phenomena generate trends when change in a population's age distribution shifts the mix of persons who experience the circumstances common to youth or the elderly.

Several chapters here point to generational or cohort turnover as a driver of change. Cohort replacement combines cohort- and age-related phenomena (Firebaugh 1989) because it simultaneously substitutes someone in a later-born cohort for an exiting member of an earlier one, and a younger person for an older one. Here, Davis finds that cohort replacement yields upward shifts in tolerance, Firebaugh and Tach observe that it implies a slight decline in happiness, Alwin and Pacheco link it to lower word knowledge, and Kalleberg and I note that it tends to reduce job satisfaction. Several of these analyses find that intracohort change due to aging and/or period-related factors counters differences implied by cohort replacement, so that only modest overall change results. Not all cohort-related trends are steady, as the cohort-reversal pattern noted by Smith illustrates.

Attributing change to cohort replacement does not specify which between-cohort differences in characteristics are behind it. Demographic explanations of change (Davis 2001) attempt this, by introducing individual sociodemographic characteristics that both predict the phenomenon of interest and vary across cohorts. Education is a very important example; Davis finds that between-cohort differences in schooling account for an appreciable portion of the growth in tolerance due to cohort replacement, while Alwin and Pacheco note that schooling is responsible for some cohort-related differences in vocabulary knowledge. Earlier, Davis (1982) pointed to pervasive education-related differences in attitudes and behaviors. Fischer and Hout (2006) presented an extended discussion of the rising salience and consequences of educational differences in U.S. society.

Period-, cohort-, and age-related aspects of change are intertwined with one another, and separating them requires that assumptions about their form be made. For example, Alwin and Pacheco argue that because vocabulary knowledge is acquired first via schooling and then gradually during the life course, it is implausible that some period-related factor would alter the verbal proficiency of all in a population at once. With that proviso, they can readily estimate age- and cohort-related differences. Srivastava and I assume that socializing has relatively smooth associations with the three sources of change and find that age-related differences appear largest.

Many authors here juxtapose attitudinal and subjective trends against contemporaneous demographic data or pertinent objective social indicators. Wright and colleagues find some correspondence between changing attitudes regarding crime and recent declines in official crime rates. Campbell and I observe that trends toward less traditional gender role orientations track changes in women's labor force participation and election to political office. Kalleberg and I note that perceived job insecurity rises and falls with unemployment rates. Steady or slightly declining happiness despite rising living standards provides a point of departure for Firebaugh and Tach.

Somewhat similar are interpretations of trends that reference particular historical events. For Manza and colleagues, election outcomes provide a basis for predicting that U.S. political attitudes and affiliations grew more conservative beginning in the 1970s. Smith concludes that fluctuations in institutional confidence have more to do with sector-specific negative and positive events—e.g., disasters, financial crises, wars, elections, economic cycles, or clergy scandals—than with broader-scope phenomena.

These chapters do not test any comprehensive theory of change, or systematically assess the types of factors that shape the trends studied. They do give more attention to cohort- and period-related phenomena than to age-linked factors. Most authors invoke multiple interpretations, none of which appears to account for change in the full range of topics examined here.

Conclusion

The trend studies in this book depict a changing but complex U.S. social fabric over nearly two generations. Tolerance of free expression, endorsement of principles of equal treatment by race, and acceptance of broadened women's roles rose markedly. Americans evince ambivalence about what role government should play in grappling with social problems, however. A few signs of growing crystallization in social divisions can be seen, but at least within the public at large studied here, middle-of-the road positions generally outnumber extreme ones. Declines in some forms of social connectivity are evident, but these are neither universal nor dramatic. Likewise, notwithstanding some rather substantial change in objective conditions, Americans give relatively steady self-assessments of their well-being.

These findings do not comprehensively portray recent social trends, of course: Many sociopolitical topics and questions are not covered by chapters in this book. Data in the GSS archive bear on many of the latter, including orientations toward the environment, health and medical care, national citizenship, change in family and household structures, sexual attitudes and behavior, media use, and many more. The trend studies included here well demonstrate the value of a sustained, prospectively planned survey data collection program. It observes change as it unfolds, rather than reconstructing it after the fact. Its findings reflect the views of representative cross sections of Americans, not only those who strive to publicize their views or succeed in gaining media attention. Replication of questions over time offers assurance that between-year differences reflect change in the subject of interest rather than variation in measuring devices. Certainly other sources can usefully supplement conclusions that rest on survey data like these, but the analyses based on the GSS archive that follow provide an invaluable perspective on how ordinary Americans viewed their society and lives between the early 1970s and the present.

Notes

1. The appendix to this book describes the study design and research methods used to collect the GSS data. They are available to researchers, students, and the public via several channels indicated there.

2. The GSS does not yet track use of new media on a regular basis, but it did collect cross-sectional data on Internet and electronic mail use in the early 2000s; see J. P. Robinson, DiMaggio, and Hargittai (2003).

3. Smith suggested that still other varieties of liberalism apply in the sphere of foreign affairs, including internationalism, multinationalism, and nonmilitarism.

4. Percentages reported here were calculated from the GSS cumulative file, available via the Survey Documentation and Analysis site maintained at the University of California, Berkeley (http://sda.berkeley.edu).

5. Not all trends were toward increased permissiveness, however. For example, just over 70% of adults regarded extramarital sexual relations as "always wrong" in the mid-1970s, a figure that rose to around 82% in the early 2000s.

6. McCall and Kenworthy (2009) argue that rising inequality does concern Americans but that they want government to address it via means other than "traditional redistributive programs."

References

Andrews, Frank M. 1974. "Social Indicators of Perceived Life Quality." *Social Indicators Research* 1 (3): 279–99.

Bellah, Robert N., Richard Madsen, William M. Sullivan, Ann Swidler, and Steven M. Tipton. 1985. *Habits of the Heart: Individualism and Commitment in American Life*. New York: Harper & Row.

Brooks, Clem, and Catherine Bolzendahl. 2004. "The Transformation of US Gender Role Attitudes: Cohort Replacement, Social-Structural Change, and Ideological Learning." *Social Science Research* 33 (1): 106–33.

Cherlin, Andrew J. 2004. "The Deinstitutionalization of American Marriage." *Journal of Marriage and the Family* 66 (4): 848–61.

Cotter, David A., Joan M. Hermsen, and Reeve Vanneman. 2011. "The End of the Gender Revolution? Gender Role Attitudes from 1977 to 2008." *American Journal of Sociology* 117:259–89.

Danziger, Sheldon, and Peter Gottschalk. 2005. "Diverging Fortunes: Trends in Poverty and Inequality." In *The American People: Census 2000*, edited by Reynolds Farley and John Haaga, 49–75. New York: Russell Sage Foundation.

Davis, James A. 1975. "Communism, Conformity, Cohorts, and Categories: American Tolerance in 1954 and 1972–73." *American Journal of Sociology* 81 (3): 491–513.

———. 1982. "Achievement Variables and Class Cultures: Family, Schooling, Job, and Forty-Nine Dependent Variables in the Cumulative GSS." *American Sociological Review* 47 (5): 569–86.

———. 1992. "Changeable Weather in a Cooling Climate atop the Liberal Plateau: Conversion and Replacement in Forty-Two General Social Survey Items, 1972–1989." *Public Opinion Quarterly* 56 (3): 261–306.

———. 2001. "Testing the Demographic Explanation of Attitude Trends: Secular Trends in Attitudes among U.S. Householders, 1972–1996." *Social Science Research* 30 (3): 363–85.

DiMaggio, Paul. 1996. "Are Art Museum Visitors Different from Other People? The Relationship between Attendance and Social and Political Attitudes in the United States." *Poetics* 24 (2–4): 161–80.

DiMaggio, Paul, John Evans, and Bethany Bryson. 1996. "Have Americans' Social Attitudes Become More Polarized?" *American Journal of Sociology* 102 (3): 690–755.

Farley, Reynolds. 1996. *The New American Reality: Who We Are, How We Got Here, Where We Are Going.* New York: Russell Sage Foundation.

Farley, Reynolds, and John Haaga, eds. 2005. *The American People: Census 2000.* New York: Russell Sage Foundation.

Firebaugh, Glenn. 1989. "Methods for Estimating Cohort Replacement Effects." In *Sociological Methodology 1989*, edited by Clifford C. Clogg, 243–62. Oxford: Basil Blackwell.

Fischer, Claude S. 2011. *Still Connected: Family and Friends in America since 1970.* New York: Russell Sage Foundation.

Fischer, Claude S., and Michael Hout. 2006. *Century of Difference: How America Changed in the Last One Hundred Years.* New York: Russell Sage Foundation.

Harding, David J., and Christopher Jencks. 2003. "Changing Attitudes toward Premarital Sex: Cohort, Period and Aging Effects." *Public Opinion Quarterly* 67 (2): 211–26.

Hout, Michael. 1999. "Abortion Politics in the United States, 1972–1994: From Single Issue to Ideology." *Gender Issues* 17 (2): 3–34.

Hout, Michael, and Claude S. Fischer. 2002. "Why More Americans Have No Religious Preference: Politics and Generations." *American Sociological Review* 67 (2): 165–90.

Hunter, James Davison. 1991. *Culture Wars: The Struggle to Define America.* New York: Basic Books.

Kalleberg, Arne L. 2009. "Precarious Work, Insecure Workers: American Employment Relations in Transition." *American Sociological Review* 74 (1): 1–22.

———. 2011. *Good Jobs, Bad Jobs: The Rise of Polarized and Precarious Employment Systems in the United States, 1970s–2000s.* New York: Russell Sage Foundation.

Kritz, Mary M., and Douglas T. Gurak. 2005. "Immigration and a Changing America." In *The American People: Census 2000*, edited by Reynolds Farley and John Haaga, 259–301. New York: Russell Sage Foundation.

Land, Kenneth C. 1983. "Social Indicators." *Annual Review of Sociology* 9:1–26.

Levy, Frank. 1998. *The New Dollars and Dreams: American Incomes and Economic Change.* New York: Russell Sage Foundation.

Lichter, Daniel T., and Zhenchao Qian. 2005. "Marriage and Family in a Multiracial Society." In *The American People: Census 2000*, edited by Reynolds Farley and John Haaga, 169–200. New York: Russell Sage Foundation.

Loftus, Jeni. 2001. "America's Liberalization in Attitudes toward Homosexuality, 1973 to 1998." *American Sociological Review* 66 (5): 762–82.

Marsden, Peter V., Arne L. Kalleberg, and Cynthia R. Cook. 1993. "Gender Differences in Organizational Commitment: Influences of Work Positions and Family Roles." *Work and Occupations* 20 (3): 368–90.

McCall, Leslie, and Lane Kenworthy. 2009. "Americans' Social Policy Preferences in the Era of Rising Inequality." *Perspectives on Politics* 7 (3): 459–84.

McPherson, Miller, Lynn Smith-Lovin, and Matthew Brashears. 2006. "Social Isolation in America: Changes in Core Discussion Networks over Two Decades." *American Sociological Review* 71 (3): 353–75.

Mitchell, Susan. 1996. *The Official Guide to American Attitudes.* Ithaca, NY: New Strategist.

Patterson, James. 2005. *Restless Giant: The United States from Watergate to Bush v. Gore*. New York: Oxford University Press.

Paxton, Pamela. 1999. "Is Social Capital Declining in the United States? A Multiple Indicator Assessment." *American Journal of Sociology* 105 (1): 88–127.

Phelan, Jo A., Bruce G. Link, Ann Stueve, and Bernice A. Pescosolido. 2000. "Public Conceptions of Mental Illness in 1950 and 1999: What Is Mental Illness and Is It to Be Feared?" *Journal of Health and Social Behavior* 41 (2): 188–207.

Phillips-Fein, Kim. 2011. "1973 to the Present." In *American History Now*, edited by Eric Foner and Lisa McGirr, 175–97. Philadelphia: Temple University Press.

Putnam, Robert D. 1995. "Bowling Alone: America's Declining Social Capital." *Journal of Democracy* 6 (1): 65–78.

———. 2000. *Bowling Alone: The Collapse and Revival of American Community*. New York: Simon & Schuster.

Robinson, John P., Paul DiMaggio, and Eszter Hargittai. 2003. "New Social Survey Perspectives on the Digital Divide." *IT & Society* 1 (5): 1–22.

Robinson, Robert V., and Elton F. Jackson. 2001. "Is Trust in Others Declining in America? An Age-Period-Cohort Analysis." *Social Science Research* 30 (1): 117–45.

Schmidt, Stefanie R. 1999. "Long-Run Trends in Workers' Beliefs about Their Own Job Security: Evidence from the General Social Survey." *Journal of Labor Economics* 17 (S4): S127–41.

Sheldon, Eleanor Bernert, and Wilbert E. Moore. 1968. *Indicators of Social Change: Concepts and Measurements*. New York: Russell Sage Foundation.

Skrentny, John. 2002. *The Minority Rights Revolution*. Cambridge, MA: Harvard University Press.

Smith, Tom W. 1990. "Liberal and Conservative Trends in the United States since World War II." *Public Opinion Quarterly* 54 (4): 479–507.

Spain, Daphne, and Suzanne M. Bianchi. 1996. *Balancing Act: Motherhood, Marriage, and Employment among American Women*. New York: Russell Sage Foundation.

Stouffer, Samuel A. 1955. *Communism, Conformity, and Civil Liberties: A Cross-Section of the Nation Speaks Its Mind*. Garden City, NY: Doubleday.

Treas, Judith, and Ramon Torrecilha. 1995. "The Older Population." In *State of the Union: America in the 1990s, Volume Two: Social Trends*, edited by Reynolds Farley, 47–92. New York: Russell Sage Foundation.

Wilentz, Sean. 2008. *The Age of Reagan: A History, 1974–2008*. New York: Harper.

Trends in Social and Political Orientations

2

On the Seemingly Relentless Progress in Americans'

Support for Free Expression, 1972–2006

James A. Davis

In the summer of 1954, some 500 interviewers fanned out to conduct the first national area probability survey of American attitudes. The timing was not accidental. That year marked the height of the "McCarthy era" of Cold War tensions, and the survey sponsor—the Fund for the Republic, a Ford Foundation spin-off—was concerned that anticommunist hysteria was dampening American support for free speech.

The study's final report, *Communism, Conformity and Civil Liberties: A Cross Section of the Nation Speaks Its Mind,* authored by Samuel A. Stouffer (1955/1992), became a landmark of sociological research. In particular, (1) the data showed that only a small minority supported textbook First Amendment rights; (2) the findings serve as a solid baseline for following trends in civil liberties opinions; (3) its major predictor variables—age and education—have held up in numerous studies (e.g., Hyman and Wright 1979; Nunn, Crockett, and Williams 1978; Nie, Junn, and Stehlik-Barry 1996); and (4) Stouffer's method for measuring tolerance has become the standard approach—although not without some controversy (see below).[1]

This is not the first follow-up study. In its first year, 1972, the General Social Survey (GSS) included some original Stouffer items. In 1975 I published an article (Davis 1975) reporting the early GSS results, showing a striking increase in tolerance during the almost two decades since Stouffer and suggesting that Stouffer's age finding might better be interpreted in terms of birth cohorts. An independent national survey in 1973 (Nunn et al. 1978) came to essentially similar conclusions. A second follow-up based on GSS data (Davis 1992) revealed continued gains in tolerance but also hinted that the trend was slowing.

Half a century after Stouffer's research and more than three decades into the GSS seems a good time for another follow-up. In this chapter I will (1) update the trend findings as of 2006, (2) scrutinize the "meaning" of the classic Stouffer items in the light of subsequent criticism, (3) see whether Stouffer's predictors account for changes in tolerance during the GSS years, and (4) explore some complexities that underlie the overall trends.

The Stouffer Items Then and Now

Stouffer recognized that generalized items about free expression (e.g., "People should be allowed to express their opinions") would probably elicit unthinking endorsement. Instead he proposed miniature vignettes about concrete situations in the general form, "Would you allow [controversial or unpopular target individual] to [specific form of public expression]?"

The 1954 study included a number of variations on "suspected communist" but the key items included three *targets*,

Atheist: "somebody who is against all churches and religion"
Communist: "a man who admits he is a communist"
Socialist: "a person who favored government ownership of the railroads and all big industries"

and three *venues* (free expression situations),

Speech: "Suppose [target] wants to make a speech in your community. Should he be allowed to speak or not?"
Library: "Suppose he wrote a book which is in your public library. Somebody in your community suggests the book be removed from the library. Would you favor removing it or not?"
College: "Suppose he is teaching in a college. Should he be fired or not?"

(Boldface labels were not read to the respondents.)

Interestingly, Stouffer's 1954 questionnaire did not ask about attitudes to communism or socialism. At the time it was reasonable to assume that most U.S. adults would find them unpalatable.

The GSS stopped asking about socialists after 1974 because they were not salient. In 1973 it added the target,

Homosexual: "a man who admits he is a homosexual"

and in 1976 it added,

Militarist: "a person who advocates doing away with elections and letting the military run the country," and

Racist: "a person who believes Blacks are genetically inferior"

The homosexual target was added because of its topicality (its **Library** version asks about "a book he wrote in favor of homosexuality," the intention being to imply the book was not pornography).[2] Militarists and racists were added because critics felt the Stouffer targets were all more palatable to liberal respondents (much more on this soon).

The Broad Picture: Tolerance Increased Steadily

Table 2.1 shows the percentages of respondents giving the more tolerant of the two possible answers for the 15 free speech questions (3 venues for each of 5 targets), from 1954 to 2006 for targets in both studies, from 1974 to 2006 for homosexuals, and from 1984 to 2006 for militarists and racists.

Table 2.1. Percentage Choosing the More Tolerant Response on Free Speech Items, 1954 (Stouffer) and 1974–2006 (GSS)

Target	Venue	1954	1964	1974	1984	1994	2004	2006
Atheist	Speech	38		63	69	74	78	78
	Library	37		61	66	71	75	73
	College	12		44	47	55	65	62
Communist	Speech	28		60	61	68	70	68
	Library	29		61	62	68	72	70
	College	6		44	47	58	66	63
Homosexual	Speech			65	71	81	84	83
	Library			57	61	71	74	76
	College			54	60	73	80	79
Militarist	Speech				59	63	63	63
	Library				60	66	70	70
	College				42	49	55	54
Racist	Speech				59	63	63	63
	Library				65	68	67	65
	College				41	44	48	48
N (unweighted)								
	Maximum	4,806		1,462	1,461	1,971	890	1,991
	Minimum	4,566		1,389	1,388	1,876	866	1,903

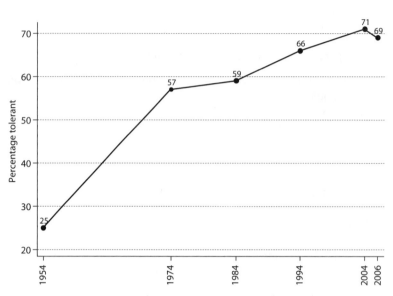

Figure 2.1. Mean percentage tolerant on Communist and Atheist items, 1954–2006.

Figure 2.1 plots the mean of the atheist and communist items in Table 2.1 against year.

With few exceptions the percentages and dots increase from left to right—Americans' expressed tolerance of free expression increased steadily throughout the last half of the 20th century. (Alas, there seem to be no studies between 1954 and 1972.) In 1954 at most one-third of the population chose the tolerant answer; by 2006 from one-half to three-quarters did. Glancing up and down Table 2.1 reveals no obvious patterns save for lesser tolerance for college teachers.

For a more precise reading I (1) constructed five target-specific indices (for tolerance of atheists, communists, homosexuals, militarists, and racists) by averaging over venues (giving each a possible range from 0 to 100 so results can be interpreted in terms of percentages) and (2) constructed a summary tolerance index, the mean of the five target-specific subscales. Because the GSS began asking about different targets in different years, the summary scale is disproportionally weighted toward the original Stouffer items targeting atheists and communists. However, Table 2.1 and the arguments below suggest that the measures are not strongly affected by selection of targets.

Table 2.2 displays regression results (ordinary least squares) showing trends in the six tolerance indices by year,[3] from which,

1. All six scales showed statistically reliable increases in tolerance.
2. The typical rate of change (slope) was about half a percentage point per year.

Table 2.2. Trends in Six GSS Tolerance Scales by Year (OLS regression)

	Atheists	Communists	Homosexuals	Militarists	Racists	Summary
Trend (slope)	0.475	0.524	0.747	0.463	0.115	0.453
Intercept	−888.3	−928.1	−141.8	−863.5	−171.5	−840.2
Correlation	0.130	0.137	0.200	0.120	0.031	0.145
t statistic	23.7	24.8	35.5	19.8	5.1	21.8
Regression predictions (% more tolerant)						
2006	66.0	68.4	80.9	64.7	59.4	68.3
1972	49.8	50.6	55.5	48.9	55.5	52.9
Gain	+16.2	+17.8	+25.4	+15.8	+3.9	+15.4
Scale statistics						
Mean	57.5	57.0	68.2	59.7	63.1	61.6
SD	3.8	4.1	4.0	4.1	3.9	3.3
N	32,355	32,096	30,262	26,936	27,029	27,241
Time span	1972–2006	1972–2006	1973–2006	1976–2006	1976–2006	1972–2006

3. From 1972 to 2006 tolerant answers increased between 4 and 25 percentage points.
4. The homosexual tolerance index rose about 10 points more than the others, the racists index about 10 points less.
5. Save for the homosexual target (68%) the index means were all close to 60% tolerant, suggesting little variation in target "palatability."
6. Although growth was steady, even as late as 2006 Americans did not appear to be especially tolerant. Despite Fourth of July oratory, as we entered the 21st century the typical tolerance item received only two-thirds endorsement. (For a cross-national comparison see Davis 1990.)

The Palatability Problem

As noted above, Stouffer's interview schedule ignored palatability—attitudes for or against particular targets. He assumed that communists, atheists, and socialists were controversial and unpopular. The assumption cannot be totally wrong—one would not ask, "Should your best friend be allowed to give a speech?" Nevertheless, the matter deserves scrutiny for two reasons: (1) if responses are target sensitive, GSS might have tarnished the time series by introducing new targets, and (2) the Stouffer items have been severely criticized in some corners for choice of targets. Sullivan, Pierson, and Marcus (1979), for example, argued that "your least liked group" should be substituted for specific targets. The notion has become widely accepted. Thus, Bishop (2005, p. 89), in a well-regarded book, writes, "Sullivan, Piereson and Marcus demonstrated that a seemingly dramatic increase in American tolerance of groups such as Communists, Socialists and Atheists over a twenty to twenty-five year period was mostly an illusion."

If tolerance is merely a function of target palatability, two implications follow:

1. Cross-target correlations should be low
2. Attitudes toward specific targets should predict tolerance of those targets, but not others

The simplest test of implication 1 would be to calculate Cronbach's alpha, the standard test for scalability. High values of alpha suggest that items about different targets are measuring the same thing, contrary to the mere palatability hypothesis.

I calculated alpha for 3 five-item scales for venues (Speech, Library, College), for 5 three-item scales for targets (Atheist, Communist, Homosexual, Militarist, Racist), and for the 15-item summary scale, with the following results:

Venue Scales (5 items)		Target Scales (3 items)		Summary Scale (15 items)	
Library	.874	Homosexuals	.819	Summary	.917
Speech	.850	Communists	.775		
College	.807	Atheists	.746		
		Racists	.728		
		Militarists	.652		

The alphas for the venue-specific scales, each of which involves five different targets, exceed the psychologists' magic number for adequate reliability, .70. (So do all but one of those for the target-specific scales based on three different venues.) These findings challenge the extreme notion that tolerance is target unique.

For a test of implication 2, I looked for GSS items that seemed to indicate favorable attitudes toward specific targets. Thus, one would expect that nonreligious people would be more tolerant of atheists, racial bigots more tolerant of racists, and so on.

Here are the items I chose (abbreviations in parentheses are GSS mnemonics):

Atheist
    Infrequent church attendance (ATTEND)
    Reject biblical inerrancy (BIBLE)
    Less fundamentalist religious denomination (FUND)
    Less religious intensity (RELITEN)

Communist
 Favorable attitude toward communism as form of government
  (COMMUN)
 Agree that government should equalize wealth (EQWLTH)
 Favor spending on cities, education, health, environment (NATS)
Homosexual
 Homosexuality not wrong (HOMOSEX)
 Premarital sex not wrong (PREMARSX)
 Extramarital sex not wrong (XMARSEX)
Militarist
 Favor spending on military (NATARMS)
 Higher confidence in military leaders (CONARMY)
 Rank "Obedience" above "Thinking for Oneself" as a value for chil-
  dren (OBEY-THNKSLF)
Racist (African American respondents excluded)
 Race differences due to inborn disability (RACDIF2)
 Race differences due to blacks' lack of will power (RACDIF4)
 Racial intermarriage should be illegal (RACMAR)
 Blacks shouldn't push "where they are not wanted" (RACPUSH)

Table 2.3 displays standardized partial regression coefficients and multiple correlations between these measures of palatability and the target-specific tolerance indexes. If the palatability critics are correct,

1. The boldface regression coefficients between an index and its corresponding palatability indicators should all be positive, and
2. The boldface multiple correlations (Rs) should be much larger than the others in their row and column.

One pattern leaps out from Table 2.3. While the top three groups of coefficients are all positive, the bottom two are *all negative*. That is, racists are *less* tolerant of racist expression, while promilitary respondents are *less* tolerant of militarist expression! The pattern is certainly fatal to the "just-palatability" hypothesis, but what is one to make of it?

If one were to reverse the scoring of the racist and militarist palatability measures, (1) all the signs in Table 2.3 would become positive, and (2) the positive end of every palatability measure would line up with "liberal" positions on issues—liberal religious positions, liberal politics, liberal sex norms, liberal stances on militarism and authority, liberal racial attitudes. Thus, I read the story in Table 2.3 as stating that specific palatabilities have little to do with tolerance, general liberalism has a lot to do with it.

To summarize, I created a liberalism index using eight liberal palatabilities from Table 2.3 and correlated it with the tolerance indices, obtaining bivariate correlations ranging from +.252 (Racists index) to +.462 (Homosexuals index).[4] Save for the Racists index, all correlations were .351 or higher. For

Table 2.3. Relationships between Palatability Items and GSS Tolerance Indices
(1972–2006)

Palatability mnemonic		Standardized partial regression coefficients (beta)[a]				
		Atheists	Communists	Homosexuals	Militarists	Racists
Atheism						
ATTEND		.041	.042	.028	.027	.025
BIBLE		.262	.255	.241	.226	.189
FUND		.090	.085	.115	.074	.058
RELITEN		.097	.073	.071	.069	.080
	R	.356	.331	.338	.297	.259
Communism						
COMMUN		.223	**.306**	.190	.221	.156
EQWLTH		.159	**.167**	.130	.123	.120
NATS		.157	**.142**	.193	.092	.034
	R	.307	**.371**	.292	.265	.196
Homosexuality						
HOMOSEX		.264	.263	**.326**	.272	.178
PREMARSX		.184	.160	**.204**	.117	.109
XMARSEX		.036	.040	**.006**	.019	.045
	R	.394	.378	**.454**	.346	.265
Militarism						
NATARMS		−.099	−.120	−.101	**−.064**	−.020
CONARMY		−.086	−.084	−.056	**−.047**	−.066
OBEY-THNKSELF		−.283	−.267	−.310	**−.253**	−.183
	R	.336	.331	.351	**.279**	.205
Racism						
RACDIF2		−.095	−.090	−.073	−.098	**−.035**
RACDIF4		−.078	−.082	−.057	−.094	**−.066**
RACMAR		−.296	−.292	−.330	−.220	**−.143**
RACPUSH		−.181	−.181	−.208	−.162	**−.080**
	R	.481	.477	.508	.411	**.237**
Item Ns						
Maximum		31,750	31,458	29,921	27,189	27,088
Minimum		9,357	9,272	9,297	9,312	9,015

[a]R denotes multiple correlation between a set of palatability items and a tolerance scale.

each tolerance index, the correlation with the liberal index was higher than its boldface R in Table 2.3. Thus, a grab bag index of liberal stances predicts tolerances for specific targets better than do target-specific palatabilities.

While *specific* palatabilities are hardly the driving force molding positions on free speech, it defies common sense to believe they have nothing to do

Table 2.4. Row Multiple Correlations in Table 2.3 Compared

Topic	Bold R in Table 2.3	Mean of other four Rs	Difference
Atheism	.356	.306	+.050
Communism	.371	.265	+.106
Homosexuality	.454	.346	+.032
Militarism	.279	.306	−.027
Racism	.237	.469	−.232

with those positions. Table 2.4 reanalyzes results in Table 2.3 to spot the effects of specific palatabilities. The first three rows of Table 2.4 say that the multiple correlation for the specific palatability (in boldface in Table 2.3) is from 3 to 11 points stronger than the others. The bottom two rows *seem* to say the opposite—but remembering that the signs of the palatability regression coefficients for militarists and racists are negative, it also could be read as, "Liberals are a bit less supportive of free expression for far right targets."

Putting it together, free speech attitudes are related to positions on social and political matters—mostly as a function of "general liberalism," only partly as a function of specific target palatabilities.[5]

But there is a less technical issue to address—how seriously should one take these answers? Saying "do not remove" does not imply the respondent is prepared to lay down his or her life to defend libraries. Taken to an extreme, one may ask whether we are *just tapping social desirability*? I don't believe we can answer this question with GSS data but say instead, *measuring long-term changes in social desirability (also known as culture) is a worthy task*. The same problem arises in studies of racial attitudes. Fischer and Hout (2006, p. 47) write,

> Social scientists argue over whether answers to surveys can accurately portray prejudice; the answers may not reflect what people really feel, much less what they actually do. Some suggest that the only thing public opinion surveys can measure is what is socially acceptable to say. Still, the trends in these public expressions of prejudice, as revealed by polls taken over a span of time, are substantial, valid and profound.

A simpler defense is that if in 2006 a third or more of Americans oppose basic constitutional rights, there is something to the Stouffer tolerance items beyond parroting platitudes.

The Demography of Tolerance Trends

Sociological analyses of trends mainly use the "demographic" approach (Davis 2001; Stinchcombe 1968, pp. 68–79), that is, attributing changing attitude levels in the population to changing proportions of people in categories with distinctive positions.[6]

Stouffer worked this way, though he did not use these words. In particular, in a famous section in chapter 4 (1955/1992, pp. 307–8) he speculated about future trends, forecasting a race between increasing education—which would raise tolerance—and future aging, which he expected would lower it. (He cautiously came down on the side of increasing tolerance.)

Stouffer did not seriously confront the now-ubiquitous distinction between age and cohort. (Ryder's [1965] seminal article on the topic came out a decade later.) Today one must consider both interpretations.

If a "demographic"[7] contributes to or explains population-level trends, (1) it must be related to the dependent variable; (2) its level must change over time (i.e., correlate with year); and (3) consequentially the correlation between the dependent variable and year will vanish or shrink when it is controlled.[8] Table 2.5 applies the rules to standard demographics and the liberalism index.

The products in the right-hand column suggest variables that might produce change in tolerance by year:[9] cohort, education, and the liberalism index seem most promising, the others less so.

Observe that cohort is the most promising predictor, age is next to last. While they are both correlated with overall tolerance (.302 and –.283), cohort shows the biggest change over time ($r = .510$), and age almost the smallest (.034). Despite popular opinion, during the GSS years the adult population was "middle-aging" not "aging," as baby boomers moved into their middle years.

Consequently we will dodge the notorious age/period/cohort conundrum by assuming that changes in population mean tolerance levels are due to cohort, not age. Note also that the correlations in the year column of Table 2.5

Table 2.5. Demographic Predictors and Trends in Summary Tolerance Scale (bivariate correlations[a])

"Demographic"	Year	Summary tolerance	Product
Cohort (birth year)	.510	.302	.154
Liberal index	.229	.446	.102
Education (years)	.206	.418	.086
Marital status (5 dummies)[a]	.157	.197	.030
Region (9 dummies)[a]	.090	.197	.018
City size (6 dummies)[a]	.081	.197	.016
Occupational prestige	.057	.244	.014
Fundamentalism of religious denomination	.049	.250	.012
Race (black)	.019	.088	.002
Sex (male)	.011	–.056	–.001
Age	.034	–.283	–.010

[a]Multiple correlations shown for demographics represented by two or more dummy variables.

are consistently smaller than those in the summary tolerance column—an example of the prime challenge in accounting for trends: a shortage of predictor variables that change much.

Table 2.5 suggests the following causal order: Year → Cohort → Education → Liberalism → Tolerance.

The appropriate sequence of four regressions implied by this model appears in Table 2.6.

> Model I, estimated from Table 2.2, gives the total gain in tolerance, in standardized scores.
> Model II shows the effects of cohort replacement.
>> Year controlled, cohort has a solid positive effect on tolerance.
>> Cohort controlled, all but one year effect (for homosexuals) becomes slightly *negative*.
> Model III shows the effect of education. It . . .
>> Drives the year coefficients down even further.
>> Reduces, but does not eliminate, the cohort coefficients.
> Model IV shows the effect of the liberalism index. It . . .
>> Has a consistent positive effect on tolerance and, net of the other variables, drives the year coefficients down even further.
>> Reduces, but does not eliminate, the cohort effects, save for tolerance of racists, for which the cohort effect is near zero.

In sum, after allowing for cohort replacement, upgraded education, and increased general liberalism, something in the GSS years operated to reduce tolerance of free expression, although it was not strong enough to reverse the overall trend toward increased tolerance.

Table 2.6. Demographic Predictors of Linear Trends in Tolerance Indices (OLS)

Model	Predictor	Standardized partial regression coefficients (beta)					
		Atheists	Communists	Homosexuals	Militarists	Racists	Summary
I	Year	+.132	+.138	+.200	+.093	+.037	+.143
II	Year	−.038	−.004	+.056	−.028	−.034	−.025
	Cohort	+.330	+.278	+.281	+.289	+.128	+.334
III	Year	−.065	−.031	+.031	−.051	−.053	−.055
	Cohort	+.249	+.197	+.205	+.219	+.072	+.244
	Education	+.330	+.331	+.312	+.285	+.233	+.369
IV	Year	−.079	−.045	+.015	−.062	−.063	−.071
	Cohort	+.170	+.121	+.117	+.159	+.020	+.156
	Education	+.254	+.258	+.226	+.227	+.184	+.284
	Liberalism	+.308	+.294	+.342	+.233	+.198	+.341
N, model IV		23,697	23,505	23,542	20,974	21,037	23,752

Cohort replacement, the ceaseless substitution of younger, more tolerant Americans for older, less tolerant ones, was the main vehicle for change—producing a better educated, more liberal adult population and having additional unmeasured positive effects.

The effects of cohort and education over and above the effect of liberalism suggest—but do not prove—the existence of some unmeasured pure tolerance variable not included in social liberalism.

For summary tolerance, Table 2.6 is nothing more (or less) than a breakdown of the first three numbers in the middle column of Table 2.5. Its coefficients estimate how much the summary scale would (in theory) change with a standard deviation change in the demographic. To see the actual effect of a demographic for all six indices, we multiply its net effect by the amount it changed during the GSS years. Specifically, I (1) transformed all six tolerance indices to percentages, for simplicity in interpretation; (2) multiplied each of the Demographic → Year coefficients in Table 2.5 by 34 (2006—1972) to give the total change in each predictor; and (3) multiplied the total change by the raw (unstandardized) slope for model IV, Table 2.6. The results appear in Table 2.7. Three predictors—year, cohort, and the liberalism index—make quite similar contributions. Each altered the percentage tolerant by about 8 points during the GSS years, cohort and liberalism increasing it, year decreasing it. The contribution of education was slightly lower, an increase of about 6 percentage points.

Table 2.7 also gives insight into the two outliers, the indices for Homosexuals and Racists. For Homosexuals the effects of three predictors are about the same as for the other items, but the year effect is slightly positive. Unmeasured forces from 1972 to 2006 tended to *reduce* other tolerance levels, but they increased tolerance of homosexuals.

The opposite holds for the Racists scale. Its year effect is negative like those for most scales, but the effects of the other three predictors are about half as large as for the other scales.

Table 2.7 underlines a theme of the analysis so far: The main drivers of tolerance were increases in education and liberalism, driven by and reinforced

Table 2.7. "Total Causal" Effects (in percentage points) of Demographic Predictors on Tolerance Indices

Predictor	Atheists	Communists	Homosexuals	Militarists	Racists	Summary
All	16.2	17.8	25.4	15.7	3.9	15.3
Cohort	10.8	8.0	7.6	10.7	1.3	8.4
Education	6.5	6.9	5.9	6.1	4.8	6.2
Liberalism	8.8	8.8	10.0	7.1	5.7	8.3
	26.1	23.7	23.5	23.9	11.8	22.9
Year	−9.8	−5.9	+1.9	−8.1	−7.9	−7.5
	16.3	17.8	25.4	15.8	3.9	15.4

by cohort succession. Attitudes toward specific targets played a role, but it was small and subtle.

Some Complexities

So far it appears that the forces of relentless progress outweighed the negative period effects. Since even by 2006, a third of U.S. adults still chose the less tolerant responses to the items (Table 2.2), it seems plausible that a Stoufferian optimism about the future is in order. Nevertheless, two complexities in the numbers—*nonlinearity* and *interactions*—cast a shadow on such sunny forecasts.

Nonlinearity

Analyses so far have used the traditional "linear" method—fitting the best possible straight line through the point cloud. This does not mean the data *are* perfectly linear or even close to it. The *best* line may not be a *good* line. For a simple test of linearity, one can (1) construct a new data set containing the mean levels of a dependent variable at each level of a predictor and (2) correlate the levels of each predictor with the means.[10] If the relationship is perfectly linear, the correlation will be +1.0 or –1.0. My experience has been that graphs appear as essentially straight lines when such correlations are larger than .90, while lower correlations merit a good look.

Table 2.8 applies this method to our key variables.

Inspection of graphs for the boldface numbers in Table 2.8 shows the following patterns:

Year → Liberalism:	Inverted U peaking in 2004
Year → Racists Index:	Plateau beginning in 1988
Cohort → Education:	Plateau beginning with birth date 1948
Cohort → Atheists Index:	Plateau beginning with birth date 1952
Cohort → Communists Index:	Plateau beginning with birth date 1952
Cohort → Militarists Index:	Plateau beginning with birth date 1952
Cohort → Summary Index:	Plateau beginning with birth date 1952
Cohort → Racists Index:	Inverted U peaking in 1952
Cohort → Homosexuals Index:	Monotonic decelerating

The story seems to be this: during the GSS years the two main drivers of tolerance trends, increasing educational attainment and the relative liberalization of newer cohorts, both stalled.

GSS education means peaked with the cohort born in 1948.[11] Cohort increases in tolerance hit the brakes with the 1952 cohort. Americans born in 1952 would reach 18 in 1972—that is, at the tail end of the legendary "1960s." Researchers have found it difficult to nail down a permanent "bulge" associated with maturing in the 1960s (Davis 2004). Rather it appears (for

Table 2.8. Linearity Assessment: Correlations between
Means for Dependent Variables and levels of Year and Cohort

Dependent Variable	Predictor	
	Year	Cohort
Cohort	.979	
Education	.970	**.803**
Liberalism	**.662**	.958
Atheists index	.948	**.859**
Communists index	.952	**.888**
Homosexuals index	.920	**.881**
Militarists index	.963	**.887**
Racists index	**.688**	**.640**
Summary index	.921	.867

Note: Values less than 0.90 appear in bold.

tolerance at least) that liberalism increased through the 1960s and then re-mained stable, rather than declining.[12]

These two brakes on ever-increasing tolerance did not appear to have much effect during the GSS years (left-hand column of Table 2.8). However, the following conjecture may be worth noting. If the relationships remain as they are, the GSS will comprise steadily increasing proportions of respondents born after 1952 and after 1948. Since they are no more tolerant than their predecessors, the overall increase in tolerance will slow down and eventually cease, settling near the 2006 mean for cohorts born after 1949, 70% tolerant on the summary scale.

Interactions and Ceilings

Linear trends in grand means may conceal quite different slopes among sub-categories. At an extreme, group B might be advancing while group A was stalled at some "ceiling" or even moving in the opposite direction. Ceilings have two meanings: (1) empirical—e.g., when a program to improve voting turnout produces 100% turnout which can not thereafter increase—and (2) artifactual—when a measurement instrument is not calibrated to catch very high values. I doubt the latter are present for the Stouffer tolerance items: only items such as "Taxpayers' money should be used to subsidize communist speeches" would suffer from that problem.

Assuming the current items are sufficiently calibrated, it could be that some groups have reached a practical upper limit while others continue to change—that is, statistically an "interaction." No one knows exactly what the maximum percentage tolerant for a practical upper limit would be. However, other GSS items give a few clues: in 2004–2006, 93% said extramarital sex was "always or almost always wrong," and 1984 questions about whether "jury duty," "voting," and "wartime military service" are citizens' obligations were

Table 2.9. Subgroup Differences in Summary Tolerance Scale

A. Means of Summary Tolerance Scale for Subgroups, 2004–2006

Education		Race		Size of place	
College Graduate	81 (779)	Nonblack	69 (2,456)	Suburb	75 (524)
Less	62 (2,016)	Black	55 (341)	Other	67 (1,441)
Region		Religion		Marital Status	
New England	74 (96)	Jewish	79 (40)	Single	70 (673)
Other	67 (2,702)	Other	68 (2,728)	Other	67 (2,123)
Cohort					
Born 1950–1988	70 (2,038)				
Born before 1950	61 (759)				

Note: Ns in parentheses.

B. Raw Slopes for Regression of Summary Tolerance Scale on Year for Subgoups, 1972–2006

Education		Race		Size of place	
College Graduate	+0.044	Nonblack	+0.579	Suburb	+0.358
Less	+0.428	Black	+0.352	Other	+0.615
Difference	−0.384	Difference	+0.227	Difference	−0.275
	(8.3)		(3.3)		(5.0)
Region		Religion		Marital Status	
New England	+0.246	Jewish	+0.201	Single	+0.201
Other	+0.558	Other	+0.551	Other	+0.593
Difference	−0.312	Difference	+0.350	Difference	−0.392
	(3.4)		(2.8)		(7.9)
Cohort					
Born 1950–1988	+0.189				
Born before 1950	+0.436				
Difference	−0.247				
	(5.4)				

Note: Numbers in parentheses are z statistics testing difference in slopes between groups.

endorsed by 95%, 96%, and 98%. My guess is that the apparent plateau in tolerance is not a question-writing artifact.

With this in mind, Table 2.9 displays the 2004–2006 mean percentages on the summary tolerance scale for key subgroups.

The upper panel shows the mean percentage more tolerant in 2004–2006 for the most tolerant subgroups on key demographic indicators. The highest mean is 81% tolerant, for college graduates. Thus, differences in slopes between subgroups do not seem to reflect artifactual ceilings.

Panel B in Table 2.9 displays slopes for the regression of the summary scale on year, separately for the two values of each dichotomy in panel A. Except for race (tolerance rose faster among nonblacks), the rate of increase was significantly greater for the less tolerant subgroups.[13]

Thus, in general, less tolerant population groups increased their tolerance at a greater rate than did more tolerant ones. The latter may have been nearing an empirical ceiling, though the GSS has subgroup percentages on other items well above them.

The same pattern may be viewed from another perspective, *depolarizing* (DiMaggio, Evans, and Bryson 1996; Evans 2003; Fiorina, Abrams, and Pope 2006; Kriner 2006), that is, a tendency for the spread in attitudes in the population to decline—or, reversing the language, an increase in consensus. To investigate, I formed a data set including *standard deviations* of the tolerance indices for each year. The correlations between year and variation in the tolerance scales turn out to be

Homosexuals	−.943
Summary	−.942
Atheists	−.916
Militarists	−.852
Communists	−.789
Racists	−.509

All correlations except that for racists ($p = .025$, the usual outlier) were significant at the .001 level despite Ns of only 19 and 20. Viewed this way, the GSS years saw not only increased liberalism but definite movement toward consensus on free expression issues.

To summarize this section, although the total population showed essentially straight-line increases in free expression tolerance 1972 to 2006 (tolerance of racists aside), several findings point toward future slowdowns and possible future stability: (1) two key drivers, cohort differences and educational attainment, reached plateaus; (2) save for race, subgroup differences showed slower progress in the more tolerant subgroups, possibly indicating a future national consensus (around 70% for the summary tolerance scale).

Summary and Conclusion

Tolerance of controversial expression is an important strand in America's official culture. Trends in it tell us a good deal about how the society is moving. The growth of replication studies allows sociologists to examine the underlying processes of social change. The classic "Stouffer questions" serve us well on both scores, as shown in this chapter.

The key findings here are the following:

1. Taking off from a low in 1954 (probably an outlier), tolerance (support for free expression) increased steadily during the GSS years 1972 to 2006.

2. The increase was observed across the ideological spectrum, although it was slower for "racist" targets.
3. Attitudes toward specific targets played a surprisingly small role, despite professional opinion. Rather, tolerance is mostly part of a package of "liberal" positions on social issues. Liberals are *more* tolerant of militarists and racists than "conservatives" more favorable to them.
4. The increase in tolerance was driven by two main forces—increasing levels of formal education and the relative liberalism of newer cohorts.
5. When "age" is reinterpreted as "cohort," Samuel Stouffer's 1955 prediction of increasing tolerance is borne out.
6. Beneath the appearance of endlessly increasing tolerance, some doubts appear.
   a. While smaller than the cohort influence, the year effects were *negative*, not positive, save for tolerance of homosexuals.
   b. The steady increases in education and arrival of more tolerant cohorts both hit plateaus during the GSS years.
   c. The increased slopes were significantly smaller among the initially more tolerant demographic groups, hinting though not proving that more tolerant groups may be approaching some ceiling well below unqualified support for First Amendment rights.

One can hardly wait for future GSSs that will allow us to discern whether these doubts are borne out, or if tolerance continues its rise.

Notes

This research was supported by the General Social Survey Project, funded in part by NSF grant SBR-9617727. Data from the 1954 Stouffer survey were provided by the Inter-University Consortium for Political and Social Research.

1. Two other key findings of less relevance here are the following: (1) despite the "hysteria," Americans showed little personal anxiety over political matters and (2) community leaders, even American Legion officers, were generally more tolerant than members of the national cross section. On the methodological side, the project carried out a powerful and unique experiment: it divided the interview assignments randomly between the National Opinion Research Center and the Gallup Organization—which got strikingly similar results.

2. The distinction may be important. The GSS item asking if pornography should be legalized shows no change during the GSS years ($r = -.006$). While a card-carrying ACLU member (the author is one) would consider pornography a First Amendment issue, the general public seems not to. One possibility is this: Americans assume the Stouffer targets, while wrongheaded, are "serious" while pornographers are considered "naughty."

3. From here on the results are for data weighted so that the sample represents individuals rather than households. The use of percentages as dependent variables in OLS analyses is a source of bitter debate. I lean to the position that with large samples,

significance tests are really a bit of a fetish since "everything is significant" and the gain in precision from using, say, logits is more than offset by inscrutable findings (see Ziliak and McClosky 2008; Hellevik 2009). I have not attempted corrections for cluster sampling (design effects) but as a rule of thumb treated t values less than 3.0 ($p < .002$) gingerly. Few turned up.

4. Namely, the eight liberal palatabilities are NATS, FUND, RELITEN, PREMARSX, XMARSEX, RACPUSH reversed, RACMAR reversed, and NATARMS reversed. Each was converted to its z score, and the eight were averaged. Alpha = .561, only moderate but suitable for a grab bag index.

5. The results for OBEY-THNKSELF suggest a totally different interpretation. If one substitutes "nonauthoritarian" for "liberal," exactly the same pattern holds. It might be that nonauthoritarians tend to hold liberal positions, one of which is generalized tolerance. Alas, the OBEY-THNKSELF item appears only for 1986–2006, and the GSS has no long-term authoritarianism item. If I were redesigning the survey, I would add items on authoritarianism even though the topic is no longer fashionable.

6. This, of course, is the totally wrong way to approach changes in attitudes for individuals.

7. I'm defining "demographic" very loosely here, following the usual practice in survey analysis.

8. This is the famous "path multiplication/it takes two to tango" rule that is the foundation of multivariate analysis.

9. The rule of thumb: the product will be a little bit larger than the reduction in the year–summary tolerance correlation obtained by controlling that particular predictor.

10. I used the "aggregate" procedure in SPSS.

11. Deleting respondents under 25, whose schooling may not be complete, gives the same plateau shape. See Goldin and Katz (2008, esp. pp. 20–21).

12. Note that the 1952 cohort entered the GSS-eligible population in 1970, just as the survey was beginning (1972). It may be no coincidence that the negative year effects revealed in this analysis coincided with the beginning of the cohort plateau.

13. The z of 2.8 for religion does not meet the promised $z = 3$ criterion (there are only 40 Jewish cases). However, from what we know about American religious groups, the finding seems plausible.

References

Bishop, George F. 2005. *The Illusion of Public Opinion*. Lanham, MD: Rowman & Littlefield.

Davis, James A. 1975. "Communism, Conformity, Cohorts and Categories." *American Journal of Sociology* 81:491–513.

———. 1990. "Attitudes toward Free Speech in Six Countries in the Mid-1980's: Australia, Austria, Great Britain, Italy, the United States, and West Germany." *European Sociological Review* 6:1–14.

———. 1992. "Changeable Weather in a Cooling Climate atop the Liberal Plateau." *Public Opinion Quarterly* 56:261–306.

———. 2001. "Testing the Demographic Explanation of Attitude Trends: Secular Trends in Attitudes among U.S. Householders, 1972–1996." *Social Science Research* 30:363–85.

———. 2004. "Did Growing Up in the 1960s Leave a Permanent Mark on Attitudes and Values? Evidence from the GSS." *Public Opinion Quarterly* 68:161–83.

DiMaggio, Paul, John Evans, and Bethany Bryson. 1996. "Have American Social Attitudes Become More Polarized?" *American Journal of Sociology* 102:690–755.

Evans, John H. 2003. "Have Americans' Attitudes Become More Polarized?—An Update." *Social Science Quarterly* 84:71–90.

Fiorina, Morris P., Samuel J. Abrams, and Jeremy C. Pope. 2006. *Culture War? The Myth of a Polarized America.* New York: Pearson/Longman.

Fischer, Claude S., and Michael Hout. 2006. *Century of Difference: How America Changed in the Last One Hundred Years.* New York: Russell Sage Foundation.

Goldin, Claudia, and Lawrence F. Katz. 2008. *The Race between Education and Technology.* Cambridge, MA: Harvard University Press.

Hellevik, Ottar. 2009. "Linear versus Logistic Regression When the Dependent Variable Is a Dichotomy." *Quality and Quantity* 43:59–74.

Hyman, Herbert, and Charles Wright. 1979. *Education's Lasting Influence on Values.* Chicago: University of Chicago Press.

Kriner, Douglas L. 2006. "Examining Variance in Presidential Approval." *Public Opinion Quarterly* 70:23–47.

Nie, Norman H., Jane Junn, and Kenneth Stehlik-Barry. 1996. *Education and Democratic Citizenship in America.* Chicago: University of Chicago Press.

Nunn, Clyde Z., Harry J. Crockett Jr., and J. Allen Williams Jr. 1978. *Tolerance for Nonconformity.* San Francisco: Jossey-Bass.

Ryder, Norman B. 1965. "The Cohort as a Concept in the Study of Social Change." *American Sociological Review* 30:843–61.

Stinchcombe, Arthur L. 1968. *Constructing Social Theories.* Chicago: University of Chicago Press.

Stouffer, Samuel A. 1955/1992. *Communism, Conformity and Civil Liberties: A Cross Section of the Nation Speaks Its Mind.* New Brunswick, NJ: Transaction.

Sullivan, John L., James Piereson, and George E. Marcus. 1979. "An Alternative Conceptualization of Political Tolerance: Illusory Increases 1950s–1970s." *American Political Science Review* 73:781–94.

Ziliak, Stephen T., and Deirdre N. McClosky. 2008. *The Cult of Statistical Significance.* Ann Arbor: University of Michigan Press.

3

The *Real* Record on Racial Attitudes

Lawrence D. Bobo, Camille Z. Charles, Maria Krysan, and Alicia D. Simmons

> But the responsibility of the historian or sociologist who studies racism is not to moralize and condemn but to understand this malignancy so that it can be more effectively treated, just as a medical researcher studying cancer does not moralize about it but searches for knowledge that might point the way to a cure.
>
> —George M. Fredrickson, *Racism: A Short History*

Anyone serious about understanding American society must at some early point engage the problem of race and racial division. These have been prominent features of U.S. social organization and culture from about as far back as the historical record allows us to go. For this reason, distinguished historian Winthrop Jordan once wrote that he wished he could have been there in 1619 "questionnaire in hand" when the first "twenty Negars" arrived at Jamestown, Virginia (Jordan 1968, p. viii). He suggested that to understand how and why race had so profoundly shaped the development of the early United States, one had to understand the racial attitudes and beliefs of actors in those times. Jordan did not, however, have a time machine. He could not directly ask people about their attitudes and beliefs on race. Instead, he had to cull available records and writings to extract how race was understood.

Modern sociologists, however, are fortunate to have systematic, repeated social surveys that provide an unusually powerful tool for assessing change in our social and cultural fabric. The full attitudinal record on race from the General Social Survey (GSS) provides a rich and complex scientific resource for analyzing one of the fundamental bases of social organization and inequality in the United States, race and racial division (Massey 2007). Unlike even the most probing ethnography or handful of in-depth interviews, or the most complex and meticulously designed laboratory experiment, surveys represent large and important population groups in a fashion that allows for rigorous multivariate analyses and hypothesis testing. Beyond these customary strengths of surveys, the GSS's repeated cross-sectional samples yield assessments of social change over a nearly 40-year time span (Davis, Smith, and Marsden 2008).[1]

Consistent with the thrust of eminent historian George Fredrickson's admonition in this chapter's epigraph, the GSS aims mainly to document and describe key features of racial attitudes in the United States; to allow scholars to pinpoint the social location of these views for such significant social attributes as age, level of education, region of the country, gender, and other factors; and, importantly, to trace patterns of change over time. No single conceptualization of racial attitudes, or racism more broadly, dominated the initial content of the GSS in this domain. With perfect hindsight, we see that its coverage of some key conceptual domains (e.g., racial stereotypes) was much thinner than it should have been (Quillian and Pager 2001). Over time, the GSS's approach to racial attitudes has changed, partly because of changes in larger social issues, partly because of empirical trends in the items measured, and partly in response to significant intellectual currents in the scientific community interested in racial attitudes. All of this is fundamentally how good, careful, empirically grounded science should develop (Lieberson 1992).

After a brief review of the pre-1972 record on racial attitudes, we organize our treatment of trends in racial topics into seven conceptual or subject areas. We first examine what Schuman, Steeh, and Bobo (1985) labeled "racial principles": basic rules that should guide black–white relations—in particular, whether the United States should be a society that segregates and openly discriminates on the basis of race, or one that is integrated and nondiscriminatory on the basis of race. The second category involves social distance feelings about potential hypothetical forms of social contact that cross the black–white divide in different domains of life (e.g., schools), often in different proportionate mixtures (i.e., majority-white settings versus majority-minority settings). The third area involves governmental policy initiatives to ameliorate racial inequality and discrimination (e.g., affirmative action). The fourth set concerns stereotypes, or beliefs about the behavioral traits and capacities of particular racial groups, while the fifth involves lay or causal explanations of racial inequality. Affective or socioemotional evaluations—that tap basic like-versus-dislike, or approach-versus-avoid reactions to members of other groups—constitute the sixth area. The final category involves collective resentments—the extent to which African Americans are perceived as trying to advance themselves unfairly by a different set of rules than those putatively followed by white Americans.

We view race as a social construction. Race, or, more generally, ethnoracial distinctions, is historically contingent and varies in exact configuration and salience over time. Such a base of social identity intersects with and is often importantly conditioned by other markers of social difference such as gender, age, class, and sexuality. Although distinctions seen as racial typically invoke consideration of physical and biological markers like skin tone and color, hair texture, eye shape, and possibly other features, none of these lends race its social meaning or significance.

This chapter will, of necessity, disproportionately emphasize the views of white Americans and the black–white divide. This emphasis is due to the design of the GSS, not our theoretical choice or priority. The GSS design represents the English-speaking population of the United States as a whole, so there are many more white respondents than black (or Hispanic or Asian) ones in every GSS sample. Our main task is to report on social change with regard to whites' attitudes and beliefs on race. At several points we also report such trends among blacks. We occasionally report group comparisons, but the GSS only recently initiated repeated attitude series referring to Hispanics or Asians, severely constraining our capacity to trace change in a more multiracial context.

This chapter does not attempt exhaustive coverage of all topics that should be addressed by a more general summary of the literature on racial attitudes. For example, we devote little attention to racial attitudes as an influence on voting behavior or over the course of political campaigns (for excellent summaries see Callaghan and Terkildsen 2002; Hutchings and Valentino 2004; Valentino and Sears 2005; Lee 2008). Much important scholarly work on race has such a political focus (Carmines and Stimson 1989; Kinder and Sanders 1996; Stoker 1996; Sears, Van Larr, Carrillo, and Kosterman 1997; Sniderman and Carmines 1997; Mendelberg 2001), but the GSS does not assess views at times proximate to major biennial national elections, nor does it focus centrally on electoral behavior.

Other topics have more immediate sociological relevance but too are largely beyond the scope of this review. We do not carefully consider the effects of actual minority group size (Fossett and Kiecolt 1989; Kinder and Mendelberg 1995; M. C. Taylor 1998; Dixon and Rosenbaum 2004; Dixon 2005; Stults and Baumer 2007) or of perceived minority group size (Gallagher 2003; Alba, Rumbaut, and Marotz 2005; Wong 2008) on racial attitudes; the impacts of urbanicity or of regional migration (Tuch 1987; Kuklinski, Cobb, and Gilens 1997; Glaser and Gilens 1997; Weakliem and Biggert 1998; Carter, Steelman, Mulkey, and Borch 2005; T. C. Wilson 1985, 1986, 1991); or debates about gender effects on racial attitudes (Stack 1997; Johnson and Marini 1998; Hughes and Tuch 2003), nor do we examine race as an aspect of social tolerance and political and cultural polarization more broadly (Davis 2004; Downey 2000; Evans 2003; Mondak and Sanders 2003; Moore and Ovadia 2006; Persell, Green, and Gurevich 2001).

We do aim to map the major dimensions of, and trends in, U.S. racial attitudes as recorded by the GSS. We assess change within race and consider black–white differences in attitudes, and report more selectively on differences in attitudes by education, region, and age. The GSS is best suited to illuminate the fundamental and general problem of race as a sociological feature of larger social organization and culture, on which we will focus.

The attitudinal record assembled in the GSS provides a remarkably rich and sociologically important lens on race in the United States. These data vividly document both significant progressive changes regarding race, as well as substantial enduring frictions and conflicts that continue to make race such a fraught terrain. While the GSS does not tap every relevant nuance of a changing American racial divide, it does provide incredible scientific purchase on what has changed, what has not, and why. This conceptually broad and analytically powerful record is a strong caution against glib generalities that try to reduce an enormously multifaceted social phenomenon to simplistic catch phrases like "racist America," "the end of racism," or most recently "postracial America."

The Pre-1972 Record and the *Scientific American* Reports

Sociological interest in matters of racial attitudes, or what might be termed "prejudice," has a very long and distinguished history. Consideration of such questions dates back at least to W.E.B. DuBois and his pioneering work *The Philadelphia Negro: A Social Study* (1899), which treated racial prejudice as one organic and contextual factor structuring American society in general and racial inequality in particular (Bobo 2000). Other early sociologists such as Robert E. Park (1924) and Emory S. Bogardus (1928) focused attention on aspects of racial attitudes. Likewise, an ambitious background report on attitudes was prepared for Swedish economist Gunnar Myrdal's (1944) massive two volume work *An American Dilemma: The Negro Problem and American Democracy* (see Horowitz 1944).

Of greatest significance for the development of the racial items in the GSS, however, was a series of surveys first launched during World War II. Conducted under the auspices of what was once called the Office of War Information and fielded by NORC, national surveys in 1942 and 1944 sought to determine if racial divisions would impede a unified U.S. war effort. The first reports were, in fact, "classified" documents.

Spanning two decades, the *Scientific American* series of four articles on racial attitudes in America provides a positive report of national sentiment and expresses great optimism about the future direction of white racial attitudes toward blacks. These four documents, penned by Herbert H. Hyman, Paul B. Sheatsley, Andrew M. Greeley, and D. Garth Taylor, present a wealth of longitudinal data that provide a fundamental baseline for national surveys of racial attitudes in the United States.

The first *Scientific American* article, written by Hyman and Sheatsley, appeared in 1956. "Attitudes toward Desegregation" covers racially integrating schools, public transportation, and neighborhoods by families with the same income and education. Examining the nation as a whole, Hyman and Sheatsley found that 60% of whites were willing to extend integration to transportation, 51% did not object to living near a black family of the same socioeconomic status, and 48% supported school integration. They also found more acceptance of integration among northerners, younger adults, and those with greater educational attainment. Comparing these findings to data collected during the 1940s, the authors found a steady trend toward more integrationist attitudes. Contributing to these gains were a growing belief that blacks and whites were equally intelligent and official institutional and legal actions eliminating segregation.

Hyman and Sheatsley released a second report in 1964, following events such as the school desegregation efforts in Little Rock, sit-ins, and the Oxford, Mississippi, riots. They asked if the subsequent tumultuous years had derailed the positive trends they found in 1956. Certainly the American public was acutely aware of these events; civil rights and race relations were mentioned more than any other issue as the most important problem facing the nation. Hyman and Sheatsley found that the tide of integrationist sentiments observed in 1956 had not only continued but in fact surged ahead in the South. Age, education, and region continued to be important determinants of racial attitudes. The authors also highlighted regional mobility, reporting that attitudes of southerners who formerly lived in the North tended to be more similar to their northern rather than southern counterparts. The 1964 report continued to express optimism for the future of racial attitudes, not only because of the positive attitude trends over time, but also because these gains resulted largely from segregationists becoming more open to integration over time.

Greeley and Sheatsley published the third entry in the series in 1971, one year before the GSS began. During the preceding seven years, riots, the Martin Luther King Jr. assassination, and rising black militancy had rocked the country. In the face of these historical events, Greeley and Sheatsley continued to have high hopes for Americans' racial attitudes, evidenced in a small but symbolic way by a change in the article's title from "Attitudes toward Desegregation" (as in 1956 and 1964), to "Attitudes toward Racial Integration" (also used in the fourth article). Their continuing optimism was buoyed by the fact that integrating transportation had been rendered a nonissue: 88% of the population rejected segregation in this area. Integration of schools remained problematic, however: a quarter of the population still supported separate schooling for whites and blacks.

Important methodological changes took place in the 1971 article. First, the sample pool expanded to include nonwhites (although they were omitted from the analysis). Second, newly collected information on respondents' ethnicity revealed little evidence of a distinctive pattern of racism among white ethnics. Differences in attitudes were also reported for groupings by religion, income level, occupation, gender, and population size of residential area. Third, Greeley and Sheatsley included a new scale of racial attitudes. Questions concerning schooling, transportation, and neighborhoods were either retained or slightly modified, while items about integration of other public spaces, inviting a "Negro" guest home for dinner, intermarriage, and whether blacks should push where they are not wanted were added. Overall, the authors found a continued rise in prointegration sentiment, with the largest gains among groups that were previously the staunchest segregationists. Notably, however, one question revealed support for the then-popular claim that black militancy was producing a backlash among whites. While in 1963 a quarter of whites rejected the idea that blacks shouldn't push themselves where they are not wanted, by 1970 such acceptance of black activism fell by almost 10 points, to 16%.[2]

The final (1978) *Scientific American* article, which drew on early GSS data, was published by D. G. Taylor, Sheatsley, and Greeley. This report found a surge of integrationist sentiment between 1970 and 1972, particularly in the South. During the 1973–1978 period liberalism on racial issues continued to increase, but at a slower, albeit steady, pace. The authors noted that while part of the change in attitudes stemmed from the entry of new cohorts of younger respondents with more liberal outlooks, older Americans were also changing their beliefs. Furthermore, they asserted that liberalization on racial issues was part of a trend encompassing a range of related social issues.

Taken together, the *Scientific American* articles report a clear and unyielding rise in the expression of integrationist sentiment among the American public between the mid-1950s and the late 1970s. As the authors predicted, racial attitudes in the domains studied continued to liberalize after the period covered by their research. Key variables such as education, region, and age remained important predictors of racial attitudes.

Contemporary research differs from these important past studies in two interesting ways, however. Hyman, Sheatsley, Greeley, and Taylor were not concerned about the social desirability bias that often worries scholars today. In regard to respondent candor, the first report notes,

> There can be little doubt that on racial segregation people honestly expressed their deeply felt opinions. They were not at all reluctant to talk about the subject to interviewers, and they consistently showed a livelier interest in this topic than in almost any other public question on which people are polled. (Hyman and Sheatsley 1956, p. 37)

Second, rising numbers of "don't know" responses in surveys are of increasing concern to present-day researchers (Berinsky 1999, 2002; Forman 2004). Such responses may express ambivalence or be attempts to give socially acceptable answers. The *Scientific American* reports did not share these concerns: their "don't know" rate was never above 4%. This does not indicate an overall assuredness in opinion among midcentury survey respondents; on the contrary, "don't know" rates were 10% to 20% for the majority of questions posed on other topics. Instead, Hyman and Sheatsley (1956, p. 37) stated that when it came to racial attitudes, "almost everyone knows exactly where he stands on the matter."

The Attitudinal Record

The GSS launched in 1972–1973 contained the 14 racial attitude questions shown in Table 3.1.[3] These items provide a snapshot of key attitudes in the United States at that time and a benchmark for viewing not only ensuing trends for these items, but responses to new questions introduced later. Most of the items measure either principles guiding race relations or social distance feelings. Only two were items on government policy, while we classify one as "miscellaneous." At this early stage, the survey did not cover racial stereotypes, explanations of racial inequality, affective orientations, or collective resentments. The latter type of question, very close in content to the question of whether blacks should "push themselves where they're not wanted," proves to be of great interpretative importance below.[4]

Seven patterns stand out in Table 3.1. First and foremost, even in 1972 endorsement by whites of segregation and open discrimination as principles guiding black–white relations had given way to preferred ideals of integration and equal treatment. Only 3% thought whites should have the "first chance" at a job, only roughly 1 in 10 (13%) endorsed separate schools, and just 1 in 4 (25%) said that they would not vote for a qualified black presidential candidate nominated by their own party. Second, the equal treatment responses for two items in this original 1972–1973 pool, about job access and neighbors of similar socioeconomic status, were endorsed at such high levels (97% and 87%, respectively) that these questions were not repeated after 1972. The repudiation of Jim Crow ideology as the guiding principle for black–white interaction, while not complete, was quite far-reaching.

Third, endorsement of integration seemed to reach beyond mere principle. Expressed openness to various forms of contact with blacks, be it a neighbor on the block, a few black children in a school, or even hosting a black dinner guest, was quite high. The principles seemed to imply more than just lofty goals, including ideals that might be put into practice in these more public and less intimate ways.

Fourth, sharp differences in outlook divided northerners from southerners, the highly from the poorly educated, and the young from the old. For example, only a third of northern whites endorsed the idea that whites have the right to keep blacks out of their neighborhood, compared to 53% of southern whites; only 24% of college educated whites endorsed this view, compared to 53% of those who had not completed high school; and only 26% of those age 18 to 33 endorsed whites' right to keep blacks out of a neighborhood, compared to 52% of those over age 50. These are all portentous trends. There were

Table 3.1. Whites' Responses to Racial Attitude Questions, GSS 1972–1973[a]

	National	Region		Education			Age		
		North	South	<12	12	13+	18–33	34–50	51+
Racial principles									
White first chances at jobs (RACJOB)	3	3	5	7	2	0.3	1	4	5
Blacks should go to separate schools (RACSHOL)	13	8	31	26	9	3	7	16	17
Not vote for black president (RACPRES)	25	18	48	36	22	15	16	24	35
Favor laws against intermarriage (RACMAR)	37	31	53	59	33	18	23	37	51
Right to segregate neighborhoods (RACSEG)	39	35	53	53	38	24	26	39	52
Home sellers can discriminate in sales (RACOPEN)	64	60	73	70	68	54	52	67	73
Social distance feelings									
Object to same SES black neighbor (RACOBJCT)	13	9	25	19	12	7	7	13	18
Object to school with few blacks (RACFEW)	7	4	16	12	5	3	4	6	11
Object to school with half blacks (RACHALF)	17	14	26	22	16	12	12	18	21
Object to school with mostly blacks (RACMOST)	41	41	45	38	43	44	40	45	40
Object to black dinner guest (RACDIN)	30	23	46	38	32	18	26	31	32
Government policy on race									
Opposes school busing (BUSING)	86	84	94	87	88	83	80	88	90
Too much spending on blacks (NATRACE)	26	22	34	33	26	19	20	28	30
Miscellaneous									
Blacks shouldn't push (RACPUSH)	74	71	83	81	75	58	61	76	84

[a]Values are the percentages supporting the intolerant response. *N* ranges between 960 and 2,583. GSS variable mnemonics in parentheses. Data are from the 1972 GSS, except for RACOPEN and NATRACE (1973).

good grounds to expect that the South would increasingly come to resemble the rest of the nation, that the highly educated would be thought leaders for the rest of the population, and that younger cohorts of individuals would gradually usher in more prointegration outlooks in this domain.

These four patterns constitute much of the case for a very optimistic interpretation of the tenor of U.S. racial attitudes in the early 1970s, as conveyed in the last *Scientific American* report. Three other noteworthy patterns, however, temper such optimism. First, the number or proportion of blacks in a social setting clearly mattered to most white respondents. Whites were much less willing to see their child(ren) attend a school where half of the other students were black. Their willingness dropped even further when asked about a majority-black school. This pattern demonstrates that whites were not blind or completely indifferent to race. It points to at least one manifestation of the durable importance of race. Nonetheless, it would be facile to interpret these results as racism. Resistance to being in a minority status, for instance, might well be found for religious (e.g., Catholic versus Jewish) or class-based social settings as well.

Second, it is telling that both items in the "government intervention" category reveal little white enthusiasm for government action to redress racial inequality. Fully 86% of white respondents rejected school busing as a tool for achieving school desegregation. Only about a quarter of white respondents thought the government was spending "too much" on assisting blacks, but most felt that such spending was already at the right level. Third, in 1972, 74% of whites nationwide agreed that "blacks should not push themselves" where they are not wanted. Despite broad acceptance of principles of equality, then, whites were reluctant to endorse actions challenging the status quo.

This snapshot portrait in 1972–1973 is telling and much more nuanced than that frequently assumed by those asserting that the survey literature portrays an overly rosy picture of racial change (Bonilla-Silva 1997; Feagin 1999). No simple description fits the full set of results in Table 3.1. Even in 1972 the careful analyst would have wisely stressed the complexity of the portrait painted by these data. Moreover, with hindsight, we can say that these data effectively foreshadowed patterns of consistent importance over the next four decades. Although the GSS eventually enriched and deepened the attitudinal record using new categories of questions, the initial pool effectively captured a number of its very durable features. Contrary to the views of survey research critics, these patterns are borne out in a variety of larger societal conditions as the trends discussed below reveal.

Racial Principles

Figure 3.1 shows trends for several key racial principle items. All show steady movement by white Americans away from supporting racial segregation and discrimination as ideals that should guide black–white interaction. A solid majority turned against segregationist or Jim Crow principles in the

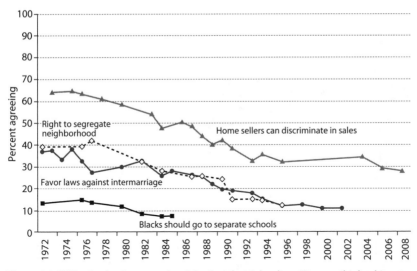

Figure 3.1. Whites' attitudes toward racial principles. Schooling: "Do you think white students and (Negro/Black) students should go to the same schools or separate schools?" ("separate schools" coded as agreeing). Intermarriage: "Do you think there should be laws against marriages between (Negroes/Blacks/African Americans) and whites?" ("yes" coded as agreeing). Neighborhood: "White people have a right to keep (Negroes/Blacks/African Americans) out of their neighborhoods if they want to, and (Negroes/Blacks/African Americans) should respect that right." ("agree strongly" and "agree slightly" coded as agreeing). Home sales: "Suppose there is a community-wide vote on the general housing issue. There are two possible laws to vote on. One law says that a homeowner can decide for himself whom to sell his house to, even if he prefers not to sell to (Negroes/Blacks/African Americans). The second law says that a homeowner cannot refuse to sell to someone because of their race or color. Which law would you vote for?" ("owner decides" coded as agreeing).

domains of schools, housing, and racial intermarriage. By 1972, fewer than 15% of whites nationwide thought that black and white children should attend separate schools. That fell below 10% by the early 1980s. By 1985, so few people endorsed the segregationist response that the GSS dropped this item. Similarly, support for laws against intermarriage and the idea that whites have a right to keep blacks out of their neighborhoods declined steadily, from around 40% in 1972 to around 15% by the mid-1990s. Substantial opposition to laws that would prohibit individual home owners from racial discrimination when selling, however, remains even in 2008 (the last point for which we have data). Just fewer than one-third of white adults nationwide then supported the idea that individual home owners should be able to discriminate. Although quite substantial, this is far below the roughly 65% of whites who advocated such a posture in 1973.

To underscore an earlier point, we examine the trend in support for a home owner's right to discriminate by education and region simultaneously

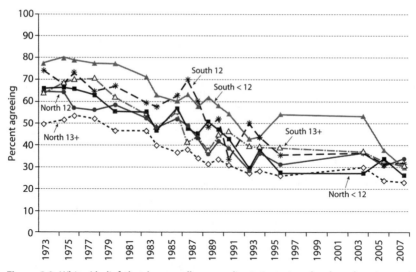

Figure 3.2. Whites' belief that home sellers can discriminate in sales, by education and region. See note to Figure 3.1 for question wording. Education is measured in years of education. "South Atlantic," "East South Central," and "West South Central" are coded as South.

(Figure 3.2). Better educated whites and those living outside the South are a good deal less likely to endorse support for discrimination. Considering education and region jointly we find that well-educated whites outside the South least support the right to discriminate in the sale of housing whereas poorly educated southern whites most support it. Within all six groups, though, the core trend moves substantially away from supporting discrimination. Indeed, among poorly educated southern whites endorsement falls from nearly 80% in 1973 to 30% in 2008. The gap between highly educated northern whites and poorly educated southern whites fell from almost 30 percentage points in 1973 to roughly 10 percentage points in 2008.

Yet these results should also caution those who would claim that segregationist sentiment has completely vanished. In 2008, a nontrivial proportion of whites nationwide, 28%, still support an individual home owner's right to discriminate on the basis of race when selling a home, and even nearly 1 in 4 highly educated northern whites adopt this position. On the basis of careful experimental data we know that many whites supporting such a right to discriminate claim to be motivated by a competing principle of limiting government authority to coerce individuals (Schuman and Bobo 1988). At a minimum, this result suggests that other commitments may check or trump principles of racial integration and equal treatment in significant ways.

Figure 3.3 shows trends in the racial principle items among African American respondents.[5] On none of the items at any point do even as many as one-third of African Americans endorse the segregationist, discriminatory,

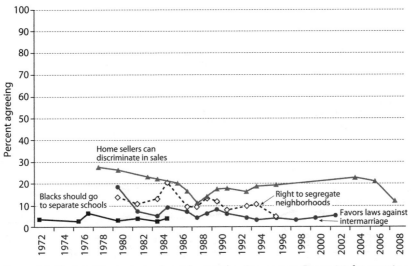

Figure 3.3. Blacks' attitudes toward racial principles. See note to Figure 3.1 for question wording.

unequal treatment response. Blacks were most likely to support discrimination by home owners in selling to whomever they like, but at levels well beneath those among whites. On the whole African Americans broadly endorsed integrationist, nondiscriminatory views on racial principle items throughout the period for which we have data.

Social Distance Feelings

Figure 3.4 maps trends among whites in openness to sending their children to a school where, variously, a few, half, or most of the other children would be black. Numbers clearly matter for most respondents; moreover, no strong secular trend toward diminishing concern with the number of black children in a school is evident, in sharp contrast to the pattern for the racial principle items. The GSS dropped these items after 1996, though the hypothetical "half black" and "mostly black" schools still elicited substantial resistance then. Objection to such schools is consistent with the notion that whites are defending their group position (Blumer 1958; A. W. Smith 1981; Bobo and Tuan 2006). Accordingly, prejudice is not just a matter of feelings of like or dislike, but rather of relative group status, positioning, and entitlement.

No long-standing set of social distance items deals with neighborhoods. The GSS item on neighborhood social distance (see Table 3.1, "Object to Same SES Black Neighbor") was not repeated after 1972. Given the accumulating evidence on the importance of racial residential segregation to larger patterns of racial inequality (Massey and Denton 1993), rich examinations of attitudes on neighborhood composition preferences in several metropolitan areas

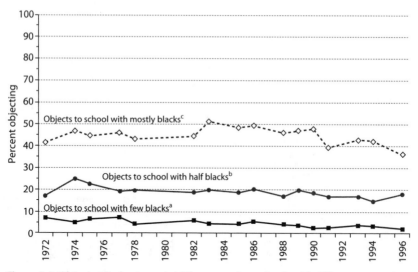

Figure 3.4. Whites' attitudes toward children attending schools with different proportions of blacks. Question a: "Would you yourself have any objection to sending your children to a school where a few of the children are (Negroes/Blacks/African Americans)?" ("yes" coded as objecting). Question b: "Would you yourself have any objection to sending your children to a school where half of the children are (Negroes/Blacks/African Americans)?" ("yes" coded as objecting). Question c: "Would you yourself have any objection to sending your children to a school where more than half of the children are (Negroes/Blacks/African Americans)?" ("yes" coded as objecting).

(Farley, Steeh, Krysan, Jackson, and Reeves 1994; Bobo and Zubrinsky 1996; Zubrinsky and Bobo 1996), and key methodological innovations (Charles 2000), the GSS later assessed residential social distance in two different ways.

First, as part of its 2000 Multiethnic America Module, the GSS replicated a key innovation from the Multicity Study of Urban Inequality project (O'Connor, Tilly, and Bobo 2001). Respondents were shown a card depicting a 15-house neighborhood with their own home in the middle and asked to indicate their preferred racial mixture by writing a "W" (for white), "B" (for black), "A" (for Asian), or "H" (for Hispanic) in the remaining homes. Results reported by Charles (2003) are reproduced in Table 3.2. Three patterns stand out. First, and arguably most encouraging, most white, black, and Hispanic respondents created neighborhoods with some degree of racial mixture. Second, all groups, on average, exhibited a degree of ethnocentrism by creating neighborhoods including substantial percentages of coracials.

Third, the results highlight the likely difficulty of creating stably integrated communities: it is not possible to achieve the mixtures preferred by all groups simultaneously. Something that looks much more like racial prejudice also appears to be involved. Thus, 1 in 5 whites nationally created an ideal neigh-

Table 3.2. Summary Statistics, Multiethnic Neighborhood Showcard Experiment, 2000 GSS[a]

Ideal neighborhood composition by target group race	Respondent race		
	White	Black	Hispanic
White			
Mean %	57	30	32
% no whites	0	9	1
% all whites	20	0	0
Black			
Mean %	27	42	19
% no blacks	25	1	18
% all blacks	0	7	0
Hispanic			
Mean %	13	15	34
% no Hispanics	32	38	3
% all Hispanics	0	0	1
Asian			
Mean %	13	13	16
% no Asians	33	32	19
% all Asians	0	0	0
N	858	152	78

Source: Charles (2003).

[a]"Now I'd like you to imagine a neighborhood that had an ethnic and racial *mix you personally* would *feel most comfortable in.* Here is a blank neighborhood card, which depicts some houses that surround your own. Using the letters A for Asian, B for Black, H for Hispanic, or Latin American and W for White, please put a letter in each of these houses to represent your preferred neighborhood where you would most like to live. Please be sure to fill in all of the houses."

borhood that was all white, 1 in 4 created a neighborhood with no blacks in it, and 1 in 3 created a neighborhood with no Hispanics or no Asians. Similarly, though fewer than 1 in 10 blacks created an all-black neighborhood or one with no whites, almost 2 out of 5 created ideal neighborhoods with no Hispanics or Asians in them. Careful multivariate models make it clear that negative racial stereotypes play an important role in structuring these neighborhood racial composition preferences (Charles 2003, 2006).[6]

The GSS has more recently begun to track changes over time in racial residential preferences. Data from the 1976, 1994, and 2004 Detroit Area Studies, however, reveal a trend toward more willingness to consider integrated neighborhoods. For example, between 1976 and 2004, the percentage of Detroit-area whites who said they would be "willing to move into" a neighborhood that was 20% African American increased from 50% to 78%. As we saw for schools (Figure 3.4), the level of integration matters: whites are far less willing to consider a 53% African American neighborhood, and such

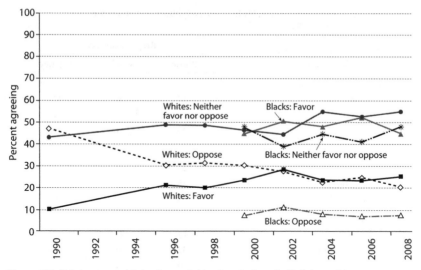

Figure 3.5. Opinion toward living in a neighborhood where half of the residents are opposite race. "Now I'm going to ask you about different types of contact with various groups of people. In each situation would you please tell me whether you would be very much in favor of it happening, somewhat in favor, neither in favor nor opposed to it happening, somewhat opposed, or very much opposed to it happening? Living in a neighborhood where (half of your neighbors were whites/half of your neighbors were blacks)?" (white responses are about black neighborhoods and black responses are about white neighborhoods).

willingness has increased less since 1976. Between 1976 and 2004, the percentage of whites willing to consider such a neighborhood increased from 16% to 34% (Farley et al. 1994; Krysan and Bader 2007).

Among African Americans, the patterns are quite different. The vast majority (ranging from 87% and 99%) of Detroit-area African Americans are willing to live in neighborhoods that were 20% black or 53% black, and this has not changed since 1976 (Farley et al. 1994; Krysan and Bader 2007). Furthermore, the majority of African Americans in Detroit—across all three periods—ranked the approximately 50–50 neighborhood as the most attractive.

The 1990 GSS Intergroup Tolerance module introduced a set of items on residential social distance and racial intermarriage that have been measured regularly since 1996. Figure 3.5 reports the trends in whites' willingness to live in a neighborhood where "half of your neighbors were blacks." Only 10% of whites said they favored living in such a neighborhood in 1990. This response rises considerably, to 25%, by 2008. The percentage of whites opposed to living in such a neighborhood falls sharply, from roughly 47% in 1990 to 20% in 2008. Black respondents were asked a parallel question about their willingness to live in a neighborhood where "half of your neighbors would

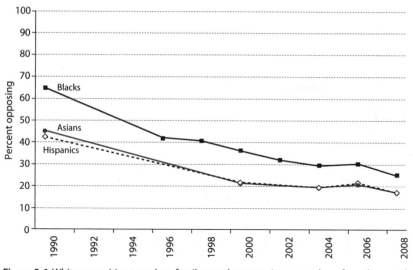

Figure 3.6. White opposition to a close family member marrying a member of another racial group. "How about having a close relative or family member marry a (Black/Asian/Hispanic) person?" ("strongly oppose" and "oppose" coded as opposing).

be whites" beginning in 2000. Fewer than 10% of black respondents oppose living in such a neighborhood, and better than 40% favor living in such a neighborhood.

A final social distance item (Figure 3.6) added in 1990 deals with inter-racial marriage: reactions to having a close relative or family member marry, variously, a black, an Asian, or a Hispanic person. When first measured in 1990, fully 65% of whites opposed a black–white union, while 40+% opposed Asian–white or Hispanic–white unions. The data since then reveal both a general decline in objection to racial intermarriage and a considerable narrowing of the size of the gap between opposition to black–white unions and either Asian– or Hispanic–white unions. Nonetheless, even in 2008 1 in 4 whites either "opposed" or "strongly opposed" a close relative or family member marrying a black person. One might expect an accelerated decline in such opposition in the aftermath of Barack Obama's election as president, given his popularity and much-commented-upon mixed racial background.

Government Policy on Race

Next, we turn to views about the role that government and social policy should play in redressing racial inequality, a longstanding topic of concern. Figure 3.7 reports trends in responses by white Americans about whether government has a special obligation to "help improve the living standards" of African Americans. The policy referent in the question is vague: it could implicate, variously, social welfare spending, affirmative-action-type policies,

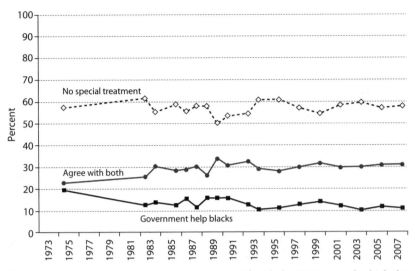

Figure 3.7. White attitudes toward government aid for blacks. "Some people think that (Blacks/Negroes/African Americans) have been discriminated against for so long that the government has a special obligation to help improve their living standards. Others believe that the government should not be giving special treatment to (Blacks/Negroes/African Americans). Where would you place yourself on this scale, or haven't you made up your mind on this?" ("1–2" coded as government help blacks, "3" coded as agree with both, and "4–5" coded as no special treatment).

or even reparations. That ambiguity notwithstanding, the trends reveal that levels of support for such an obligation to uplift African American communities is low and indeed slightly declining over time. At no point over the more than 30-year time span did as many as 1 in 4 whites endorse such an obligation; solid majorities of whites select the "no special treatment" category over the entire period.

Beginning with the 1990 Intergroup Tolerance Module, the GSS posed a more pointed question about affirmative-action-type policies. It asked, "What do you think the chances are these days that a white person won't get a job or promotion while an equally or less qualified black person gets one instead? Is this very likely, somewhat likely, or not very likely to happen these days?" The modal and slightly increasing response (Figure 3.8) has been "somewhat likely." Slightly over 40% of whites nationally took this position in 1990, rising to nearly 50% by 2008. In addition, nearly 1 in 5 whites consistently take the even stronger position that affirmative action for blacks is "very likely" to hurt a white person's chances of getting a job or promotion, providing clear evidence that affirmative action policies face steep public opinion obstacles.

To pin down the meaning of the perception that affirmative action for blacks was costly for whites, the 1990 GSS asked a follow-up question of those

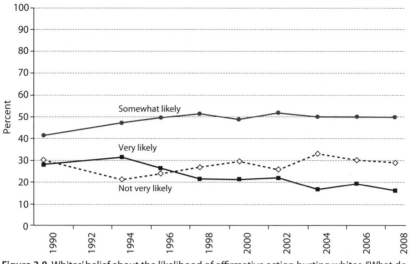

Figure 3.8. Whites' belief about the likelihood of affirmative action hurting whites. "What do you think the chances are these days that a white person won't get a job or promotion while an equally or less qualified black person gets one instead? Is this very likely, somewhat likely, or not very likely to happen these days?"

who thought it "very" or "somewhat likely" to harm whites: "Do you feel this way because of something that happened to you personally, because it happened to a relative, family member or close friend, or because you have heard about it from the media or other sources?" The results were somewhat surprising. Most whites said that they had "heard about it in the media" (40%) or from other unspecified sources (35%). Much smaller fractions reported that their beliefs were grounded in their personal experience, or that of their personal contacts.

It is certainly fair to conclude that affirmative action is controversial on the basis of these data and, furthermore, that much white opposition to it is rooted not in concrete bad experiences but rather vague, mass-mediated resentments of the policy, but it would nonetheless be a mistake to infer that opposition to government action seeking to ameliorate black disadvantage is completely implacable. For example, the 1990 GSS also tested the relative popularity of race-targeted and income-targeted social policy interventions. The results (Table 3.3) show that the income- or class-targeted policy interventions are always more popular among whites than race-targeted ones. This holds whether an intervention involves tax breaks for businesses locating in certain areas, enhanced spending on preschool and early education programs, or college scholarships for students who maintain good grades. However, clear majorities of whites supported two such interventions—early education programs and college scholarships—even when targeted specifically on blacks. This led Bobo and Kluegel (1993) to emphasize the distinction

Table 3.3. Summary Statistics, Race Targeting Experiment, 1990 GSS[a]

	Giving businesses and industry special tax breaks for locating in [poor and high unemployment/largely black] areas			Spending more money on the schools in [poor/black] neighborhoods especially for pre-school and early education programs			Provide special college scholarships for [children from economically disadvantaged backgrounds/black children] who maintain good grades		
	Class cue	Race cue	Difference	Class cue	Race cue	Difference	Class cue	Race cue	Difference
Whites									
Favor (%)	70	43	−27	87	68	−19	92	70	−22
Neither favor nor oppose (%)	16	25	9	8	15	7	6	14	8
Oppose (%)	14	32	18	5	16	11	2	16	14
N	557	549		567	555		568	559	
Blacks									
Favor (%)	73	70	−3	93	92	−1	92	96	4
Neither favor nor oppose (%)	14	21	7	3	5	2	5	4	−1
Oppose (%)	14	10	−4	4	3	−1	3	0	−3
N	73	74		74	78		74	78	

[a]"Here are several things that the government in Washington might do to deal with the problems of poverty and unemployment. I would like you to tell me if you favor or oppose them. . . . Would you say that you strongly favor it, favor it, neither favor nor oppose it, oppose it, or strongly oppose it?" (*strongly favor* and *favor* coded as favoring, *strongly oppose* and *oppose* coded as opposing).

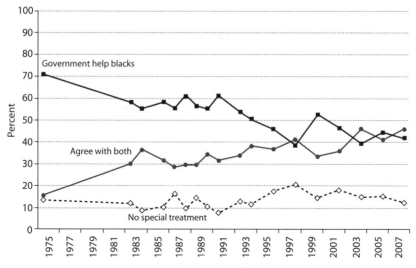

Figure 3.9. Blacks' attitudes toward government aid for blacks. See note to Figure 3.7 for question wording.

between policies following an "opportunity enhancing" logic and those seeming to affect "outcomes."

The views of African Americans help illuminate some of the public controversy surrounding affirmative action. Black and white levels of support for government efforts to improve economic outcomes for African Americans differ dramatically. Figure 3.9 shows trends among blacks in support for a government obligation to improve the living standards of blacks. In 1975 approximately 72% of African American endorsed such an obligation (far more than the 20% of whites who did so; see Figure 3.6). The percentage of blacks espousing such an obligation declines steadily, however, falling well below 50% by 2008. The percentage opposing such an obligation largely holds steady, while more blacks selected a somewhat ambiguous middle response.

Beginning in 1994 the GSS posed a question on strong versions of workplace affirmative action that would actually give blacks "preference in hiring and promotion" in order to make up for past discrimination. A very high and essentially unchanging fraction of whites opposes such "preferences" (Figure 3.10). Fewer than 2 out 5 blacks opposed such preferences when first asked in 1994, but this rises somewhat over time, with approximately 55% opposition among blacks by 2008. Thus, the black–white gap in opposition to preferential hiring and promotion policies narrowed, though it remains large.

The results on attitudes toward affirmative action reported here are limited in one important respect. Apart from the question on government's special obligation to help blacks, the GSS trend data focus on a very specific, strong

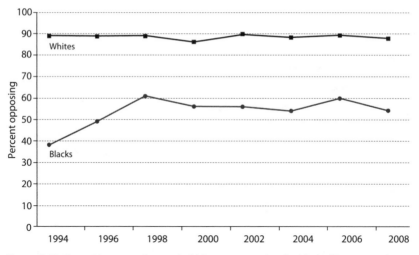

Figure 3.10. Opposition to preference in hiring or promotion for blacks. "Some people say that because of past discrimination, blacks should be given preference in hiring and promotion. Others say that such preference in hiring and promotion of blacks is wrong because it discriminates against whites. What about your opinion—are you for or against preferential hiring and promotion of blacks? If favors: Do you favor preference in hiring and promotion strongly or not strongly? If opposes: Do you oppose preference in hiring and promotion strongly or not strongly?" ("strongly oppose" and "oppose" coded as opposing).

form of affirmative action: preferences in hiring and promotion for African Americans. This likely conjures up the notion of "quotas," a policy that is both illegal (except in specific, court-ordered situations) and extremely unpopular. The long-term survey record includes no questions about the full range of programs, such as enhanced outreach and recruitment efforts and policies envisioned under the rubric of "affirmative action."

Other scholars note that support for affirmative action in surveys depends on how specifically a program is described, the type of policy involved (preferences versus quotas versus economic aid versus job training and educational assistance), and the target (women or blacks or minorities). All of these factors can affect expressed support for race-targeted policies (Bobo and Kluegel 1993; Bobo and Smith 1994; Steeh and Krysan 1996). When questions starkly contrast abilities with race-based preferential treatment, fewer than 10% of whites favor the race-based policy. Support is far higher when questions ask about affirmative action that specifically would *not* include rigid quotas. Indeed, when last asked in 1988, 73% of whites favored affirmative action thus described. These contrasting figures reveal the complexity of attitudes toward affirmative action, something often missed because questions asked regularly in national surveys refer to only a few specific policies or very general issues of "government spending."

Racial Stereotypes

Examinations of racial stereotypes have long been at the center of work on intergroup attitudes and relations (Allport 1954). The *Scientific American* reports included a key item on whether blacks were inherently less intelligent than whites. They found such a sweeping decline in endorsement of the "less intelligent" response that the item was not included in early GSSs. Indeed, the rapid decline in this belief is credited as an important basis for future prointegration changes in other aspects of racial attitudes (Schuman, Steeh, Bobo, and Krysan 1997).

Sociologist Mary Jackman (Jackman and Crane 1986, Jackman and Senter 1983) argued that older models and measures of stereotypes had a dichotomous, either/or, nature. She proposed that stereotypes may, in fact, be more gradational, identifying degrees of difference between groups. Based on this theoretical reconceptualization, the 1990 Intergroup Tolerance Module included a series of 7-point bipolar rating scales asking respondents to rate groups on a series of traits. This innovation revealed that stereotypes remain alive and well (T. W. Smith 1991; Sniderman and Piazza 1993; Bobo and Kluegel 1997).

Ratings on two traits—how "hardworking" or "lazy" members of a group tend to be, and how "intelligent" or "unintelligent" they tend to be—have been obtained regularly since 1990. Figure 3.11 reports the percentages of white respondents who rate whites as more intelligent or more hardworking than blacks. This more gradational or qualified expression of racial stereotypes reveals that whites are still very apt to attribute negative traits to blacks more often than to whites. In 1990, when first assessed, roughly 65% of whites rated blacks as less hardworking than whites, while just under 60% rated blacks as less intelligent than whites. Such negative stereotyping subsequently falls for both traits, particularly between 1990 and 1996, remaining relatively stable over the ensuing decade.

Jackman's (1994) general treatise on race, class, and gender relations makes a strong case that the perception of even small differences between groups can be a basis for consequential differential treatment. These negative stereotypes have been shown to play a powerful role in supporting social distance preferences (i.e., the neighborhood composition preferences discussed above) and opposition to social policies targeted to assist African Americans (Bobo and Kluegel 1993; Tuch and Hughes 1996; T. C. Wilson 2006). The more negative the racial stereotypes individuals hold about members of a particular group, the less willing they are to share residential space with members of that group, and the less likely they are to see members of that group as deserving of government assistance or intervention.

To these dispositional or behavioral trait beliefs we should add one other important observation: most white Americans are indeed aware that, on average, African Americans lag behind whites in economic status. When asked how "rich" or "poor" members of each race tend to be, a substantial

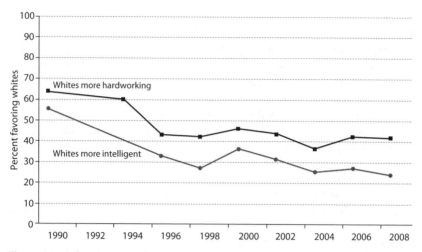

Figure 3.11. Whites' ratings of whites' industriousness and intelligence in comparison to blacks. The figure plots percentages of whites who rated whites higher than blacks on a given trait (industriousness or intelligence). "Industriousness" question: "The second set of characteristics asks if people in the group tend to be hard-working or if they tend to be lazy. Where would you rate whites in general on this scale? Blacks?" "Intelligence" question: "Do people in these groups tend to be unintelligent or tend to be intelligent? Where would you rate whites in general on this scale? Blacks?" In all, 7% of whites rated blacks as more hard-working than whites, and 6% rated blacks as more intelligent.

and largely stable fraction of the white adult population rates blacks as less well-off financially than whites (Figure 3.12). Just 1 in 5 whites see the two groups as equal in economic status, so they are, broadly speaking, mindful of black–white economic inequality. Just as there has been no broad secular trend toward a diminishing gap in black–white median family incomes (Darity and Myers 1998), the perception of a clearly more advantaged status for whites persists.

Explanations of Racial Inequality

Social psychologists stress that the meaning of observable social phenomena depends heavily on the causal accounts people construct for what they see (Nisbett and Ross 1980). That is, attributions about an individual's behavior or even a larger societal condition have strong implications for fundamental understandings of what we observe. Kluegel and Smith's (1986) pioneering work showed that how people perceive and explain social inequality powerfully structures what (if anything) they want to see done to address it.

Scholars of racial attitudes began to take an interest in how people perceived and explained black–white inequality in the late 1960s and early 1970s. Schuman (1969) provided the first systematic evidence that whites tend to explain black disadvantage in terms of the free will or the choices made by

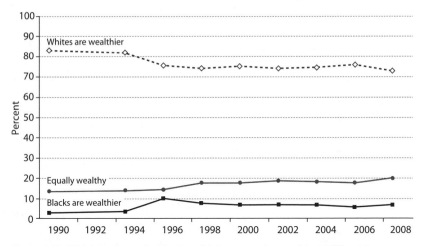

Figure 3.12. Whites' ratings of whites' wealth in comparison to blacks. "Now I have some questions about different groups in our society. I'm going to show you a seven-point scale on which the characteristics of people in a group can be rated. In the first statement a score of 1 means that you think almost all of the people in that group are 'rich.' A score of 7 means that you think almost everyone in the group are 'poor.' A score of 4 means you think that the group is not towards one end or another, and of course you may choose any number in between that comes closest to where you think people in the group stand. Where would you rate whites in general on this scale? Blacks?" The figure plots the percentages of whites who rate blacks higher than whites on the 1–7 wealth scale, who rate the two groups equally, and who rate whites higher than blacks.

blacks themselves. This constitutes a significant departure from the presumed traditional biological or Jim Crow racist ideology of black inferiority. Thereafter, Charles Glock and his students developed a more elaborate typology of "modes of explanation" of racial inequality (Apostle, Glock, Piazza, and Suelzle 1983; see also Sniderman and Hagen 1985; Schuman and Krysan 1999).

As shown above, white Americans by and large recognize black economic disadvantage. The key question then becomes one of how they explain it. Beginning in 1977, the GSS asked about four possible causes of black–white socioeconomic inequality: discrimination, less in-born ability to learn, lack of educational opportunity, and insufficient motivation and willpower. Trends in the percentages of whites endorsing each of the four explanations appear in Figure 3.13.

First, lack of "motivation or willpower" is the most commonly endorsed explanation of black disadvantage across the 1977–2008 time span. Support for this motivational account declines slightly, particularly after 1990. Second, the "less in-born ability" account is least popular at each time point, and its acceptance changes most over time; endorsement of it begins at about 25% in 1977 and falls to around 10% by 2008. Third, the strongest structural account

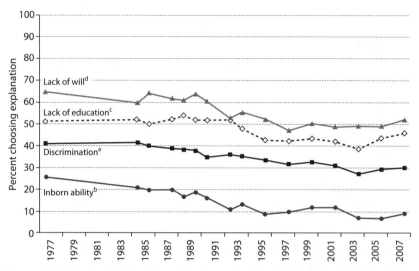

Figure 3.13. White explanations for racial socioeconomic inequality. Question a: "On the average (Negroes/Blacks/African Americans) have worse jobs, income, and housing than white people. Do you think these differences are . . . Mainly due to discrimination?" ("yes" coded as choosing). Question b: ". . . Because most (Negroes/Blacks/African Americans) have less in-born ability to learn?" ("yes" coded as choosing). Question c: ". . . Because most (Negroes/Blacks/African Americans) don't have the chance for education that it takes to rise out of poverty?" ("yes" coded as choosing). Question d: ". . . Because most (Negroes/Blacks/African Americans) just don't have the motivation or will power to pull themselves up out of poverty?" ("yes" coded as choosing).

for black–white inequality, "discrimination," was endorsed by about 2 in 5 whites in 1997 but only about 1 in 3 by 2008. The more ambiguous no "chance for education" account is always second most commonly endorsed, but its acceptance too appears to decline slightly.

These patterns make it clear that most white Americans do not embrace a single account of black–white economic inequality. Most attribute it to multiple possible sources. Kluegel's (1990) analyses of 1977–1989 GSS data developed a set of modes of explaining racial inequality that can be divided into three key groupings (Hunt 2007): person centered (attributions to ability or motivational differences), mixed (attributions to both ability and structural bases or to both motivational and structural differences), and structuralist (attributions to structural factors, educational chances, or racial discrimination). Hunt (2007) reports a substantial rise in the percentage of respondents who reject all four possible accounts of racial inequality, from 5% (1977) to 15% (2004). This pattern may reflect the emergence of what Forman (2004) has characterized as "racial apathy" (see also Forman and Lewis 2006), a growing indifference to talk of race and racial distinctions altogether.

Black–white differences in attributions for racial inequality can be large. In the 2000–2008 period, African Americans, as Table 3.4 shows, were far more likely to endorse discrimination as a cause of group inequality (59%) than were whites (30%). Interestingly, the tendency to endorse discrimination as an account of black–white inequality declines among blacks as well as whites. More surprisingly (and unlike whites), the percentage of blacks attributing racial inequality to "lack of motivation and willpower" rises. Reporting a similar pattern of decline in attributions to discrimination among Hispanic respondents, Hunt (2007) suggests that this trend may be most pronounced among younger and politically conservative blacks.

Table 3.4 sheds some light on this matter. The percentage of blacks attributing inequality to discrimination declines over time within each education level, though somewhat less among the best educated. Similarly, the percentage of blacks attributing inequality to motivation increases within each education level, slightly more among the better educated. The differences by age are even more pronounced, however: attributions to discrimination decline fully 23 percentage points among the youngest blacks, but only 11 points among the oldest. Likewise, the percentage of young blacks attributing inequality to motivation rises by a full 17 percentage points, but this attribution actually declines by 5 points among the oldest blacks.

These trends are open to several plausible interpretations. At a minimum, they show that polarization between blacks and whites in attributions for racial inequality is narrowing to a degree. They may or may not reflect a greatly reduced sensitivity to or actual exposure to discrimination among young African Americans, the increasingly distant heyday of the civil rights movement and its strong galvanizing effect on group solidarity, or growing class and political heterogeneity in the black population. But better educated, and especially younger, African Americans show the clearest drift toward less structuralist and more motivational accounts for black–white inequality.

Socioemotional Evaluations

Concern with the emotional or affective tenor of reactions to members of different groups lies at or near the core of the concept of prejudice (Adorno, Frenkel-Brunswik, Levinson, and Sanford 1950; Allport 1954; Sears 1988; Jackman 1994; Bobo and Tuan 2006). Many commentators on race and social scientists regard affect measures as a part of any full portrait of racial attitudes.

The original GSS items emphasize issues of broad public discourse, rather than testing theories of racial prejudice per se, so none of those items (Table 3.1) measured socioemotional or affective responses to minority groups. Questions asked once in the 1994 Multiculturalism Model and trend items on emotional closeness added in 1996 began to give some purchase on change in whites' affective responses to blacks. Distinguished social psychologist Thomas Pettigrew (Pettigrew and Meertens 1995) proposed that in the modern

Table 3.4. Explanations for Racial Socioeconomic Inequality, by Education and Age across Selected Years

	Whites							Blacks						
		Years of education			Years of age				Years of education			Years of age		
	Pooled	<12	12	13+	18–33	34–50	51+	Pooled	<12	12	13+	18–33	34–50	51+
Due to discrimination (%)														
1977–1989	40	40	37	43	46	39	36	77	82	72	76	75	79	79
1990–1999	35	47	32	36	35	34	35	71	74	68	73	67	74	72
2000–2008	30	30	27	32	31	28	32	59	62	54	62	52	58	69
Less in-born ability (%)														
1977–1989	21	36	22	11	12	16	35	16	31	9	4	8	12	26
1990–1999	13	27	16	6	7	8	22	11	16	12	6	10	8	15
2000–2008	9	20	13	5	6	7	13	13	23	13	8	11	11	17
Lack of chance for education (%)														
1977–1989	52	42	48	63	55	52	49	68	69	65	70	63	68	75
1990–1999	47	37	41	55	46	49	47	60	63	61	57	55	55	72
2000–2008	43	33	36	49	41	45	44	52	56	46	55	47	50	61
Lack of motivation or willpower (%)														
1977–1989	63	74	67	51	54	62	72	35	44	34	26	30	33	44
1990–1999	55	70	63	46	50	50	65	38	43	40	33	45	32	38
2000–2008	50	66	61	41	45	45	57	44	51	50	38	49	42	42

Note: N for whites ranges between 5,307 and 16,906. *N* for blacks ranges between 517 and 2,387. For wording of explanations for racial socioeconomic inequality, see Figure 3.13. For education: years of education. For age: years of age.

Table 3.5. Whites' feelings of Sympathy and Admiration for Blacks, by Education and Region, 1994 GSS

	National	North			South		
		< 12 years	12 years	13+ years	< 12 years	12 years	13+ years
Very often on both	6%	5	5	7	7	4	8
Combination	60	50	54	65	61	59	66
Not very often/ never on both	34	54	41	29	32	37	27
N	1,169	102	258	429	87	108	184

For feelings of sympathy: "Now, I would like to ask whether you have ever felt the following ways about blacks and their families. For each of the feelings that I ask you about, please tell me whether you have felt that way very often, fairly often, not too often, or never? How often have you felt sympathy for blacks?" For admiration for blacks: "How often have you felt admiration for blacks?" For education: years of education. For region: "South Atlantic," "East South Central," and "West South Central" coded as South.

era, withholding positive emotions from members of a minority group is more telling than expressing active emotional hostility. Accordingly, GSS respondents were asked how often they felt "sympathy" and "admiration" for blacks.

Very few whites embrace African Americans on an emotional level (Bobo 2004). A quite low percentage of whites say "very often" on *both* the admiration and sympathy items, fewer than 1 in 10 in 1994. Even within region and education groupings, no segment of white America strongly embraces blacks emotionally. Also, fairly high percentages of white respondents report "not very often" or "never" feeling both admiration and sympathy for blacks.

Beginning in 1996, the GSS asked respondents to rate their "closeness" to whites and blacks as groups on a 1 to 9 scale. Figure 3.14 reports trends among whites for the difference in closeness to whites and blacks. The largest group of whites expresses equal closeness to both groups: between 40% and 50% do so between 1996 and 2008. This means that roughly between 50% and 60% of whites rate themselves as closer to other whites, however. Tellingly, a substantial percentage of whites favor other whites by at least 3 points on this 9-point scale, though this fraction falls slightly by the 2000s.

To the extent that basic affect is a fundamental foundation for an array of other racial attitudes and outlooks, the GSS provides clear evidence of a large socioemotional gap or bar to comity across the racial divide. These data arguably indicate that the sort of socioemotional bond essential to a sense of basic common humanity and worth is lacking for a large number of white Americans regarding their fellow black citizens.

Collective Racial Resentments

During the 1980s survey researchers began exploring new forms of anti-black sentiment that may be taking shape. Research on symbolic racism is the most prominent work advancing such a claim (Kinder and Sears 1981;

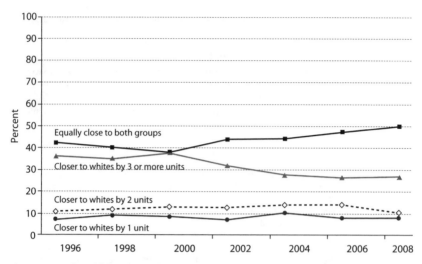

Figure 3.14. Whites' difference in closeness to whites and blacks. The question asked was, "In general, how close do you feel to blacks? And in general, how close do you feel to whites?" The figure plots percentages of whites who rated themselves as equally close to whites and blacks, or 1, 2, or 3 points closer to whites on the 1–9 closeness scale. Between 3% and 4% of whites each year indicated that they were closer to blacks.

McConahay 1986; Sears 1988; Sears and Jessor 1996), what some characterize more concretely (and less provocatively) as racial resentment (Kinder and Sanders 1996). It suggests that with waning advocacy of Jim Crow and openly biological racism, a new discourse for expressing animosity toward African Americans developed. Central to this new type of attitude are a sense of antagonism to political demands by blacks, rejection of the assumption that real discriminatory barriers impede black advancement, and hostility to any favor or benefit blacks might now receive from government. Although the subject of intensive controversy (see Bobo 1983 and 1988b; Sniderman and Tetlock 1986; Jackman 1996; Hughes 1997; E. R. Smith 1993; Krysan 2000; Feldman and Huddy 2005), the idea that group or collective resentments are an important feature of contemporary racial attitudes has endured.

The GSS added an item that taps such collective racial resentments in 1994. The question asks whether respondents agree or disagree that "Irish, Jewish, and many other minorities overcame prejudice and worked their way up. Blacks should do the same without special favors." This item taps collective racial resentments because it implies that "other groups made it in America without special favors, blacks should too." Throughout the 1994–2008 time span, roughly three-fourths of white Americans agreed with this assertion (Figure 3.15). In the main, the item shows no meaningful trend, despite a slight dip in 2004: the lopsided majority view among whites is that blacks need to make it all on their own.

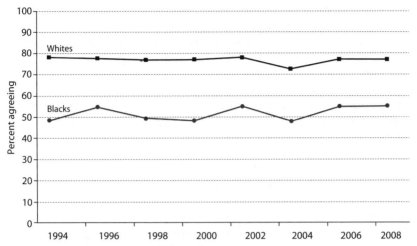

Figure 3.15. Belief that blacks should overcome prejudice without special favors. "Do you agree strongly, agree somewhat, neither agree nor disagree, disagree somewhat, or disagree strongly with the following statement: Irish, Italians, Jewish and many other minorities overcame prejudice and worked their way up. Blacks should do the same without special favors" ("agree strongly" and "agree somewhat" coded as agree).

Figure 3.15 also reports the trend in agreement with the "no special favors" assertion among blacks. Throughout the 14-year time span, whites are always substantially more likely to endorse this viewpoint than blacks, but not only do a nontrivial number of blacks agree with it (about 50%): the black–white gap actually narrows slightly over time. We suspect that important qualitative differences exist between black and white respondents in the meaning and import of agreeing with this statement. It is clear, for instance, that among those who agree with it, blacks are more likely than whites to believe that significant racial discrimination still occurs and perceive only minor behavioral differences between the races (in, e.g., the traits of intelligence and industriousness). Moreover, such views may carry less powerful consequences for views on important policy questions (e.g., support for the death penalty) among blacks than among whites (Bobo and Johnson 2004). Hunt, Jackson, Powell, and Steelman (2000) caution against assuming that measures have equivalent meaning for minority and white respondents in the absence of direct data. Similarly, Sidanius and Pratto (1999) make a strong case that members of dominant or privileged groups and of subordinate or minority ones respond asymmetrically about prominent, ideologically central beliefs like that tapped by the "no special favors" question.

Because it resonates with several other predominant beliefs about race among white Americans—stereotypes, explanations of inequality, and affective distinctions—this collective resentment item merits extended reflection. In light of several key trends among whites discussed above, it is clearer why high endorsement of the "no special favors" position expresses collective racial resentment. It is part racial stereotype, part normative judgment or evaluation, and part perception of current or future threat. The sentiment identifies a moral shortcoming of blacks that threatens to impinge upon the well-being of putatively hardworking white Americans. Recall first the evidence of negative stereotyping, the clear-cut recognition of economic inequality favoring whites, the wide acceptance of person-centered, largely cultural/volitional accounts of black–white inequality, and the substantial expressed emotional distance from blacks. Such sentiments declare that blacks are singularly and indeed pointedly undeserving of sympathy or assistance. Following this logic, the perception that blacks are successful in getting the attention or resources of government is at least judged inappropriate and unfair to whites, if not more severely as a costly or burdensome imposition. Second, other correlational work shows that the "no special favors" position has much in common with other perceptions that members of a minority group are getting ahead at the expense of other groups (Bobo and Tuan 2006). Third, the broad endorsement of this position is consistent with other survey evidence indicating that many white Americans view blacks as disproportionately welfare dependent and as undeserving recipients of government benefits (Gilens 1999; Fox 2004; Federico 2004).

Evidence from other sources helps to illuminate what respondents mean when they say members of a minority group should "receive no special favors." One 1990 sample survey in Wisconsin about Indian treaty rights (Bobo and Tuan 2006) included open-ended probes of such responses, though they pertained to Native Americans, not blacks. The probes followed a question on whether Indians received "unfair advantages given to them by the government." Though not aimed at blacks, the replies are instructive. Among them were remarks to this effect:

> "Well, they sit on their lazy butts and do nothing and they get their welfare checks and go sit in bars all night" or "Well, I think that they feel they're owed this, and I don't think it's fair. It's the same people who are on AFDC and keep collecting and don't bother to do anything to get out of it." (Bobo and Tuan 2006, pp. 146–47)

Probes following a question on whether Native Americans were getting ahead at the expense of non-Indians elicited very similar remarks. Bobo and Tuan quote one respondent: "If they are getting food stamps and welfare coming out of our taxes, I'm paying for them living without working. I'm working for them," and yet another as follows: "They are asking too much from the government. Niggers don't get all that. This was their land a long time ago, but that is past" (Bobo and Tuan 2006, pp. 156–57).

Other nonsurvey data reveal collective racial resentments of blacks more directly. Evidence of such sentiments appears in a number of recent influential qualitative works. Cultural sociologist Michèle Lamont's (2000, pp. 60–61)

The Dignity of Working Men: Morality and the Boundaries of Race, Class, and Immigration illustrates how these collective racial resentments blend stereotype, normative or moral judgment, and perceived threat. She writes of one of her subjects,

> Vincent is a workhorse. He considers himself "top gun" at his job and makes a very decent living. His comments on blacks suggest that he associates them with laziness and welfare and with claims to receiving special treatment at work through programs such as affirmative action. He says: "Blacks have a tendency to . . . try to get off doing less, the least possible . . . to keep the job where whites will put in that extra oomph. I know this is a generality and it does not go for all, it goes for a portion. It's this whole unemployment and welfare gig. A lot of the blacks on welfare have no desire to get off it. Why should they? It's free money. I can't stand to see my hard-earned money [said with emphasis] going to pay for someone who wants to sit on his ass all day long and get free money."

Lamont (2000, p. 62) concludes that a number of the white working-class men she interviewed "underscore a concrete link between the perceived dependency of blacks, their laziness, and the taxes taken from their own paychecks."

This is not an isolated finding. For example, Mary Waters (1999, p. 177) observed a very similar pattern among white managers and employers. She writes, "Most white respondents were much more able to tap into their negative impressions of black people, especially 'underclass' blacks whom they were highly critical of. These opinions were not just based on disinterested observation. There was a direct sense among many of the whites that they personally were being taken advantage of and threatened by the black population."

Likewise, William Julius Wilson reported directly parallel sentiments in his study of Chicago-area neighborhoods and race relations. One subject voiced collective racial resentments very directly:

> This whole city is going down the fucking toilet. . . . If [Mayor Daley's] dad knew what he was doing he would turn in his grave. Now old man Daley, he was for the blue-collar worker. Used to be that when you had those jobs you had 'em for life and you could raise a family. It's all different now, taxes and all that shit is killing the workingman. We're paying to support all the fucking niggers and minorities. . . . Yeah, but I'll tell ya, if this city keeps going the way it is, it's going to drive all the good working people right out of it. It's all fucked up and I tell ya why: too many niggers an' Mexicans an' minorities in this city. I mean niggers don't pay taxes, spics don't pay taxes. If we leave there'll be nothing in this goddamn city. (W. J. Wilson and Taub 2006, pp. 23–24)

This language couples attributions of traits (laziness), violations of values (hard work and self-reliance), and moral condemnation. As well, group comparisons, sense of threat, and identity-engaging elements are clearly present.

Social scientists arguably have been slow to appreciate the full significance of collective resentments. Political pollsters and journalists identified them as a broad-gauge outlook of powerful political import. In their memorable book *Chain Reaction*, Edsall and Edsall (1991, p. 182) focus on resentments, quoting Democratic pollster Stanley Greenberg's description of a significant segment of white voters at length:

> These white Democratic defectors express a profound distaste for blacks, a sentiment that pervades almost everything they think about government and politics. . . . Blacks constitute the explanation for their [white defectors] vulnerability and for almost everything that has gone wrong in their lives; not being black is what constitutes being middle class, not living with blacks is what makes a neighborhood a decent place to live. . . . The special status of blacks is perceived by almost all of these individuals as a serious obstacle to their personal advancement. Indeed, discrimination against whites has become a well-assimilated and ready explanation for their status, vulnerability and failures.

We focus attention on these collective resentments here because of the central and almost era-defining quality. Support for segregation, revulsion at interracial marriage, and belief in the inherent inferiority of blacks were the ideological cornerstones of the Jim Crow era. Collective racial resentments are among the centerpieces of the new laissez-faire racism era (Bobo, Kluegel, and Smith 1997).

Multidimensionality and Scientific Progress

What does it mean? Have racial attitudes improved, or stagnated, or worsened? Is there more or less prejudice now than in the past? In trying to characterize racial attitudes in the United States—even that very particular subset of them measured by the GSS—no admonition could be more apt than Alfred North Whitehead's phrase "seek simplicity and distrust it." Long ago, social psychologist Gordon Allport (1954) cautioned against searching for "simple and sovereign" explanations of racial attitudes. Yet to a surprising degree, scholarly discourse mirrors the popular penchant for sweeping simplistic generalizations asserting, variously, that racism is either implacable or diminishing. We believe, first and foremost, that keeping the full record in view provides a strong corrective against oversimplification and inferential errors.

Patterns in the lion's share of the initial (1972) GSS racial attitude items suggested an America finished with formally institutionalized segregation and discrimination, and increasingly endorsing the opposite. Jim Crow attitudes and de jure bias appeared to be in clear retreat. Yet, to conclude that antiblack prejudice or racism was gone would have been a mistaken inference, far beyond what the data directly showed. That era's GSS did not measure many key aspects of racial attitudes, including beliefs about the causes of black–white economic inequality, attitudes on affirmative action, racial stereotypes, and affective or socioemotional orientations. Only one item (on blacks "pushing" where they were unwanted) arguably tapped any collective or racial resentments then present. Moreover, responses to some items still revealed nontrivial levels of support for antiblack or segregationist postures (e.g., support for an individual home owner's right to sell on a discriminatory basis).

Second, the multidimensional nature of racial attitudes should be borne in mind constantly (Jackman 1977), against the temptation to array all attitudes along a single prejudice-to-tolerance continuum (Bobo 1983). Configurations of views prove to be complex. Whether racial prejudice has increased, decreased, or remained the same is perhaps a wrong, or at least misspecified, question. Better is to ask about the key domains of attitudes and the significant distributions and configurations of those outlooks (Bobo 2001).

Third, good social science emerges from the regular interaction of theory building and empirical research and hypothesis testing (Lieberson 1992). The over-time development of racial attitude items in the GSS illustrates this process: it has incorporated measures of entirely new conceptual domains and items that better address intergroup attitudes in a multiethnic and multiracial America. On a more ad hoc basis, one-time modules have illuminated key questions via survey-based experiments, follow-up probes, and other innovations. Choices of both the new trends to measure and the items for topical modules have been driven by changes in U.S. society, scientific feedback, and findings from earlier rounds of data collection. Measuring these emerging conceptual types of attitudes has much illuminated critical patterns in attitudes and actual social relations alike.

Attitudes and Behavior

We posit that racial attitudes are important in their own right. It is of vital sociological utility to know what basic principles guiding race relations people assume, their willingness to enter situations with varying racial mixtures in different domains of life, and the role that most white Americans deem appropriate for government in addressing extant racial inequality. The full meaning of responses to such questions can be assessed only once we know the behavioral traits and expectations individuals hold about members of minority or out-groups, and how they perceive and explain patterns of intergroup inequality. Configurations of attitudes yield information on the social climate, political context, and identities and assumptions that individuals bring into many varied social interactions and settings.

Nonetheless, it is fair to ask what bearing these attitudes have on behavior. The attitude–behavior connection has been controversial in the past (La Piere 1934) and occasionally still is (Quillian 2006) despite otherwise compelling evidence that attitudes are relevant to behavior (Schuman 1995). In what remains the best sociological examination of this linkage, Schuman and Johnson (1976, p. 199) concluded, "Our review has shown that most [attitude-behavior] studies yield positive results. The correlations that do occur are large enough to indicate that important causal forces are involved, whatever one's model of the underlying causal process may be."

It would be a mistake, however, to posit a mechanistic and invariant attitude-behavior relationship. Schuman and Johnson identify several conditions to bear in mind in considering attitude-to-behavior connections. First, seriously assessing an attitude–behavior relation requires reliable, multi-item measures of both the underlying attitude and the underlying behavior of interest. Many, if not most, prominent failures to link attitudes to behavior involve simplistic attitude measurements and a single behavioral act, a pattern still evident in some critical literature (e.g., Quillian 2006). Truly meaningful tests of the attitude–behavior association require equally strong measurement of both concepts.

Second, Schuman and Johnson stress the importance of measuring attitude and behavior at the same level of specificity. Again, an attitude–behavior connection may not be found when, for instance, one very specific behavior is predicted by a single very general attitude measure. Third, attributes of the attitude and the social context may importantly condition the strength of an attitude–behavior relation. For example, attitudes that are highly central or salient to an individual may be linked far more consistently to potentially relevant behaviors than those that are not very salient or central (see Bobo and Tuan 2006, chap. 4). Likewise, particular situational constraints may impinge upon the attitude–behavior congruence. For example, a prejudiced restaurant owner may face financial and legal sanctions for overtly acting on this attitude. This does not render the attitude meaningless or prevent this person from acting in an attitude-consistent fashion in more subtle, less observable ways, or in less readily monitored settings.

Hence the key question for us is less about what specific individual behaviors racial attitudes predict and much more about the extent to which our portrait of the patterning and trend in attitudes is consistent with relevant societal behavioral trends and conditions. From this standpoint, we believe that the real attitudinal record strongly corresponds to many major social patterns, conditions, and trends regarding race and racial division in American society.

The attitudinal record on race, sociologically speaking, is a key ingredient in the basic constitution and experience of race relations in the United

States. Much as employment rates, earnings, and occupational data help to flesh out the economic conditions and structure of a society, a multidimensional mapping of racial attitudes and beliefs elucidates the racial conditions and structure of a society. The broad patterns we identify are features of social organization that, ceteris paribus, we expect to have implications for related behaviors and outcomes.

The broad correspondence between attitudinal trends and other related social trends appears very strong. For example, at an early point the attitudinal record indicated that government efforts to substantially desegregate schools and communities would likely face resistance. Survey data certainly captured well the level of opposition to school busing for purposes of integration. Moreover, they pointed to likely controversy over the reach and nature of affirmative action efforts regarding both educational opportunity and employment/workplace opportunity.

Likewise, patterns indicating persistent racial stereotyping, appreciable affective differentiation, and widespread collective resentment suggest considerable bases for often fraught, tension-filled, and conflictual interactions along the color line. Views on interracial marriage parallel behavioral outcomes in three respects: (1) black–white intermarriage remains infrequent relative to white intermarriage with either Asians or Hispanics, (2) the number of black–white intermarriages is rising, and (3) social apprehension about such unions is ongoing but lessening.

The full record also strongly points to a large and growing orbit of social and political acceptance for African Americans. This too is borne out by manifold behavioral evidence: the growth and size of the black middle class, declining levels of racial residential segregation, and even the election of Barack Obama as the 44th (and first African American) president of the United States.

We are not claiming that attitudes caused or created these other outcomes, though in general we expect that individual attitudes and behaviors exhibit an important degree of consistency. Our point is twofold: First, the all-too-common sociological assertion that the attitudinal record paints a purely and unduly optimistic picture of race relations at odds with actual behavioral data on segregation, inequality, and discrimination is simply wrong. Second, analytically these attitude data provide a very rich and robust portrait of the sociological state of race relations.

Indeed the frequent assumption that attitudinal data either tell one simple story or are too contradictory to parse sensibly is curious. Certainly an examination of median family incomes by race would yield useful information on the extent of race-related economic inequality. But careful analysts would surely insist on data from numerous indicators that capture the multidimensionality of economic standing and inequality. Information on hours worked, wage rates, work force experience, job titles and status, authority in the work place, benefits packages, wealth holdings, and the like would all contribute to a full sociological portrait of economic inequality. Similar remarks apply to most other domains of social existence. It is thus deeply puzzling that so many sociologists disregard the complexity and multidimensionality of racial attitudes (Schuman 1972).

Conclusions

Taking stock of thinking on race during the late 19th and early 20th centuries, historian George Fredrickson (1971, p. 321) identified six key elements of then-dominant social thought. He noted the widespread acceptance of ideas that blacks were different from and inferior to whites and that such differences would not be quickly or easily changed. Consequently, race mixing and intermarriage were to be avoided at all costs, hostility to or prejudice against blacks was presumed natural and inevitable, and biracial civic equality was simply inconceivable.

American society has moved a very long distance away from that deeply racialized and overtly racist ideology. The benchmark NORC surveys that informed the early *Scientific American* reports show the degree of national acceptance of such ideas at the time of World War II. By then support for proposals such as the colonization, or the near-complete removal, of the American black population to Africa—at one time very serious matters—had largely vanished. But U.S. whites endorsed many other aspects of what Fredrickson terms a "white supremacist" position as recently as the early 1940s, particularly in southern states.

We offer seven broad conclusions about the attitudinal record on race among white Americans. First and foremost, it documents a sweeping fundamental change in norms regarding race. A Jim Crow–era commitment to segregation, explicit white privilege, revulsion against mixed marriages, and the categorical belief that blacks were inherently and biologically inferior to whites collapsed. Broad support for equal treatment, integration, and a large measure of tolerance supplanted these views. Second, despite accepting integration as a general principle and a small minority presence in schools, neighborhoods, or other public social spaces, whites express strong social distance preferences; indeed, a racial hierarchy of association remains, with African Americans at or near its bottom (Charles 2006).

Third, support for a strong, active government role in ameliorating racial inequality and segregation is limited, with little movement in a prointervention direction. Policies aimed at enhancing the human capital attributes of African Americans, especially those that involve "playing by the rules of the game," are reasonably popular. The GSS data indicate, however, that affirmative action and other vigorous efforts by government to bring about integration or reduce racial inequality face an uphill struggle for public acceptance (Bobo 1991).

Fourth, negative racial stereotypes remain widespread, but they differ from past stereotyping in two important ways. Contemporary negative views of blacks have a gradational or qualified, rather than categorical, character. The basis for such perceptions also appears to have shifted away from presumed biological or natural differences toward presumptions rooted in group culture. Fifth, and closely related, core accounts or explanations of black–white socioeconomic inequality have moved decisively from biology to culture. Hence a core element of what might be labeled racial prejudice remains but has undergone a noteworthy qualitative shift to a more porous and potentially modifiable stance.

Sixth, most white Americans maintain a significant affective or socioemotional distance from African Americans. Seventh, a broad and widely shared cultural motif among white Americans involves collective racial resentments. Accompanying persistent negative stereotypes, predominantly cultural explanations of black disadvantage, and rejection of a strong government role in redressing racial inequality, the sine qua non of the new racial ideological regime in America is a belief that blacks are singularly undeserving of "special treatment" and should just sink or swim in the modern free market.

Important changes appear to be under way in the attitudes of African Americans as well. Three patterns stand out. First, blacks are less and less likely to explain racial inequality in structural, discrimination-based terms. Second, blacks have shifted discernibly toward more motivational and cultural accounts of racial inequality. Third, black support for certain forms of government intervention to advance the status of African Americans has declined. These are quite portentous trends indeed that call for more careful investigation with large black samples. Is it really a rise in conservatism among blacks? Is it a concession by blacks to largely implacable white opposition to vigorous desegregation and affirmative-action-type policies? Is it a weakening of the sense of common fate and group consciousness among blacks? Educational and especially age differences in some views are suggestive, but more fine-grained analyses than we can conduct here are necessary.

The GSS provides an important sociological lens on race in the United States, one that allows insight into critical aspects of the meaning of racial division over the past four decades. The initial GSS pool of questions on race largely reflected topical concerns of the early 1970s, but nonetheless covered significant terrain with regard to race relations. It broadened over the years to incorporate wholly new theoretical concepts and subject matter, while items on which overwhelming popular consensus had been reached were removed. Special modules in 1990, 1994, and 2000 explored key issues in greater depth, sometimes by systematic experimentation. Some of these innovations later became new trend items. Others examined intergroup attitudes toward Hispanics and Asians. As GSS samples accumulate, the capacity to examine the views of black and Hispanic respondents in detail by pooling data across years rises steadily. The substantive contribution and analytical power of the

GSS lens on U.S. intergroup relations, in fact, grow increasingly with continued biennial administration of the survey and its continued practice of scientific innovation.

Notes

We wish to thank Howard Schuman, Tyrone Forman, Matthew Hunt, and Jennifer Hochschild for their careful read and comments on an earlier draft of this chapter. The authors, of course, are responsible for any remaining shortcomings.

1. Since many GSS items are drawn from earlier surveys, it is of course possible to extend some trends back over 40 years, particularly the early set of race-related items.

2. This trend coincided with the rising black activism of the time, especially the emergence of the "black power" slogan and movement (see Bobo 1988a for related attitude trend analyses).

3. Most items in Table 3.1 were in the first (1972) GSS. Two (RACOPEN and NATRACE) were first measured in 1973.

4. We follow Schuman, Steeh, and Bobo (1985) in examining data for respondents age 21 and over. We also report percentages excluding don't know responses, as we could discern no systematic rise in don't know responses for the items we examine.

5. Many of these items were not initially asked of black respondents either out of apprehension about potentially insulting them or on the assumption that black responses would be obvious. The trends for blacks are based on much smaller annual sample sizes than those for whites, and hence show much greater volatility.

6. The wording of the "multiethnic showcard" itself does not expressly equate the social class background of potential neighbors. Respondents are asked to specify the mixture "that you personally would feel most comfortable in." Multivariate analyses, however, usually include direct controls for perceived differences in class background between groups as well as for direct measures of in-group attachment. The strong effects of racial stereotypes are net of both of these factors (Charles 2006).

References

Adorno, Theodor W., Else Frenkel-Brunswik, Daniel J. Levinson, and R. Nevitt Sanford. 1950. *The Authoritarian Personality*. New York: Harper.

Alba, Richard, Ruben G. Rumbaut, and Karen Marotz. 2005. "A Distorted Nation: Perceptions of Racial/Ethnic Group Sizes and Attitudes toward Immigrants and Other Minorities." *Social Forces* 84:901–19.

Allport, Gordon W. 1954. *The Nature of Prejudice*. Reading, MA: Addison-Wesley.

Apostle, Richard A., Charles Y. Glock, Thomas Piazza, and Marijean Suelzle. 1983. *The Anatomy of Racial Attitudes*. Berkeley: University of California Press.

Berinsky, Adam J. 1999. "The Two Faces of Public Opinion." *American Journal of Political Science* 43:1209–30.

———. 2002. "Political Context and the Survey Response: The Dynamics of Racial Policy Opinion." *Journal of Politics* 64:567–84.

Blumer, Herbert. 1958. "Race Prejudice as a Sense of Group Position." *Pacific Socio-logical Review* 1:3–7.

Bobo, Lawrence D. 1983. "Whites' Opposition to Busing: Symbolic Racism or Realis-tic Group Conflict?" *Journal of Personality and Social Psychology* 45:1196–1210.

———. 1988a. "Attitudes toward the Black Political Movement: Trends, Meaning, and Effects on Racial Policy Preferences." *Social Psychology Quarterly* 51:287–302.

———. 1988b. "Group Conflict, Prejudice, and the Paradox of Contemporary Racial Attitudes." In *Eliminating Racism: Profiles in Controversy*, edited by Phyllis A. Katz and Dalmas A. Taylor, 85–114. New York: Plenum.

———. 1991. "Social Responsibility, Individualism, and Redistributive Policies." *Sociological Forum* 12:147–76.

———. 2000. "Reclaiming a Du Boisian Perspective on Racial Attitudes." *Annals of the American Academy of Political and Social Science* 568:186–202.

———. 2001. "Racial Attitudes and Relations at the Close of the Twentieth Century." In *America Becoming: Racial Trends and Their Consequences*, edited by Neil Smelser, William Julius Wilson, and Faith Mitchell, 264–301. Washington, DC: National Academy Press.

———. 2004. "Inequalities That Endure? Racial Ideology, American Politics, and the Peculiar Role of the Social Sciences." In *The Changing Terrain of Race and Ethnicity*, edited by Maria Krysan and Amanda E. Lewis, 13–42. New York: Russell Sage Foundation.

Bobo, Lawrence D., and Devon Johnson. 2004. "A Taste for Punishment: Black and White Americans' Views on the Death Penalty and the War on Drugs." *Du Bois Review* 1:151–80.

Bobo, Lawrence D., and James R. Kluegel. 1993. "Opposition to Race-Targeting: Self-Interest, Stratification Ideology, or Racial Attitudes?" *American Sociological Review* 58:443–64.

———. 1997. "Status, Ideology, and Dimensions of Whites' Racial Beliefs and At-titudes: Progress and Stagnation." In *Racial Attitudes in the 1990s: Continuity and Change*, edited by Steven A. Tuch and Jack K. Martin, 93–120. Westport, CT: Praeger.

Bobo, Lawrence D., James R. Kluegel, and Ryan A. Smith. 1997. "Laissez-Faire Rac-ism: The Crystallization of a Kindler, Gentler, Antiblack Ideology." In *Racial Attitudes in the 1990s: Continuity and Change*, edited by Steven A. Tuch and Jack K. Martin, 15–44. Westport, CT: Praeger.

Bobo, Lawrence D., and Ryan A. Smith. 1994. "Antipoverty Policy, Affirmative Ac-tion, and Racial Attitudes." In *Confronting Poverty: Prescriptions for Change*, edited by Sheldon H. Danziger, Gary Sandefur, and Daniel Weinberg, 365–95. Cambridge, MA: Harvard University Press.

Bobo, Lawrence D., and Mia Tuan. 2006. *Prejudice in Politics: Group Position, Public Opinion, and the Wisconsin Treaty Rights Dispute*. Cambridge, MA: Harvard University Press.

Bobo, Lawrence D., and Camille L. Zubrinsky. 1996. "Attitudes on Residential In-tegration: Perceived Status Differences, Mere in-Group Preference, or Racial Prejudice?" *Social Forces* 74:883–909.

Bogardus, Emory S. 1928. *Immigration and Race Attitudes*. Boston: D.C. Heath.

Bonilla-Silva, Eduardo. 1997. "Rethinking Racism: Racial Structure in the United States." *American Sociological Review* 62:465–80.

Callaghan, Karen, and Nayda Terkildsen. 2002. "Understanding the Role of Race in Candidate Evaluation." *Political Decision Making, Deliberation, and Participation* 6:51–95.

Carmines, Edward G., and James A. Stimson. 1989. *Issue Evolution: Race and the Transformation of American Politics*. Princeton, NJ: Princeton University Press.

Carter, J. Scott, Lala Carr Steelman, Lynn M. Mulkey, and Casey Borch. 2005. "When the Rubber Meets the Road: Effects of Urban and Regional Residence on Principle and Implementation Measures of Racial Tolerance." *Social Science Research* 34:408–25.

Charles, Camille Z. 2000. "Neighborhood Racial-Composition Preferences: Evidence from a Multiethnic Metropolis." *Social Problems* 47:379–407.

———. 2003. "The Dynamics of Racial Segregation." *Annual Review of Sociology* 29:167–207.

———. 2006. *Won't You Be My Neighbor? Race, Class, and Residence in Los Angeles*. New York: Russell Sage Foundation.

Darity, William A., and Samuel L. Myers. 1998. *Persistent Disparity: Race and Economic Inequality in the U.S. since 1945*. Northampton, MA: Edward Elgar.

Davis, James A. 2004. "Did Growing Up in the 1960s Leave a Permanent Mark on Attitudes and Values?" *Public Opinion Quarterly* 68:161–83.

Davis, James A., Tom W. Smith, and Peter V. Marsden. 2008. *General Social Surveys 1972–2008* [Cumulative file]. Chicago: NORC.

Dixon, Jeffery C. 2005. "The Ties That Bind and Those That Don't: Toward Reconciling Group Threat and Contact Theories of Prejudice." *Social Forces* 84:2179–2204.

Dixon, Jeffery C., and Michael S. Rosenbaum. 2004. "Nice to Know You? Testing Contact, Cultural, and Group Threat Theories of Anti-Black and Anti-Hispanic Stereotypes." *Social Science Quarterly* 85:257–80.

Downey, Dennis J. 2000. "Situating Social Attitudes toward Cultural Pluralism: Between Culture Wars and Contemporary Racism." *Social Problems* 47:90–111.

DuBois, W.E.B. 1899. *The Philadelphia Negro: A Social Study*. Philadelphia: University of Pennsylvania Press.

Edsall, Thomas B., and Mary D. Edsall. 1991. *Chain Reaction: The Impact of Race, Rights and Taxes on American Politics*. New York: Norton.

Evans, John H. 2003. "Have Americans' Attitudes Become More Polarized? An Update." *Social Science Quarterly* 84:71–90.

Farley, Reynolds, Charlotte Steeh, Maria Krysan, Tara Jackson, and Keith Reeves. 1994. "Stereotypes and Segregation: Neighborhoods in the Detroit Area." *American Journal of Sociology* 100:750–80.

Feagin, Joe R. 1999. "Soul-Searching in Sociology: Is the Discipline in Crisis?" *Chronicle of Higher Education* 46:4–6.

Federico, Christopher M. 2004. "When Do Welfare Attitudes Become Racialized? The Paradoxical Effects of Education." *American Journal of Political Science* 48:374–91.

Feldman, Stanley, and Leonie Huddy. 2005. "Racial Resentment and White Opposition to Race-Conscious Programs: Principles or Prejudice?" *American Journal of Political Science* 49:168–83.

Forman, Tyrone A. 2004. "Color-Blind Racism and Racial Indifference: The Role of Racial Apathy in Facilitating Enduring Racial Inequalities." In *Changing Terrain of Race and Ethnicity*, edited by M. Krysan and A. E. Lewis, 43–66. New York: Russell Sage Foundation.

Forman, Tyrone A., and Amanda E. Lewis. 2006. "Racial Apathy and Hurricane Katrina: The Social Anatomy of Prejudice in the Post–Civil Rights Era." *Du Bois Review* 3:175–202.

Fossett, Mark A., and K. Jill Kiecolt. 1989. "The Relative Size of Minority Populations and White Racial Attitudes." *Social Science Quarterly* 70:820–35.

Fox, Cybelle. 2004. "The Changing Color of Welfare? How Whites' Attitudes toward Latinos Influence Support for Welfare." *American Journal of Sociology* 110:580–625.

Fredrickson, George M. 1971. *The Black Image in the White Mind: The Debate on Afro-American Character and Destiny, 1817–1914*. New York: Harper & Row.

———. 2002. *Racism: A Short History*. Princeton, NJ: Princeton University Press.

Gallagher, Charles A. 2003. "Miscounting Race: Explaining Whites' Misperception of Racial Group Size." *Sociological Perspectives* 46:381–96.

Gilens, Martin. 1999. *Why Americans Hate Welfare: Race, Media, and the Politics of Antipoverty Policy*. Chicago: University of Chicago Press.

Glaser, James M., and Martin Gilens. 1997. "Interregional Migration and Political Resocialization: A Study of Racial Attitudes under Pressure." *Public Opinion Quarterly* 61:72–86.

Greeley, Andrew M., and Paul B. Sheatsley. 1971. "Attitudes toward Racial Integration." *Scientific American* 225:13–19.

Horowitz, Eugene L. 1944. "Race Attitudes." In *Characteristics of the American Negro*, edited by Otto Klineberg, 141–247. New York: Harper & Row.

Hughes, Michael. 1997. "Symbolic Racism, Old-Fashioned Racism, and Whites' Opposition to Affirmative Action." In *Racial Attitudes in the 1990s: Continuity and Change*, edited by Steven A. Tuch and Jack K. Martin, 45–75. Westport, CT: Praeger.

Hughes, Michael, and Steven A. Tuch. 2003. "Gender Differences in Whites' Racial Attitudes: Are Women's Attitudes Really More Favorable?" *Social Psychology Quarterly* 66:384–401.

Hunt, Matthew O. 2007. "African-American, Hispanic, and White Beliefs about Black/White Inequality, 1977–2004." *American Sociological Review* 72:390–415.

Hunt, Matthew O., Pamela Braboy Jackson, Brian Powell, and Lala Carr Steelman. 2000. "Color-Blind: The Treatment of Race and Ethnicity in Social Psychology." *Social Psychology Quarterly* 3:352–64.

Hutchings, Vincent L., and Nicholas A. Valentino. 2004. "The Centrality of Race in American Politics." *Annual Review of Political Science* 7:383–408.

Hyman, Herbert H., and Paul B. Sheatsley. 1956. "Attitudes toward Desegregation." *Scientific American* 195:35–39.

———. 1964. "Attitudes toward Desegregation." *Scientific American* 211:16–23.

Jackman, Mary R. 1977. "Prejudice, Tolerance, and Attitudes toward Ethnic Groups." *Social Science Research* 6:145–69.

———. 1994. *The Velvet Glove: Paternalism and Conflict in Gender, Class and Race*. Berkeley: University of California Press.

———. 1996. "Individualism, Self-Interest, and White Racism." *Social Science Quarterly* 77:760–67.

Jackman, Mary R., and Marie Crane. 1986. "'Some of My Best Friends Are Black . . .': Interracial Friendship and Whites' Racial Attitudes." *Public Opinion Quarterly* 50:459–86.

Jackman, Mary R., and Mary S. Senter. 1983. "Different, Therefore Unequal: Beliefs about Trait Differences between Groups of Unequal Status." *Research in Social Stratification and Mobility* 2:309–35.

Johnson, Monica K., and Margaret M. Marini. 1998. "Bridging the Racial Divide in the United States: The Effect of Gender." *Social Psychology Quarterly* 61:247–58.

Jordan, Winthrop D. 1968. *White over Black: American Attitudes toward the Negro, 1550–1812.* Chapel Hill: University of North Carolina Press.

Kinder, Donald R., and Tali Mendelberg. 1995. "Cracks in American Apartheid: The Political Impact of Prejudice among Desegregated Whites." *Journal of Politics* 57:402–24.

Kinder, Donald R., and Lynn M. Sanders. 1996. *Divided by Color: Racial Politics and Democratic Ideals.* Chicago: University of Chicago Press.

Kinder, Donald R., and David O. Sears. 1981. "Prejudice and Politics: Symbolic Racism versus Racial Threats to the Good Life." *Journal of Personality and Social Psychology* 40:414–31.

Kluegel, James R. 1990. "Trends in Whites' Explanations of the Black–White Gap in Socioeconomic Status, 1977–89." *American Sociological Review* 55:512–25.

Kluegel, James R., and Eliot R. Smith. 1986. *Beliefs about Inequality: Americans' Views of What Is and What Ought to Be.* New York: Aldine.

Krysan, Maria. 2000. "Prejudice, Politics, and Public Opinion: Understanding the Sources of Racial Policy Attitudes." *Annual Review of Sociology* 26:135–68.

Krysan, Maria, and Michael Bader. 2007. "Perceiving the Metropolis: Seeing the City through a Prism of Race." *Social Forces* 86:699–733.

Kuklinski, James H., Michael D. Cobb, and Martin Gilens. 1997. "Racial Attitudes and the 'New South.'" *Journal of Politics* 59:323–49.

La Piere, Richard T. 1934. "Attitudes vs Actions." *Social Forces* 13:230–37.

Lamont, Michèle. 2000. *The Dignity of Working Men: Morality and the Boundaries of Race, Class, and Immigration.* New York: Russell Sage Foundation.

Lee, Taeku. 2008. "Race, Immigration, and the Identity-to-Politics Link." *Annual Review of Political Science* 11:457–78.

Lieberson, Stanley. 1992. "Einstein, Renoir, and Greeley: Some Thoughts about Evidence in Sociology: 1991 Presidential Address." *American Sociological Review* 57:1–15.

Massey, Douglas S. 2007. *Categorically Unequal: The American Stratification System.* New York: Russell Sage Foundation.

Massey, Douglas S., and Nancy Denton. 1993. *American Apartheid: Segregation and the Making of the American Underclass.* Cambridge, MA: Harvard University Press.

McConahay, J. B. 1986. "Modern Racism, Ambivalence, and the Modern Racism Scale." In *Prejudice, Discrimination, and Racism,* edited by John F. Dovidio and Samuel L. Gaertner, 91–125. New York: Academic Press.

Mendelberg, Tali. 2001. *The Race Card: Campaign Strategy, Implicit Messages, and the Norm of Equality*. Princeton, NJ: Princeton University Press.

Mondak, Jeffery J., and Mitchell S. Sanders. 2003. "Tolerance and Intolerance, 1976–1998." *American Journal of Political Science* 47:492–502.

Moore, Laura M., and Seth Ovadia. 2006. "Accounting for Spatial Variation in Tolerance: The Effects of Education and Religion." *Social Forces* 84:2205–22.

Myrdal, Gunnar. 1944. *An American Dilemma: The Negro Problem and American Democracy*. New York: Harper.

Nisbett, Richard, and Lee Ross. 1980. *Human Inference: Strategies and Shortcomings of Human Judgment*. Englewood Cliffs, NJ: Prentice Hall.

O'Connor, Alice, Chris Tilly, and Lawrence D. Bobo. 2001. *Urban Inequality: Evidence from Four Cities*. New York: Russell Sage Foundation.

Park, Robert E. 1924. "The Concept of Social Distance as Applied to the Study of Racial Relations." *Journal of Applied Sociology* 8:339–44.

Persell, Caroline Hodges, Adam Green, and Liena Gurevich. 2001. "Civil Society, Economic Distress, and Social Tolerance." *Sociological Forum* 16:203–30.

Pettigrew, Thomas F., and Roel Meertens. 1995. "Subtle and Blatant Prejudice in Western Europe." *European Journal of Social Psychology* 25:57–75.

Quillian, Lincoln. 2006. "New Approaches to Understanding Racial Prejudice and Discrimination." *Annual Review of Sociology* 32:299–328.

Quillian, Lincoln, and Devah Pager. 2001. "Black Neighbors, Higher Crime? The Role of Racial Stereotypes in Evaluations of Neighborhood Crime." *American Journal of Sociology* 107:717–67.

Schuman, Howard. 1969. "Sociological Racism." *Society* 7:44–48.

———. 1972. "Attitudes vs. Actions versus Attitudes vs. Attitudes." *Public Opinion Quarterly* 36:347–54.

———. 1995. "Attitudes, Beliefs, and Behavior." In *Sociological Perspectives on Social Psychology*, edited by Karen A. Cook and Gary A. Fine, 68–79. Boston: Allyn & Bacon.

Schuman, Howard, and Lawrence D. Bobo. 1988. "Survey-Based Experiments on White Racial Attitudes toward Residential Integration." *American Journal of Sociology* 94:273–99.

Schuman, Howard, and Michael P. Johnson. 1976. "Attitudes and Behavior." *Annual Review of Sociology* 2:161–207.

Schuman, Howard, and Maria Krysan. 1999. "A Historical Note on Whites' Beliefs about Racial Inequality." *American Sociological Review* 64:847–55.

Schuman, Howard, Charlotte Steeh, and Lawrence D. Bobo. 1985. *Racial Attitudes in America: Trends and Interpretations*. Cambridge, MA: Harvard University Press.

Schuman, Howard, Charlotte Steeh, Lawrence D. Bobo, and Maria Krysan. 1997. *Racial Attitudes in America: Trends and Interpretations*. Rev. ed. Cambridge, MA: Harvard University Press.

Sears, David O. 1988. "Symbolic Racism." In *Eliminating Racism: Profiles in Controversy*, edited by Phyllis A. Katz and Dalmas A. Taylor, 53–84. New York: Plenum.

Sears, David O., and Tom Jessor. 1996. "Whites' Racial Policy Attitudes: The Role of White Racism." *Social Science Quarterly* 77:751–59.

Sears, David O., Collette Van Larr, Mary Carrillo, and Rick Kosterman. 1997. "Is It Really Racism? The Origins of White Americans' Opposition to Race-Targeted Policies." *Public Opinion Quarterly* 61:16–53.

Sidanius, Jim, and Felicia Pratto. 1999. *Social Dominance: An Intergroup Theory of Social Hierarchy and Oppression.* New York: Cambridge University Press.

Smith, A. Wade. 1981. "Racial Tolerance as a Function of Group Position." *American Sociological Review* 46:558–73.

Smith, Eliot R. 1993. "Social Identity and Social Emotions: Toward New Conceptualizations of Prejudice." In *Affect, Cognition, and Stereotyping: Interactive Processes in Group Perception,* edited by Diane M. Mackie and David L. Hamilton, 297–315. New York: Academic Press.

Smith, Tom W. 1991. "Ethnic Images." GSS Topical Report No. 19. Chicago: NORC.

Sniderman, Paul M., and Edward G. Carmines. 1997. *Reaching Beyond Race.* Cambridge, MA: Harvard University Press.

Sniderman Paul M., and Michael G. Hagen. 1985. *Race and Inequality: A Study in American Values.* Chatham, NJ: Chatham House.

Sniderman, Paul M., and Thomas Piazza. 1993. *The Scar of Race.* Cambridge, MA: Harvard University Press.

Sniderman, Paul M., and Paul E. Tetlock. 1986. "Symbolic Racism: Problems of Motive Attribution in Political Analysis." *Journal of Social Issues* 42:129–50.

Stack, Steven. 1997. "Women's Opposition to Race-Targeted Interventions." *Sex Roles* 36:543–50.

Steeh, Charlotte, and Maria Krysan. 1996. "Trends: Affirmative Action and the Public, 1970–1995." *Public Opinion Quarterly* 60:128–58.

Stoker, Laura. 1996. "Understanding Differences in Whites' Opinions across Racial Policies." *Social Science Quarterly* 77:768–77.

Stults, Brian J., and Eric P. Baumer. 2007. "Racial Context and Police Force Size: Evaluating the Empirical Validity of the Minority Threat Perspective." *American Journal of Sociology* 113:507–46.

Taylor, D. Garth, Paul B. Sheatsley, and Andrew M. Greeley. 1978. "Attitudes toward Racial Integration." *Scientific American* 238:42–51.

Taylor, Marylee C. 1998. "How White Attitudes Vary with the Racial Composition of Local Populations—Numbers Count." *American Sociological Review* 64:512–35.

Tuch, Steven A. 1987. "Urbanism, Region, and Tolerance Revisited: The Case of Racial Prejudice." *American Sociological Review* 52:504–10.

Tuch, Steven A., and Michael Hughes. 1996. "Whites' Racial Policy Attitudes." *Social Science Quarterly* 77:723–45.

Valentino, Nicholas A., and David O. Sears. 2005. "Old Times There Are Not Forgotten: Race and Partisan Realignment in the Contemporary South." *American Journal of Political Science* 49:672–88.

Waters, Mary. 1999. *Black Identities: West Indian Dreams and American Realities.* Cambridge, MA: Harvard University Press.

Weakliem, David L., and Robert Biggert. 1998. "Region and Political Opinion in the Contemporary United States." *Social Forces* 77:863–86.

Wilson, Thomas C. 1985. "Urbanism and Tolerance: A Test of Some Hypotheses Drawn from Wirth and Stouffer." *American Sociological Review* 50:117–23.

———. 1986. "Interregional Migration and Racial Attitudes." *Social Forces* 65:177–86.

———. 1991. "Urbanism, Migration, and Tolerance: A Reassessment." *American Sociological Review* 56:117–23.

———. 2006. "Whites' Opposition to Affirmative Action: Rejection of Group-Based Preferences as well as Rejection of Blacks." *Social Forces* 85:111–20.

Wilson, William Julius, and Richard P. Taub. 2006. *There Goes the Neighborhood: Racial, Ethnic, and Class Tensions in Four Chicago Neighborhoods and Their Meaning for America*. New York: Knopf.

Wong, Cara J. 2008. "Objective vs. Subjective Context: Questions about the Mechanism Linking Racial Context to Political Attitudes." Unpublished manuscript, Department of Political Science, University of Illinois at Urbana-Champaign.

Zubrinsky, Camille L., and Lawrence D. Bobo. 1996. "Prismatic Metropolis: Race and Residential Segregation in the City of the Angels." *Social Science Research* 25:335–74.

4

Gender Role Attitudes since 1972

Are Southerners Distinctive?

Karen E. Campbell and Peter V. Marsden

In January 2007, Nancy Pelosi became the first woman to serve as speaker of the U.S. House of Representatives (Center for American Women and Politics [CAWP] 2007). In 2008, Hillary Clinton emerged as a viable candidate for the Democratic nomination for the presidency; Sarah Palin was the Republican nominee for the vice presidency. Neither Clinton nor Palin was elected, but their candidacies—and Pelosi's four-year tenure as Speaker of the House— reflect significant progress since the 1970s in women's representation among elected officials at both the state and national levels. In 1975, for example, just 8.1% of elected state legislators, 3.6% of U.S. representatives, and no U.S. senators were women (CAWP 1975). After the 2010 midterm elections, women hold 24.5% of seats in state legislatures, 16.8% of the U.S. House of Representatives, and 17% of U.S. Senate seats (CAWP 2010a, 2010b).

The story is more complex, however. During the 1990s and early 2000s, women's movement into state legislatures apparently leveled off (Paxton, Painter, and Hughes 2009). After substantial and steady gains from the mid-1970s to the early 1990s, the percentage of women among state legislators rose by just 2 points between 1999 (22.4) and 2010 (24.5; CAWP n.d.; see also Carroll 2004). And women's share of seats in the U.S. Congress, at a historic high during the 111th Congress, declined slightly as an outcome of the 2010 elections (CAWP 2010b; Women in Congress 2011).

A similar but even more dramatic story can be told with regard to American women's involvement in paid employment. During the 20th century, employment for women (especially married women and those with young children) became a relatively routine rather than uncommon experience (Oppenheimer 1970; Abrams 2006; Cotter, Hermsen, and Vanneman 2005; Fischer and Hout 2006). During the first half of that century, the likelihood of a woman's employment varied greatly, depending on her marital and parental statuses.[1] Fewer than 12% of wives (with husband present) with children under the age of 6 were in the labor force in 1950, but about 30% of such women were employed by 1970 (U.S. Bureau of the Census 1975, p. 134). Single women with no children at home have long had the highest labor force participation rate, and married mothers the lowest. These differences narrowed sharply after World War II (Cotter et al. 2005; Oppenheimer 1970, chap. 1), however: By 2000, 60% of wives with children younger than 6 years old were in the labor force, as were 80% of childless never-married women (Cotter et al. 2005; Fischer and Hout 2006).

Here, too, scholars of gender and work have pointed to a leveling off in married women's labor force participation rates during the 1990s (e.g., Cotter et al. 2005; Lee and Mather 2008; Stone 2007; Boushey 2008). This plateau has occasioned much discussion in the popular media, best illustrated by a 2003 *New York Times Magazine* essay on the "opt-out revolution" (Belkin 2003), which claimed that well-educated women with high-status jobs were increasingly leaving full-time employment to be full-time mothers (for a review of the media coverage, see Kuperberg and Stone 2008). Social scientists debate whether this stasis is permanent or passing, which women (if any) are "opting out" of employment, and why (see, e.g., Hoffman 2009; Stone 2007; Boushey 2008). Since at least the early to mid-1980s, in any event, mothers of young children have typically been *in* rather than *out* of the labor force (e.g., Hayghe and Bianchi 1994, p.28; Mosisa and Hipple 2006, p. 47),[2] a radical shift since the 1960s. Indeed, the movement of married mothers into the labor force is widely regarded as a signal social change of the second half of the 20th century (e.g., Fischer and Hout 2006, p. 98; Hayghe 1997, p. 41; Boushey 2008, p. 1; Bianchi 2000, p. 401).

The dramatic rise in married mothers' employment directs greater attention to women's and men's responsibilities within the household, particularly in regard to parenting. U.S. gender culture has long defined caring for children as a central capacity and responsibility of women, and sees it at odds (at least for white women) with full-time employment (e.g., Bernard 1974; Risman 1998).[3] Many anticipated that negative consequences for children would accompany rises in mothers' labor force participation, assuming that employed mothers would spend less time with their children (see Bianchi 2000 and Bianchi and Milkie 2010 for reviews).

Yet increased labor force participation by married women with children in the 1960s and beyond was not initially accompanied by greater participation by fathers in household chores or daily child care. Analyzing 1981 time-diary data, for example, Nock and Kingston (1988, p. 81) concluded, "Our findings counter the sense that the emergence of the dual-earner family has fostered a new, involved paternal role for fathers" (see also Hochschild 1989; Risman 1998). More recent research (e.g., Bianchi 2000; Sandberg and Hofferth 2001, 2005; Sayer, Bianchi, and Robinson 2004), however, suggests both that time spent with children by employed mothers has held stable or increased *and* that employed fathers now spend more time with their children than did similar men in the 1980s. Though the gap may have narrowed, women continue to provide the majority of all types of child care in dual-earner couples (Bianchi 2000; Sayer et al. 2004; Sandberg and Hofferth 2005). Married mothers remain the primary parents in such families despite their dramatically increased employment levels.

With these broad trends in women's participation in elective office, the labor market, and child care as background, this chapter examines changing attitudes about women's involvement in politics, paid employment, and child rearing and notably about the interplay between maternal employment and family roles. The General Social Survey (GSS; J. A. Davis, Smith, and Marsden 2009) provides rich trend data on gender role attitudes during a pivotal era.[4] Its initial round (1972) probed adults' attitudes toward women as presidential candidates and the propriety of married women's employment. That coverage broadened to include eight gender role items measured regularly between 1985 and 1998, five of which remained as of the 2008 round. Our analyses assess trends as well as individual differences in these attitudes, with special attention to comparisons between adults living in the South and elsewhere in the United States. Previous research on gender roles using GSS data documents substantial change in Americans' views of women's roles over more than three decades (Bolzendahl and Myers 2004; Brooks and Bolzendahl 2004; Vanneman and Kling 2010). These trends indicate increased acceptance of less traditional views about gender, but are uneven over the period: In general, the steepest rise in more liberal notions of gender roles took place by the early to mid-1990s. Thereafter, the percentages of adults giving liberal responses fluctuated within a narrow band, increasing slightly for some items, while remaining virtually level for others. Their general pattern mirrors trends in women's share of elective office and in women's labor force participation.

Extant research also establishes that several sociodemographic factors predict the likelihood of holding less traditional stances. Women (e.g., Mason and Lu 1988; Brooks and Bolzendahl 2004), younger adults (Mason and Lu 1988; Kozimor-King and Leicht 1999; Powers et al. 2003), the more highly educated (Harris and Firestone 1998; Brooks and Bolzendahl 2004), non-southerners (Hurlbert 1989; Rice and Coates 1995; Powers et al. 2003), and those who have migrated away from the South (Rice and Pepper 1997) hold more liberal attitudes. Brooks and Bolzendahl (2004) carefully demonstrate that while cohort replacement accounts for much of the aggregate over-time change in gender role attitudes, adults' attitudes also change through a process of "ideological learning."[5]

Little prior research has closely examined the role of region in shaping gender role attitudes. In particular, the tendency of those living in the South to take conservative stances on gender roles goes largely unremarked. Many writers control for regional differences in their analyses of gender role attitudes (e.g., Brooks and Bolzendahl 2004), but only a few focus on regional differences in these orientations (Hurlbert 1989; Rice and Coates 1995; Rice and Pepper 1997; Powers et al. 2003). Fewer still look with care at possible factors that might account for regional variation in views regarding gender.

This chapter first describes aggregate changes over time in the eight gender role attitudes that the GSS has tracked since the 1970s. We then turn attention to South–non-South differences, first asking about whether these have lessened over time and then examining the extent to which rurality and religion account for differences in gender role attitudes between southerners and those living elsewhere. We address both change in Americans' views about women's roles in politics, employment, and family since 1972, and the degree to which southerners maintain distinctive stances about appropriate roles for women.

The General Landscape of U.S. Gender Role Attitudes

The GSS measured eight items about women's roles over much of the 1972–2008 span, although not all appeared in each survey round. We organize these into three clusters in our discussion.[6] Table 4.1 presents the full wording of each question. Three items tap attitudes about women and politics: willingness to vote for qualified women as presidential candidates, the relative emotional suitability of women and men for politics, and whether men should run the country while women run their homes. Another set of three questions focuses on the appropriate mix of marriage, family, and employment roles for women: whether it is acceptable for married women to be employed, whether wives should give priority to their husbands' careers over their own, and whether "everyone involved" benefits when men achieve outside the home while women care for home and family. Finally, two questions ask specifically about how employment affects relationships between mothers and their children: whether employed mothers can have relationships with their children that are as warm and secure as those that nonemployed mothers have, and whether preschool children suffer if their mothers are employed.

Attitudes about Women and Politics

Two GSS questions ask specifically about women's involvement in politics, while a third addresses the traditional notion that men should occupy the

Table 4.1. GSS Gender Role Questions

	Nontraditional response	# Years measured	Years covered	GSS mnemonic
Women and politics				
"If your party nominated a woman for President, would you vote for her if she were qualified for the job?"	Yes	18	1972–2008	FEPRES
"Tell me if you agree or disagree with this statement: Most men are better suited emotionally for politics than are most women."	Disagree	21	1974–2008	FEPOL
"Do you agree or disagree with this statement?: Women should take care of running their homes and leave running the country up to men."	Disagree	16	1974–1998	FEHOME
Employment, marriage, and family				
"Do you approve or disapprove of a married woman earning money in business or industry if she has a husband capable of supporting her?"	Approve	17	1972–1998	FEWORK
"It is more important for a wife to help her husband's career than to have one of her own."	Strongly disagree	11	1977–1998	FEHELP
"It is much better for everyone involved if the man is the achiever outside the home and the woman takes care of the home and family."	Strongly disagree	16	1977–2008	FEFAM
Maternal employment and children				
"A working mother can establish just as warm and secure a relationship with her children as a mother who does not work."	Strongly agree	16	1977–2008	FECHLD
"A preschool child is likely to suffer if his or her mother works."	Strongly disagree	16	1977–2008	FEPRESCH

Note: In 1974 and 1982, the GSS asked a subsample of respondents to answer an alternate version of this item. These respondents are omitted in most analyses in this chapter but are part of the summary analyses (Figures 4.4 and 4.8).

public sphere while women remain within the private realm. Figure 4.1 graphs trends for all three items.

As already noted, gender role attitudes have liberalized since 1972, but even in the early 1970s, majorities of U.S. adults held nontraditional stances regarding women's roles in the political sphere. In 1972, almost 80% of U.S.

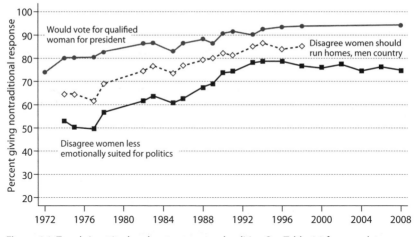

Figure 4.1. Trends in attitudes about women and politics. See Table 4.1 for complete question wordings.

adults indicated that they would vote for a (qualified) woman for president; this rose to 93.7% by 1998, and slightly further to 94.2% by the 2008 survey. A substantially smaller share (though still a majority, 53.1%) of respondents in 1974 rejected the notion that men are generally better suited for politics than women; this rose to a peak of 78.7% in 1994 and 1996, but has declined slightly since (to 74.6% in 2008). The gap between the percentages giving liberal responses to these items suggests robust differences in adults' views on these two issues. More than 1 in 5 respondents in both 1974 and 2008 agreed that most men are more emotionally suited for politics than are most women, while *also* saying that they would support a qualified female presidential candidate from their party. Thus, a notable share of adults saw men as generally better qualified—at least emotionally—for politics, but were willing to entertain the possibility that a *particular* woman could be qualified for the presidency.

The third question included in Figure 4.1 does not ask about the suitability of women for political office per se, but instead about support for a "separate spheres" ideology holding that men belong in the public sphere ("running the country") while women inhabit the domestic/private one ("running their homes"). Responses to this question, measured until 1998, fall into the same general pattern seen for the two explicitly political items, however. In 1974, a majority (64.5%) of American adults rejected this traditional division of labor, a share that rose fairly steadily until 1993 (to 85.1%) and then leveled off.

Attitudes about Women's Employment, Marriage, and Family Roles

Figure 4.2 displays trends in three items that tap adults' attitudes about appropriate roles for women in combining paid employment with marriage and

Figure 4.2. Attitudes about employment, marriage, and family. See Table 4.1 for complete question wording.

family commitments. Of the three, U.S. adults are most accepting of wives' employment, even when it is not financially necessary. In 1972, more than two-thirds (67.1%) endorsed wives' employment.[7] When first measured five years later in 1977, attitudes regarding the relative priority of wives' and husbands' careers were substantially more conservative than those regarding wives' employment. Fewer than one-half (43%) of American adults then disagreed or strongly disagreed with the proposition that a wife should be willing to forgo her own career in order to advance her husband's.[8] Acceptance of a traditional household division of labor was likewise widespread: Only 34.1% disagreed that men should achieve outside the home while women specialize in caring for household and family. Thus, while U.S. adults of the 1970s did not roundly object to the notion of employment among married women, they held that husbands' careers should take priority and that a division of labor in which men were earners and women responsible for the domestic front was preferable.

Over the subsequent two decades, however, views on the priority of men's careers and the desirability of a traditional division of household labor shifted very substantially toward more liberal positions. Most dramatically, an increased share of adults endorsed nontraditional attitudes about whether women should prioritize their husbands' careers over their own. By 1998, more than 80% of adults disagreed that women should advance their husbands' careers at the expense of having careers of their own. Views of the appropriate division of household labor shifted similarly: More than half of adults disputed the claim that "everyone involved" benefits from a conventional division of responsibilities between women and men by 1986. Beginning in 1993, however, a plateau akin to that seen for views about women and politics (Figure 4.1) emerged here as well. Moreover, the nontraditional position on the household division of labor lost ground at times. In 2008, the percentage of adults who disputed a traditional gender-based division of labor (59.8) was virtually the same as that found two decades earlier, in 1989 (59.7).

Employed Mothers and Their Children

Two final gender role questions focus on the consequences of women's employment for their children. Figure 4.3 displays trends in these items since 1977. One item asks how strongly respondents agree or disagree that "[a] working mother can establish just as warm and secure a relationship with her children as a mother who does not work." The other asks if a preschool child is likely to suffer if his or her mother works. U.S. adults gave consistently more conservative answers with regard to preschool-aged children; mothers' employment was seen as especially problematic when children are young (see also Charles and Cech 2010). In 1977, fewer than one-third (31.8%) disagreed with the claim that mothers' employment is detrimental for their young children, while nearly one-half (48.9%) *agreed* that employed mothers could have relationships with their children on a par with those enjoyed by mothers who are not employed. Both figures rose somewhat during the 1980s, but during the 1990s increases in beliefs that maternal employment has benign effects on children ceased, in keeping with the patterns seen for attitudes about women's participation in politics, and on employment, marriage, and family.

Attitudes about how mother's employment affects children grew notably more liberal after 2000, however. In fact, the share of respondents giving liberal answers to these two items was higher in 2008 than in any prior GSS;

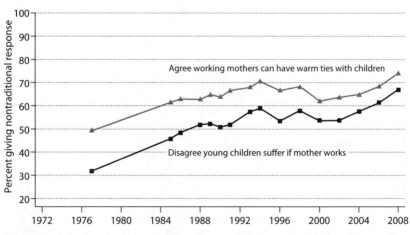

Figure 4.3. Attitudes about employed mothers and children. See Table 4.1 for complete question wording.

nearly three-quarters then agreed that employed mothers can have warm and secure relationships with their children, while two-thirds rejected the idea that preschool children suffer as a result of their mothers' employment. Of particular interest is that these two trends—the most steadily upward of the eight examined—continued while media attention increasingly focused on the problems that employment poses *for mothers* (and less on the problems it creates for children; Vanneman and Kling 2010) and on the so-called "opting out" of employment by women in favor of full-time mothering (Stone 2007; Kuperberg and Stone 2008). Notwithstanding this media climate, U.S. adults became increasingly confident during the 2000s that mothers' employment was not detrimental for their children. This is the only realm among those measured by the GSS in which gender role attitudes grew *more* liberal during the early 2000s.

In sum, then, four general over-time patterns are evident. First, all gender role attitudes among U.S. adults have liberalized substantially since the 1970s. Second, much of that trend toward liberal (or nontraditional) views unfolded by the early to mid-1990s, with limited increases (and even modest conservative shifts in some domains) in the late 1990s and early 2000s. Third, while U.S. adults shed traditional attitudes about women's roles as helpmates and women's suitability for politics relatively quickly, they were more circumspect about how a woman's employment affects children. But fourth, Americans grew somewhat more liberal regarding these very issues about employed mothers and child rearing during the early 2000s, contrary to trends on the other three items that were then measured by the GSS.

Crafting a single conclusion about the 1972–2008 trend in gender role attitudes is challenging because the GSS posed different questions about these issues over time. In 1972, it measured only willingness to vote for a qualified

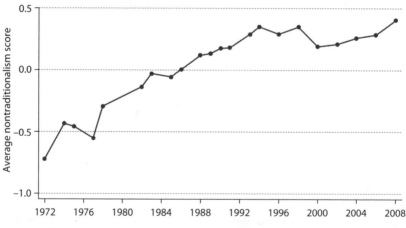

Figure 4.4. Summary trend in nontraditional gender attitudes.

woman for president and the propriety of wives' employment in the absence of financial need. All eight items appeared in 1977, and again between 1985 and 1998; subsets of four or five of them were included in other survey years. Using a graded response model described in the appendix to this chapter, Figure 4.4 graphs trends in a latent nontraditionalism variable over the full 1972–2008 period. We see relatively steady upward movement in nontraditionalism between 1972 and 1994, albeit with a slight dip in the later 1970s; but after 1994, the trend abruptly levels off and even falls a bit, before rising after 2000 to a high in 2008. The rising nontraditionalism level of the 2000s reflects increasingly optimistic beliefs about the compatibility of maternal employment and responsible child rearing.

The following sections examine variation in gender role attitudes *among* adults. We focus particularly on one aspect of that variation, differences between southerners and nonsoutherners.

The Enduring South?

Historically, southern states were slow to embrace significant change in women's social roles. No southern state, for example, granted full suffrage to women prior to ratification of the Nineteenth Amendment (Flexner 1973).[9] Around the turn of the 20th century, women in the South were less apt to be physicians than those elsewhere, net of other state-level factors (Campbell and McCammon 2005); southern states resisted efforts to raise the age of consent for girls to marry (Odem 1995, pp. 35–37) and to include women on juries (Kenyon and Murray 1966; McCammon, Muse, Newman, and Terrell 2007). More recently, the effort to ratify the Equal Rights Amendment to the U.S. Constitution during the 1970s and 1980s was particularly fruitless in the South. Of the 35 states that ratified the amendment, only 5 were southern; of those, 2 (Kentucky and Tennessee) later voted to rescind ratification. Conversely, 10 of the 15 states that never ratified the amendment were in the South (Thomas 1991, p. 377). Finally, women have historically been, and remain, rarer in state legislatures in the South. In 2010, for example, 7 of the 10 states with the lowest representation of women among state legislators were in the South, along with one state from each of the other three census regions (CAWP 2010a).[10]

Regional variation in women's labor force participation is narrower than in political representation. Nonetheless, in 1960, women in the South were slightly less apt to be in the labor force (33.4%) than were women in the Northeast (36.1%) or West (35.1%) (at 33.7%, women's labor force participation rate in the north-central states was virtually identical to that among southern women; calculated from U.S. Bureau of the Census 1961, p. 1-243, table 101). Although labor force participation rates among women nearly doubled by 2000, a small regional gap remains: 62.7% of women in southern states were in the labor force, compared with 63.2%, 66.4%, and 63.9% in the Northeast, Midwest, and West, respectively (U.S. Bureau of the Census 2003, p. 4, table 4).

In addition to describing these state and regional variations, sociologists and historians have long noted the more conservative attitudes of southerners themselves, compared to residents of other regions in the United States (e.g., Odum 1947; Vance 1932; Reed 1972, 1983; Weakliem and Biggert 1999; Edgell and Tranby 2007). Historically, southerners have held more traditional attitudes and beliefs, particularly with regard to relations between whites and blacks (e.g., Reed 1983; see also Bobo et al., chapter 3 of this volume) and to appropriate roles for women and men (e.g., Scott 1970). The regional gap in both racial and gender role attitudes has narrowed over time, however (Firebaugh and Davis 1988; Hurlbert 1989; Bolzendahl and Myers 2004), due to both migration of nonsoutherners into the South and liberalizing trends among southerners themselves. Most research on region and gender role attitudes, however, focuses on the extent of contemporary differences and/or on whether these are diminishing over time (e.g., Rice and Coates 1995; Rice and Pepper 1997; Powers et al. 2003). It gives less attention to possible explanations for such differences.

Past work reports varied findings about regional differences in attitudes toward women's and men's appropriate roles. Brooks and Bolzendahl (2004) found no regional difference in changes in gender role attitudes between 1977 and 1998; Bolzendahl and Myers (2004) found that net of other relevant factors, residence in the South was associated with more conservative gender role attitudes. Powers and her colleagues found a weak regional difference in gender ideology during the 1990s, although it was stronger among whites than blacks. They concluded that the "absence of important effects of region may be explained by the fact that we controlled for the variables that greatly account for the 'distinctive southern culture' characteristics" (Powers et al. 2003, p. 52).[11] Fischer and Hout (2006, pp. 220–23) reported substantial regional gaps in the 1970s for two GSS items studied here (whether adults would vote for a qualified woman for president, and whether they approve of married women's employment), with southerners and midwesterners the most conservative; these gaps closed by 2000.

Perhaps because regional differences in gender role attitudes are typically smaller than those linked to age, education, sex, or labor force participation, social scientists have been content primarily to document them, accepting regional differences—particularly the conservative consequences of living in the South—at face value.[12] Here, we explore possible routes through which region shapes gender role attitudes, including the influences of religion and rurality, two aspects of the South and its residents that may undergird its more traditional gender role orientations.

We first briefly describe differences in how southerners and nonsoutherners answer the eight GSS gender role questions. Then we consider whether southerners' stronger religiosity and/or their residence in more rural communities help to explain regional differences in those attitudes.

Differences between Southerners and Nonsoutherners

Figures 4.5 through 4.7 depict over-time differences in gender role attitudes between adults living in the South and those living elsewhere.[13] We illustrate these regional differences for one question drawn from each of the three clusters of gender role items discussed earlier: whether men are better suited for politics than women (Figure 4.5), the desirability of a traditional gender division of labor (Figure 4.6), and whether employed mothers can have relationships with their children comparable in warmth and security to relationships that homemakers have with their children (Figure 4.7). These graphs suggest that (1) gender role attitudes among southerners tend to be a bit more conservative than those of nonsoutherners, (2) these differences are not large (certainly not nearly so large as regional differences in some racial attitudes discussed by Bobo et al., chapter 3 in this volume) and have narrowed over time, and (3) southerners and nonsoutherners differ *least* in their responses to questions about employed mothers and their children (Figure 4.7).

First, greater percentages of nonsouthern adults than southerners took the more liberal position on gender roles for almost all questions in almost all survey years. Thus, when there *are* regional differences in gender role attitudes, southerners are typically more conservative than nonsoutherners.

Second, regional differences are generally small. In numerous cases, the difference between southerners and nonsoutherners is just a few percentage points; the largest difference was less than 20 percentage points (in 1988, on gender and politics, with more nonsoutherners giving the liberal response; see Figure 4.5).[14] The largest one in which southerners responded *more*

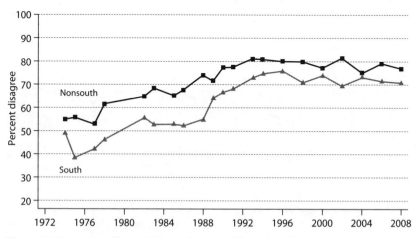

Figure 4.5. Percentage disagree: Women less suited for politics, by region. See Table 4.1 for complete question wording.

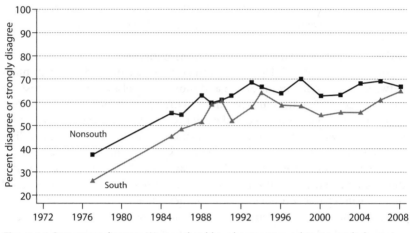

Figure 4.6. Percentage disagree: Women should run homes, men achieve outside, by region. See Table 4.1 for complete question wording.

liberally—for the question about employed mothers' relationships with their children—was only 4.3 percentage points, in 1989 (Figure 4.7).

As well, the regional gap in gender role attitudes, while never stark, clearly has narrowed over time on most questions. The trend in whether it is better for men to achieve outside the home and women to focus on home and family in Figure 4.6 illustrates this pattern clearly. In 1977, 26.4% of southern adults disagreed (the liberal position), compared to 37.9% of adults living outside the South. As adults in both groups moved toward more liberal positions over time, the regional gap fluctuated but generally shrank. By 2008,

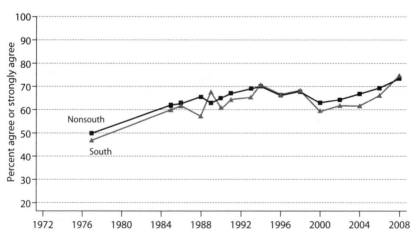

Figure 4.7. Percentage agree: Employed mothers can have warm relationships with children, by region. See Table 4.1 for complete question wording.

similar percentages in the two regions disagreed with the statement: 64.9% of southerners and 66.8% of nonsoutherners.

Lastly, regional *similarity* in answers to the two questions about relationships between employed mothers and their children is particularly interesting. Figure 4.7 demonstrates that even in 1977, southerners and nonsoutherners gave virtually identical answers to the question about the potential warmth and security of employed mothers' relationships with their children. They have not diverged in the 30 years since. This similarity exists despite the consistently more conservative responses of southerners to other gender role questions and the historically lower labor force participation rates among southern women. Likewise, southerners were more apt to agree that all involved benefit when women focus on home and family yet were no more likely than nonsouthern adults to agree that women's employment negatively affects their children.

In sum, then, consistent and somewhat persistent differences between the responses of southerners and nonsoutherners exist for five of the eight gender role items (all three questions about women and politics, and two questions about women's employment, marriage, and family roles). Regional differences in approval of married women's employment wax and wane, but are generally small. On just two items—those about employed mothers' relationships with their children—are no regional differences apparent over the three-decade span covered here.

To summarize overall regional differences in gender role orientations, we again estimate a graded response variable for a latent nontraditionalism variable, utilizing all of those indicators measured in each GSS round (see the appendix to this chapter), with results shown in Figure 4.8. The overall pattern among both southerners and nonsoutherners is similar to that for all

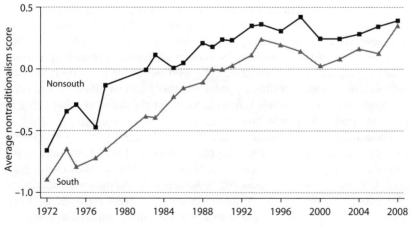

Figure 4.8. Summary trend in nontraditional gender attitudes, by region.

adults (Figure 4.4): relatively steady rises in nontraditional views between 1972 and the mid-1990s, stasis or slight decline (especially among southerners) until 2000, and moderate increases during the 2000s. While the gray line for southerners always lies beneath the black one for nonsoutherners, the rate of increase is somewhat higher among southerners, so that a substantial gap between the lines in the 1970s and early 1980s narrows during the later 1980s and 1990s, and virtually closes by 2008. This finding is consistent with the regional convergence in two of these items previously reported by Fischer and Hout (2006).

We have seen, then, that since 1972 southerners have held modestly more conservative gender role attitudes than adults living outside the South. The size of the gap varies over time, and nearly vanishes by 2008. Our finding is consistent with Fischer and Hout's (2006) recent suggestion that many regional differences in attitudes and beliefs have given way to other dimensions of difference, especially that between residents of center cities and of suburbs (e.g., Fischer and Hout 2006, pp. 220, 244). Modest regional gaps remain on some individual items we analyze, however, so we next investigate what accounts for those differences. In particular, we ask if part or all of those regional gaps in gender role orientations can be traced to rural residence or religious beliefs.

Why Are Southern Gender Attitudes Distinctive?

Historically, observers of the South have offered several explanations for its distinctiveness as a region: its antebellum plantation economy, social and economic isolation following the Civil War, slower rates of industrialization and of urbanization, resistance to "northern" intervention, poorer educational infrastructure, deeper religious conviction (at least among Protestants, the strong majority in southern states), and deep reverence for the past (see, e.g., Twelve Southerners 1930; Reed 1972, 1983; Grasmick 1973; Cobb 2005). To assess the continuing impact of structural factors (e.g., slower rates of industrialization) on southern culture and on southerners' attitudes would require state-level data that span many decades and aggregate indicators reflective of gender role attitudes (such as the content of state laws regarding married women's property rights), something beyond our scope here. With the GSS data we can, however, readily consider whether regional differences in rural residence or religious beliefs help to account for the difference that living in the South makes for gender role attitudes.

Though large metropolitan areas in the South such as Atlanta and Dallas have grown rapidly, as of 2000 the region remained the most rural in the United States by a slim margin over the Midwest (Northeast Midwest Institute 2002; U.S. Bureau of the Census 2005). Among GSS respondents interviewed after 2000, 17% of those from the South reside in areas classified as "open country" or places having fewer than 2,500 residents, compared to about 9% of those in nonsouthern regions. Decades of social science research extending from Louis Wirth's (1938) "Urbanism as a Way of Life" to more recent work (Fischer 1995; Stephan and McMullin 1982; Wilson 1985, 1991; Fischer and Hout 2006) demonstrate that residents of rural areas tend to have more conservative beliefs and practices than those living in metropolitan places.

Adherents of religions that most staunchly espouse traditional religious and gender beliefs (particularly evangelical Protestants; see Steensland et al. 2000) are more often found in the South than elsewhere, while Jews (typically more liberal on many social issues) are underrepresented in southern states (Jones et al. 2002). Strong professions of faith and religious practice (e.g., attendance at religious services) have long been a hallmark of the South (Friedman 1985; Reed 1972, chap. 6; Spruill Wheeler 1993, pp. 5–11; Twelve Southerners 1930).[15] Religiosity is associated with numerous conservative or traditional attitudes and beliefs (but see Karpov 2002), from weaker support for civil liberties (Reimer and Park 2001) to lower tolerance for homosexuality (e.g., Burdette, Ellison, and Hill 2005) to more traditional gender beliefs (e.g., Peek, Lowe, and Williams 1991).

Regional differences in religiosity are clearly evident in the most recent GSSs. Some 37% of southerners interviewed after 2000 were evangelicals according to the Steensland et al. (2000) classification, compared to fewer than 20% of nonsoutherners. Over 43% of recent southern respondents described their religious beliefs as "strong"; fewer than 34% of those living elsewhere did so. Similarly, over 31% of post-2000 interviewees in the South reported attending religious services at least weekly, by contrast to 23% of those from other regions.

The more rural and religious ecology of the South, together with the greater intensity of religious beliefs and practices among those residing there, may contribute to southern gender conservatism. To date, however, few researchers have sought to determine whether rurality, religiosity, or both help to account for the more conservative attitudes found among southerners (but see Moore and Ovadia 2006).

We illustrate the interplay of region, rural residence, religion, and gender role attitudes for the question about women and politics, which asks whether respondents agree or disagree that "[w]omen should take care of running their homes and leave running the country up to men." Across all GSS years, nearly 80% of nonsoutherners but only 70% of southerners gave the liberal response (disagree) to this question. Figures 4.9 and 4.10 depict regional differences in disagreement with the statement, separately by rural/nonrural residence, strength of religious belief, frequency of attending worship services (Figure 4.9), and religious denomination (Figure 4.10).

The comparisons at the left of Figure 4.9 confirm the greater traditionalism of rural and southern respondents regarding this separate spheres vision of gender roles. As anticipated, those who live in rural areas were less likely to disagree with the statement. We see that residents of nonrural communities outside the South gave the most liberal responses; over 80% disagreed. Just

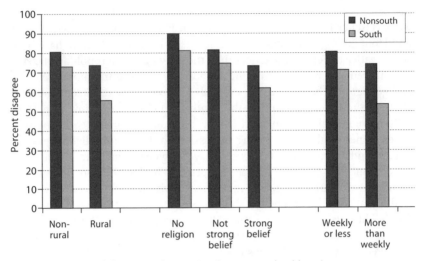

Figure 4.9. Regional difference in disagreeing that women should run homes, men country, by rurality, religious belief, and attending services.

over 73% of both nonrural southerners and rural nonsoutherners disagreed, but only a bit more than half (55.7%) of rural southerners took the nontraditional stance. While living in rural areas is linked to responses to this statement, a regional gap in attitudes remains, as shown by the different heights of the regional bars for both rural and nonrural residents. In both types of

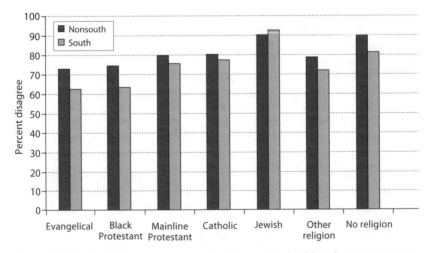

Figure 4.10. Regional difference in disagreeing that women should run homes, men country, by religious denomination.

settings, adults living in the South expressed more conservative views than those residing elsewhere, with a particularly notable regional gap among rural dwellers. Adults living outside the South were more likely to dispute the proposition that women should focus on running homes while men run the country, regardless of whether they lived in rural or nonrural places.

Similar patterns are apparent when we compare southerners and non-southerners while holding constant indicators of religiosity. Disagreement with the separate spheres proposition was less common among adults who held stronger religious beliefs (middle, Figure 4.9), attended religious services more often (right, Figure 4.9), and affiliated themselves with religious denominations that tend to be overrepresented in the South (Figure 4.10). Notwithstanding this, at any level of belief and at both levels of attendance shown in Figure 4.9, southerners were less apt than those in other regions to reject the separate spheres vision of men running the country while women run homes.

Likewise, in Figure 4.10 we see that in most of the Steensland et al. (2000) denominational groupings, southerners were less likely to challenge the conservative conception of men's and women's appropriate roles. For example, about 73% of nonsouthern evangelicals disagreed, compared to only 63% of southern evangelicals. Jewish people represent an exception—slightly over 90% of both southern and nonsouthern Jews disagree—but they constitute only about 2% of GSS respondents. While regional differences in religiosity may account for some regional variation in this gender role attitude, they offer less than a full account of it.

The illustrative comparisons in Figures 4.9 and 4.10 adjust South–non-South differences for only one indicator of rurality or religiosity at a time. We examine those differences more comprehensively in Table 4.2, which summarizes the results of three logistic regression analyses for each of the eight gender role items. These analyses shed some light on whether living in the South contributes to more conservative gender role attitudes, taking several sociodemographic variables into account, together with tendencies for southerners to live in rural areas, belong to religious denominations that encourage gender conservatism, express stronger religious beliefs, and attend worship services more frequently. These analyses, like those in Figures 4.9 and 4.10, combine respondents from all GSSs in which gender role attitudes were measured.

For each gender role item, Table 4.2 reports "discrete changes" (Long 1997) associated with the difference between southerners and nonsoutherners. The first column displays the overall regional differences in percentages of respondents who gave the more nontraditional response. For all three questions about women and politics, all three dealing with women's roles in marriage and family, and one of the two about employed mothers, southerners in the aggregate responded more conservatively than did those living outside

Table 4.2. Discrete Change in Gender Role Items Associated with Region, Adjusting for Rurality, Religiosity, and Sociodemographic Factors

Item[a]	Overall (%)	Adjusted for sociodemographic factors (%)[b]	Adjusted for rurality, religiosity, sociodemographics (%)[c]	Number of cases
Would vote for woman for president	−5.3*	−1.3*	−0.1	21,710
Disagree women run homes, men country	−9.2*	−4.4*	−4.0*	24,657
Disagree women less suited for politics	−10.4*	−4.2*	−3.2*	20,603
Approve of married woman working	−3.1*	−1.0	−1.4	20,877
Disagree wives should prioritize husband's career	−5.9*	−3.9*	−3.3*	14,017
Disagree men should achieve, women stay home	−7.1*	−4.1*	−3.4*	20,147
Agree working mothers can have warm ties to children	−1.8*	−0.9	−0.9	20,366
Disagree young children suffer if mother works	0.4	−0.5	0.2	20,131

*Regional difference significant at $p < .05$. Negative values indicate that nontraditional responses are less common among southerners than among nonsoutherners, with control variables indicated held constant at their means.

[a]For full question wording, see Table 4.1. Responses were dichotomized as in Figures 4.1–4.3.

[b]Sociodemographic factors include southern residence at age 16, gender, education, employment status, decade of birth, and year of survey.

[c]Indicators of rurality and religiosity include current rural residence, rural residence at age 16, current religious denomination, current attendance at religious services, and current intensity of religious belief.

the South. Even in this large sample that pools 16 GSSs, however, southerners and nonsoutherners did not hold significantly different views about whether preschoolers suffer when their mothers are employed.

Column 2 of Table 4.2 demonstrates that these overall differences are much reduced by statistical adjustments for sociodemographic factors examined in previous research, including gender, year of birth, education, employment status, and southern residence during adolescence. For instance, a 9.2-percentage-point regional difference in disagreement with the assertion that men should run the country while women run their homes (the "separate spheres" item that appears in Figures 4.9 and 4.10) falls to an estimated 4.4 percentage points when we assume that the mean levels of sociodemographic variables are the same in the South and non-South. For two items—approving of a married woman's employment in the absence of need and agreeing that working mothers can have warm relationships with their children—sociodemographic adjustments alone leave only a negligible regional difference. For these two items, what initially appear to be regional differences can instead be attributed to greater traditionalism among those who were *raised* in the South, were of older generations, were not in the labor force, or had less education.

Our question here is whether regional differences in rurality and religiosity help to interpret the five remaining differences (three questions about women and politics, two about women in marriage and family). They do: For all five, the discrete change associated with region becomes even smaller after rurality and religiosity, in addition to the sociodemographic factors, are held constant. Adjusting for rurality and religiosity reduces the small but statistically significant 1.3-percentage-point difference in willingness to vote for a qualified woman for president to virtually nil. For the other four items, this adjustment serves to shrink, but not eliminate, the regional difference in nontraditionalism.

Thus, regional differences in responses to four of the gender questions persist even after rural residence (both at age 16 and in adulthood) and religious preferences and practices (in adulthood) are taken into account. Adults who lived in rural settings (or who lived there while teenagers), were evangelical Protestants, attended worship services more often, and professed strong religious convictions typically expressed more traditional views about appropriate gender roles. These underlying tendencies, however, do not fully account for greater southern gender conservatism on two of the three questions about women and politics, and two of the three about women's employment and family roles. What emerges from this multivariate analysis, then, is the conclusion that southerners and nonsoutherners differ most persistently in views regarding women's involvement in politics and their primary roles in the domestic sphere. Southerners were comparatively sanguine about wives being employed in the absence of financial necessity and possible negative effects of mothers' employment on children. Further efforts to understand the differences shown in the last column of Table 4.2 might consider factors that our analysis could not capture, such as regional differences in historical or structural features, or differences in regional cultures not linked with rural residence or religious belief, practice, and affiliation.

The analyses in Table 4.2 combine respondents across GSS years, and so elide changes in regional differences over time. They do demonstrate that over the 1972–2008 time span, southerners took more conservative stances on matters of gender related to the political sphere and women's roles in marriage and family. Moreover, they show that rurality and religiosity account for some, though far from all, of these regional gaps in gender role attitudes.

Discussion and Conclusion

The GSS data cover a period of dramatic change in U.S. women's social, economic, and political roles. Gender role ideology among U.S. adults has undergone substantial change since the early 1970s. On several of the gender role questions examined here, the traditional view was the majority position in early GSSs (see Figures 4.2 and 4.3). The more liberal stance is now the more common one on all eight of the gender role items. Most shifts toward more liberal views, however, took place by the mid-1990s, with only modest movement—if any—since then. Others have noted this "stalling" of the movement toward less traditional gender role attitudes (e.g., Vanneman and Kling 2010; Cotter et al. 2005). Scholars and journalists have written extensively about the "end of feminism" and the retrenchment of progress toward gender equality in multiple spheres of U.S. life (e.g., Faludi 1991; Douglas 2010). A critical question for future research is whether the plateau documented here preceded, lagged, or coincided with changes in more tangible indicators (e.g., the flattening of labor force participation rates, slowing gains in state legislatures) of the engagement of women in U.S. society.

Apart from bringing these trends up to date and documenting some recent movements of interest—most notably the upturn in nontraditional views about the compatibility of women's employment with motherhood—we have examined the regional differences in attitudes that social scientists often estimate but rarely dwell upon. Evidence of southern conservatism is apparent for some gender matters, though like others (Fischer and Hout 2006) we find that even those regional differences in gender role attitudes may have narrowed recently.

We use the GSS data in an initial attempt to unravel *why* southerners have held more tightly to conservative gender role attitudes than their counterparts elsewhere. Gross regional differences in attitudes are only partially attributable to regional differences in rural residence, denominational affiliation, and religiosity (strength of religious belief and frequency of attending worship services). For half the items measured repeatedly in the GSS, greater traditionalism among southerners could be explained by appealing to regional differences in these variables, together with disparities in education and employment status, among other factors. But for the other half—items dealing with the priority of husbands' careers, the desirability of separate spheres for women and men, and the emotional suitability of women and men for politics—neither rural residence nor measures of religion nor sociodemographic differences could fully account for aggregate differences between adults living in the South and those living outside the South. A distinctive and more conservative gender ideology thus appears to remain at work among southerners, if perhaps to a muted extent.

Notwithstanding our references to the comparative "conservatism" of the South, the majority of U.S. adults, both southern and nonsouthern, now hold nontraditional positions on the continuing gender role questions tracked by the GSS (see, e.g., Figures 4.5–4.7). Going forward, it will be of interest to see whether the relative stasis since the mid-1990s continues, or if it is replaced by further liberalization (as suggested by recent upward movement in nontraditional responses to the employment and motherhood items) or conceivably even a neoconservative trend. Beyond that, complementary inquiry into attitudes regarding men's roles is sorely needed. None of the current GSS items asks directly about men's appropriate roles as fathers, while just one of them (a separate spheres item) refers indirectly to men's roles as husbands. The GSS questions are invaluable for tracking changing attitudes about women's roles since the 1970s; adding items that more directly assess views about men's roles as fathers and partners would complement this strength by establishing a benchmark for trends over the coming decades, as change in the political, employment, and family spheres of U.S. society continues.

Appendix: Graded Response Models for Trends in Gender Nontraditionalism

Over time, the GSS has measured gender role orientations using six distinct, though overlapping, sets of items; here we refer to these sets of items as "tests." The shortest of them (test 1), consisting of just the items FEWORK and FEPRES,[16] was used in only the 1972 GSS. The longest and most often-used one (test 2) consists of the eight items shown in Table 4.A.1, trends on which are depicted in Figures 4.1–4.3. Test 2 appeared in 11 GSSs: 1977, 1985–1986, and 1988–1998. A four-item subset consisting of the first four items in Table 4.A.1 (GSS mnemonics FEPRES, FEPOL, FEHOME, and FEWORK; test 3) was administered in 1975, 1978, and 1983; the 1974 and 1982 GSSs used substantially the same four-item subset, except that some randomly selected respondents answered an alternate form of the "emotionally suited for politics" item, FEPOLY (test 4).[17] A different four-item subset including FEPOL, FEFAM, FECHLD, and FEPRESCH (test 5) was asked between 2000 and 2006; FEPRES was added to that subset in 2008 (test 6).

Because the wording of items remains identical over time, we can readily track trends in each, as shown in Figures 4.1–4.3, but most of those trends do not extend through the entire 1972–2008 period covered here. Depicting a single overall trend in gender role attitudes is more challenging due to differences between tests (sets of items) across years. Comparing values of a simple additive index that averages responses to the items administered in any given year could be misleading because of between-year differences in the "difficulty" of the items included in the respective tests. That is, higher percentages of respondents give nontraditional answers to some items (e.g., FEPRES), making them "easier" to answer nontraditionally than some others (e.g., FEFAM, FEPRESCH). One rationale for changing the items measured

Table 4.A.1. Estimated Item Parameters for GSS Gender Role Items

Item/GSS mnemonic	Nontraditional response	Difficulty threshold parameters			Discrimination parameter
		1	2	3	
FEPRES	Yes	−1.54	—	—	1.81
FEPOL	Disagree	−0.71	—	—	1.53
FEPOLY	Women	−1.01	2.72	—	1.31
FEHOME	Disagree	−0.83	—	—	3.15
FEWORK	Approve	−1.53	—	—	0.95
FEHELP	Strongly disagree	−2.02	−0.62	1.09	2.23
FEFAM	Strongly disagree	−1.47	−0.20	1.19	2.84
FECHLD	Strongly agree	−2.07	−0.47	1.22	1.48
FEPRESCH	Strongly disagree	−1.73	−0.05	1.84	1.73

Note: Based on 32,346 respondents and 183,257 item responses from the pooled 1972–2008 GSSs.

after 1998 was that near consensus had been reached on items like FEPRES and FEWORK, so that they had become relatively uninformative. Removing them—or replacing them with more "difficult" items on which respondents are more evenly divided—would reduce the numerical value of a simple additive index; that reduction, however, would reflect the difference in item "difficulty," rather than a change in the underlying gender role orientation.

This appendix outlines methods used to construct the composite trend plots shown in Figures 4.4 and 4.8. We draw on methods for constructing and equating test forms developed under item response theory (Embretson and Reise 2000). In our context, the "invariance" property of these methods is especially valuable: It allows the use of different sets of items drawn from an appropriate domain of content to make comparable measurements of a latent variable ("ability") of interest. Under appropriate specifications, the "ability" values are invariant to the particular items used to measure them, just as the "difficulty" values of items (and other item properties) are invariant to the pool of subjects/respondents used to calibrate them.

We assume that a single, unidimensional latent nontraditionalism construct underlies responses to the distinct GSS gender role orientation tests. Low values on this construct represent a "traditional" orientation toward gender roles, including beliefs that men and women should occupy "separate spheres" (with women enacting domestic, home-centered roles while men specialize in paid employment and politics) and that children require full-time, stay-at-home mothering. High values on the continuum represent a "nontraditional" orientation that accords equal status to women and men in workplaces and politics and holds that such multifaceted women's roles are fully compatible with motherhood.

The six distinct gender role orientation tests administered in different years by the GSS constitute an (unplanned) common-item nonequivalent group design (Kolen and Brennan 2004); different GSS years are the comparison groups. Because the distinct tests overlap, each test is linked to others by one or more common items; this overlap provides a basis for interleaving them. Though each test was administered to a random sample of respondents drawn in the year(s) it was used, these groups are not necessarily directly comparable since there is reason to expect that the mean level of nontraditionalism, as well as the sociodemographic composition of GSS samples, differs by year.

To compare values of the latent construct across years, we must first "calibrate" the nine items (including FEPOLY, the alternate form of FEPOL) that appear (in various combinations) in the six tests, such that they lie on a common latent scale. We then allow for between-year differences in values of the latent construct.

We simultaneously assess the measurement properties of all nine gender role items via "concurrent calibration," assuming stability of an item's properties when it appears in the distinct tests. We estimate a two-parameter graded response model assuming that responses to items reflect a single latent variable or common factor, formulated as follows,

$$\Pr[x_i > j \,|\, \theta] = \frac{\exp(\alpha_i(\theta - \beta_{ij}))}{1 + \exp(\alpha_i(\theta - \beta_{ij}))}, \; j = 1, \dots k_i - 1 \tag{1}$$

where x_i is the response to item i with categories numbered 1 to k_i, θ is the value of the latent variable ("ability"), β_{ij} is the "difficulty threshold" separating responses j and $j+1$ on item i, and α_i is the "discrimination parameter" for item i. Equation 1 posits that the probability that a subject's response to an item is above category j rises with the extent to which the subject's ability θ exceeds the jth difficulty threshold for the item. The difficulty threshold β_{ij} gives the value of the latent variable at which the probability of responding above category j to item i is 0.5; in our application, items for which nontraditional responses are relatively common will have low β_{ij} values. The larger the discrimination parameter α_i, the more abruptly a given difference between ability and a difficulty threshold translates into differences in the item response.

This measurement model bears a close resemblance to the latent variable formulation of an ordinal logistic regression model (Long 1997), with the important proviso that the *same* underlying latent variable affects responses to different items. The model readily accommodates items with different numbers of response categories, as found in our application.

We estimate the model using marginal maximum likelihood, using methods described by Zheng and Rabe-Hesketh (2007) and gllamm statistical software (Rabe-Hesketh, Skrondal, and Pickles 2004), assuming that the latent variable θ is normally distributed with mean 0 and variance 1. Table 4.A.1 displays estimates of item properties for the nine GSS gender role items under model 1.

One threshold parameter is estimated for each pair of adjacent response categories of each item. It gives the predicted value of a standard normal variable separating those categories, in the sense that a subject whose ability level θ equals the threshold value β_{ij} would have a probability of 0.5 of responding in the higher category (or above) and likewise a probability of 0.5 of responding in the lower one (or below). Interpreting the thresholds is particularly straightforward for dichotomous items. For FEPRES, for example, a subject with a well-below-average nontraditionalism score of –1.54 nonetheless would have a probability of 0.5 of saying that she or he would vote for a qualified woman for president; hence this is a relatively "easy" item to answer in the nontraditional direction. FEWORK has a similarly low difficulty threshold, while it is somewhat more difficult to answer liberally to FEHOME and FEPOL. The thresholds for polytomous items have a similar interpretation. Answers more nontraditional than "strongly agree" to the separate spheres item asserting that women should care for homes while men achieve outside them (FEFAM) are quite common, as the low first threshold value of –1.47 for this item indicates. A relatively high θ value of 1.19, however, would be required before the most nontraditional response, strongly disagree, would be as likely as any less nontraditional one.

The estimated discrimination parameters in the last column of Table 4.A.1 show how abruptly the probability of a more positive (nontraditional) response rises as a subject's ability θ exceeds a threshold (or, conversely, how rapidly the probability of a less positive (more traditional) one grows as ability falls beneath a threshold). All nine items discriminate relatively well, with a one-standard-unit difference in θ corresponding to a 1- to 3-logit difference in responding above or below a given division between categories. The sharpest distinctions are seen for three items—FEHOME, FEHELP, and FEFAM—that most explicitly invoke separate spheres ideology. The lowest estimated discrimination parameter is for the item about the legitimacy of paid work by married women in the absence of need.

Following Zheng and Rabe-Hesketh (2007), we next elaborate model 1 by allowing the mean level of the latent variable θ to depend on covariates,

$$\theta = \sum_m \gamma_m w_m + \varepsilon \qquad (2)$$

where w_m is the mth covariate, γ_m is its regression coefficient, and ε is a disturbance term. Estimating model 1-2 with covariates w_m representing differences among years yields estimates that allow us to construct the overall nontraditionalism trend shown in Figure 4.4. Including additional covariates that represent regional differences and the interaction of region and year leads to the region-specific trends displayed in Figure 4.8.

Because of the invariance property of item response models, the θ values for different years are comparable, though they are assessed using different items.[18] The estimates of annual average nontraditionalism adjust for item difficulty differences across years. Note, for example, the low average non-traditionalism level in 1972 (Figure 4.4), despite the fact that roughly 70% of GSS respondents then gave the liberal answer to each of the two items administered that year (FEPRES and FEWORK; see Figures 4.1 and 4.2). This reflects the fact that these items have relatively low difficulty values (Table 4.A.1), so that nontraditional answers to them are relatively common even among more traditionally oriented respondents.

Our approach assumes a unidimensional underlying nontraditionalism construct, and that the items in the different tests vary with year and region in the same way. The general contours of change shown in Figures 4.1–4.3 and 4.5–4.7 are broadly consistent with this assumption, but there are also some hints that it may not hold precisely—notably the upward trend since 2000 in the two items about employed mothers and children (while trends on other items are more or less flat), and the smaller regional differences for those items (Figure 4.7). Additionally, the distinct tests include relatively small numbers of items, so estimates of nontraditionalism levels in any given year may lack precision; this is especially the case in 1972 when the GSS included only two items that measure nontraditionalism at the relatively low difficulty values shown in Table 4.A.1. Nonetheless, this method does serve to summarize how a single gender role nontraditionalism construct varies over the full course of the GSS, while making appropriate allowances for differences in the properties of the particular items used to measure it.

Notes

1. And on her race. Until recently, nonwhite women have had higher labor force participation rates than white women, but only 37% of nonwhite women were in the labor force in 1950 (U.S. Bureau of the Census 1953, p. 1-254, table 120).

2. Mothers' (and women's) labor force participation rates vary with their age and marital status, and the age of their children. For example, in 1975, 56.1% of mothers with children under age 18 were employed (Bianchi, Robinson, and Milkie 2006, p. 44). Of *married* mothers with children under age 18, 53.7% were employed (Hayghe and Bianchi 1994, p. 28).

3. Hays (1996) terms this orientation "intensive motherhood." Charles and Cech (2010) report that U.S. women were more apt to endorse full-time mothering of pre-school children than were women in many other developed and formerly socialist societies. U.S. women were less apt than average to believe that mothers of school-age children should stay at home, however.

4. We use the phrase "gender role attitudes" because it is common in the literature, though none of the items we study measures attitudes about the roles of *men* in families and employment.

5. See the recent review article by S. N. Davis and Greenstein (2009). Also, using panel data from the 1979 National Longitudinal Study of Youth, Vespa (2009) demonstrates how adults' gender ideology changes over the life course as a consequence of life experiences such as marriage, parenthood, and employment.

6. Only one repeated GSS question asks about *men's* roles: Since 1994, respondents have been asked whether they agree that "[f]amily life often suffers because men concentrate too much on their work." Roughly 60% of respondents agreed or strongly agreed in all years except 1996, when more than 70% endorsed the statement. No trend in the responses is evident.

7. This marked a dramatic increase from the pre–World War II era. The identical question was asked of national samples by the American Institute of Public Opinion in 1937 and 1938. Only 18% and 22% of U.S. adults, respectively, then approved of wives' employment in the absence of financial need (Oppenheimer 1970, pp. 43–44).

8. In Figures 4.2 and 4.3, we ignore degrees of agreement and disagreement, therefore combining "strongly agree" and "agree" responses (and likewise for "disagree" answers).

9. Oklahoma extended full suffrage to women in 1918, but was then clearly a western rather than a southern state.

10. From the South, South Carolina, Oklahoma, Alabama, Mississippi, Kentucky, Louisiana, and West Virginia; from other regions, Pennsylvania, North Dakota, and Wyoming. For over-time evidence of the dearth of women in state legislatures in the South, see the annual fact sheets on women in state legislatures at the website of the Center for American Women and Politics (n.d.).

11. Powers and her colleagues (2003, p. 46) controlled for religiosity (strength of belief) but not for religious preference or for frequency of attendance at religious services.

12. Rice and Pepper's (1997) study of attitudinal differences among migrants into and out of the South is one exception. In addition, Moore and Ovadia (2006) recently explored contextual factors (such as the educational composition of respondents' areas of residence) that could explain the conservative effects of southern and rural residence on support for civil liberties.

13. The southern states, as designated by the U.S. Census Bureau, are Alabama, Arkansas, Delaware, District of Columbia, Florida, Georgia, Kentucky, Louisiana, Maryland, Mississippi, North Carolina, Oklahoma, South Carolina, Tennessee, Texas, Virginia, and West Virginia. Using other definitions (such as omitting Delaware and D.C.) did not produce substantially different patterns.

14. Although not every gap between southern and nonsouthern responses is statistically significant, southerners tended to give more conservative answers to the three questions about women and politics, and to those about women's employment, marriage, and family roles. In all years but one, however, *no* significant regional differences were found for either of the questions about employed mothers and their children.

15. The recent growth of "megachurches" in southern cities and suburbs (Thumma n.d.) is additional evidence of at least a very public religiosity among southerners. See

also the database of megachurches at the website of the Hartford Institute (http://hirr
.hartsem.edu/megachurch/database.html); of the 1,378 megachurches listed, 671 are in
southern states.

16. See Table 4.1 for a key to abbreviations for items; FEPRES, for example, refers to the item asking whether the respondent would vote for a qualified woman for
president.

17. The wording of item FEPOLY is, "Would you say that most men are better
suited for politics than are most women, that men and women are equally suited, or
that women are better suited than men in this area?" Of 1,628 persons answering this
item in 1974 and 1982, 28% said that men were better suited, 5% said that women were
better suited, and 67% chose "equally suited."

18. The fact that different items appear in different years raises questions about
how missing data might affect our estimates. The vast bulk of missing data on the
gender role items in the GSS are missing by design, however, because the questions
either were not asked at all in particular years or were asked only of randomly selected
respondents. Survey year is among the covariates in model 2, and Allison (2010) indicates that no missing data bias arises under these conditions.

References

Abrams, Richard M. 2006. *America Transformed: Sixty Years of Revolutionary Change,
    1941–2001.* Cambridge: Cambridge University Press.
Allison, Paul D. 2010. "Missing Data." In *Handbook of Survey Research*, 2nd ed., edited
    by Peter V. Marsden and James D. Wright, 631–57. Bingley, UK: Emerald.
Belkin, Lisa. 2003. "The Opt-Out Revolution." *New York Times Magazine*, October 26,
    pp. 42–47, 58, 85–86.
Bernard, Jessie. 1974. *The Future of Motherhood.* New York: Dial Press.
Bianchi, Suzanne M. 2000. "Maternal Employment and Time with Children: Dra-
    matic Change or Surprising Continuity?" *Demography* 37:401–14.
Bianchi, Suzanne M., and Melissa A. Milkie. 2010. "Work and Family Research in the
    First Decade of the 21st Century." *Journal of Marriage and Family* 72:705–25.
Bianchi, Suzanne M., John P. Robinson, and Melissa A. Milkie. 2006. *The Changing
    Rhythms of American Family Life.* New York: Russell Sage Foundation.
Bolzendahl, Catherine I., and Daniel J. Myers. 2004. "Feminist Attitudes and Support
    for Gender Equality: Opinion Change in Women and Men, 1974–1998." *Social
    Forces* 83:759–90.
Boushey, Heather. 2008. " 'Opting Out?': The Effect of Children on Women's Employ-
    ment in the United States." *Feminist Economics* 14:1–36.
Brooks, Clem, and Catherine Bolzendahl. 2004. "The Transformation of U.S. Gender
    Role Attitudes: Cohort Replacement, Social-Structural Change, and Ideologi-
    cal Learning." *Social Science Research* 33:106–33.
Burdette, Amy M., Christopher G. Ellison, and Terrence D. Hill. 2005. "Conservative
    Protestantism and Tolerance toward Homosexuals: An Examination of Poten-
    tial Mechanisms." *Sociological Inquiry* 75:177–96.
Campbell, Karen E., and Holly J. McCammon. 2005. "Elizabeth Blackwell's Heirs:
    Women as Physicians in the United States, 1880–1920." *Work and Occupations*
    32:290–318.

Carroll, Susan J. 2004. "Women in State Government: Historical Overview and Current Trends." In *The Book of the States, 2004; Volume 36*, 389–97. Council of State Governments, Lexington, KY.

Center for American Women and Politics. 1975. "Numbers of Women in Office: State Summaries." Rutgers University, New Brunswick, NJ. http://www.cawp.rutgers.edu/fast_facts/levels_of_office/documents/stleg75.pdf.

———. 2007. "Nancy Pelosi: Two Heartbeats from the Presidency." Rutgers University, New Brunswick, NJ. http://www.cawp.rutgers.edu/press_room/news/documents/archives/07-01-04_ABCNews.pdf.

———. 2010a. "Fact Sheet: Women in State Legislatures 2010." Rutgers University, New Brunswick, NJ. http://www.cawp.rutgers.edu/fast_facts/levels_of_office/documents/stleg.pdf.

———. 2010b. "Fact Sheet: Women in the U.S. Congress 2010." Rutgers University, New Brunswick, NJ. http://www.cawp.rutgers.edu/fast_facts/levels_of_office/documents/cong.pdf.

———. n.d. "Women in State Legislatures 1975–2009." Rutgers University, New Brunswick, NJ. http://www.cawp.rutgers.edu/fast_facts/levels_of_office/documents/stleghist.pdf.

Charles, Maria, and Erin Cech. 2010. "Beliefs about Maternal Employment." In *Dividing the Domestic: Men, Women, and Household Work in Cross-National Perspective*, edited by Judith Treas and Sonja Drobnič, 147–74. Stanford, CA: Stanford University Press.

Cobb, James C. 2005. *Away Down South: A History of Southern Identity*. Oxford: Oxford University Press.

Cotter, David A., Joan M. Hermsen, and Reeve Vanneman. 2005. "Gender Inequality at Work." In *The American People; Census 2000*, edited by Reynolds Farley and John Haaga, 107–37. New York: Russell Sage Foundation.

Davis, James Allan, Tom W. Smith, and Peter V. Marsden. 2009. *General Social Surveys, 1972–2008* [Machine-readable data file]. Chicago: NORC (producer). Storrs, CT: Roper Center for Public Opinion Research, University of Connecticut (distributor).

Davis, Shannon N., and Theodore N. Greenstein. 2009. "Gender Ideology: Components, Predictors, and Consequences." *Annual Review of Sociology* 35:87–105.

Douglas, Susan J. 2010. *Enlightened Sexism: The Seductive Message That Feminism's Work Is Done*. New York: Times Books, Henry Holt.

Edgell, Penny, and Eric Tranby. 2007. "Religious Influences on Understandings of Racial Inequality in the United States." *Social Problems* 54:263–88.

Embretson, Susan E., and Steven P. Reise. 2000. *Item Response Theory for Psychologists*. Mahwah, NJ: Lawrence Erlbaum.

Faludi, Susan. 1991. *Backlash: The Undeclared War Against American Women*. New York: Crown.

Firebaugh, Glenn, and Kenneth E. Davis. 1988. "Trends in Anti-Black Prejudice, 1972–1984: Region and Cohort Effects." *American Journal of Sociology* 94:251–72.

Fischer, Claude S. 1995. "The Subcultural Theory of Urbanism: A Twenty-Year Assessment." *American Journal of Sociology* 101:543–77.

Fischer, Claude S., and Michael Hout. 2006. *Century of Difference: How America Changed in the Last One Hundred Years*. New York: Russell Sage Foundation.

Flexner, Eleanor. 1973. *Century of Struggle: The Woman's Rights Movement in the United States*. New York: Atheneum.

Friedman, Jean E. 1985. *The Enclosed Garden: Women and Community in the Evangelical South, 1830–1900*. Chapel Hill: University of North Carolina Press.

Grasmick, Harold G. 1973. "Social Change and Modernism in the American South." *American Behavioral Scientist* 16:913–33.

Harris, Richard J., and Juanita M. Firestone. 1998. "Changes in Predictors of Gender Role Ideologies among Women: A Multivariate Analysis." *Sex Roles* 38:239–52.

Hayghe, Howard V. 1997. "Developments in Women's Labor Force Participation." *Monthly Labor Review* 120 (9): 41–46.

Hayghe, Howard V., and Suzanne M. Bianchi. 1994. "Married Mothers' Work Patterns: The Job-Family Compromise." *Monthly Labor Review* 117 (6): 24–30.

Hays, Sharon. 1996. *The Cultural Contradictions of Motherhood*. New Haven, CT: Yale University Press.

Hochschild, Arlie Russell. 1989. *The Second Shift: Working Parents and the Revolution at Home*. New York: Viking.

Hoffman, Saul D. 2009. "The Changing Impact of Marriage and Children on Women's Labor Force Participation." *Monthly Labor Review* 132 (2): 3–14.

Hurlbert, Jeanne S. 1989. "The Southern Region: A Test of the Hypothesis of Cultural Distinctiveness." *Sociological Quarterly* 30:245–66.

Jones, Dale E., Sherri Doty, Clifford Grammich, James E. Horsch, Richard Houseal, Mac Lynn, John P. Marcum, Kenneth M. Sanchagrin, and Richard H. Taylor, eds. 2002. *Religious Congregations and Membership in the United States 2000: An Enumeration by Region, State and County Based on Data Reported for 149 Religious Bodies*. Nashville, TN: Glenmary Research Center.

Karpov, Vyacheslav. 2002. "Religiosity and Tolerance in the United States and Poland." *Journal for the Scientific Study of Religion* 41:267–88.

Kenyon, Dorothy, and Pauli Murray. 1966. *The Case for Equality in State Jury Service: Memorandum in Support of ACLU Proposal to Amend S.2923 (Civil Rights Protection Act of 1966)—To Wit Exclusion of Women from Service on State Juries*. New York: American Civil Liberties Union.

Kolen, Michael J., and Robert L. Brennan. 2004. *Test Equating, Scaling, and Linking: Methods and Practices*. 2nd ed. New York: Springer.

Kozimor-King, Michele, and Kevin T. Leicht. 1999. "Sources of Convergence and Divergence in Attitudes about Work and Family Roles among Women." *Research in the Sociology of Work* 7:85–108.

Kuperberg, Arielle, and Pamela Stone. 2008. "The Media Depiction of Women Who Opt Out." *Gender & Society* 22:497–517.

Lee, Marlene A., and Mark Mather. 2008. "U.S. Labor Force Trends." *Population Bulletin* 63 (2): 1–16.

Long, J. Scott. 1997. *Regression Models for Categorical and Limited Dependent Variables*. Thousand Oaks, CA: Sage.

Mason, Karen Oppenheim, and Yu-Hsia Lu. 1988. "Attitudes toward Women's Family Roles: Changes in the United States, 1977–1985." *Gender & Society* 2:39–57.

McCammon, Holly J., Courtney Sanders Muse, Harmony D. Newman, and Teresa M. Terrell. 2007. "Movement Framing and Discursive Opportunity Structures: The

Political Successes of the U.S. Women's Jury Movements." *American Sociological Review* 72:725–49.

Moore, Laura M., and Seth Ovadia. 2006. "Accounting for Spatial Variation in Tolerance: The Effects of Education and Religion." *Social Forces* 84:2205–21.

Mosisa, Abraham, and Steven Hipple. 2006. "Trends in Labor Force Participation in the United States." *Monthly Labor Review* 129 (10): 35–57.

Nock, Steven, and Paul W. Kingston. 1988. "Time with Children: The Impact of Couples' Work-Time Commitment." *Social Forces* 67:59–83.

Northeast-Midwest Institute. 2002. "Rural Population as a Percent of State Total by State, 2000." Northeast-Midwest Institute, Washington, DC. http://www.nemw.org/images/issues/roc/2002-10-24 - Rural Population as a Percent of State Total By State.pdf.

Odem, Mary E. 1995. *Delinquent Daughters: Protecting and Policing Adolescent Female Sexuality in the United States, 1885–1920*. Chapel Hill: University of North Carolina Press.

Odum, Howard W. 1947. *The Way of the South*. New York: Macmillan.

Oppenheimer, Valerie Kincade. 1970. *The Female Labor Force in the United States: Demographic and Economic Factors Governing Its Growth and Changing Composition*. Westport, CT: Greenwood.

Paxton, Pamela, Matthew A. Painter II, and Melanie M. Hughes. 2009. "Year of the Woman, Decade of the Man: Trajectories of Growth in Women's State Legislative Representation." *Social Science Research* 38:86–102.

Peek, Charles W., George D. Lowe, and L. Susan Williams. 1991. "Gender and God's Word: Another Look at Religious Fundamentalism and Sexism." *Social Forces* 69:1205–21.

Powers, Rebecca S., J. Jill Suitor, Susana Guerra, Monisa Shackelford, Dorothy Mecom, and Kim Gusman. 2003. "Regional Differences in Gender-Role Attitudes: Variations by Gender and Race." *Gender Issues* 21 (2): 40–54.

Rabe-Hesketh, Sophia, Anders Skrondal, and Andrew Pickles. 2004. "GLLAMM Manual." Working Paper 160, University of California, Berkeley Division of Biostatistics. http://www.bepress.com/ucbbiostat/paper160/.

Reed, John Shelton. 1972. *The Enduring South: Subcultural Persistence in Mass Society*. Lexington, MA: Lexington Books.

———. 1983. *Southerners: The Social Psychology of Sectionalism*. Chapel Hill: University of North Carolina Press.

Reimer, Sam, and Jerry Z. Park. 2001. "Tolerant (In)civility? A Longitudinal Analysis of White Conservative Protestants' Willingness to Grant Civil Liberties." *Journal for the Scientific Study of Religion* 40:735–45.

Rice, Tom W., and Diane L. Coates. 1995. "Gender Role Attitudes in the Southern United States." *Gender & Society* 9:744–56.

Rice, Tom W., and Meredith L. Pepper. 1997. "Region, Migration, and Attitudes in the United States." *Social Science Quarterly* 78:83–95.

Risman, Barbara. 1998. *Gender Vertigo: American Families in Transition*. New Haven, CT: Yale University Press.

Sandberg, John F., and Sandra L. Hofferth. 2001. "Changes in Children's Time with Parents: United States, 1981–1997." *Demography* 38:423–36.

——. 2005. "Changes in Children's Time with Parents: A Correction." *Demography* 42:391–95.

Sayer, Liana C., Suzanne M. Bianchi, and John P. Robinson. 2004. "Are Parents Investing Less Time in Children? Trends in Mothers' and Fathers' Time with Children." *American Journal of Sociology* 110:1–43.

Scott, Anne Firor. 1970. *The Southern Lady: From Pedestal to Politics, 1830–1930*. Chicago: University of Chicago Press.

Spruill Wheeler, Marjorie. 1993. *New Woman of the New South: The Leaders of the Woman Suffrage Movement in the Southern States*. New York: Oxford University Press.

Steensland, Brian, Jerry Z. Park, Mark D. Regnerus, Lynn D. Robinson, W. Bradford Wilcox, and Robert D. Woodberry. 2000. "The Measure of American Religion: Toward Improving the State of the Art." *Social Forces* 79:291–318.

Stephan, G. Edward, and Douglas R. McMullin. 1982. "Tolerance of Sexual Nonconformity: City Size as a Situational and Early Learning Determinant." *American Sociological Review* 47:411–15.

Stone, Pamela. 2007. *Opting Out? Why Women Really Quit Careers and Head Home*. Berkeley: University of California Press.

Thomas, Claire Sherman. 1991. *Sex Discrimination in a Nutshell*. 2nd ed. St. Paul, MN: West.

Thumma, Scott. n.d. "Exploring the Megachurch Phenomena: Their Characteristics and Cultural Context." http://hirr.hartsem.edu/bookshelf/thumma_article2 .html.

Twelve Southerners. 1930. *I'll Take My Stand: The South and the Agrarian Tradition*. New York: Harper.

U.S. Bureau of the Census. 1953. *Census of Population: 1950—Volume II, Characteristics of the Population—Part 1, United States Summary*. Washington, DC: Government Printing Office. http://www2.census.gov/prod2/decennial/ documents/21983999v2p1.pdf.

——. 1961. *Census of Population: 1960—Volume I, Characteristics of the Population— Part 1, United States Summary*. Washington, DC: Government Printing Office. http://www2.census.gov/prod2/decennial/documents/11085788v1p11.pdf.

——. 1973. *Census of Population: 1970—Volume I, Characteristics of the Population— Part 1, United States Summary, Section 2*. Washington, DC: Government Printing Office. http://www2.census.gov/prod2/decennial/documents/1970a_us2- 08.pdf.

——. 1975. *Historical Statistics of the United States, Colonial Times to 1970, Bicentennial Edition, Part 2*. Series D63-74. Washington, DC: Government Printing Office.

——. 2003. *2000 Census of Population and Housing, Summary Social, Economic, and Housing Characteristics, PHC-2-1, United States Summary*. Washington, DC: Government Printing Office. http://www.census.gov/prod/cen2000/phc-2- 1-pt1.pdf.

——. 2005. *Statistical Abstract of the United States, 2004–2005*. Table 25. Washington, DC: Government Printing Office. http://www.census.gov/prod/2004pubs/ 04statab/pop.pdf.

Vance, Rubert B. 1932. *Human Geography of the South*. Chapel Hill: University of North Carolina Press.

Vanneman, Reeve, and Joanna Kling. 2010. "Popular Culture and the Gender Shift of the 1990s." Paper presented at the annual meeting of American Sociological Association, Atlanta.

Vespa, Jonathan. 2009. "Gender Ideology Construction: A Life Course and Intersectional Approach." *Gender & Society* 23:363–87.

Weakliem, David L., and Robert Biggert. 1999. "Region and Political Opinion in the Contemporary United States." *Social Forces* 77:863–86.

Wilson, Thomas C. 1985. "Urbanism and Tolerance: A Test of Some Hypotheses Drawn from Wirth and Stouffer." *American Sociological Review* 50:117–23.

———. 1991. "Urbanism, Migration, and Tolerance: A Reassessment." *American Sociological Review* 56:117–23.

Wirth, Louis. 1938. "Urbanism as a Way of Life." *American Journal of Sociology* 44:1–24.

Women in Congress. 2011. "Historical Data." http://womenincongress.house.gov/historical-data/representatives-senators-by-congress.html.

Zheng, Xiaohui, and Sophia Rabe-Hesketh. 2007. "Estimating Parameters of Dichotomous and Ordinal Item Response Models with gllamm." *Stata Journal* 7:313–33.

5

Public Opinion in the "Age of Reagan"

Political Trends 1972–2006

Jeff Manza, Jennifer A. Heerwig, and Brian J. McCabe

In March 1972, when the first General Social Survey went into the field, important shifts in the American political landscape were well under way. Forty years of liberal dominance in national politics—represented most vividly in the reforms of the New Deal and Great Society eras—had fundamentally changed the U.S. political system in place prior to the Great Depression. Almost continuous Democratic Party control of Congress, a liberal Supreme Court, and three influential presidencies (Roosevelt, Kennedy, Johnson) produced major liberal social policy breakthroughs that built the modern American welfare state.

By 1972, though, liberalism as a dominant governing philosophy was fraying at the seams. The turmoil of the 1960s, and the tensions between the "new left" and New Deal liberalism have been widely chronicled. The Watergate scandal gave liberals and Democrats a brief reprieve (and large congressional majorities) in the mid-1970s, but from the late 1970s through 2006 an increasingly powerful conservative coalition gained influence over the national policy agenda, and increasingly set the terms of political debate. The 1980 election of Ronald Reagan and a Republican Senate majority (breaking nearly 50 years of virtually uninterrupted Democratic control of Congress) was the first of a series of conservative breakthroughs. In 1994, Republicans won majorities in both houses of Congress for the first time since 1932. With the subsequent election of George W. Bush in 2000 and the appointment of a conservative majority on the Supreme Court, conservative political influence reached an apex.

Surveying this era, historian Sean Wilentz (2008) has characterized it as the "Age of Reagan." Significant public policy shifts in a sharply conservative direction occurred, including reductions in governmental regulation of economic markets, renewed U.S. assertiveness in foreign and military affairs, and repeated tax cutting that would dramatically reduce tax burdens for corporations and high-earning households. The Republican majority also halted the steady expansion of New Deal/Great Society–era government efforts to reduce poverty, racism, sexism, and socioeconomic problems, and trimmed rights-based reforms at the margins. Together, these shifts helped to produce levels of income and wealth inequality that were unprecedented among the world's rich democracies (Neckerman 2004).

While its political and policy successes were considerable, the era of conservative political dominance failed to achieve many of the more ambitious goals of conservative activists. Though budget cutting and fiscal discipline were conservative priorities (at least in principle), in practice they were seldom achieved; even nonmilitary domestic spending would grow in real terms under Republican presidents. Combined with increased defense spending and major tax cuts in 1981 and 2001–2003, ballooning budget deficits inevitably resulted. The most visible "welfare" program, Aid to Families with Dependent Children (AFDC), was reformed in 1996 by instituting new work requirements and setting time limits on benefit receipt, but overall federal and state spending on the poor grew slightly in real terms. In 2004, the Bush administration and the Republican Congress even passed a significant (and costly) expansion of Medicare to cover certain prescription drugs for program recipients. Workplace legal protections for women and minorities were threatened rhetorically, but only partially rolled back, and the long-anticipated assault on affirmative action was surprisingly limited. Calls to revive traditional family norms and ban abortion went largely unheeded, while other "social issues" goals of religious conservatives were never seriously entertained.

To what extent are the successes—and failures—of the conservative policy initiatives of the 1972–2006 period reflected in, or even guided by, changes in public attitudes? Research on the general relationship between public opinion and public policy shows strong, if mixed, evidence that public preferences impact policy outcomes (cf. Page and Shapiro 1983; Erikson, MacKuen, and Stimson 2002; Brooks and Manza 2007; Sroka and Wlezien 2009). Whether shifts in public opinion are associated with, or perhaps even caused by, changes in the political environment since the 1970s is a complicated and oft-debated question (cf. Jacobs and Shapiro 2000; Bartels 2005; Hacker and Pierson 2005; Hacker and Pierson 2010). For most political sociologists, the conservative drift in public policy during this period is best accounted for by organizational factors such as the rise of the "new" Christian Right, the political mobilization of business interests beginning in the mid-1970s, and the vastly expanded role of money in the political system.

But it would indeed be surprising if there were *no* evidence of public support for at least some of the conservative political momentum from the late 1970s to the early 2000s. This chapter explores what General Social Survey (GSS) data can tell us about the evolution of some important general political orientations and public attitudes toward government, public policy, and political parties over the past 35 years. The principal puzzle facing analysts of public opinion in this era is how to reconcile a number of *contradictory* trends in the policy and political attitudes that citizens express in surveys. We explore several key questions. To what extent, and on what issues, did public opinion shift in a conservative direction, and how well can we identify those trends? Conversely, when and to what extent did the political attitudes of Americans resist the overall political trend to the right over this same period? As we will see, some significant trends in general political orientations begin in the 1970s and persist, while others reflect short-lived conservative shifts specific to particularly decisive moments—especially the election of President Reagan in 1980 but also Republican control of Congress starting in 1994 and Republican dominance in all three branches of government starting in the early 2000s.

Other chapters in this book tell important components of the larger story about the political implications of trends in American public opinion with respect to confidence in public institutions (Smith), attitudes toward crime and punishment (Wright, Jasinski, and Lanier), racial attitudes (Bobo, Charles, Krysan, and Simmons), and civil liberties (Davis). We add to these chapters an analysis of other political and policy attitudes regularly measured in the GSS. We begin by examining trends in political ideology and general orientations toward government. Next, we turn to attitudes toward specific policy areas as reflected in the GSS's unique battery of spending items, and examine trends in "social issue" attitudes (which have frequently been sources of political controversy in the past 30 years). We conclude with some brief reflections on which political trends did (and did not) move in a conservative direction during this period and speculations about the future.

Political Orientations and Ideology

We start by examining trends in Americans' general political orientations, focusing specifically on three important areas: ideology, party identification, and opinions about the general responsibilities of government. The last item captures well a critical aspect of Americans' changing overall political orientations in this era, as later sections of the chapter suggest.

The terms "liberalism" and "conservatism" have represented the dominant ideological poles in American politics since the New Deal. However, individuals identifying as "liberal" or "conservative" need not hold entirely consistent ideological worldviews: self-described "liberals" do not take the liberal position on every issue, and likewise for conservatives. Nevertheless, liberals and conservatives do tend to adopt fairly consistent policy positions. So the overall distribution of ideological identification in the mass public tells us something about the general drift in political orientations.[1]

Since 1974, the GSS has measured ideological identification using the following question:

> We hear a lot of talk these days about liberals and conservatives. I'm going to show you a seven-point scale on which the political views that people might hold are arranged from extremely liberal—point 1—to extremely conservative—point 7. Where would you place yourself on this scale?

Figure 5.1 displays trends in ideological identification.[2] The bold line shows the percentage of respondents identifying themselves as "slightly liberal," "liberal," or "extremely liberal," the line with the diamond marker shows the percentage of moderates, and the broken line the percentage of respondents identifying themselves as "slightly conservative," "conservative," or "extremely conservative." In 1974, 40% of Americans identified as moderates, with conservatives and liberals each making up about 30% of the population. The figure confirms the widely held image of America as a centrist nation; throughout the period, "moderate" has almost always been the modal identification.

But some striking trends among those identifying as more liberal or conservative are apparent. During this period, the percentage of liberals fluctuated within a narrow range (just under 25% to 30%). However, the percentage

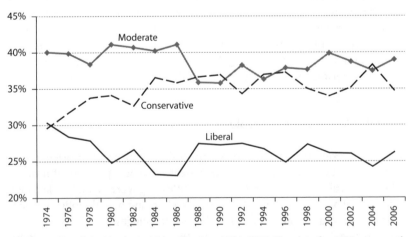

Figure 5.1. Trends in ideological identification, 1974–2006. The data for 1992 average the 1991 and 1993 data.

of conservative identifiers grew notably between 1974 and 2004, starting at 30%, climbing and staying above 35% in the early 1980s, and peaking at 38% in 2004 before falling in 2006. The increase in conservative identification occurred mainly in the 1980s during the Reagan presidency (reaching 36% in 1985), bounced around that level during the presidencies of George H. W. Bush and Bill Clinton in the late 1980s and 1990s, and then climbed again in the early 2000s during the first half of the presidency of George W. Bush. The average gap separating liberals and conservatives during this period was 7%, but at times it was much larger—peaking in 2004 at a very substantial 14%.

Notably, the rise in conservative identification was largely concentrated among southern whites.[3] Initially, 30% of southerners identified as conservatives, but this increased to 45% in 2004—a startling growth of 15 percentage points over this 30-year period. In nonsouthern states, on the other hand, conservative identification grew only modestly. In the 1970s, 29% of nonsoutherners identified as conservative—about the same as southerners. The nonsouthern percentage of conservatives climbed to the mid-30s by the early 1980s, and then remained near that level for the next two decades.

Ideology and Partisanship

We will see shortly that rising conservative identification in the mass public has *not* been accompanied by a corresponding decline in support for many important government programs. But what about trends in party identification?[4] Between the New Deal era in the 1930s and the 1970s, a much larger share of the electorate identified as Democrats than as Republicans; to be electorally competitive during this period at the national level, Republicans had to capture a larger share of votes from Independents (see Fiorina 2002). But this traditional Democratic advantage in party identification began to weaken beginning in the 1970s. One large source of this was the movement of southerners from the Democratic to the Republican Party, a slow but steady process over a long period of time (Katznelson 1997; Knuckey 2001). Republicans also gained outside the South, winning and holding greater allegiance among virtually all subgroups except African Americans.

To track changes in party identification, we utilize the following GSS question:

> Generally speaking, do you usually think of yourself as a Republican, Democrat, Independent, or what?

Figure 5.2 shows the marked shift away from the Democratic Party during this period, alongside growth in the percentages identifying as Republicans and Independents.[5] Democrats held an enormous advantage throughout the 1970s: twice as many respondents then identified as Democrats than as Republicans. The Republican share increased during the 1980s, from 23% at the decade's outset to 33% at its end. Notably, too, Independents surged in the 1990s, becoming the modal identification by 1996. Beginning in the early

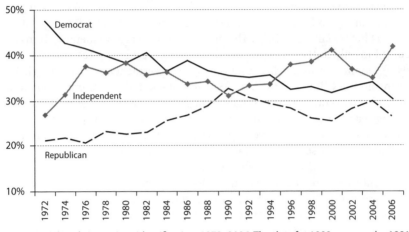

Figure 5.2. Trends in partisan identification, 1972–2006. The data for 1992 average the 1991 and 1993 data.

1990s, identification with the two major parties steadily declined, save for small upward bounces for both in 2002 and 2004.

A number of factors may account for increased Republican partisanship from the mid-1970s onward. We examine one possibility here: that during this period, citizens increasingly sorted themselves into their "natural" party based on ideological identification (i.e., liberals into the Democratic Party and conservatives into the Republican Party) (see also Levendusky 2009). Figure 5.3 highlights this ideological polarization in party identification. It displays trends in the "natural" ideological identification of Democrats, In-

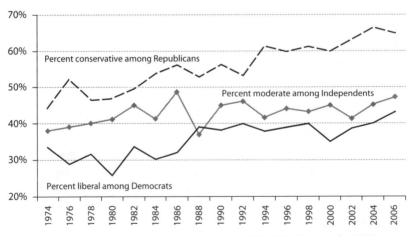

Figure 5.3. Ideological polarization by political party, 1974–2006. The data for 1992 average the 1991 and 1993 data.

dependents, and Republicans. Between 1974 and 2006, the linkages between ideology and partisanship became much tighter. The percentage of Independents identifying as moderates increased slightly during this period, from about 40% at its beginning to 47% by 2006. The coupling of party and ideology rose more for the two major parties: the percentage of Democrats identifying as liberals increased from 33% to 43%, while the tendency of Republicans to identify as conservatives *dramatically* rose, from 44% in 1974 to over 65% in 2006.

Taken together, the trends displayed in Figures 5.1 and 5.3 provide one clue to improved Republican electoral performance from the late 1970s onward. A modest increase in ideological conservatism in the mass public, *coupled* with a tightened connection between conservative identification and Republican partisanship, provided a small but significant boost in the potential Republican vote share in elections. Identification with the Republican Party rose both because the mass public included more conservatives *and* because conservatives were increasingly likely to vote for Republican candidates. The converse, however, did *not* hold for Democrats. While the linkage of liberal ideology to Democratic voting strengthened somewhat, the share of liberals in the mass public declined (albeit only slightly) during this period, providing no net gain.

Accounting for trends in the improved "sorting" of conservatives and liberals into parties has both "micro" (changes among individuals) and "macro" (changes in the party system and other organizational and institutional factors) components. A full analysis would require a more extensive discussion than we can provide here. But we will suggest a couple of possibilities. At the individual level, rising education levels make it easier for individuals to discern which party is "liberal" and which is "conservative" (cf. Weakliem 1995). An American National Election Survey (ANES) item about perceived differences between the parties offers some evidence of this. Among ANES respondents, the perception that differences between parties are significant has steadily risen over time (see Manza and Brooks 1999, p. 29).

The larger explanation for the changing ideology–party link, however, is likely to lie in changes in the party system itself. The pre-1960s "solid South"—in which the Democratic Party dominated southern politics—dampened the correspondence between ideology and partisanship. Its disappearance increasingly sorted citizens into parties by ideological identification. Moreover, with respect to the special case of conservatives and the Republican Party, strong evidence indicates that the Republican Party moved to the right from the 1980s onward. For example, Republicans in Congress became increasingly unified and more conservative during this period than at any time in the 20th century (Poole and Rosenthal 1997). The so-called "liberal" wing of the party, represented in the post–World War II period by figures like Dwight Eisenhower, Nelson Rockefeller, and Jacob Javits, largely disappeared from the national scene (Rae 1989; Hacker and Pierson 2005).

This bloc of Republicans, disproportionately from the Northeast and West Coast, was moderate on civil rights questions and supported both internationalism abroad and a moderate welfare state at home. This rightward drift of the Republican Party at the national level (and the virtual disappearance of congressional Republicans from the Northeast) thus magnified the differences between the parties (see Layman, Carsey, and Horowitz 2006; Hetherington 2007).

General Orientations toward Government

Trends in another GSS item illuminate a related, and potentially important, shift in American public opinion toward greater conservatism. First fielded in 1975, the item asks respondents whether the responsibility for solving social problems rests with government or with individuals and the market:

> Some people think that the government in Washington is trying to do too many things that should be left to individuals and private businesses. Others disagree and think that the government should do more to solve our country's problems. Still others have opinions somewhere in between. Where would you place yourself on this scale, or haven't you made up your mind on this?

Respondents are asked to place themselves on a 5-point scale where 1 represents a position that government should do more, 5 a preference for government to do less, and 3 agreement with both views. After 1975, the question was not asked again until 1983, but it appears consistently in the GSS thereafter.

This item nicely captures the competing frames dominating public discourse of the past three decades about the role of government versus the responsibility of markets/individuals. The three lines in Figure 5.4 represent

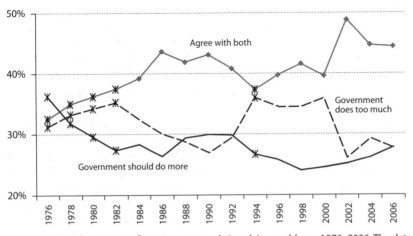

Figure 5.4. Trends in support for government role in solving problems, 1976–2006. The data for 1992 average the 1991 and 1993 data.

the percentages of respondents believing that government should do more, believing that it does too much, and taking the middle view.[6]

The proportion of respondents believing that government should do more fell sharply, from 39% to 25%, between 1975 and 1983, a period during which President Reagan and his conservative allies encouraged skepticism about the effectiveness of government. Thereafter, it fluctuates within a narrow range between 25% and 30%. This did not lead to a corresponding increase in the belief that government does too much, however. The fraction of those holding that view rose somewhat between 1975 and 1983, but then fell to near 30% in most remaining GSSs, save for a modest rise in the mid- to late 1990s. Instead, the primary shift was toward the middle position; the percentage selecting that climbed from 31% to 39% between 1975 and 1983. It rose more modestly thereafter, often exceeding 40% and reaching the mid-40s after 2000.[7]

It is unfortunate that this item about government's role in solving problems was asked only once before 1983, limiting our ability to assess longer-term trends. But after the sharp drop in support for government activism between 1975 and 1983, such support holds remarkably steady. This gives us confidence that a real and significant development occurred in the early part of this period, intersecting with Reagan's election and first term in office. The antigovernment rhetoric that emerged in that era shifted a significant number of Americans away from the view that government should do more. To be sure, only some of them adopted the polar opposite view that government should do less, however. The main rise was in those taking the moderate view.

Public Spending Preferences

While trends in general political orientations provide one view of political shifts since the early 1970s, other GSS data allow us to analyze trends in a number of other important orientations. One of the GSS's most original and salient batteries of core items asks respondents about their preferences regarding national spending in a variety of policy domains. First fielded in 1973, these questions are introduced as follows:

> We are faced with many problems in this country, none of which can be solved easily or inexpensively. I'm going to name some of these problems, and for each one I'd like you to tell me whether you think we're spending too much, too little, or about the right amount on [item].

Each GSS since 1973 has asked about (1) space-exploration programs; (2) improving and protecting the environment; (3) improving and protecting the nation's health; (4) solving the problems of big cities; (5) halting the rising crime rate (a factually misleading item); (6) dealing with drug addiction; (7) improving the nation's education system; (8) improving the conditions of Blacks; (9) the military, armaments, and defense; (10) foreign aid; and (11) welfare.[8]

We constructed a domestic spending index that includes the nine domestic policy items (all except military/defense and foreign aid).[9] The index measures preferences for increased domestic spending. Items were scored +1 for respondents favoring more spending, –1 for those favoring less spending, and 0 for those viewing spending as about right, so scale scores range between +9 (those wanting more spending on all 9 domestic items) to –9 (those wanting reduced spending on all). A respondent wanting increased spending in 4 areas, decreased spending in 2, and no change in the remaining 3 would be scored +2. As such, the scale scores represent the difference between the number of areas in which the respondent prefers spending increases and the number in which he or she opts for decreases.

Figure 5.5 displays trends in average domestic spending preferences over time. In all years, the mean spending index score is positive, indicating that GSS respondents wanted to increase spending in more areas than they wanted to decrease it. Despite this pronounced prospending bias, over-time movements reflect important contrasts in the public spending mood. From the mid-1970s to the early 1980s, at the outset of the Reagan era, the desire for more spending is at its lowest point. The political market for more spending declined during this period. But since the early 1980s, Americans have moved toward wanting *more* spending, varying only in *how much* additional spending they want, and on what issues. Following Reagan's election in 1980, and in the aftermath of ongoing battles over Reagan administration proposals to cut spending on many domestic programs (including Social Security, Medicare/Medicaid, and federal support for education), average support for more spending rose by more than a point on the spending scale, reaching its

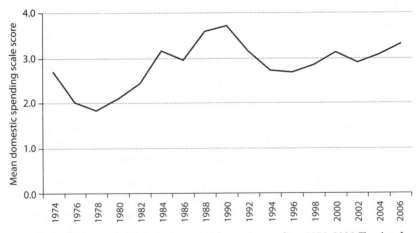

Figure 5.5. Trends in preferences for increased domestic spending, 1974–2006. The data for 1992 average the 1991 and 1993 data.

first peak in the early 1990s. Support for more spending declined a bit during the Clinton presidency, when the president proposed a sweeping national
health insurance plan, but began to grow slightly after the Republican sweep
of Congress in 1994 and the rejection of Clinton's more ambitious proposals.
Support for more spending again grew slightly after the election of George W.
Bush in 2000. By 2006, it had risen nearly to its 1990 peak.

These aggregate trends in the domestic spending index may, of course,
mask significant movements in public attitudes toward spending in individual areas. We thus examined trends in each of the nine domestic spending items available for the 1973–2006 period, but found few differences in
the trends within specific areas. Figure 5.6 illustrates this by displaying the
trends for health, where more spending is most desired, and welfare, among
the areas where expanded spending is least desired. As a reference point, the
trend in domestic spending preferences from Figure 5.5 is rescaled to the
range –1 to 1 (from –9 to 9) for comparability with the individual spending
items here. While there is some significant variation on welfare, the preference for health spending moves more or less in line with the overall spending
trend. It declines in the late 1970s, then increases throughout the 1980s, before
falling a bit in the 1990s during the Clinton presidency and rising slightly
since the late 1990s.

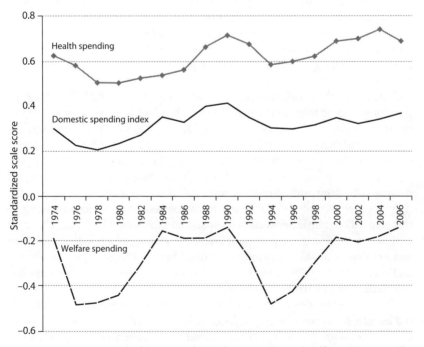

Figure 5.6. Trends in support for increased spending on health and welfare, 1974–2006. The
data for 1992 average the 1991 and 1993 data.

Spending preferences on "welfare" have been the most volatile of all those measured on the GSS, perhaps not surprising in an era where seemingly everyone found something not to like in the major welfare program, AFDC. A desire for less welfare spending peaks in the mid-1990s, as both Bill Clinton and the Republican Congress debated plans to significantly change the program. But following the welfare reform of 1996, support for more welfare spending rises, suggesting that the introduction of work requirements for welfare recipients made "welfare" a less toxic spending issue than before. The "welfare" item also illustrates how changes in question wording impact spending preferences. When framed as providing "assistance to the poor" rather than "welfare" spending, opposition to this spending item decreases dramatically (Smith 1987). Still, the volatility of the "welfare" spending item captures an important sentiment toward government assistance during this period.

Support for "more spending" on these domestic items is not necessarily a uniformly liberal position; for example, conservatives may favor increasing spending on reducing crime (e.g., putting more convicted offenders in prison) or "dealing with drug addiction," at least since Ronald Reagan declared a "war on drugs" in 1985, and a corresponding reduction in tolerance for drug offenders ensued (e.g., see Tonry 1995; Gottschalk 2007). The liberal position on these two spending questions is also complex. A liberal respondent could well favor *more* spending to reduce crime by programs to reduce unemployment, improve postincarceration transitions, or create new alternatives to prison. Similarly, a liberal position on drug offenses could favor increased spending on drug treatment programs as opposed to increased policing.

We explore these different possibilities in Figure 5.7, which displays support for spending to combat drug addiction by ideological identification. The question is not nuanced enough to indicate *how* conservatives and liberals would spend increased funding to combat drug addiction.[10] Still, the trend lines by ideological identification are revealing. From the early 1980s, the percentages of both conservatives and liberals favoring increased spending on dealing with drug addiction grew, although there seems to be more volatility among conservatives. For much of the period, support for spending in this area differed little between liberals and conservatives. However, the early 1990s saw a decline in support for increased spending, and the decline among conservatives was starker than that among liberals. The gap between liberals and conservatives widens the most in the mid-1990s, shortly after Republicans recaptured control of the Congress.

One of the puzzles of the spending items is the pronounced prospending bias in preferences they produce. Because actual expenditures in some of these areas are much higher than in others, preferences for more spending in the abstract may be even greater than the raw data imply. Among the spending items measured regularly since 1973, the four most unpopular (for-

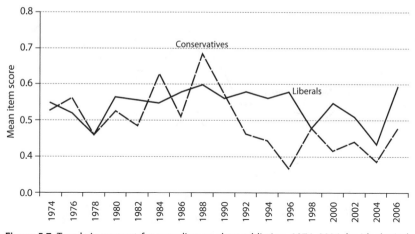

Figure 5.7. Trends in support for spending on drug addiction, 1974–2006, by ideological orientation. The data for 1992 average the 1991 and 1993 data.

eign aid, welfare, improving the conditions of blacks, and space exploration) refer to areas where relatively little actual government spending occurs. By contrast, annual expenditures in some of the most favored areas (education, health, Social Security [measured only since 1984], and national defense) are very large. If we were to weight spending preferences by the actual spending involved, the American public could be said to favor considerably more government—and government spending—than it is currently getting, even in conservative eras.

But preferences for "more spending" in the abstract do not always translate into concrete support for greater governmental activism. In addition to the health care spending item discussed above, the GSS also asks specifically about expanding the government's role in providing health care. It asks respondents,

> In general, some people think that it is the responsibility of the government in Washington to see to it that people have help in paying for doctors and hospital bills; they are at point 1. Others think that these matters are not the responsibility of the federal government and that people should take care of these things themselves; they are at point 5. Where would you place yourself on this scale, or haven't you made up your mind on this?

As Figure 5.8 shows, this second item produces dramatically lower support for increased government involvement when juxtaposed against the trend line for the earlier item measuring support for increased spending on health care.

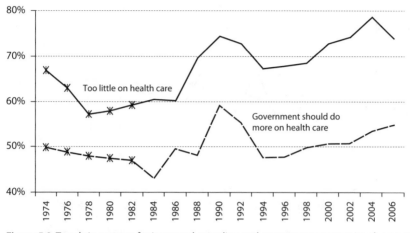

Figure 5.8. Trends in support for increased spending and greater government involvement in health care, 1974–2006. The data for 1992 average the 1991 and 1993 data.

The difference between the two items is striking, especially since the early 1990s. It helps to explain why a political market for health reform always exists, but also why it is so difficult to garner support from a significant majority of the public for a national, federally administered health program. The most important thing to notice is the large gap between the two lines. On average, respondents are 18 percentage points less likely to say that the "government should do more" about health care than to support generic spending increases in this area.

There also appears to be an important trend in the gap between the two lines. It has increased from 10–12 percentage points throughout much of the 1980s to over 20 percentage points after 2000, peaking at 25 percentage points during the reelection campaign of George W. Bush in 2004. In 1993, President Bill Clinton advanced his ill-fated proposal for a national health plan, which met with powerful opposition from conservative and industry sources. They mounted an all-out campaign against the proposal, emphasizing antigovernment frames that highlighted how it would significantly expand government bureaucracies (Skocpol 1996; Hacker 1997; Jacobs and Shapiro 2000). The campaign against the Clinton proposal seems to have an enduring effect; while a general desire to spend more on health care exists, the proportion of Americans endorsing a greater government role has grown more slowly.[11]

Of the 11 spending items asked consistently since 1973, 2 concern foreign affairs: one asks about foreign aid, the other about military spending. These items engage different issues, and might be expected to move in a different direction than domestic social problem spending preferences, both because foreign policy questions are inherently different and because the timing of overseas developments requires different government responses. As Fig-

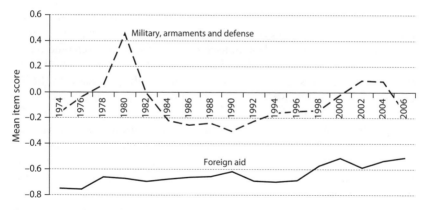

Figure 5.9. Trends in preferences for increased spending on foreign aid and defense, 1974–2006. The data for 1992 average the 1991 and 1993 data.

ure 5.9 suggests, opposition to increased spending on foreign aid is very strong; in every year, more than twice as many Americans want less foreign aid spending than want more.[12] While levels of such opposition remain fairly consistent across the series, we do see a slight movement toward supporting more spending on foreign aid beginning in the late-1990s. Support for more spending on the military and national defense, by contrast, shows some very sharp and pointed movements. The two most dramatic shifts are in the late 1970s and following September 11, 2001. The extraordinarily large shift toward a preference for increased military spending peaking in 1980 is especially notable. Concerted conservative attacks during this period on the alleged failure of the United States to maintain its military strength and respond to the "Soviet threat" appeared to have a big, if short-lived, impact.[13] After this, preferences in the early 1980s shift toward decreased military spending and level off by the middle of the Reagan presidency. The post–September 11 jump in support for more military spending is a second critical shift. It too may be of short duration, as such support begins to weaken after 2004.

The overall impression produced by an examination of trends in the spending preference items is partially at odds with the sharper conservative trends in general political orientations. Americans generally want more spending, especially on large and expensive programs. While the general spending index does move in a more prospending or antispending direction from time to time, at all points in the series Americans favor more spending, and frequently by a large margin. How can we reconcile the two? One hint can be found in the differences between general support for increased spending on health care but much lower support for increased governmental involvement in that field. The availability of antigovernment frames to challenge arguments for an expanded public sector is critical. Second, the GSS does not assess the relative salience of each of these areas to respondents; one cannot tell *how* important increases in any of the individual areas are to them. Respondents' political behavior may be more influenced by their general political orientations and salient spending preferences than by more mildly or loosely held preferences. Third, we should note that the preference for increased spending does *not* uniformly coincide with the liberal position. Conservatives could favor more spending on dealing with drug addiction or halting the (hypothetical) rising crime rate, for example. Finally, the spending items offer a "cost-free" analysis of government spending. Individuals are *not* reminded that increased spending is oftentimes accompanied by increased taxation or government debt. Thus, the spending preferences recorded by the GSS are abstracted away from the real-world implications of increased national spending.

Social Issue Attitudes

The past 35 years have seen greatly increased contention over "social issue" questions, such as gay/lesbian rights, family breakdown and changing gender roles, abortion, and the role of religion in public life (including, for example, prayer in the public schools and the teaching of evolution in biology curricula). Political mobilization around social issues is generally traced to the rise of the Moral Majority, an evangelical Christian organization founded by the Rev. Jerry Falwell in the late 1970s. Shortly thereafter, Ronald Reagan openly embraced much of the evangelical issue agenda in his 1980 presidential campaign and received the endorsement of Falwell's conservative coalition (Bruce 1988). The integration of the evangelical issue agenda into mainstream political discourse has spawned new electoral cleavages. Linked to the cultural divide over social issues are debates about rising political polarization and "red–blue" America, replete with colorful maps of the country allegedly showing how the two coasts and parts of the upper Midwest are moving in one direction on contentious social issues while the rest of the country shifts in another.

The image of a growing "culture war" between religious conservatives and secular Americans has periodically captured the fancy of scholars and journalistic commentators on American politics (e.g., Hunter 1991; Himmelfarb 2001; Frank 2004). Variations on the culture/values conflict perspective have been sharply criticized (e.g., DiMaggio, Evans, and Bryson 1996; Fiorina, Abrams, and Pope 2006; Fiorina and Abrams 2008; Gelman 2008), but it is nonetheless among the most widely debated topics in recent studies of American public opinion (see, for example, the attention devoted to Frank's [2004] version of this thesis in *What's the Matter with Kansas?*).

Much debate over the polarization/values conflict thesis concerns either (1) whether the public has, in fact, become more *divided* on these issues (e.g., whether distributions of attitudes have become more bimodal, or whether cleavages between sociodemographic groups have sharpened) or (2) whether social/cultural issues have become more *salient*, such that citizens and voters weigh them more heavily when deciding whether they are "liberals" or "conservatives," or "Republicans" or "Democrats." These are both important, widely debated questions. While measures of issue salience are not routinely available in the GSS, participants in the polarization/values conflict debate often draw on GSS data to examine questions of overall trends and the patterning of cleavages in public opinion over contested social issues (cf. Fiorina et al. 2006).

Most relevant to the theme of this chapter is whether conservatives succeeded in moving public opinion on social issues to the right during this period. We begin with an overall picture of the changing social issue mood by examining trends in a social issues index that takes advantage of repeated GSS items on attitudes toward (1) homosexual relationships, (2) laws that make it easier (or harder) to obtain a divorce, (3) laws limiting (or expanding) access to pornography, (4) the death penalty, and (5) abortion rights under a variety of circumstances. For each item, a standardized liberalism score is calculated as 100 plus the percentage of liberal responses minus the percentage of conservative responses (cf. Stimson 1999); higher scores indicate a more liberal social issue climate. The appendix to this chapter provides further details.[14] The five attitudes in the scale were all measured in 1976, and then regularly beginning in 1988.[15]

Figure 5.10 displays the mean social issues index score for 1976 and 1988–2006. (For the years 1978–1986 in which all of the index items are not available, we plot a dashed line depicting a projected linear trend based on the

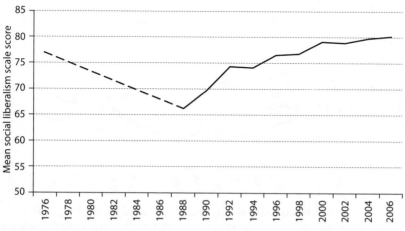

Figure 5.10. Trends in the social issues index, 1976–2006.

difference between the 1976 and 1988 data points.) Although the social issues index shows that, on average, a greater percentage of respondents gave the conservative response than the liberal response, the index also exhibits some interesting over-time movements. Figure 5.10 shows, for instance, that American social issue attitudes grew increasingly more liberal after 1988. Parallel analyses of ANES data suggest that these liberalizing trends have helped offset some of the other pro-Republican trends and helped keep the Democrats electorally competitive in the 1980s and 1990s (Brooks 2000).

Equally striking, however, is the conservative movement in the index between 1976 and 1988. During this era—highlighted again by the rise of Ronald Reagan and the political mobilization of the Christian Right—Americans became less liberal on these social issues.

Trends for individual items in the index—available for more years than the index scores themselves—yield a better sense of the timing and source of this conservative shift. Figure 5.11 highlights trends in three individual items included in the social issues index—attitudes toward abortion, capital punishment, and homosexual relationships. Two of these—attitudes toward abortion and capital punishment—shift in the conservative direction beginning in the mid- to late 1970s, and drop by at least 10 points by the late 1980s. The percentage of respondents who oppose the death penalty for convicted murderers drops over 20 points by 1985, not rebounding to pre-Reagan era levels until the beginning of the 2000s. Attitudes toward abortion rights exhibit considerably more fluctuation but show a similar over-time trend until the 1990s. Unlike attitudes toward capital punishment, however, attitudes toward abortion shift in the liberal direction in the early 1990s, only to fall

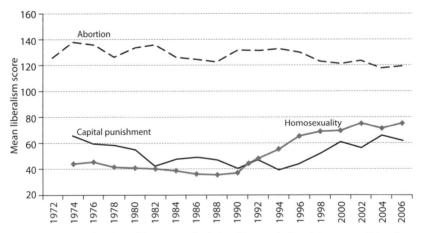

Figure 5.11. Attitudes toward homosexual relationships, capital punishment, and abortion, 1972–2006. The data for 1992 average the 1991 and 1993 data for all items. Additionally, the data for 1978 (1977/1980) and 1986 (1985/1987) are averages for attitudes toward homosexual relationships as well as 1986 (1985/1987) for attitudes toward abortion.

precipitously in the next decade. By 2006, support for abortion rights is at an all-time low, below even the levels found during the socially conservative Reagan years. In contrast, attitudes toward homosexual relationships were flat from 1974 through the 1980s but grew steadily more liberal since the early 1990s.

The overall index may, however, mask important subgroup variation. Seculars and people with limited religious commitments, or the better educated,

(a)

(b)

Figure 5.12. Panel a: Trends in social issues index by partisan affiliation, 1976–2006. Panel b: Trends in social issues index by ideological identification, 1976–2006. Panel c: Trends in social issues index by religious attendance, 1976–2006. Panel d: Trends in social issues index by education, 1976–2006.

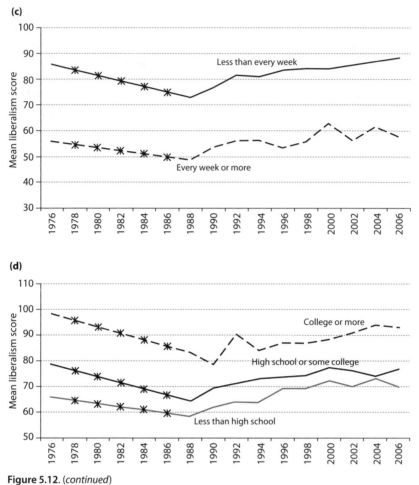

(c)

(d)

Figure 5.12. (*continued*)

might be becoming more liberal at a much faster rate than everyone else, such that the recent upward trend in Figure 5.10 gives a false impression of a society-wide movement. Brooks and Manza (2007) show that between 1972 and 1992 professionals became significantly more liberal on social issue attitudes (as measured in the ANES) than did those in other classes, driving them toward the Democratic Party.

Figure 5.12 considers this important possibility. Its four panels plot average scores on the social issues index for subgroups defined by partisan affiliation, ideological identification, frequency of attending religious services, and educational attainment. Again, we plot a line that averages the total difference between the available 1976 and 1988 data points for the years 1978–1986 with asterisks indicating the predicted values for the unavailable data points. Most of the subgroup trends closely resemble one another, falling between 1976 and 1988 and increasing thereafter. Some substantial differences in the *rate* of increase after 1988 for certain subgroups are apparent, however. Trends by ideological identification, for example (panel b), show that conservatives, liberals, and moderates all moved in the liberal direction on social issues, but not at the same pace. The gap between conservatives and liberals increases rapidly after 1988 and by 2006 reaches over 40 points. The story for partisan affiliation (panel a) is similar: Democrats and Independents moved upward on the social liberalism scale, while Republicans all but plateaued, so the gap between Democrats and Republicans more than doubled between 1988 and the end of the series. Fewer differences are evident for groups defined by attendance at religious services or education; indeed, there is some suggestion in panel d that educational differences in social liberalism shrank between the 1970s and 2006.

Conclusions

Trends in GSS items provide some evidence of a rightward shift in orientations toward government and social issues in the late 1970s. Particularly striking in this regard are the declining percentage of Americans who saw government as the appropriate vehicle to solve social problems, the small but significant increase in conservative identification, and the tightening of the linkage between ideology and party identification. Some of these trends were short-lived, while others continued for much longer periods, even into the mid-2000s.

The imprint of Ronald Reagan's rise to national political power on these trends jumps out in these data, justifying Wilentz's characterization of the entire period as the Age of Reagan. While some of the Reagan impact appears short-lived, other components endured. For example, increasing conservatism on social issues or declining support for increased national spending would reverse in the 1990s and 2000s. But the larger Reagan impact can be seen in the discrediting of both government in general and "liberalism" as a governing philosophy. Already under way by the early 1970s, these trends deepened later in the decade and would continue into the early 2000s (and even since the election of Democrat Barack Obama in 2008, liberals have had a harder time reestablishing a positive connotation for "liberalism"). Democratic politicians generally disdained the "liberal" label, while Republicans routinely embraced the label of "conservative," with the mass public moving in similar directions. These shifts provided Republicans with a small but significant boost. In a competitive two-party system, even small shifts can, however, be of considerable importance.

The sources of rising rates of conservative identity and antigovernment orientations are complex, and cannot be fully explored here (see Smith's chapter on public confidence in major institutions for discussion of the latter). Attitudinal trends explored in other chapters of this volume (see, e.g., Wright et al., chapter 6, on attitudes toward crime, and Bobo et al., chapter 3, on attitudes toward racial egalitarianism) contribute other factors. A critical element paving the way for rising conservative political influence was the delegitimation of government as an institution in this era. Widely held antigovernment sentiments provided conservatives with a powerful tool for challenging liberal arguments favoring government-based solutions to social problems. Research on issue framing or priming suggests that declining support for government is a key pathway that can override many other values and beliefs (see, e.g., Jacobs and Shapiro 2000; Page and Jacobs 2009) when people answer issue questions, by manipulating what they consider or increasing the accessibility of certain ideas.

An important source of conservative momentum in this era concerns the relative *salience* of particular issues. Beginning in the late 1970s, conservative political entrepreneurs succeeded in raising the salience of concerns about bloated government, crime, taxes, and threats to national security. Citizens generally view the Republican Party as stronger in terms of such issues. Because the GSS does not measure salience, our analysis does not reveal how changes in issue salience tended to favor conservatives during this period.

But perhaps the most important lesson of this chapter is that successful conservative mobilization from the late 1970s onward was *not* rooted in a massive or widespread shift in public opinion toward conservative positions. Many political journalists and commentators have depicted America as moving to the right on diverse cultural values and opposition to "big" government. We do not find such changes, however, in many specific domestic policy arenas. Movement away from belief in an expanded government role in solving social problems has been mainly toward a more moderate view, not a belief that government should substantially contract. In terms of "operational" questions about national spending, our trends show that Americans, if anything, became more liberal about increasing spending in areas where it is already large, including health care, education, and Social Security.[16] GSS data offer less evidence about trends in support for military and defense policy, but the available evidence here indicates that movements in a conservative direction were at most cyclical: prodefense sentiment rises markedly during the early phases of the Reagan and George W. Bush presidencies, only to fall back to lower levels soon thereafter. And finally, while Americans did become more conservative on heated social issue questions between the mid-1970s and late 1980s, we find clear evidence of a liberalizing trend since then. Abortion attitudes do seem to have moved in the conservative direction since the late 1990s, but on other social issues, American attitudes have had a decidedly liberal drift.

Postscript

In the brief interval since the analysis for this chapter ends, America has undergone two profoundly contradictory political shifts. Democratic congressional victories in 2006 and 2008 and the election of Democrat Barack Obama as president seemed to signal that the conservative policy ideas associated with the Republican majority since 1980 had exhausted themselves. Indeed, commentators in the immediate aftermath of the 2008 election suggested that Democratic control of the House, the Senate, and the presidency marked a fundamentally new era in American politics. To some, the return of the presidency and both houses of Congress to Democratic control suggested the possibility for a "new New Deal" in response to the deep economic and financial crisis that gripped the nation. Many commentators predicted the Democratic victories would renew the role of government in social and economic life by combining short-term job creation programs with larger structural and regulatory reforms. In particular, discussions of national health care reform underscored the possibility of "big government" initiatives reawakening American liberalism after 30 years of decline.

But if Democratic control of Congress signaled the return of liberalism, it did not last long. The ascent of the conservative Tea Party movement in reaction to the perceived emergence of "big government" initiatives helped renew the conservative assault on "big government," even as the new Obama administration moved extremely cautiously and remained firmly in a centrist position. The outcome of the 2010 midterm election, which returned the House of Representatives to Republican control, suggests that the four-year period of Democratic renewal that began in 2006 may represent only a brief interruption of the Age of Reagan rather than a fundamental shift away from it. In either case, it remains an open question over the next few years whether Democrats can revive the spirit of New Deal liberalism and restore faith in the role of government, or whether the strength of the Tea Party movement signals the further entrenchment of conservative politics in the United States.

Appendix

Table 5.A.1. Coding of Variables in Social Issues Index

GSS mnemonic	Question	Coding (+ = Liberal, – = Conservative)
HOMOSEX	What about sexual relations between two adults of the same sex—do you think it is always wrong, almost always wrong, wrong only sometimes, or not wrong at all?	(+ = Not wrong at all, – = Always wrong)

(*continued*)

Table 5.A.1. (*continued*)

GSS mnemonic	Question	Coding (+ = Liberal, – = Conservative)
PORNLAW	Which of these statements comes closest to your feelings about pornography laws: 1. There should be laws against the distribution of pornography whatever the age. 2. There should be laws against the distribution of pornography to persons under 18. 3. There should be no laws forbidding the distribution of pornography.	(+ = Legal to all, – = Illegal to all)
DIVLAW	Should divorce in this country be easier or more difficult to obtain than it is now?	(+ = Easier, – = More difficult)
CAPPUN	Do you favor or oppose the death penalty for persons convicted of murder?	(+ = Oppose, – = Favor)
ABDEFECT	Please tell me whether or not you think it should be possible for a pregnant woman to obtain a legal abortion if: There is a strong chance of serious defect in the baby?	(+ = Yes, – = No)
ABNOMORE	Please tell me whether or not you think it should be possible for a pregnant woman to obtain a legal abortion if: She is married and does not want any more children?	(+ = Yes, – = No)
ABHLTH	Please tell me whether or not you think it should be possible for a pregnant woman to obtain a legal abortion if: The woman's own health is seriously endangered by the pregnancy?	(+ = Yes, – = No)
ABPOOR	Please tell me whether or not you think it should be possible for a pregnant woman to obtain a legal abortion if: The family has a very low income and cannot afford any more children?	(+ = Yes, – = No)
ABRAPE	Please tell me whether or not you think it should be possible for a pregnant woman to obtain a legal abortion if: She became pregnant as a result of rape?	(+ = Yes, – = No)
ABSINGLE	Please tell me whether or not you think it should be possible for a pregnant woman to obtain a legal abortion if: She is not married and does not want to marry the man?	(+ = Yes, – = No)

Notes

1. The issue of ideological and issue consistency within the American public is one of the most widely debated—and still unresolved—questions in public opinion research. The seminal work of Converse (1964) and his "Michigan School" colleagues in *The American Voter* (Campbell, Converse, Miller, and Stokes 1960), portrayed most survey respondents as inconsistent and incoherent in their responses. By contrast, the authors of *TAV* argued, party identification was the best and most consistent predictor of both behavior and attitudes. Later scholarship challenged the Converse thesis, by either providing a more sophisticated model of the survey response (e.g., Zaller 1992) or finding much stronger response consistency using better survey questions (Ansolabehere, Rodden, and Snyder 2008).

2. Throughout this chapter, we weight the GSS data using the variable "wtssall." We also correct for oversampling of African American respondents in 1982 and 1987 using the variable "sample."

3. Using the GSS's "region" variable, we define the "South" as the South Atlantic, East South Central, and West South Central census regions. The states included are Delaware, Maryland, West Virginia, Virginia, North Carolina, South Carolina, Georgia, Florida, Washington D.C., Kentucky, Tennessee, Alabama, Mississippi, Arkansas, Oklahoma, Louisiana, and Texas. Ideally we would not include Delaware, Maryland, West Virginia, and Washington D.C. as southern states, but publicly available GSS data do not allow us to distinguish them from other states in the South Atlantic.

4. The GSS also regularly asks respondents if and how they voted in the most recent presidential election. This retrospective question asks respondents to recall their voting behavior over a period of time ranging between six months and three and a half years. While valuable for some purposes, such retrospective reports are subject to well-known recall biases and errors, so we do not examine voting in this chapter.

5. Follow-ups to the party affiliation question measure the strength of that identification for Republicans and Democrats, and the leaning (if any) of Independents. We categorize respondents based only on their partisan identification, not its strength (see Keith et al. 1991).

6. Respondents answering either 1 or 2 on the 5-point scale are coded as believing that government should do more, those answering either 4 or 5 are coded as believing that government does too much, and those answering 3 are coded as agreeing with both positions.

7. Although the series in Figures 5.4, 5.8, and 5.12 begin in 1975 and pick up consistently in 1983, we plot values only for even years to maintain consistency with the other figures presented in the chapter. Asterisks indicate predicted values for even-numbered years between 1976 and 1982 based on the observed 1975–1983 difference.

8. Since 1984, a number of alternatively worded spending items have been asked as part of an ongoing question wording experiment. Typically, these items are "terse" versions of the "verbose" descriptions of the original spending items given in the text, although several are "verbose" versions of originally "terse" items. For several of the question wording experiments, previous research finds that changes in the wording makes a dramatic difference—particularly when contrasting spending on "welfare" versus "assistance to the poor" (Smith 1987). For the sake of parsimony, we focus on the original question wording rather than comparing "verbose" and "terse" wordings through the experiment.

9. Several other spending items—on highways and bridges, Social Security, mass transportation, and parks and recreation—were added to this battery in 1984. One on assistance to children was added in 2000, and another on supporting scientific research in 2002. We do not include these items in the domestic spending index because they were not asked during most of the period covered by the chapter.

10. For further analysis of the question wording experiments with reference to crime and drug policy, see Timberlake, Rasinski, and Lock (2001).

11. An updated analysis of the two health care items shows substantial movement after the passage of the Obama administration's health care reform act. The percentage of respondents who wanted "more spending" on the generic item that does *not* refer to government involvement—and typically exhibits an overwhelming prospending bias—declined from 77% in 2008 to 60% in 2010. The alternative item that refers directly to government action declined more modestly from 54% in 2008 to about 47% in 2010. By 2010, the gap between the two items had thus closed significantly and returned to the level typical of the Reagan years. The passage of the health care legislation—or the failure of the Obama administration to set the terms and tone of the debate surrounding it—seems to have turned back the clock on Americans' increasingly liberal attitudes toward health care spending.

12. Kull and Destler (1999) note that Americans are unusually poorly informed about foreign aid; few realize that the United States provides far less aid as a proportion of GDP than other rich democracies do. It is also striking that Americans are among the most generous in the world in terms of *private* charitable giving, including giving to foreign causes.

13. In the mid-1970s, a group of prominent conservative defense analysts came together in a group called the Committee on the Present Danger, which broadcast claims of declining U.S. capacity to respond to the Soviet military threat (Sanders 1983). In his 1980 campaign, Ronald Reagan stridently attacked incumbent Jimmy Carter and the Democratic Congress for allowing America to become weak. The 1978 seizure of the American embassy in Iran and the subsequent holding of U.S. hostages for 444 days provided daily evidence that appeared to underscore U.S. weakness.

14. Following Best (1999), the abortion item in the social issues index averages responses to six questions about whether it should be possible for a pregnant woman to obtain a legal abortion under different circumstances, including a strong chance of a serious birth defect, a pregnancy that seriously endangers the woman's health, a desire to have no more children, a pregnancy that resulted from rape, an inability to afford more children, and an unwillingness to marry the man involved. The combined abortion item receives the same weight as does each of the other four items in the social issues scale.

15. Between 1977 and 1987, at least one of the component variables of the social issue index was not measured in any given year. The GSS rotated many of its replicating core items during this period, measuring them in only two out of every three years. We thus use a broken line that averages the difference between the 1976 and 1988 data points in Figure 5.10. When constructing index scores for survey years 1976 and 1988–2006, we dropped respondents with missing values on seven or more component variables from the analysis and imputed missing values for other respondents using the "ice" command in Stata version 9.0.

16. In the case of Social Security, steep declines in global financial and real estate wealth after 2008 may prompt even more future support for improving public pensions.

References

Ansolabehere, Stephen, Jonathan Rodden, and James Snyder. 2008. "The Strength of Issues: Using Multiple Measures to Gauge Preference Stability, Ideological Constraint, and Issue Voting." *American Political Science Review* 102:215–32.

Bartels, Larry M. 2005. "Homer Gets a Tax Cut: Inequality and Public Policy in the American Mind." *Perspectives on Politics* 3:15–31.

Best, Samuel J. 1999. "The Sampling Problem in Measuring Public Mood: An Alternative Solution." *Journal of Politics* 61:721–40.

Brooks, Clem. 2000. "Civil Rights Liberalism and the Suppression of Republican Political Realignment in the United States, 1972–1996." *American Sociological Review* 65:482–505.

Brooks, Clem, and Jeff Manza. 2007. *Why Welfare States Persist*. Chicago: University of Chicago Press.

Bruce, Steve. 1988. *The Rise and Fall of the Christian Right*. New York: Oxford University Press.

Campbell, Angus, Philip E. Converse, Warren E. Miller, and Donald E. Stokes. 1960. *The American Voter*. Chicago: University of Chicago Press.

Converse, Philip E. 1964. "The Nature of Belief Systems in Mass Publics." In *Ideology and Discontent*, edited by David E. Apter, 206–61. New York: Free Press.

DiMaggio, Paul, John Evans, and Bethany Bryson. 1996. "Have Americans' Social Attitudes Become More Polarized?" *American Journal of Sociology* 102:690–755.

Erikson, Robert, Michael MacKuen, and James Stimson. 2002. *The Macro Polity*. New York: Cambridge University Press.

Fiorina, Morris. 2002. "Parties and Partisanship: A Forty Year Retrospective." *Political Behavior* 24:93–115.

Fiorina, Morris, and Samuel Abrams. 2008. "Political Polarization in the American Public." *Annual Review of Political Science* 11:563–88.

Fiorina, Morris, Samuel Abrams, and Jeremy Pope. 2006. *Culture War? The Myth of a Polarized America*. 2nd ed. New York: Pearson Longman.

Frank, Thomas. 2004. *What's the Matter with Kansas?* New York: Metropolitan Books.

Gelman, Andrew. 2008. *Red State, Blue State, Rich State, Poor State: Why Americans Vote the Way They Do*. Princeton, NJ: Princeton University Press.

Gottschalk, Marie. 2007. *The Prison and the Gallows: The Politics of Mass Incarceration in the United States*. New York: Cambridge University Press.

Hacker, Jacob. 1997. *The Road to Nowhere: The Genesis of President Clinton's Plan for Health Security*. Princeton, NJ: Princeton University Press.

Hacker, Jacob, and Paul Pierson. 2005. *Off-Center: The Republican Revolution and the Erosion of American Democracy*. New Haven, CT: Yale University Press.

———. 2010. *Winner-Take-All Politics*. New York: Simon & Schuster.

Hetherington, Marc J. 2007. "Turned Off or Turned On? The Effects of Polarization on Political Participation, Engagement, and Representation." In *Red and Blue Nation?* Vol. 2 of *Consequences and Correction of America's Polarized Parties,* edited by Pietro S. Nivola and David W. Brady, 1–33. Washington, DC: Brookings Institution.

Himmelfarb, Gertrude. 2001. *One Nation, Two Cultures: A Searching Examination of American Society in the Aftermath of Our Cultural Revolution.* New York: Vintage Books.

Hunter, James D. 1991. *Culture Wars: The Struggle to Define America.* New York: Basic Books.

Jacobs, Lawrence, and Robert Shapiro. 2000. *Politicians Don't Pander: Political Manipulation and the Loss of Democratic Responsiveness.* Chicago: University of Chicago Press.

Katznelson, Ira. 1997. "Reversing Southern Republicanism." In *The New Majority: Toward a Popular Progressive Politics,* edited by Stanley B. Greenberg and Theda Skocpol, 238–63. New Haven, CT: Yale University Press.

Keith, Bruce, E., David B. Magleby, Candice J. Nelson, Elizabeth Orr, Mark C. Westyle, and Raymond E. Wolfinger. 1991. *The Myth of the Independent Voter.* Berkeley: University of California Press.

Knuckey, Jonathan. 2001. "Ideological Realignment and Partisan Change in the American South, 1972–1996." *Politics and Policy* 29:337–58.

Kull, Stephen, and I. M. Destler. 1999. *Misreading the Public: The Myth of a New Isolationism.* Washington, DC: Brookings Institution.

Layman, Geoffrey, Thomas M. Carsey, and Juliana Menasce Horowitz. 2006. "Party Polarization in American Politics: Characteristics, Causes, and Consequences." *Annual Review of Political Science* 9:83–110.

Levendusky, Matthew. 2009. *The Partisan Sort: How Liberals Became Democrats and Conservatives Became Republicans.* Chicago: University of Chicago Press.

Manza, Jeff, and Clem Brooks. 1999. *Social Cleavages and Political Change: Voter Alignments and U.S. Party Coalitions.* New York: Oxford University Press.

Neckerman, Kathryn M., ed. 2004. *Social Inequality.* New York: Russell Sage Foundation.

Page, Benjamin, and Lawrence Jacobs. 2009. *Class War? Economic Inequality and the American Dream.* Chicago: University of Chicago Press.

Page, Benjamin, and Robert Shapiro. 1983. "Effects of Public Opinion on Policy." *American Political Science Review* 77:175–90.

Poole, Keith T., and Howard Rosenthal. 1997. *Congress: A Political-Economic History of Roll Call Voting.* New York: Oxford University Press.

Rae, Nicole. 1989. *The Decline and Fall of the Liberal Republicans.* New York: Oxford University Press.

Sanders, Jerry W. 1983. *Peddlers of Crisis.* Boston: South End Press.

Skocpol, Theda. 1996. *Boomerang: Health Care Reform and the Turn Against Government.* New York: Norton.

Smith, Tom W. 1987. "That Which We Call Welfare by Any Other Name Would Smell Sweeter: An Analysis of the Impact of Question Wording on Response Patterns." *Public Opinion Quarterly* 51:75–83.

Sroka, Stuart, and Christopher Wlezien. 2009. *Degrees of Democracy: Politics, Public Opinion, and Policy.* New York: Cambridge University Press.

Stimson, James. 1999. *Public Opinion in America: Moods, Cycles, and Swings.* 2nd ed. Boulder, CO: Westview.

Timberlake, Jeffrey M., Kenneth A. Rasinski, and Eric D. Lock. 2001. "Effects of Conservative Sociopolitical Attitudes on Public Support for Drug Rehabilitation Spending." *Social Science Quarterly* 82:184–96.

Tonry, Michael. 1995. *Malign Neglect: Race, Crime and Punishment in America.* New York: Oxford University Press.

Weakliem, David. 1995. "Two Models of Class Voting." *British Journal of Political Science* 25:259–70.

Wilentz, Sean. 2008. *The Age of Reagan: A History, 1974–2008.* New York: Harper.

Zaller, John R. 1992. *The Nature and Origins of Mass Opinion.* New York: Cambridge University Press.

6

Crime, Punishment, and Social Disorder

Crime Rates and Trends in Public Opinion over More Than Three Decades

James D. Wright, Jana L. Jasinski, and Drew Noble Lanier

In 1980, Arthur Stinchcombe, Tom Smith, Garth Taylor, and several additional coauthors published *Crime and Punishment—Changing Attitudes in America* (Stinchcombe et al. 1980). The book reviewed public opinion data from the first five or six waves of the General Social Survey (GSS), plus a large number of pre-GSS polls and surveys dating back to the 1930s, all dealing with attitudes of the American public toward crime, punishment, and social disorder. This chapter revisits the principal findings, themes, and conclusions of *Crime and Punishment* in light of what is now 30-plus years worth of GSS data—a stocktaking, as it were, of what we have learned about these topics from the GSS over its first three and a half decades. In addition, for the first time since *Crime and Punishment* was published, the United States has recently experienced a sharp decline in crime rates that began in about 1994 and continued for a decade. So in addition to stocktaking, we also explore the apparent effects of declining crime rates on Americans' attitudes about crime, punishment, and related matters.

The Fundamental Puzzle

The principal observation, or "fundamental puzzle," with which *Crime and Punishment* began is that while American attitudes toward a variety of social and cultural matters were clearly "liberalizing" throughout the 1970s (a trend that has continued to the present day), attitudes toward crime, criminals, and punishment were becoming harsher and more punitive.[1] The obvious explanation at the time was that crime and fear of crime were on the rise and were associated with people's becoming more punitive in their outlooks.

The difficulty with this line of explanation is that there was (and is) no significant correlation between fear of crime, or victimization by crime, and attitudes about how severely to punish criminals. To illustrate, probably the best indicator of punitiveness toward criminals available in the GSS is a question that asks whether the courts are "too harsh" or "not harsh enough." The GSS "fear" question states, "Is there anywhere right around here, that is, within a mile, where you would be afraid to walk alone at night?"[2] In 1972, the correlation between these two indicators was $r = .070$, statistically significant but insubstantial. In 2006, more than 30 years later, the correlation was .083. Similarly, in 1973 and 1994, the first and last years the GSS measured victimization (being forcefully robbed or burglarized) together with punitive attitudes, the correlations between victimization and punitive attitudes were not significant. So on this point, Stinchcombe and his associates were clearly correct—"fear" is not a compelling explanation of punitiveness, or vice versa. Some other explanation for the then-recent trends in punitiveness was clearly in order.

The book attempts to resolve the puzzle by reference to urbanization and what happens when large, racially mixed urban neighborhoods replace relatively homogeneous, small-town, racially segregated neighborhoods as the modal type. The authors argue that living in large cities and in proximity to racial minorities increases the salience of crime as a social problem. While these forces may promote increased tolerance and liberalism in many matters (civil liberties, religion, what Scammon and Wattenberg [1970] once referred to as famously as the Social Issue), when it comes to crime, they are associated with a preference for harsh, punitive, illiberal solutions. Most people want the crime problem solved—as soon as possible, by whatever means necessary, without much regard for the civil liberties of the accused. Or as Scammon and Wattenberg (1970, p. 287) themselves put it almost 40 years ago, "Law and order has become a nonnegotiable demand by voting Americans." Roberts, Stalans, Indermaur, and Hough (2003) argue that many penal policies are in fact reactions by policy makers based on their inaccurate perceptions of the view of the general public, resulting in calls for harsher and more unrelenting punishments than the public actually favors.

The seminal chapter 2 of *Crime and Punishment* reviews then-recent trends on five loosely related crime-like topics, as follows:

- Crime, especially violent crime, had been increasing.
- Fear of crime was also increasing, especially among women.
- The perception of crime as a major national problem was on the rise.

- Most social attitudes on things like civil liberties, abortion, race relations, gender, and the like had been moving in a generally liberal direction, a trend that has clearly continued.[3]
- Support for gun control, specifically for gun registration and for laws requiring police permits in order to purchase a gun, had been neither increasing nor decreasing but was, at the time, basically flat.

The concluding chapter describes the "principal intellectual puzzle of the book" as the apparent "mismatch" between the "personal variables" of crime (e.g., fear of crime, and actual victimization by crime) and the outlooks that represent "demands on the political system" (e.g., opinions about courts, capital punishment, and gun control) (Stinchcombe et al. 1980, p. 137). Actual victimization is rare and highly concentrated in specific social groups. Fear is somewhat more widespread (but not closely related to actual victimization); however, "demands for local improvement or change in the judicial system are nearly uniformly distributed across all categories of the population" (p. 138). The unfortunate result (from the perspective of public policy) is that widespread and fairly uniform "pressure in public opinion is brought to bear on policy makers to solve what is actually an extremely localized problem." In other words, the policy response to crime becomes disproportionate to the true extent and location of the crime problem—certainly a prescient observation on what American crime policy became in the subsequent three decades.

In this chapter, we first review trends in several of the content domains covered in *Crime and Punishment*, covering the period from the original GSS in 1972 through its 2006 administration—from roughly where Stinchcombe and his associates ended through to the present day. The early years of the new millennium have posed a new "fundamental puzzle," namely, that crime rates have fallen to levels substantially lower than any encountered in the United States in more than forty years (Rosenfeld 2004). Unlike the era covered in *Crime and Punishment*, in which crime rates went up and up, recently they have trended downward. A second major question taken up in this chapter, then, is whether these drastically falling crime rates have had any discernible effects on trends in public opinion about crime and punishment issues. In most but not all cases, they clearly have.

Crime Rates: Violent Crime, Property Crime, and Index Offenses

In 1980, Stinchcombe and colleagues described the recent crime trends as a "great surge in crime." Table 6.1 and Figure 6.1 illustrate the index crime rate for the nation from 1960 to 2006. These data indicate the number of index crimes divided by the country's population, reported in units of crimes per 100,000 population.[4] We calculated the rates of violent crime and property crime and an index rate combining both categories of offenses.

Table 6.1. Annual Crime Rates for Index Offenses, Violent Crimes and Property Crimes, 1960–2006

Time period	Violent crime rate[a]	Property crime rate[a]	Index crime rate[a]
1960s	**214.06**[b]	2340.06	2554.12
1970s	451.72	4296.75	4748.47
1980s	**592.32**	**4933.74**	**5526.06**
1990s	**673.02**	**4567.8**	**5240.82**
2000s	485.28	3672.17	4161.98
Overall	482.94	3960.86	4443.79

　[a]Rates are the aggregated annual average of the total number of index, violent, and property crimes per 100,000 population, as reported in the FBI's annual Uniform Crime Reports. The index crime rate is the sum of the violent crime and property crime rates. The rates for decades are the simple arithmetic average of the annual averages within the corresponding time periods. The "overall" averages are for the entire period between 1960 and 2006.

　[b]Cell entries in bold differ significantly from the relevant category total at $p < .05$ based on difference of means tests. For example, the mean violent crime rate in the 1960s (214.06) is significantly different from the mean violent crime rate for the 1960 to 2006 period (482.94).

Table 6.1 shows the decade-by-decade averages for each category of crime. The violent crime rate in particular was significantly lower in the 1960s (mean rate = 214.06) than that for the entire period, and it rose substantially during the 1970s, 1980s, and 1990s. The averages for the latter two decades are significantly above the overall mean for the series. Property crime rates show a similar pattern.

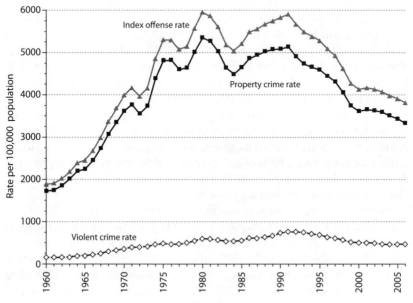

Figure 6.1. Index offense, violent crime and property crime rates, 1960–2006.

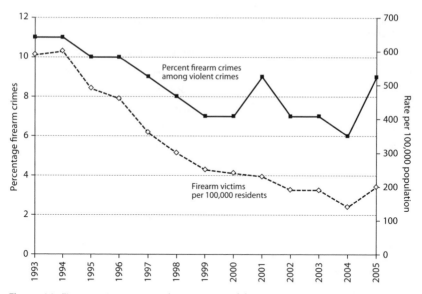

Figure 6.2. Firearm crime rates and percentage of firearm crimes of all violent offenses, 1993–2005.

Figures 6.1 and 6.2 show these changes graphically. The property crime rate is always much higher than the violent crime rate. The index offense rate is driven more by property crime than by violent crime. The index offense rate and the property crime rate each increased rather consistently through 1980, then again from 1984 through the early 1990s, after which they began to decline and did so consistently through to the end of the series in 2006. The slope of the function line for both series becomes less negative after 1999. Lanier and Dietz (2012) have argued that the declining crime rate may be due to the passage and incremental implementation of the U.S. Crime Bill of 1994; Rosenfeld (2004) considers a number of additional hypotheses (changing demography, more aggressive police practices, abatement of the crack cocaine epidemic) and finds them all lacking to some degree. Looking at the violent crime rate separately, one sees an equivalent, although perhaps slightly less dramatic, decline since the early 1990s. Thus, at least since 1993 or 1994, all three indices show a decreasing crime trend.

Figure 6.2 displays trends in the *firearms* crime rate—the number of firearm crimes per 100,000 residents—and firearm crimes as a percentage of all violent incidents, from 1993 to 2005. These data depict declines since the mid-1990s, similar to those for the crime rates in Figure 6.1. Both the rate of firearms crimes and the percentage of firearm incidents among all violent crimes decline across this period. Like the violent crime, property crime, and index offense rates, there is a general downward trend in gun crime.

Intuitively, one might anticipate that public opinion on gun control issues, and crime issues more generally, would track this general decline in crime of all sorts. If, as Stinchcombe and colleagues suggested, increasing crime rates made people more punitive toward criminals, perhaps decreasing crime rates will have made them less punitive. Thus, from 1994 (or thereabouts) forward, one might expect declining fear of crime, declining support for capital punishment, muted demands to spend more to fight crime, and a diminished sense that the courts are too lenient on criminals. We test each of these hypotheses in turn, first for the U.S. adult population, then separately for men, women, whites, and nonwhites, since studies have consistently shown that gender and race are the most important demographic correlates of opinions about crime (e.g., Unnever and Cullen 2007; Cochran and Chamlin 2006; Ferraro 1995; Haynie 1998).

Public Opinion and Crime

Fear of Crime

Given the backdrop of declining crime rates, we turn now to trends in public opinion about crime and criminal justice issues to assess our general hypothesis that the decline in crime rates eventually has *some* noticeable effect on public opinion, perhaps with some lag as opinions catch up to reality. However, this logic assumes that views about crime and criminal justice are driven principally by the objective probabilities or perceived risks of becoming a crime victim, and there is precious little evidence in the literature to suggest that such is the case (Unnever, Cullen, and Fisher 2007; Stack 2003). Indeed, this is the precise "mismatch" that gave Stinchcombe and his colleagues the conclusion for *Crime and Punishment*. Are crime opinions and reality more closely "matched" now than they were then? If yes, what is the implication?

Table 6.2 and Figures 6.3 and 6.4 show the GSS trends in fear of crime or, more specifically, fear of walking around alone at night, which is usually interpreted as a fear of crime measure.[5] We examine the overall trend, then separate trends by gender and race. From 1972 to 2004, the percentage of respondents saying that there is somewhere "around here, that is, within a mile, where you would be afraid to walk alone at night" ranged from a high of 45% (1994) to a low of 30% (2004). Warr (1995, p. 297) reviewed this same time series through 1993 while the range of variation was even narrower, and concluded, "The most striking feature . . . is the relative constancy of fear during the past two decades." The constancy was particularly striking since real crime rates were in fact consistently increasing up to the early 1990s.

In contrast to Warr's conclusion about relative constancy, there has been a definite *decline* in fear from a 1994 peak, evident for both men and women (and for both blacks and whites). Visual inspection of Figures 6.3 and 6.4 strongly suggests that declining fear is a lagged reaction to declining real

Table 6.2. Mean GSS Respondent Views on Fear of Crime and Crime Spending in the United States, 1970s–2000s

Respondent view	1970s	1980s	1990s	2000s	Overall
Fear of crime—total	**42.17** (0.83)[a]	40.00 (0.99)	41.38 (0.99)	**33.50**[b] (1.76)	39.57 (0.86)
Males	21.80 (0.72)	19.53 (1.18)	24.65 (1.58)	21.60 (0.88)	21.82 (0.75)
Females	**60.57** (0.99)	56.54 (1.03)	55.40 (1.27)	**44.95** (2.43)	54.78 (1.31)
Whites	40.65 (1.00)	38.11 (1.07)	39.23 (0.90)	**31.25** (2.12)	37.61 (0.92)
Blacks	54.97 (3.24)	54.90 (1.78)	51.98 (2.00)	**41.00** (0.61)	51.43 (1.51)
Too little spending on halting rising crime—total	69.40 (0.54)	71.10 (1.21)	70.53 (1.96)	**59.30** (0.99)	68.67 (1.05)
Males	67.62 (0.62)	67.70 (1.58)	66.22 (2.30)	**53.87** (1.66)	65.11 (1.28)
Females	70.97 (0.80)	74.21 (0.97)	74.18 (2.03)	**63.95** (0.85)	71.78 (0.96)
Whites	68.93 (0.57)	70.39 (1.18)	69.35 (2.05)	57.22 (1.20)	67.68 (1.14)
Blacks	73.22 (1.08)	77.56 (2.32)	77.85 (1.78)	73.78 (2.20)	75.98 (1.08)
Too little spending on law enforcement—total	—	58.87 (1.38)	59.37 (1.31)	**52.42** (1.58)	56.69 (1.03)
Males	—	52.68 (1.34)	55.85 (1.47)	**48.02** (1.59)	52.71 (1.11)
Females	—	59.87 (1.69)	62.38 (1.36)	56.25 (1.63)	59.91 (1.05)
Whites	—	56.47 (1.43)	59.00 (1.58)	**51.95** (1.71)	56.29 (1.10)
Blacks	—	64.50 (2.64)	64.10 (1.76)	60.77 (2.88)	63.42 (1.35)

[a]Numbers in parentheses are standard errors. The results indicate the percentage of respondents expressing the indicated view, based on weighted data; weighting procedures are discussed in note 5. No results are reported for the question on law enforcement spending in the 1970s as that question was first asked in 1984.
[b]Numbers in bold represent significant differences between the indicated time period and the mean for the overall period, based on difference of means tests, at $p < .05$ or better. For example, the mean percentage of females expressing fear of crime during the 1970s (60.57) is significantly different from the overall mean percentage of females fearing crime across the period of analysis (54.78)

crime rates. This is perhaps the strongest evidence anywhere in the literature that "fear of crime" has much to do with actual crime rates or that actual crime trends might have some influence on public thinking about crime, and is thus a signal result. Crime and fear of crime might have some actual relationship after all!

But note too, the time series spiked in 1994, coincident with crime rates starting to fall. We have no ready-to-hand explanation for the 1994 spike, but some of the subsequent decline must be regression to more typical levels. Note also that the falloff in fear since 1994 is by no means as dramatic as the falloff in real crime. But these points granted, it does at least appear that lower crime rates are associated with some decline in fear of crime.

It is also obvious that the link between real crime and fear of crime cannot be *very* strong or *very* direct, whatever the recent trends. Nearly every "fear of crime" study has noted the paradox that while men are far more likely than

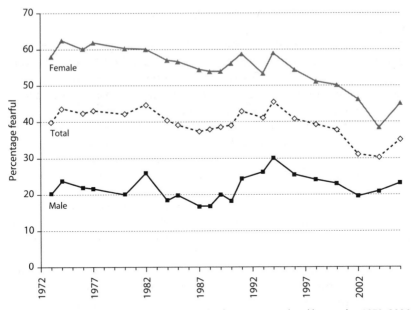

Figure 6.3. Percentage of GSS respondents who fear crime, total and by gender, 1972–2006.

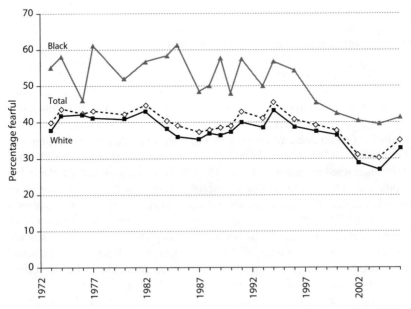

Figure 6.4. Percentage of GSS respondents who fear crime, total and by race, 1972–2006.

women to be actual victims of crime, women express more fear (Bachman, Dillaway, and Lachs 1998; Parker, McMorris, Smith, and Murty 1993; Dowler 2003, Rountree and Land 1996; Stanko 1995). Generally speaking, women are 40 points more fearful than men, year after year, and this has not changed in the past 30 years (Figure 6.3). So while some portion of fear might be attributable to real crime risks, another and perhaps larger portion is a gendered trait, possibly a consequence of gender socialization, not a stimulus-response-style reaction to true crime or actual victimization risks.

The gender differences in fear sharply contrast with racial differences (Figure 6.4), which are also clear and reasonably consistent over time, but do reflect empirical differences in victimization risk. Nonwhites are more fearful than whites, presumably because nonwhites live in more crime-riddled and thus more fear-engendering neighborhoods (May and Dunaway 2000; Chiricos, Hogan, and Gertz 1997; Ferraro 1995; Hale 1996). There is also an interesting race–gender interaction (data not shown): white women are by far the most fearful (but also by far the least likely to be actual victims). These differences in fear by gender and race are generally stronger than any relationship between fear and actual victimization or trends in real crime. Note finally that all groups—men, women, nonwhites, whites, and the overall U.S. population—show some falloff in fear levels after 1994 that continues through to 2004, with some reversal of the downward trend evident in 2006. Thus, while the race and gender groups' fear levels start at different points, those trends over time are similar. All groups register unmistakable and very similar declines in fear from 1994 to 2004. The decline in fear in general and across all groups at precisely the time when national crime rates were plummeting is the strongest evidence yet that fear of crime responds in some (obviously complicated) way to actual crime trends.

Crime as an Important National Problem

With regard to crime as a major national problem, Stinchcombe and associates remarked at some length on an apparent upsurge of people after 1969 naming crime or crime-like things as the "most important national problem" in a series of Gallup polls, an upsurge that seemed to be an obvious response to the then-recent "great surge in crime." Some years ago, Hamilton and Wright (1986) examined several decades worth of Gallup and other poll data on what people see as the leading national problems. They reported that responses to these kinds of items depend heavily on method and cuing effects. If one asks people to pick the most important problem from a preset list, the pattern of responses is different than if the question is completely open-ended (as in the Gallup version). Even if the question is left open-ended, responses are sensitive to question context: asking it right after six questions about the local crime problem will cause crime to come up higher on the list.

The open-ended "most important problem" question is asked as the initial question in the Gallup interview, thus avoiding the cuing effects of embedding the item inside other sequences. The series based on this item is hence least subject to extraneous effects and most comparable over time. The majority, and usually the large majority, of Americans always cite some aspect of the economy as the most important problem facing the nation. Crime and issues related to crime (e.g., drugs, juvenile delinquency) are never very high on the list of concerns. Indeed, even in Stinchcombe et al.'s "surge years" (1966–1973), the percentage of persons mentioning crime and like things as the most important problem was never higher than 7.2%. To quote Warr's (1995, p. 300) review of the same material, "[C]rime is rarely ranked as the major problem facing the country, an honor that is ordinarily reserved for economic issues." There are some exceptions to this general rule, but not many.

The GSS series on whether too little, too much, or just the right amount is being spent to "halt the rising crime rate" is another often-studied and much more tractable time series measuring the salience of crime in the public mind. As an aside of some significance, the GSS has continued to ask this question even though the crime rate was not actually "rising" between 1994 and 2004. Perhaps in anticipation of this problem, an alternative question was posed beginning in 1984 about whether too much, too little, or just the right amount was being spent on "law enforcement."

In most years, large majorities ranging upward from 65% think "too little" is being spent to "fight rising crime," and hardly anyone thinks that "too much" is. The percentage indicating that too little was being spent began just below 70% in 1973 (Figure 6.5). In the early part of the period, it increased, although erratically: the series rose through 1982, then dropped precipitously until 1985, at which point it resumed its upward climb. It peaked at 78% in 1994 and declined thereafter until 2002, at which point it was under 60%. Table 6.2 shows the decade-based averages: in no decade was the percentage "too little" significantly different from the overall mean except for the 2000s, when it is significantly lower than the overall series average. We also considered whether this trend was observed post-1994 when the crime rate decrease began. A significantly lower percentage of respondents felt that crime spending was too low in the years after 1994. Although hardly dramatic, these trends constitute some evidence that demands to spend more to "halt the rising crime rate" abate when the crime rate is not empirically rising. Note again the spike in 1994 but also the clear falloff since then. Even with allowances for regression toward the mean, the fraction of persons believing that too little is being spent to "halt the rising crime rate" is clearly declining, apparently in response to the falling crime rate.

The trends in opinions about spending on "law enforcement" are more erratic (Figure 6.5), with peaks in the view that the United States is "spending too little" on this in 1989 and 1994, a clear decline from 1994 to 2002, and increases since. Evidently, the stimuli "halt the rising crime rate" and "law enforcement" evoke different responses. One plausible (although entirely ad hoc) possibility is that the post-2002 upward trend on "law enforcement"

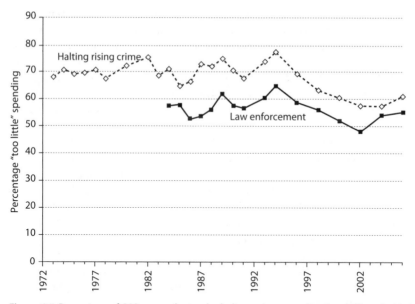

Figure 6.5. Percentage of GSS respondents who believe crime spending "too little on halting the rising crime rate" and "too little on law enforcement," 1972–2006.

taps general security concerns secondary to the events of September 11, 2001, whereas the long-term downward trend on spending for "halting the rising crime rate" reflects declining anxieties about garden-variety crime.

Note finally that women are more likely than men, and blacks more likely than whites, to think that too little is being spent both to halt the rising crime rate and on law enforcement (see Table 6.2). The relative differences among these groups are largely constant over the period studied here, so all groups show essentially equivalent trends.

Sometime shortly after 2004, firearm crime rates began to increase once again and have generally increased since that time (see Figure 6.2). So after a decade when crime rates were not increasing, the GSS core question about spending "to halt the rising crime rate" is again pertinent. Our guess is that as long as the GSS keeps asking about "the rising crime rate," a fair number of people will keep saying that not enough money is being spent to halt it, regardless of what the actual crime rate is doing, especially among that presumably broad swath of the public that has no objective idea what has been happening recently in the Uniform Crime Report (UCR) or the crime victimization surveys. One Canadian study found that even when presented with conflicting statements on whether crime was getting worse or not, 90% of those polled believed that crime had increased (Focus Canada 1998, as cited in Roberts et al. 2003). Roberts and colleagues (2003) argue that these misperceptions of the crime problem result in public demands for punitive criminal justice policies and a justice system that reacts to pressure from elected officials trying to appease their constituents, exactly the same argument advanced in *Crime and Punishment* nearly 30 years ago.

Are the Courts Too Harsh or Not Harsh Enough?

"Getting tough" or "cracking down" on things one does not like (such as crime, drugs, premarital sex, welfare recipients, the homeless) is a cost-free way to register one's rage in a survey context, and questions of the general form, "Should we get tough on X?" or "Should we crack down on Y?" always elicit large YES majorities. True to form, when GSS respondents are asked whether "the courts in this area deal too harshly or not harshly enough with criminals," large majorities consistently state, "Not harshly enough." Since 1972, the majority saying "not harshly enough" has never fallen below 60% and is usually well more than 70%. Clearly, the people want the courts to Get Tough!

That said, the recent trend in punitiveness has been sharply and unmistakably downward (Figure 6.6), beginning once again in 1994. In 1994, 89% of U.S. adults thought the courts were not harsh enough, and that number has fallen steadily to 68% in the 2006 survey, the smallest majority on record. Here, then, is apparently another example where falling real crime rates have softened the public's views on crime and criminals.

Figure 6.6. Percentage of GSS respondents who believe that courts are not harsh enough on criminal defendants, total and by gender, 1972–2006.

It is a virtual certainty that when people say the courts are "not harsh enough," they are expressing a general opinion that criminals deserve the harshest possible treatment, not an informed opinion that the actual sentencing practices of local area courts and judges are somehow deficient. Many commentators on the "not harsh enough" majority (e.g., Gaubatz 1995) have wondered just what comparison standard people have in mind when they say that courts need to be harsher than they are, considering that American sentencing standards are harsher than those to be found in practically any other Western nation. The U.S. jails proportionally more of its people for longer periods of time than almost any other advanced society, South Africa being about the only exception (Walmsley 2003). Moreover, while sentencing policies have changed over time to include more and more mandatory sentences, the widespread perception that courts are not harsh enough has remained (Roberts et al. 2003).

We examine the recent trends more closely in Table 6.3 and Figure 6.6, with data again shown separately for men, women, whites, and nonwhites. The percentage of respondents thinking that the courts are too lenient

Table 6.3. GSS Respondent Views on Treatment of Criminal Defendants, and Support for Capital Punishment, 1970s–2000s

Respondent view	1970s	1980s	1990s	2000s	Overall
Courts not harsh enough—total	83.77 (21.12)[a]	87.45[b] (0.66)	84.80 (1.26)	71.07 (2.34)	83.33 (1.28)
Males	83.94 (2.20)	85.48 (0.95)	83.00 (1.50)	67.77 (1.38)	81.77 (1.42)
Females	83.61 (2.09)	89.20 (0.69)	86.37 (1.09)	74.07 (1.73)	84.71 (1.21)
Whites	84.86 (1.81)	88.34 (0.71)	85.90 (1.12)	73.17 (1.30)	84.51 (1.17)
Blacks	77.03 (3.66)	80.52 (1.90)	79.37 (1.26)	63.78 (2.43)	76.74 (1.66)
Support for capital punishment—total	68.64 (1.40)	76.32 (0.78)	77.28 (0.92)	69.22 (0.31)	73.78 (0.91)
Males	74.52 (1.48)	81.25 (0.75)	81.33 (0.69)	74.62 (0.61)	79.77 (0.80)
Females	63.40 (1.46)	72.24 (0.98)	73.82 (1.29)	64.35 (0.62)	69.48 (1.07)
Whites	71.56 (1.35)	79.79 (0.72)	80.88 (0.73)	74.10 (0.73)	77.40 (0.89)
Blacks	41.84 (1.58)	50.42 (1.61)	56.45 (1.96)	43.42 (0.86)	48.97 (1.40)
White males	77.58 (1.64)	84.77 (0.74)	84.48 (0.64)	79.37 (0.56)	82.30 (0.78)
White females	66.30 (1.41)	75.53 (0.90)	77.62 (0.99)	69.22 (1.22)	73.08 (1.05)
Black males	44.94 (2.42)	51.38 (1.95)	61.72 (2.90)	48.30 (1.21)	52.11 (1.67)
Black females	39.64 (2.50)	49.59 (2.67)	52.70 (1.66)	40.25 (0.62)	46.74 (1.61)

[a]Numbers in parentheses are standard errors. The results indicate the percentage of respondents expressing the indicated view, based on weighted data; weighting procedures are discussed in note 5.

[b]Numbers in bold represent significant differences between the indicated time period and the mean for the overall period, based on difference of means tests, at $p < .05$ or better.

increased for both men and women from around 75% in 1972 to over 90% in 1978, varied erratically within a narrow band from 1978 to 1994, and then plummeted from 1994 to the end of the time series, ending at just about 70% for females and approximately 65% for males. From 1972 to about 1982, the gender difference in the percentage feeling that the courts are not harsh enough was insignificant, but in most years since 1982, women have been more likely than men to hold this view. In 2004, the proportion of men thinking the courts are not harsh enough was about 67% versus 72% for women, a small but generally consistent difference. There is also a consistent racial gradient, with whites 6 to 10 percentage points more likely than nonwhites to believe that the courts are not harsh enough (Table 6.3).

Capital Punishment

Stinchcombe and associates (1980) pointed out that support for capital punishment and the feeling that the courts were not harsh enough were fairly strongly correlated and could be taken as two indicators of relative punitiveness. (In the 1974 GSS, the two items were correlated at a robust .305, but by 2004 the correlation had declined to .155—significant but certainly not as strong as in the earlier years.) They concluded, "The overall impression from these two rather spotty time series—attitudes on capital punishment and on the courts—is that increased salience of crime is associated with increased punitiveness in the most recent years. Increased salience has homogenized the white population behind a law-and-order position" (p. 32).

Certainly the harshest punishment that the courts can mete out is the death penalty. What the public does or does not believe about capital punishment is among the more widely researched and hotly debated topics in this area of public opinion research (Radelet and Borg 2000; Lifton and Mitchell 2000). Since 1974, the GSS capital punishment question has been asked: "Do you favor or oppose the death penalty for persons convicted of murder?" Large majorities ranging from 64% (1975) to 80% (1985) favor it (Figure 6.7). Since 1994, the pro–death penalty percentage has declined slightly (Figure 6.7), from 79% down to 74% (1998), then 69.6%, 69.8%, and 68.4% (in 2000, 2002, and 2004, respectively). The recent trend is not dramatic but is in the general direction of increasing doubts about the viability of the death penalty in the United States. Whether this "increasing doubt" is a response to falling crime rates is, of course, a separate matter, but that is at least a viable hypothesis; the recent trend, while muted, is again consistent with the view that declining crime has softened the public mood about crime.

The Gallup organization's version of the capital punishment question states, "Are you in favor of the death penalty for persons convicted of murder?"[6] The Gallup series extends back to 1953. In 1966, 42% of respondents said they favored it and 47% were opposed to the death penalty; the 1966 survey is the only one conducted in the last half century where a plurality opposed capital punishment (see Warr 1995; M. D. Smith and Wright 1992).

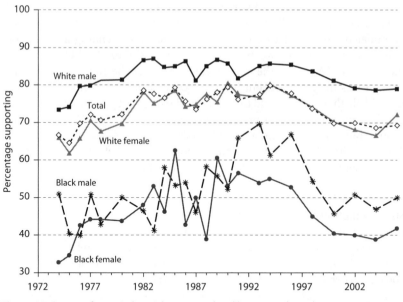

Figure 6.7. Support for capital punishment, total and by race and gender, 1972–2006.

Figure 6.7 and Table 6.3 show trends in capital punishment attitudes over three decades with breakdowns by gender and race. These patterns generally persist throughout the time series. Consistent with all previous studies, blacks are less supportive of the death penalty than whites by about 30 points and women less supportive than men by about 10 points. The elevated fear of crime among women clearly does not predispose them to be more supportive of the death penalty, contrary to what might be expected.

Moreover, the difference between males and females in their relative support of the death penalty varies for whites and blacks (Figure 6.7 and Table 6.3). Among whites, the gap between male and female support is relatively uniform, but support declined among both men and women after 1994. White male support for the death penalty declined by 6% from 1996 to 2006, while white female support declined by 5% during the same period. The shift among whites of both genders is consistent with the drop in the overall crime. Black male and female support levels, on the other hand, moved in somewhat opposite and erratic directions. There was little gender difference among blacks until about 1990; after that, the level of support that black males expressed became closer to that among whites and, thus, substantially more distant from the views of black females. Note also that white and black women came to express somewhat more similar support levels toward the end of the period.

It has been said that support for capital punishment is a mile wide and an inch deep. Large majorities favor the death penalty *in principle*, but equally large majorities oppose its application in all but the most heinous crimes. Publicity surrounding the Timothy McVeigh execution pointed out that at least some people who said they favored the death penalty in the abstract also said that McVeigh should have gotten life without parole instead of death. If McVeigh—convicted of the wanton and remorseless slaughter of 168 people including 19 small children in what was until September 11 the deadliest act of terrorism ever committed on U.S. soil—did not deserve the death penalty, then who would?

Guns, Gun Ownership, and Gun Control

Many people naturally connect guns and gun control with the crime domain since many crimes are committed with guns and (or so it is commonly assumed) many people possess guns for self-defense against crime. *Crime and Punishment* devotes an entire chapter to the question. The first question on gun ownership in a national survey was asked in a 1959 Gallup poll: just over one-half of all respondents affirmed that there was at least one firearm in their home. The 1973 GSS showed that 47.3% of U.S. households kept "guns or revolvers" in their homes (Wright and Marston 1975). Thus, in the 1970s, it was safe to conclude that about one-half of all U.S. households possessed one or more firearms.

Table 6.4 shows trends in the percentages of adults, males, and unmarried females who report that there is a gun in the home. As indicated, there is a marked gap between men and women, with males reporting a higher percentage of household gun ownership than unmarried females. Since the question seems to ask about *household* ownership, not *personal* ownership, there should not be much difference between men and women, and certainly not much between married men and married women.[7] But there is: men (even married men) are consistently more likely to say there is a gun in the house than are women (even married women), and, if anything, this gap has widened over the decades.[8] Entire articles have been written on this topic with no certain resolution (Coyne-Beasley, Baccaglini, Johnson, Webster, and Wiebe 2005; Trent, VanCourt, and Kim 1999; Ludwig, Cook, and Smith 1998). Some evidence indicates that some married women are simply unaware of guns kept in the home, car, or garage by their husbands; another possibility is that women are relatively more "embarrassed" by gun ownership than men and therefore less likely to report it; a third possibility is that women misinterpret the question as asking about their personal ownership of a gun and therefore fail to report guns possessed by males in the household. Whatever the reason, the higher reported rate of household gun ownership among men is a consistent pattern through all years of our analysis.

From 1973 to 1991, the percentage of respondents admitting household gun ownership in the GSS was never less than 40% or more than 51% (Figure 6.8).

Table 6.4. GSS Respondent Rates of Gun Ownership, Presence of a Hunter in Household, and Support for Gun Permits, 1970s–2000s

Respondent view	1970s	1980s	1990s	2000s	Overall
Gun owner in household—total	**48.10** (0.93)[a]	**45.28**[b] (0.88)	40.30 (1.14)	**33.95** (0.50)	42.24 (1.18)
Reported by married males	57.95 (1.31)	**58.96** (0.55)	55.13 (1.80)	**48.47** (2.89)	55.68 (1.30)
Reported by married females	54.95 (1.02)	**55.24** (0.81)	49.43 (1.16)	**40.70** (1.19)	50.75 (1.72)
Reported by unmarried males	45.42 (2.45)	47.76 (2.26)	43.11 (1.95)	**35.33** (1.62)	43.62 (1.42)
Reported by unmarried females	25.97 (3.58)	27.17 (3.51)	22.50 (0.94)	**17.75** (0.64)	23.81 (1.51)
No hunter in household	36.40 (—)	**33.01** (0.64)	29.40 (0.99)	**24.75** (0.36)	30.16 (0.83)
Hunter in household	85.40 (—)	84.80 (1.19)	83.15 (1.04)	77.95 (1.59)	82.76 (0.91)
Hunter in household— total	29.20 (—)	23.78 (0.81)	20.33 (0.59)	**17.45** (0.59)	21.53 (0.83)
Support gun permits— total	73.77 (0.69)	73.67 (1.26)	**81.40** (0.66)	**80.90** (0.16)	76.97 (0.90)
Males	**65.63** (0.81)	**66.26** (1.10)	**74.45** (1.01)	74.35 (1.06)	69.64 (1.01)
Females	81.43 (0.85)	**79.44** (1.33)	**87.25** (0.37)	**87.00** (0.73)	83.31 (0.87)
Whites	**65.63** (0.81)	72.43 (1.28)	**80.35** (0.68)	79.12 (0.23)	73.89 (1.32)
Blacks	81.43 (0.85)	**80.58** (0.47)	84.48 (1.11)	**86.27** (0.90)	82.81 (0.61)

[a]Numbers in parentheses are standard errors. The results indicate the percentage of respondents expressing the indicated view, based on weighted data; weighting procedures are discussed in note 5. No standard error is reported for the rates of hunters living in the respondent's household or gun ownership rates by hunters and nonhunters as those questions were asked only once during the 1970s (in 1977).

[b]Numbers in bold represent significant differences between the indicated time period and the mean for the overall period, based on difference of means tests, at $p < .05$ or better.

In the early 1990s, however, the time series tilted downward, and the gun-owning fraction has now declined to about a third of all households. Gun ownership declines substantially when reported by both men and women across that period. Among males, the 1970s average percentage owning a gun was 54%; by the 2000s, the percentage had dropped significantly to 42% (Table 6.4). The mean ownership rate reported by unmarried women dropped slightly more than 7 percentage points (from 22% to 15%) across these same decades.

Is the decline in gun ownership shown here yet another consequence of falling crime rates and softening attitudes about crime and punishment? Probably not. First, it is clear that reported gun ownership began to decline in 1991, several years before the crime rates began to fall. More significantly,

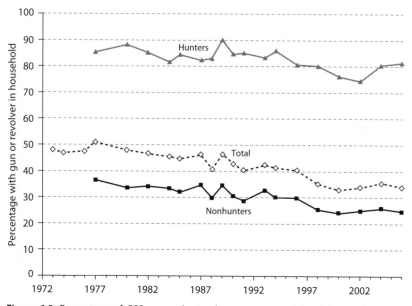

Figure 6.8. Percentage of GSS respondents who own guns, total and by involvement in hunting, 1972–2006.

it has been known for more than 25 years that at least three-quarters of all firearms in America are owned principally for sport and recreational reasons, not in response to or for defense against crime (see Wright, Rossi, and Daly 1983). It would be strange indeed if softening attitudes about crime were somehow responsible for the gun ownership trend.

The only direct evidence in the GSS on what people do with their guns is a question about whether the respondent or the respondent's spouse hunts. As shown in Table 6.4, the fraction of hunters has dropped off quite considerably over the years, from almost a third in the early years of the GSS to fewer than 20% in the 2000s. The gun sports magazines have noted this same trend with some alarm. So it is not just the GSS that has registered the declining popularity of hunting.

Figure 6.8 shows gun ownership trends separately for self-described hunters and nonhunters. Predictably, hunters are much more likely to own guns than nonhunters. The ownership gap between hunters and nonhunters averages around 50 percentage points across the years. However, the cross-time averages are telling: among nonhunters, the mean gun ownership rate declined from near 40% in 1977 to under 30% by 2006, ending up nearly 13 percentage points lower than where the series began. Hunters also reported a diminished rate of gun ownership, but their decline was on the order of only 2 to 3 percentage points across the period. These results make it clear that declining interest in hunting is partly responsible for the declining rate of reported gun ownership, not falling crime rates. Additional analyses (not reported here) suggest that the increasing percentage of female-headed households accounts for most of the rest of the long-term household gun ownership trend.

Gun Control

When Stinchcombe et al. were writing *Crime and Punishment*, the public had recently become more likely to endorse harsher treatment of criminals and it seemed reasonable, therefore, to expect them to have become more supportive of gun control as well. But on the two measures then available (whether respondents favor or oppose requiring a police permit to buy a gun, and whether they support or oppose registration of new gun sales), there was in fact no discernible trend: majorities of about 75% endorsed both measures, and that fraction had been essentially constant as far back as opinion data were collected and reported.

Figures 6.9 and 6.10 and Table 6.4 display findings on the question of whether a gun owner should be required to obtain a police permit in order to purchase a weapon, both for the total sample and separately for men, women,

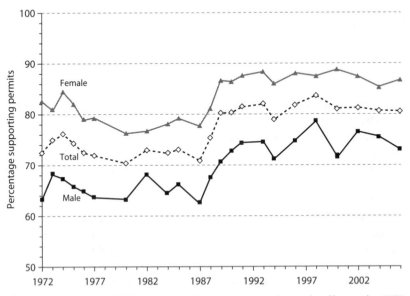

Figure 6.9. Percentage of GSS respondents favoring gun permits, total and by gender, 1972–2006.

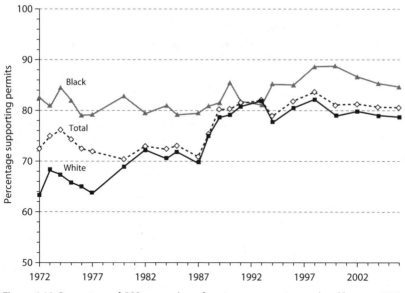

Figure 6.10. Percentage of GSS respondents favoring gun permits, total and by race, 1972–2006.

whites, and nonwhites. Women and nonwhites are generally more favorable to the idea of police permits than are men and whites. After 1987 both series trend positively, with the male series more erratic than the female series. Women expressed a relatively stable level of support for requiring gun permits after 1987; their 1990s and 2000s averages, however, were significantly higher than the overall mean for the 1972–2006 period. The aggregate level of support among women increased only marginally from 1972 (83%) to 2006 (87%); males, on the other hand, shifted their aggregate level of support from 63% to 73% across this same period, with a significant increase during the last two decades. Thus, the male–female gap narrowed substantially through time.

Figure 6.10 displays trends in support of gun permits for whites and non-whites. Nonwhites were more favorable toward gun permits than whites across all years. Both whites and nonwhites showed increased support after 1987, peaking in 1998 with an overall 84% in support of gun permits. However, after 1987 support for gun permits increased somewhat among nonwhites and simultaneously increased dramatically for whites. The white–nonwhite gap was substantially narrower at the end than at the beginning of the period.

Interpreting "gun control" questions is often problematic since much depends on wording and context. More than 30 years ago, Cook and Blose

(1981) pointed out an obvious problem with the "police permit" question. Their calculations suggested that about three-quarters of the U.S. population already lived in jurisdictions that required purchasers to obtain a police permit in order to buy a gun. The authors suggested, and to our knowledge no one has yet argued otherwise, that many people who endorsed the item were not endorsing some new, more restrictive firearms law but simply endorsing their status quo ante. So while it is true, for example, that majorities on the order of 3 in 4 favor a police permit in order to buy a gun, majorities on the order of 9 in 10 also believe they have a right to own guns and that the Constitution guarantees them that right (Wright 1981). Nevertheless, examining changes over time for questions such as these remains informative.

Political Ideology and Attitudes about Crime

American views on most matters of civil liberties, race, and other so-called social issues continue to liberalize (Bolzendahl and Myers 2004; Yang 1997). A question taken up at length in the Stinchcombe et al. volume is whether political ideology (what they call subscription to the Enlightenment tradition) accounts for views about crime or relative punitiveness toward criminals. Their conclusion was that it does not. Our version of the question is whether changing political and ideological views, rather than, say, falling crime rates, can account for the crime opinion trends we have documented. And that answer is also no.

Stinchcombe and associates (1980) develop several measures of political ideology (including a civil liberties scale, a racial attitudes scale, and others) and correlate each of them with crime attitudes. The resulting correlations are usually somewhere in the .10 to .15 range—that is, large enough to be statistically significant, but not large enough to be interesting or theoretically meaningful. Moreover, "even the slight relationship between punitiveness and liberalism seems to be due mostly to a very few extreme liberals"—that is, to a handful of people who give liberal responses to every question asked, who also support more lenient treatment of criminals and oppose capital punishment. Taking out this tiny group (a few percent at most) causes the remainder of the relationship to disappear. Creating similar scales in the 2000-era GSS surveys yields the same general result when they are correlated with the crime questions: a small and uninteresting increase in leniency toward criminals with increasing political liberalism (data not shown).

Most people, we think, do not frame questions about crime in terms of some larger political philosophy or coherent ideology. For most people, the GSS crime questions are viewed as pragmatic or simple moral issues. When people say the courts need to toughen up on crime, it is not because they are compelled to this conclusion by virtue of their political views but because they believe, rightly or wrongly, that tougher courts would produce less crime and fewer criminals. When they say they support the death penalty, they are not enunciating their enthusiasm for political conservatism but rather their conviction that some crimes are so heinous that death is the only equitable punishment.

Discussion and Conclusion

Stinchcombe and his associates concluded *Crime and Punishment* with a nuanced and evocative discussion of *attribution* and *salience* and argued that the opinion questions available for analysis could not capture subtleties involving these factors. Consider the GSS capital punishment question: "Do you favor or oppose the death penalty for persons convicted of murder?" The *attribution* process that defines the "average murderer" as a jealous husband defending his rights of sexual exclusivity to his wife might lead one to a firm NO response. The process that defines the "average murderer" as a drug-addled homicidal psychopath would lead to quite a different response. Over the years, the capital punishment question has been asked time and time again, but we have yet to systematically explore what attributions the average respondent makes to the phrase "persons convicted of murder." Absent this "rich map of the cognitive content of these attitudes, our trends go in one direction and our correlations in another" (Stinchcombe et al. 1980, p. 143). It is unfortunate that more attention has not been paid to this admonition!

Salience, Stinchcombe et al. argued, is "the central variable in this book" (p. 144) and likewise, at least in part, the central variable in this chapter. The "great surge of crime" had increased the salience of the crime problem, and as the authors so aptly put it, much sociological theorizing at the time predicted that if salience and the consequent strain increase, "*something* will happen" (p. 145). Just what would happen was less clear, but increasingly punitive views about crime and criminals were taken as the likeliest response. The argument advanced here is just the obverse: as crime declines, the salience of the crime problem likewise decreases, and in consequence, attitudes toward crime and criminals soften. In this sense, the work reported here confirms the central thesis of *Crime and Punishment*.

Granted, our findings are somewhat mixed. Many of the questions we have analyzed show significant trends over time that are consistent with the "central thesis." A few questions have remained more or less constant; and in a few more cases, the time series seems to change somewhat erratically. In some important cases (fear of crime, courts too harsh, whether too much or too little is being spent on crime), the trends mirror the absolute declines in crime rates registered in the 1990s and early 2000s, but in the other cases examined (gun ownership and gun permits), the data show no such trend. But we have argued that these latter questions have very little to do with attitudes about crime in any case. So if the question is whether public opinion about the crime problem responds to objective changes in the crime rate, the answer must be "yes" in most cases, but "maybe not" in a few cases.

Many trends that we have examined might reflect large-scale societal changes other than those in crime rates. Average levels of education have increased, ethnic heterogeneity has grown, female-headed households have become more numerous, suburbanization has accelerated, and so on. We have not systematically analyzed any of these factors but recommend them to the attention of future researchers.

For reasons that no one has quite determined, the American crime rate declined substantially in the early to middle 1990s and continued to decline for the subsequent decade, reaching 40-year lows. The decline in violent crime, the kind of crime that people fear most, has been especially dramatic. Although entire books have now been written on the decline, the exact explanation has yet to be isolated. Rosenfeld (2004) reviews a half dozen theories and finds all of them wanting to some degree.

As interesting as the causes of the decline might be, its possible effects are just as intriguing. Students of public opinion and crime have grown accustomed over the years to believing that public thinking about the crime problem has relatively little to do with actual crime; rather than crime itself, media depictions of the crime problem, various local circumstances and issues, a more general political philosophy, or sheer racial bigotry are thought to shape the contours of public views about crime (see, e.g., Unnever et al. 2007).

This chapter has presented some interesting data, one plausible interpretation of which is that public views about the crime problem have altered, at least somewhat, because real crime is just not the problem it was one or two decades ago. Obviously, we cannot prove this causal relationship: but since the crime rate began to decline, fear of crime has waned, the proportion believing that too little is being spent to halt crime has fallen, support for capital punishment has dropped off among some groups, and the number of people thinking that the courts are not harsh enough on criminals has ebbed. It is hard to believe that the simultaneous change in all these time series is purely coincidental or that the falling real crime rates have had nothing to do with these opinion trends.

But then again, we have also seen some increase in public support for a law that would require people to obtain a police permit in order to buy a gun; while it might also seem logical that this too is somehow linked to the falling crime rate, we have argued that it is not. Our analysis implies that increasing support for the police permit concept is mainly the result of the increasing proportion of U.S. households that do not possess a gun. And that trend too, it appears, has less to do with falling crime rates than with (at least in substantial part) declining interest in hunting (and possibly the increase in female-headed households). Once these factors are taken into account, there is very little left in the gun ownership trend for anything else to explain.

Stinchcombe and associates argued a quarter century ago that increased crime would add to the salience of the crime problem, and that the inability of "the system" to fix the problem might lead to public distrust and a search for other possibly extralegal "solutions" such as vigilantism and like movements. Certainly the years in which crime was getting worse were also years in which "crime" was turned into a potent political symbol, one that awakened some fairly unattractive passions. Does the name Willie Horton ring any bells anymore? How about Bernhard Goetz? That these names no longer have much salience, indeed that no similar political symbols from the new millennium can even be cited, may be the most compelling evidence yet that public views on crime have softened.[9] So far as we can remember, no one alleged in the 2000, 2004, or 2008 presidential campaigns that the Democratic candidates were "soft on crime," although this was a staple theme in presidential elections from 1968 through to the end of the 1990s.

Men and women differ pretty consistently in their views of crime and criminal justice issues, as do blacks and whites. These race and gender differences tend to be substantially constant over the decades, although in some cases (especially attitudes about capital punishment) the trends differ by race and gender. One example is that black males have become more supportive of the death penalty than they were in the past, moving away from the low support rate among black females and closer to the levels of support among whites, males and females alike.

To date, we have analyzed only three GSS surveys in the post-9/11 era. What effect increased international terrorism may have on public thinking about "crime" is yet to be determined. We have noted slight upticks in several of the time series in the most recent year we reviewed (2006); perhaps these are indicative of 9/11 effects. Then again, maybe they are just normal fluctuations in time series that do seem to change somewhat erratically from year to year. Unsure just what the effect of international terrorism might be on domestic attitudes about crime, we can at least take some comfort in knowing that 10 or 20 years hence, the GSS may well have accumulated enough data to infer an answer to that question.

Notes

1. For early evidence on the "liberalizing" trends, see Davis (1975), Taylor, Sheatsley, and Greeley (1978), T. W. Smith (1976)—all sources cited in *Crime and Punishment* (Stinchcombe et al. 1980, p. 83). For evidence that these trends have continued, see Davis (2001, 2004), Bolzendahl and Myers (2004), Yang (1997).

2. Although the "fear" question does not specifically reference crime as the source of fear, the question is widely interpreted as a "fear of crime" measure. See, e.g., Irving (2001), Warr (1995).

3. See note 1.

4. Index crimes are those tracked by the FBI and the U.S. Department of Justice. They are reported in the annual Uniform Crime Reports and include (among others) the major offenses of homicide, sexual assault, aggravated assault, and numerous property crimes. We obtained those data from the Bureau of Justice Statistics and the National Archive of Criminal Justice Data (http://www.ucrdatatool.gov/Search/Crime/State/StateCrime.cfm).

5. Our analyses of the GSS data employed the weights suggested by NORC. We used the weight WTSSALL for all years, and an additional weighting factor based on OVERSAMP to adjust for the oversampling of black respondents in 1982 and 1987 (see Davis and Smith 2006; Davis, Smith, and Marsden 2006). This produces nationally representative estimates for U.S. adults across the years. Our statistical approach was to calculate the percentages of each year's respondents who answered the various crime and crime-related questions in particular ways and then to compare each decade's mean annual percentage with the overall mean percentage for that question across the time series. Differences of means tests were used to determine whether the percentage in any one year differed significantly from the overall mean for that question. Because not all questions of interest to us were asked in all years, the number of observations for each decade varies, which is reflected in the reported standard errors shown in Tables 6.2–6.4 for each percentage in different decades.

6. The GSS included the Gallup version of the question in 1972 and 1973, registering 57% and 63% endorsement of the death penalty, respectively.

7. The exact question wording is marvelously ambiguous: "Do you happen to have in your home [or garage] any guns or revolvers?" The "you" implies personal ownership in the sense that it does not ask, "Do you, your spouse, or any other family members happen to have. . . ." But clearly, if the spouse keeps a firearm, the other spouse might be expected to say yes to a question whose second part specifies clearly "in your home. . . ." So it is not entirely clear whether the question measures individual or household gun possession. In most years since 1980, respondents answering yes are asked, "Do any of these guns personally belong to you?" Over all administrations, 61% of respondents say yes when asked about whether a gun in the household is theirs. So empirically, the question picks up more personal ownership than household ownership.

8. Across all GSS years, 55.7% of married men, but only 50.8% of married women, say that a gun or revolver is in their household. In the 1970s the difference between the average percentage of married men compared to married women owning a gun was 3.0%. By the 2000s, this difference had increased to 7.8%.

9. Willie Horton was a convicted Massachusetts murderer who, on a weekend furlough authorized by Democratic governor Michael Dukakis, raped a woman after pistol whipping and stabbing her fiancé, then stole the fiancé's car. Much was made of this incident in the 1988 presidential campaign that pitted Dukakis against George W. Bush. "Willie Horton" was a potent symbol of the Democrat's alleged "softness" on crime. Bernhard Goetz was dubbed the "Subway Vigilante" when, in 1984, he shot four men who were trying to rob him on the New York subway, an eerie instance of life imitating art (the "art" in this case being the 1974 Charles Bronson movie *Death Wish*). That Goetz more or less immediately became a folk hero was oft-cited evidence in the 1980s that the public was fed up with crime and prepared to end it by whatever means necessary.

References

Bachman, Ronet B., Heather Dillaway, and Mark Lachs. 1998. "Violence Against the Elderly: A Comparative Analysis of Robbery and Assault across Age and Gender Groups." *Research on Aging* 20:183–98.

Bolzendahl, Catherine I., and Daniel J. Myers. 2004. "Feminist Attitudes and Support for Gender Equality: Opinion Change in Women and Men, 1974–1998." *Social Forces* 83 (2): 759–89.

Chiricos, Ted, Michael Hogan, and Marc Gertz. 1997. "Racial Composition of Neighborhood and Fear of Crime." *Criminology* 35 (1): 107–31.

Cochran, John, and Mitchell B. Chamlin. 2006. "The Enduring Racial Divide in Death Penalty Support." *Journal of Criminal Justice* 34:85–99.

Cook, Phillip, and James Blose. 1981. "State Programs for Screening Handgun Buyers." *Annals of the American Academy of Political and Social Science* 455:80–91.

Coyne-Beasley, Tamera, Lorena Baccaglini, Renee M. Johnson, Briana Webster, and Douglas J. Wiebe. 2005. "Do Partners with Children Know about Firearms in Their Home? Evidence of a Gender Gap and Implications for Practitioners." *Pediatrics* 115:662–67.

Davis, James A. 1975. "Communism, Conformity, Cohorts, and Categories." *American Journal of Sociology* 81:491–513.

———. 2001. "Testing the Demographic Explanation of Attitude Trends: Secular Trends in Attitudes among US Householders, 1972–1996." *Social Science Research* 30:363–85.

———. 2004. "Did Growing Up in the 1960s Leave a Permanent Mark on Attitudes and Values? Evidence from the General Social Survey." *Public Opinion Quarterly* 68:161–83.

Davis, James A., and Tom W. Smith. 2006. *General Social Surveys, 1972–2006* [Machine-readable data file]. Chicago: NORC (producer). Storrs, CT: Roper Center for Public Opinion Research, University of Connecticut (distributor).

Davis, James A., Tom W. Smith, and Peter V. Marsden. 2006. *General Social Surveys, 1972–2006* [Cumulative file] (ICPSR 4697). Ann Arbor, MI: Inter-University Consortium for Political and Social Research. http://www.icpsr.umich.edu.

Dowler, Kenneth. 2003. "Media Consumption and Public Attitudes toward Crime and Justice: The Relationship between Fear of Crime, Punitive Attitudes, and Perceived Police Effectiveness." *Journal of Criminal Justice and Popular Culture* 10 (2): 109–26.

Ferraro, Kenneth F. 1995. *Fear of Crime: Interpreting Victimization Risk.* Albany: State University of New York Press.

Gaubatz, Kathlyn. 1995. *Crime in the Public Mind.* Ann Arbor: University of Michigan Press.

Hale, Chris. 1996. "Fear of Crime: A Review of the Literature." *International Review of Victimology* 4:79–150.

Hamilton, Richard F., and James D. Wright. 1986. *The State of the Masses.* Hawthorne, NY: Aldine.

Haynie, Dana L. 1998. "The Gender Gap in Fear of Crime, 1973–1994: A Methodological Approach." *Criminal Justice Review* 23 (1): 29–50.

Irving, Barrie. 2001. *Fear of Crime: Theory, Measurement, and Application*. London: Police Foundation of the United Kingdom.

Lanier, Drew Noble, and Tracy L. Dietz. 2012. "Time Dynamics of Elder Victimization: Evidence from the NCVS, 1992 to 2005." *Social Science Research* 41:444–63.

Lifton, Robert Jay, and Greg Mitchell. 2000. *Who Owns Death? Capital Punishment, the American Conscience, and the End of Executions*. New York: William Morrow.

Ludwig, Jens, Phillip J. Cook, and Tom W. Smith. 1998. "The Gender Gap in Reporting Household Gun Ownership." *American Journal of Public Health* 88:1715–18.

May, David C., and Gregory R. Dunaway. 2000. "Predictors of Fear of Criminal Victimization at School among Adolescents." *Sociological Spectrum* 20 (2): 149–68.

Parker, Keith, Barbara McMorris, Earl Smith, and Komanduri S. Murty. 1993. "Fear of Crime and the Likelihood of Victimization: A Bi-ethnic Comparison." *Journal of Social Psychology* 133:723–32.

Radelet, Michael L., and Marian J. Borg. 2000. "The Changing Nature of Death Penalty Debates." *Annual Review of Sociology* 26:43–61.

Roberts, Julian V., Loretta J. Stalans, David Indermaur, and Mike Hough. 2003. *Penal Populism and Public Opinion: Lessons from Five Countries*. New York: Oxford University Press.

Rosenfeld, Richard. 2004. "The Case of the Unsolved Crime Decline." *Scientific American* 290:82–89.

Rountree, Pamela Wilcox, and Kenneth C. Land. 1996. "Perceived Risk versus Fear of Crime: Empirical Evidence of Conceptually Different Reactions to Survey Data." *Social Forces* 74:1353–76.

Scammon, Richard, and Ben J. Wattenberg. 1970. *The Real Majority: An Extraordinary Examination of the American Electorate*. New York: Coward, McCann, and Geoghegan.

Smith, M. Dwayne, and James D. Wright. 1992. "Capital Punishment and Public Opinion in the Post-Furman Era: Trends and Analyses." *Sociological Spectrum* 12:127–44.

Smith, Tom W. 1976. "A Study of Trends in the Political Role of Women." In *Studies of Social Change since 1948*, edited by James A. Davis, 215–54. Chicago: National Opinion Research Center.

Stack, Steven. 2003. "Authoritarianism and Support for the Death Penalty: A Multivariate Analysis." *Sociological Inquiry* 66:267–84.

Stanko, Elizabeth A. 1995. "Women, Crime, and Fear." *Annals of the American Academy of Political and Social Science* 539:46–58.

Stinchcombe, Arthur L., Rebecca Adams, Carol A. Heimer, Kim L. Scheppele, Tom W. Smith, and D. Garth Taylor. 1980. *Crime and Punishment—Changing Attitudes in America*. San Francisco: Jossey-Bass.

Taylor, D. Garth, Paul B. Sheatsley, and Andrew M. Greeley. 1978. "Attitudes towards Racial Integration." *Scientific American* 238:42–49.

Trent, Roger B., Jason C. Van Court, and Allegra N. Kim. 1999. "Household Gun Ownership." *American Journal of Public Health* 89:1442.

Unnever, James D., and Francis T. Cullen. 2007. "Reassessing the Racial Divide in Support for Capital Punishment: The Continuing Significance of Race." *Journal of Research on Crime and Delinquency* 44:124–58.

Unnever, James D., Francis T. Cullen, and Bonnie S. Fisher. 2007. "'A Liberal Is Someone Who Has Not Been Mugged': Criminal Victimization and Political Beliefs." *Justice Quarterly* 24:309–34.

Walmsley, Roy. 2003. "Global Incarceration and Prison Trends." *Forum on Crime and Society* 3:65–78.

Warr, Mark. 1995. "Poll Trends: Public Opinion on Crime and Punishment." *Public Opinion Quarterly* 59:296–310.

Wright, James D. 1981. "Public Opinion and Gun Control: A Comparison of Results from Two Recent National Surveys." *Annals of the American Academy of Political and Social Science* 455:24–39.

Wright, James D., and Linda L. Marston. 1975. "The Ownership of the Means of Destruction: Weapons in the United States." *Social Problems* 23:93–107.

Wright, James D., Peter H. Rossi, and Kathleen M. Daly. 1983. *Under the Gun: Weapons, Crime, and Violence in America.* Hawthorne, NY: Aldine.

Yang, Alan S. 1997. "Trends: Attitudes toward Homosexuality." *Public Opinion Quarterly* 61:477–507.

Changes in Confidence and Connections

7

Trends in Confidence in Institutions, 1973–2006

Tom W. Smith

On July 15, 1979, in what became known as his "malaise" speech, President Jimmy Carter spoke of "a crisis of confidence . . . that strikes at the very heart and soul and spirit of our national will." Many scholars have picked up his refrain and extended it to the present (Lipset and Schneider 1987; Blendon et al. 1997; Shribman 1999; Moy and Pfau 2000; Newton and Norris 2000; Rosenthal, Pittinsky, Purvin, and Montoya 2007). For example, Moy and Pfau (2000, p. 24) contend that "this nation is in the throes of a crisis of confidence in democratic institutions" and that there have been "three decades of unparalleled cynicism towards public institutions." Rosenthal et al. (2007) describe a "crisis of leadership," and Shribman (1999) finds that confidence in "all institutions" has fallen.

Explanations advanced for a general decline in institutional confidence include a societal failure model that contends that institutional systems have been unable to manage an increase in societal problems, assertions that political leaders have reduced confidence by exploiting distrust and cynicism for political advantage (Fried and Harris 2001), and media influence (e.g., Moy and Pfau 2000). Others cite rising expectations (Lipset and Schneider 1987) or a shift in the locus of legitimacy from hierarchical authority toward inclusion (Dalton 2000). A distinct, complementary possibility is that trends in confidence are guided by institutionally specific historical events affecting only some sectors.

This chapter examines trends in institutional confidence measured by the General Social Survey between 1973 and 2006. It begins by considering the construct of institutional confidence and describing the items and scales used to measure it here. After presenting overall levels of confidence in 13 institutions during this period, it examines trends in general confidence scales and in individual institutions. Cohort analysis helps to illuminate these trends. The chapter next investigates correlates of institutional confidence, including experiences with specific institutions, party-in-power effects, education, misanthropy, opinionation, and a general demographic model. It briefly considers the relationship between institutional confidence and support for government programs and political matters. It closes by assessing the state and role of institutional confidence in contemporary society, and both general and event-driven models of trends in confidence.

Institutional Confidence

As Cooper (1999, p. 185) has noted, "[P]ublic trust is a complex and layered entity, not a simple and uniform one." First, there are different levels or foci of confidence. At the highest and most abstract level are broad systems such as democracy in the political realm, capitalism in the economic, or American culture in the social. Next are the institutions that make up these systems including the presidency and Congress, corporations and labor unions, the media, and universities. Then there are the people running these institutions, for example, the party in power in the White House and Congress, CEOs, union leaders, media executives, and university presidents. Finally, there are the policies and products that emerge from these leaders and institutions—laws and executive orders, corporate strategies and initiatives, editorial output and programs, curricula, and so on. Confidence can be directed to any and all of these levels. Levels of confidence in different sectors (such as the political, economic, or social) may or may not be closely tied. Moreover, within a sector evaluations may be uniform or differentiated. For example, people could have a view on corporations that they apply generally, or might sharply distinguish between types of enterprises (e.g., multinationals, foreign firms, small businesses) or individual businesses (e.g., Enron, General Electric, Ben & Jerry's).

Institutional confidence research focuses on the middle level, trust in institutions, not the higher level of systems or the lower level of specific policies (Lipset and Schneider 1987).[1] It covers a wide range of entities in various sectors (e.g., political, economic, media, education) and thus considers society in general rather than just one realm.

Measuring Confidence

The General Social Survey (GSS) measured institutional confidence in 24 rounds from 1973 to 2006, asking respondents to rate their confidence in "the people running" select institutions (Smith 1993). The question asked about 12 institutions in 1973–1974, adding banks and financial institutions in 1975. Since then it has covered 13 institutions as indicated below:

> I am going to name some institutions in this country. As far as the people running these institutions are concerned, would you say you have a great deal of confidence, only some confidence, or hardly any confidence at all in them?
> a. Banks and financial institutions
> b. Major companies
> c. Organized religion
> d. Education
> e. Executive branch of the federal government
> f. Organized labor
> g. Press
> h. Medicine
> i. TV
> j. U.S. Supreme Court
> k. Scientific Community
> l. Congress
> m. Military

Subsequent analyses of these items score the responses as follows: "a great deal of confidence," 3; "only some confidence," 2; and "hardly any confidence," 1.

Overall Institutional Confidence Rankings

Table 7.1 summarizes levels of confidence in the 13 institutions across the 1972–2006 period. It ranks institutions from highest to lowest mean confidence. Differences in the confidence people have in different institutions are considerable. Medicine tops the list: 47.8% of GSS respondents express a great deal of confidence in it. Second is the scientific community (40.3%), while the military is third (37.6%). Next, the Supreme Court and education are close; 30.5–31.8% of respondents have a great deal of confidence in them. In sixth to eighth position are organized religion (28.3%), banks/finance (26.6%) and major companies (24.5%). In 9th to 11th place are the press, the executive branch, and Congress: 13.3–16.9% express a great deal of confidence in these three. Confidence is lowest in television (13.5%) and organized labor (11.7%).

What might be called knowledge and authority institutions (medicine, the scientific community, the Supreme Court, and education) hold four of the top positions along with the military. The two business institutions, major companies and banks/finance, are in the middle with organized religion. At the

Table 7.1. Ranking of Confidence in Institutions, All Years

Institution	Mean confidence (1973–2006)	Difference from mean (1975–2006)	% great deal of confidence (1973–2006)
Medicine	2.40	+0.333	47.8
Scientific community	2.36	+0.301	40.3
Military	2.26	+0.196	37.6
Supreme Court	2.18	+0.132	31.8
Education	2.17	+0.093	30.5
Major companies	2.12	+0.060	24.5
Banks/finance	2.11	+0.040	26.6
Organized religion	2.09	+0.009	28.3
Press	1.88	−0.205	16.5
Executive branch	1.87	−0.191	16.9
Congress	1.87	−0.213	13.3
Television	1.82	−0.276	13.5
Organized labor	1.80	−0.279	11.7

Source: GSS, 1973–2006.

Note: Means based on GSS years 1973–2006, except for banks/finance (1975–2006). Difference scores give the mean score for an institution minus the mean for all 13 institutions for 1975–2006. % great deal of confidence is calculated relative to a total that includes "don't know" responses and covers 1973–2006 (except for banks/finance, 1975–2006).

bottom are the two media institutions (the press and television), two political institutions (the executive branch and Congress), and organized labor.

Institutional Confidence Factors and Scales

There has been considerable debate over the structure of institutional confidence. Some favor a unidimensional model (Bennett, Rhine, Flickinger, and Bennett 1999; Lipset and Schneider 1987), while others subdivide confidence into various domains. The most common subset consists of the three governmental institutions (executive branch, Congress, and Supreme Court) (Brehm and Rahn 1997; Brooks and Cheng 2001; Jiobu and Curry 2002; Price and Romantan 2004), but a variety of other scales have been advanced (Cook and Gronke 2001; Gronke and Cook 2002; Cook and Gronke 2005). As factor analyses summarized in this section illustrate, however, the complex and variable structure of institutional confidence presents empirical obstacles to both of these approaches.

Table 7.2 shows top factor loadings extracted from correlations of confidence ratings across all GSS years. Three factors emerge when analyzing either 12 or 13 items. The first is clearly a general confidence factor combining the two political institutions, two economic institutions (banks/finance and organized labor), and three other institutions (military, education, and

Table 7.2. Main Factor Loadings of Confidence Items (varimax rotation)

A. 13 institutions (1975–2006)

General		Knowledge		Media	
Executive branch	0.653	Scientific community	0.796	Press	0.773
Congress	0.590	Medicine	0.564	Television	0.740
Military	0.579	Supreme Court	0.538		
Organized religion	0.546	Major companies	0.481		
Education	0.490				
Organized labor	0.461				
Banks/finance	0.441				

B. 12 institutions (1973–2006)

General		Knowledge		Media	
Executive branch	0.686	Scientific community	0.818	Press	0.770
Congress	0.595	Medicine	0.557	Television	0.743
Military	0.595	Supreme Court	0.547		
Organized religion	0.523	Major companies	0.456		
Education	0.490				
Organized labor	0.462				

Source: GSS, 1973–2006.

organized religion). The second involves primarily knowledge/authority institutions—the scientific community, medicine, and the Supreme Court—and also includes major companies. The third factor covers media institutions, the press and television.

These factors are not sharply or clearly defined, either conceptually or quantitatively. Many of the top loadings are not very strong. Four of them are under 0.5. The factors themselves have notable cross loadings. All 13 confidence items are positively correlated. Even institutions that might be seen as opposing or adversarial have statistically significant and nontrivial positive associations. Examples are organized labor and major companies (Pearson's $r = .122$), the scientific community and organized religion ($r = .124$), the scientific community and television ($r = .108$), and the press and the executive branch ($r = .153$). The lowest correlation is between the military and the press ($r = .088$). Moreover, cross loadings are high for many individual institutions. For example, in the analysis involving 12 institutions, major companies loads almost as strongly on the first factor (0.381) as on the second (0.456), organized labor almost as strongly on the third (0.447) as on the first (0.462), and the Supreme Court 0.386 on the first and 0.547 on the second.

Finally, the factor loadings are very unstable across years. In no two years did the 13 confidence items form the same factors. From two to four factors emerged in different years, and their composition varied quite a bit. The most consistent factor was for the media: the press and television loaded together in 21 of 22 years. But in 17 years they were joined by organized labor, in 8 by education, and in one or more years by medicine, the scientific community, banks/finance, Congress, or the executive branch. Other pairings are even less stable (e.g., Congress with the executive branch in 19 years, the Supreme Court with the executive branch and Congress in 14 years, the Supreme Court with the scientific community and medicine in 11 years, major companies with banks/finance in 16 years). In sum, the search for factors is generally not very illuminating. Subsequent analysis in this chapter focuses on overall confidence scales and items for individual institutions.

Three additive scales measure general confidence levels. The first includes all 13 institutions and covers the years 1975–2006. Scale scores range from 13 to 39. The second (12-item) scale, with scores between 12 and 36, covers the years 1973–2006, including all institutions except banks and finance. The third scale includes the 11 nonmedia institutions, covering the years 1975–2006 and ranging from 11 to 33. A fourth two-item scale measures confidence in media institutions, press and television, with scores between 2 and 6.

Confidence Trends

This section examines trends in the general institutional confidence scales and then in confidence for each of the 13 separate institutions. Four trend models were considered. The first tested to see if mean confidence was the same in all years; if so, the trend was described as constant. If the trend was not constant but there also was no statistically significant linear component, it was labeled nonconstant, nonlinear (NCNL). If there was a statistically significant linear trend without statistically significant variation around it, it was said to be a significant linear trend (SLT). Finally, with both a statistically significant linear element and some additional statistically significant variation, the trend was said to fit a significant linear component (SLC) model. Most of the trends described below conform to the last of these models.

Trends in Confidence Scales

As Table 7.3 shows, a statistically negative SLC is present for each of the general scales (i.e., with 11, 12, or 13 items). It is weakest ($r = -.055$) for the 11-item scale that excludes the two media items, because confidence in media institutions declines more strongly ($r = -.232$ for the 2-item media scale). The 13-item scale which includes banks/finance has a $-.103$ correlation with year over the 1975–2006 time span. The association for the 12-item scale is slightly stronger ($r = -.129$) because overall confidence levels were high in 1973 and 1974, which helped to anchor the declining trend.

Table 7.3. Trends in Mean Confidence Scale Scores

Year	13-item scale	12-item scale	11-item scale	2-item media scale
1973	—	26.1	—	4.1
1974	—	26.2	—	4.1
1975	27.2	25.0	23.1	4.0
1976	27.7	25.4	23.7	4.0
1977	28.6	26.3	24.6	4.0
1978	26.9	24.7	23.0	3.8
1980	27.0	24.9	23.1	3.9
1982	27.2	25.1	23.3	3.8
1983	26.7	24.6	23.0	3.7
1984	27.5	25.3	23.7	3.8
1986	27.0	24.9	23.2	3.8
1987	27.7	25.5	23.9	3.8
1988	27.2	25.1	23.4	3.8
1989	26.9	24.9	23.2	3.7
1990	26.8	24.9	23.1	3.8
1991	27.0	25.2	23.3	3.7
1993	25.7	23.8	22.2	3.5
1994	26.0	24.0	22.6	3.4
1996	25.9	23.8	22.5	3.4
1998	26.2	24.2	22.9	3.4
2000	26.8	24.6	23.4	3.4
2002	26.7	24.6	23.4	3.4
2004	26.5	24.3	23.2	3.3
2006	26.3	24.1	22.9	3.4
Model	SLC	SLC	SLC	SLC
r	−.103	−.129	−.055	−.232

Source: GSS, 1973–2006.
Note: SLC = significant linear component.

Table 7.4 shows the overall trends another way, reporting the average percentages of respondents having a great deal of confidence in the included institutions.[2] For the set of 12 institutions, confidence is highest (30–33.5%) in 1973, 1974, and 1977 and lowest (22–23%) in 1993–1996. For the 13 institutions measured since 1975, the high points (29.5–32%) are in 1976–1977 and the low ones (21–23%) in 1993–1996.

Table 7.4. Trends in Average Percentage with a Great Deal of Confidence, 1973–2006

	12 institutions	13 institutions
1973	30.3	—
1974	33.5	—
1975	25.4	25.9
1976	28.7	29.5
1977	31.4	32.3
1978	24.2	24.8
1980	26.0	26.4
1982	26.0	26.0
1983	24.2	24.1
1984	27.2	27.4
1986	25.5	25.1
1987	28.4	28.3
1988	26.1	26.1
1989	25.9	25.3
1990	25.3	24.7
1991	28.9	27.6
1993	22.0	21.4
1994	23.1	22.7
1996	22.8	22.9
1998	23.8	24.0
2000	25.1	25.4
2002	25.0	24.8
2004	25.7	26.0
2006	24.1	24.5

Source: GSS, 1973–2006.

These negative overall trends are both modest in magnitude and far from steady. As indicated, the highest scores for the 12- and 13-item scales are in the 1970s, while their lowest points occur in the 1990s. A slight rebound in the 2000s still leaves them well below their 1970s levels. There are other statistically significant departures from linear declines. A major reason for this is that the overall scales mix diverse idiosyncratic trends for specific institutions. Linear declines are statistically significant for only 10 of the 13 institutions (Table 7.5). Confidence grows for two, and one has no net direction. Of the 10 with net declines, 9 have high points in the 1970s (2 in 1973, 5 in 1974, 2 in 1977), and 1 in 1984. The low points for these decreasing trends are at very different times: 1975, 1978, 1980, 1988, 1991, 1993, 1996, 2002, and 2004.

Table 7.5. Trends in Individual Confidence Measures, 1973–2006

Institution	Mean trend (r)	Model	Linearity as % of sum of squares
Television	−.152	SLC	85.1
Press	−.230	SLC	90.2
Medicine	−.094	SLC	66.4
Scientific community	−.014	SLC	7.4
Education	−.093	SLC	47.0
Executive branch	−.059	SLC	9.8
Congress	−.099	SLC	28.0
Supreme Court	+.012	SLC	2.1
Military	+.087	SLC	35.0
Major companies	−.014	SLC	1.4
Banks/finance (1975+)	−.069	SLC	13.4
Organized labor	+.000	NCNL	0.0
Organized religion	−.089	SLC	36.6

Source: GSS, 1973–2006.

Note: SLC = significant linear component; NCNL = nonconstant, nonlinear.

The overall confidence trends are a weak amalgamation of many distinct trends. One must focus on individual institutions to really understand trends in confidence. The next section shows that movements in confidence often track events within specific domains.

Trends for Individual Institutions

As Table 7.5 shows, the SLC model describes 12 of the 13 confidence trends. None moves consistently in one direction, and many linear components are weak. In 10 cases, statistically significant declines are accompanied by significant variation around the linear trend. For two institutions, the military and the Supreme Court, confidence rose with an SLC. For organized labor, the trend was NCNL: variation was greater than expected by chance, but there was no significant movement up or down between 1973 and 2006. Table 7.6 reports percentages having a great deal of confidence in each institution in each year.[3]

The strongest linear declines are for the two media institutions, television and the press. Confidence in them correlates with year at −.15 and −.23, respectively. High points for both trends are in the early to mid-1970s, with nadirs in the late 1990s and the 2000s (Table 7.6) (Cook and Gronke 2001; Gronke and Cook 2002; Gronke and Cook 2007). The percentage having a great deal of confidence in television slipped from 23% in 1974 to 9% in 2002 and 2006. For the press it declined from 28% in 1976 to 9% in 1998 and 2004. The two-item confidence-in-media scale falls, with an SLC ($r = -.23$,

Table 7.6. Percentage Having a Great Deal of Confidence in Individual Institutions, by Year (ranks within years in parentheses)

Year	TV	Press	Banks	Major companies	Medicine	Scientific community	Education	Organized religion	Executive branch	Congress	Supreme Court	Military	Organized labor
1973	18.2 (11)	22.7 (10)		29.2 (7)	53.8 (1)	37.0 (2)	36.9 (3)	34.5 (4)	28.9 (8)	23.4 (9)	30.9 (6)	31.9 (5)	15.6 (12)
1974	23.0 (9)	25.4 (8)		31.3 (7)	61.0 (1)	45.5 (3)	49.0 (2)	44.5 (4)	13.6 (12)	17.0 (11)	33.0 (6)	39.3 (5)	19.0 (10)
1975	17.9 (10)	23.8 (7)	31.4 (4)	19.4 (9)	51.0 (1)	37.3 (2)	31.0 (5)	23.8 (7)	13.1 (12)	13.2 (11)	30.4 (6)	34.7 (3)	9.6 (13)
1976	18.2 (10)	28.3 (8)	39.0 (4)	21.2 (9)	54.6 (1)	42.8 (2)	37.7 (5)	30.2 (7)	13.1 (12)	13.3 (11)	34.1 (6)	39.8 (3)	11.5 (13)
1977	17.6 (12)	24.8 (10)	42.0 (2)	27.1 (9)	52.8 (1)	41.3 (3)	40.5 (4)	39.6 (5)	27.5 (8)	19.1 (11)	35.9 (7)	36.3 (6)	14.8 (13)
1978	14.4 (10)	19.8 (9)	32.0 (3)	21.2 (8)	45.8 (1)	35.7 (2)	28.3 (7)	30.6 (4)	12.3 (12)	12.8 (11)	28.6 (6)	29.6 (5)	11.3 (13)
1980	15.2 (10)	22.0 (9)	31.8 (4)	26.9 (7)	53.2 (1)	40.9 (2)	29.9 (5)	35.2 (3)	12.0 (12)	8.9 (13)	24.2 (8)	28.3 (6)	15.1 (11)
1982	14.1 (11)	18.6 (10)	26.7 (7)	22.9 (8)	45.2 (1)	39.1 (2)	33.7 (3)	32.2 (4)	19.2 (9)	12.9 (13)	30.9 (5)	29.9 (6)	13.1 (12)
1983	12.4 (11)	13.3 (10)	23.4 (8)	24.4 (7)	51.9 (1)	41.9 (2)	28.3 (5)	28.6 (4)	13.5 (9)	9.9 (12)	27.3 (6)	30.1 (3)	8.4 (13)
1984	13.1 (11)	17.5 (10)	30.5 (7)	30.7 (6)	51.0 (1)	44.5 (2)	27.9 (8)	30.7 (5)	18.8 (9)	12.8 (12)	33.6 (4)	36.7 (3)	8.5 (13)
1986	14.8 (12)	18.6 (10)	20.7 (9)	24.7 (7)	46.8 (1)	39.5 (2)	28.1 (5)	25.0 (6)	21.3 (8)	16.2 (11)	30.4 (4)	31.2 (3)	8.8 (13)
1987	11.1 (12)	18.2 (10)	27.5 (8)	30.4 (6)	52.5 (1)	45.1 (2)	34.8 (5)	29.0 (7)	18.8 (9)	16.8 (11)	37.3 (3)	35.7 (4)	10.5 (13)
1988	14.1 (12)	18.9 (9)	26.9 (6)	24.8 (7)	52.6 (1)	39.3 (2)	29.7 (5)	20.5 (8)	16.5 (10)	15.9 (11)	35.1 (3)	34.7 (4)	10.9 (13)
1989	13.7 (12)	16.6 (11)	18.5 (9)	25.0 (6)	47.5 (1)	41.0 (2)	30.2 (5)	21.7 (7)	20.5 (8)	17.5 (10)	34.7 (3)	32.8 (4)	9.3 (13)
1990	13.6 (12)	14.4 (11)	16.7 (9)	25.6 (6)	45.3 (1)	37.8 (2)	26.7 (5)	22.7 (8)	23.9 (7)	15.7 (10)	34.4 (3)	33.2 (4)	10.7 (13)
1991	14.7 (11)	16.0 (10)	12.0 (12)	19.8 (8)	47.9 (2)	40.0 (3)	29.8 (5)	25.1 (7)	26.6 (6)	17.6 (9)	37.5 (4)	60.6 (1)	11.3 (13)
1993	11.6 (9)	10.6 (11)	14.5 (8)	21.3 (7)	40.4 (2)	37.6 (3)	22.3 (6)	22.6 (5)	11.4 (10)	6.5 (13)	30.2 (4)	41.2 (1)	7.8 (12)
1994	9.6 (12)	10.0 (11)	18.1 (8)	26.3 (5)	42.6 (1)	39.2 (2)	25.6 (6)	25.0 (7)	11.3 (9)	8.0 (13)	31.2 (4)	37.6 (3)	10.6 (10)
1996	10.5 (11)	10.6 (10)	24.5 (6)	24.0 (7)	45.2 (1)	39.7 (2)	23.3 (8)	25.3 (5)	9.8 (12)	7.2 (13)	28.3 (4)	38.6 (3)	11.1 (9)
1998	10.0 (12)	9.0 (13)	26.0 (8)	26.5 (7)	45.0 (1)	39.7 (2)	26.9 (5)	26.6 (6)	13.3 (9)	10.4 (11)	31.2 (4)	36.3 (3)	10.9 (10)
2000	10.3 (12)	10.0 (13)	29.5 (5)	28.4 (6)	44.6 (1)	41.5 (2)	27.2 (8)	27.6 (7)	13.5 (9)	12.7 (11)	32.4 (4)	39.7 (3)	13.0 (10)
2002	9.4 (13)	9.9 (12)	22.3 (7)	17.3 (9)	37.2 (2)	37.2 (2)	25.7 (6)	18.9 (8)	27.3 (5)	13.7 (10)	36.0 (4)	55.8 (1)	11.6 (11)
2004	10.2 (12)	8.9 (13)	29.3 (5)	18.4 (9)	37.8 (3)	41.8 (2)	28.8 (6)	23.5 (7)	21.7 (8)	14.7 (10)	31.7 (4)	58.3 (1)	12.9 (11)
2006	9.0 (13)	10.2 (12)	29.7 (5)	17.9 (8)	39.8 (3)	41.0 (2)	28.2 (6)	24.1 (7)	15.7 (9)	11.6 (11)	32.6 (4)	47.1 (1)	11.7 (10)

Source: GSS, 1973–2006.

Table 7.3). Fan, Wyatt, and Keltner (2001) link the decline in press confidence to rising generalized "self-criticism" by the media, perhaps linked to conservative charges of "liberal media bias." They do not address the television trend, however, and the similarity of trends for the two media institutions calls for an explanation that applies to both. Another possibility is that the development of new Internet-based media has undermined confidence in traditional media.

The linear declines represent rather small parts of the total changes for the other eight institutions having negative SLCs. The trend in confidence in banks/finance was driven largely by the savings and loan (S&L) crisis of the late 1980s/early 1990s (Table 7.6). The decline in confidence after 1988 was especially notable. During this time, the collapse of S&Ls progressed, and criminal charges followed some of the failures (e.g., the bankruptcy of Charles Keating's Lincoln Savings in 1989). In 1989 the Resolution Trust Corporation (RTC) was created to handle the many insolvent S&Ls, and the new Office of Thrift Supervision assumed responsibility for regulating the industry. Confidence slid to a low of 12% by 1991. The crisis abated in the early 1990s, and the RTC dissolved in 1995. Confidence in banks/finance recovered to 29.5% in 2000, remaining around that level through 2006.

Confidence in major companies is mostly a function of the business cycle and corporate scandals (Lipset and Schneider 1987; Wolfers 2003). The linear component of this trend is significant but very small ($r = -.014$). The proportion with a great deal of confidence in companies fell during recessions (i.e., 19% in 1975, 23% in 1982, 20% in 1991, and 17% in 2002).[4] In each case save one, confidence in companies rose during the subsequent recovery and expansion phases—to 27% in 1980, 30–31% in 1984 and 1987, and 28% in 2000. There was no rebound after the 2001–2002 recession, however: the percentage having a great deal of confidence remained at 18% in 2004 and 2006. This lagging confidence probably reflected the spate of corporate failures and criminal cases during 2002–2005, such as the scandals involving Enron, WorldCom, Tyco, and Adelphia and high-profile prosecutions such as Martha Stewart's 2004 insider-trading case.

The percentage having a great deal of confidence in medicine declined from 51–61% in 1973–1977 to 40–48% by 1989–2000, and to under 40% in the 2000s (Tables 7.5 and 7.6). The linear component is weak ($r = -.094$). Given rising life expectancies and some well-documented medical advances, the reason for this decline in confidence is unclear. The rising cost of medical coverage is one possibility: medical inflation has exceeded the general rise in the cost of living for more than 30 years, and medical expenditures rose from 7.2% of the gross domestic product in 1970 to 16.0% by 2004. Pescosolido, Tuch, and Martin (2001, p. 11) argue that the decline is due to changes such as "changing insurance profiles and the penetration rate of managed care." Schlesinger (2002, p. 225) finds it due to "the public's direct experience with the American health care system" and "well-publicized reports about medical error."

Confidence in the scientific community also shows only a very weak linear decline ($r = -.014$) (Tables 7.5 and 7.6). It varies little across years: the highest percentage with a great deal of confidence in science is 45.5% (1974) and the lowest is 37.0% (1973). Linearity accounts for only 7% of its variation over time (Table 7.5). High and low points are fairly evenly distributed across decades. There is some suggestion that ratings are responsive to events. The Challenger spacecraft exploded on January 28, 1986, and the percentage with a great deal of confidence dropped from 44.5% in 1984 to a postdisaster 39.5% in 1986. It then rebounded to 45.1% in 1987. No parallel drop followed the destruction of the Columbia spacecraft on reentry on February 1, 2003, but the GSS did not measure confidence until over a year after that event. In 2002, 37.2% had a great deal of confidence in science, compared to 41.8% in 2004.

The percentage of respondents who "don't know" their confidence in science (7.3%) is higher than for any of the other institutions, more than twice the average level (3.0%). This probably indicates that people have a harder time rating the scientific community than the other institutions.

Confidence in education also shows a moderate linear decline over time ($r = -.093$) with a substantial linear component (Tables 7.5 and 7.6). The highest levels are in the early to mid-1970s, when the percentage with a great deal of confidence averaged 39%. It then fell, bottoming out in the mid-1990s at around 22–23%, and then rose to 28–29% by 2004–2006. This decline may reflect the long series of critical educational reports (e.g., National Commission 1983; DeMint 2008) and international comparisons that typically identify the U.S. educational system as underperforming (e.g., the Trends in International Mathematics and Science Study).

Tables 7.5 and 7.6 show that confidence in organized religion declined over time ($r = -.089$; see also Chaves and Anderson, chapter 8 in this volume). It varied erratically in the early 1970s,[5] but mainly responds to positive and negative religious events. Among positive events were the election of John Paul II as the new pope and the Nobel Peace Prize awarded to Mother Teresa in late 1978. Afterward, the percentage of Catholics with a great deal of confidence rose from 34.0% in 1978 to 43.2% in 1980. Among negative events were the televangelist scandals of 1987–1988, mainly involving Jim Bakker and Jimmy Swaggart. They notably lowered the public's perception of religious leaders in general and televangelists in particular (Smith 1992). The percentage with a great deal of confidence decreased from 29.0% in 1987 to 20.5% in 1988, and that with hardly any rose from 18.3% in 1987 to a high of 29.4% in 1989. Likewise, the Catholic sex abuse scandals received massive attention in early 2002. The percentage with a great deal of confidence in religion dropped from 27.6% in 2000 to 18.9% in 2002, but recovered to 24.1% by 2006. Among Catholics, the decline (from 31.4% in 2000 to 19.0% in 2002) and the rebound (to 31.2% in 2006) were especially strong. The rebounds after these scandals testify to the resiliency of this institution.

For the executive branch, confidence has a slight downward trend ($r = -.059$), but linear trends explain little of the change over time (Tables 7.5 and 7.6). Confidence in the executive branch is largely shaped by presidential popularity, as the subsequent analysis of party-in-power effects documents. The presidential job approval literature finds that objective events such as foreign and security crises, economic conditions, and scandals strongly influence presidential popularity (Mueller 1973; Lipset and Schneider 1987; Edwards 1990; Mansbridge 1997; Gronke and Newman 2000). Particularly powerful is the so-called rally 'round the flag effect: foreign and security crises boost presidential job approval. Newly sworn-in presidents typically start out with relatively positive ratings, a honeymoon or inaugural effect. Similar results emerge for confidence in the executive branch. For example, 29% had a great deal of confidence in early 1973 after Nixon's reelection. This fell to 14% in 1974 after the full exposure of the Watergate scandal that preceded his resignation. In 1977 after Carter's election it rose to 28%, but by 1980—after stagflation, the Iran hostage seizure, and his "malaise" speech—only 12% had a great deal of confidence in the executive branch.

Also linked to rising confidence in the executive branch are entry into wars and/or the emergence of external threats. Confidence rose in 1991 at the time of the Persian Gulf War and in 2002 in the aftermath of the 9/11 terrorist attacks and in the midst of the ousting of the Taliban from control in Afghanistan. The percentage having a great deal of confidence more than doubled from 13.5% in 2000 to 27% in 2002. The National Tragedy Study (NTS) showed that 51.5% had a great deal of confidence in the executive branch in the weeks immediately following the 9/11 terrorist attacks (Smith, Rasinski, and Toce 2001; Cook and Gronke 2002; Rasinski, Smith, Berktold, and Albertson 2002). At the same time, confidence in the military also soared. Confidence falls, though, when wars drag out without clear success: from its post-9/11 NTS high of 51.5% in the fall of 2001 (Smith et al. 2001), the percentage with a great deal of confidence in the executive branch dropped to 16% in 2006.

Over time, confidence in Congress has declined ($r = -.099$), but the linear component is not pronounced (Tables 7.5 and 7.6). Presumably confidence in the Congress is shaped by its successes and failures, but no analysis to date relates congressional events to confidence ratings as closely as the presidential job approval literature does for the executive branch. There is some clear indication of the political fallout of low congressional confidence, however. From 1987 to 1993–1994 the percentage with hardly any confidence in Congress grew from 15% to 39–41%, and in 1994 the Republican Party gained control of the House of Representatives for the first time in over 40 years. Likewise, from 2002 to 2006 the "hardly any" percentage grew from 25% to 33%, and the Republicans lost their majority in the House in 2006.

Confidence in two institutions—the Supreme Court and the military—increased (Tables 7.5 and 7.6). For the Supreme Court, confidence rose by a small but statistically significant amount ($r = .012$), but its linear component is quite small. Moreover the overall variation is moderate: the percentage with a great deal of confidence in the Court ranges between only 24% and 37.5%. Most research on Supreme Court confidence focuses on what the confidence level implies for the operation of the political system, rather than factors behind shifts in confidence in the judiciary (Gibson, Caldeira, and Spence 2003a, 2003b; Nicholson and Howard 2003; Price and Romantan 2004).

The one clear positive shift over time ($r = .087$) is for confidence in the military (Tables 7.5 and 7.6). This trend was largely a response to military involvements and their successes and failures (Torres-Reyna and Shapiro 2002; King and Karabell 2003). The low point (at which less than 30% expressed a great deal of confidence) came in the late 1970s/early 1980s, in the face of military reversals and failures such as the Soviet occupation of Afghanistan and the botched rescue attempt of the Iran hostages. It rose modestly to around 34% during the Reagan–Bush expansion of the military and soared to 61% during the 1991 Gulf War. After that war confidence returned to more typical levels, but remained higher than its pre–Gulf War level, averaging 39% for 1993–2000. The 9/11 terrorist attacks and subsequent war in Afghanistan pushed confidence in the military up to 77% on the NTS immediately following the 9/11 terrorist attacks. It stood at 56% in 2002 and reached 58% during the following Iraq War in 2004. But by 2006 it was down to 47%, probably reflecting the limited success achieved in Iraq.

For organized labor, confidence shows no net direction over time; its trend is NCNL (Tables 7.5 and 7.6). Levels of confidence for labor do not vary greatly but are higher in the early 1970s and 2000s and reach a low point in 1983–1986. The 1981 strike by the Professional Air Traffic Controllers Organization is not clearly related to this decline since confidence in organized labor dropped only marginally from 1980 to 1982. It fell more notably from 1982 to 1983, well after the strike and disbanding of the union. The political climate has no apparent effect as the high and low points all occurred during Republican administrations. Unlike confidence in major companies, trends in confidence in organized labor do not follow the business cycle.

Trends in Ranking of Institutions

We next consider changes in the ranking of institutions in terms of confidence; the numbers in parentheses in Table 7.6 show where each institution ranked in each year. Most institutions have tended to remain within the same relative tier (e.g., the top, middle, or bottom third), but variations in ranking occurred for all institutions and several clear trends are evident (see Smith 2008a for details).

Institutions with high and relatively stable rankings include medicine, which is most often first and always in the top three positions. It was outranked by the military in 1991, 1993, and 2002–2006 and nudged into third position by the scientific community in 2004 and 2006. The scientific community is usually second, and never lower than third.

Relative confidence in the military grew over the decades: it ranked 3rd–6th until the early 1980s, rose to 3rd–4th in the mid-/late 1980s, and to 1st–3rd after 1991. Likewise, the ranking of the Supreme Court improved from about 6th until the mid-1980s to 3rd or 4th position since then. The ranking of organized labor, generally lowest until the early 1990s, rose to 9th–11th after 1993.

Comparative levels of confidence in education vary considerably, but its ranking fell from 2nd and 3rd in 1973–1974 to as low as 8th in 1984, 1996, and 2000. Organized religion slipped from a rank as high as 3rd in 1980 to between 5th and 8th after 1988. Both the press and television lost relative as well as absolute standing. The press dropped from 7th in 1975 to last in 1998, 2000, and 2004. Television never ranks above 9th in confidence, and ranks lowest in 2002 and 2006.

The relative position of the remaining institutions fluctuates, trending neither up nor down. Major companies always rank in the middle in terms of confidence, falling during recessions. The ranking of banks/finance varies more than for any other institution, from a high of 2nd in 1977 to a low of 12th in 1991. Mirroring absolute confidence levels, it drops notably from the 1970s to the early 1990s due to the S&L crisis, and then recovers to 5th by 2006. The rank of the executive branch has undergone considerable ups and downs, from as high as 5th or 6th when wars start in 1991 and 2002 to as low as 12th in 1974–1976, 1978–1980, and 1996. Congress never ranks above 9th and is frequently lowest ranked (1980–1982, 1993–1996).

Overall the absolute and relative trends are similar. The military and the Supreme Court, for example, rose on both, while for medicine, education, the press, television, and organized religion absolute confidence trended downward and ranking slipped. Some differences can be seen, however: absolute confidence in organized labor exhibits no trend, but its rank rose somewhat as confidence in other institutions fell. For the scientific community there was a downward trend, but no drop in rank. The wide and continuing fluctuations in rankings of institutions such as major companies, banks/finance, executive branch, and Congress underscore the fact that linear trends compose only minor parts of overall changes in confidence.

Birth Cohorts and Confidence

For most institutions, confidence is highest in the earliest and latest birth cohorts and lower in middle cohorts. Table 7.7 shows, for both the 12- and 13-item scales, that mean confidence declines from the pre-1923 generation to a nadir in the 1943–1952 cohort. It then rises to a high for the cohort born after 1983. Cohort-related trends for individual institutions all accord with this

Table 7.7. Confidence in Institutions by Birth Cohort, 1973–2006

	Percentage with a Great Deal of Confidence							
	Pre-1923	1923–1932	1933–1942	1943–1952	1953–1962	1963–1972	1973–1982	1983+
Banks/finance	40.3	29.4	26.5	20.7	21.6	25.6	35.8	47.0
Major companies	31.4	28.3	26.4	22.3	22.0	25.4	26.5	24.7
Organized religion	41.2	33.6	30.2	25.0	24.3	23.6	27.8	32.0
Education	38.6	33.5	30.1	27.5	27.1	27.9	36.2	41.7
Executive branch	21.0	18.7	17.2	15.0	15.2	18.2	18.0	22.0
Organized labor	15.5	12.4	9.4	9.5	11.6	14.4	19.8	23.6
Press	20.3	16.5	16.6	17.2	16.3	14.7	12.6	13.6
Medicine	48.6	46.3	46.7	47.7	49.1	49.9	51.5	61.9
Television	17.5	13.1	12.4	11.6	13.4	14.3	14.8	12.1
Supreme Court	32.6	32.3	30.2	31.0	33.5	33.7	41.3	41.3
Scientific community	42.2	40.4	40.1	44.0	45.3	45.3	47.6	57.0
Congress	16.6	14.7	12.8	11.0	12.1	15.0	17.1	26.4
Military	42.3	40.1	38.2	31.9	36.1	43.7	49.0	64.3
Mean, 13-item scale	27.5	27.1	26.7	26.3	26.6	27.0	27.5	28.9
Mean, 12-item scale	25.5	25.0	24.7	24.4	24.7	24.9	25.3	26.3

Source: GSS, 1973–2006.

summary pattern to some extent, but differ considerably in detail. For only five institutions is the confidence level lowest for the 1943–1952 cohort. For three, the 1933–1942 cohort expresses least confidence, while the 1953–1962 cohort does so for two. This dispersion of low points across cohorts, together with the modest decline from the 1933–1942 cohort to the 1943–1952 ("Vietnam" cohort) makes it hard to simply characterize the confidence decline as a Vietnam War effect (King and Karabell 2003). The effect of the Vietnam War on the middle generations may, however, be part of the general decline, notably for the cohort differences in confidence in the military.

For nine institutions (banks/finance, education, executive branch, organized labor, medicine, Supreme Court, scientific community, Congress, and military) the most recent cohort has the greatest confidence, while the earliest cohort is most confident in the remaining four (major companies, organized religion, press, and television). The decline and subsequent reversal across cohorts is sometimes deep and other times shallow. The decline for banks/finance, organized religion, and military was over 10 percentage points, while the recovery was over 10 points for banks/finance, education, organized labor, medicine, Supreme Court, scientific community, and military. The largest swings (summing absolute declines and rises across cohorts) were for banks/ finance (45.9 points), military (42.8 points), education (26.1 points), and organized religion (26.0). Without these recoveries among recent cohorts, the over-time declines in confidence discussed above would have been much deeper and more consistent. The recoveries have not generally driven confidence upward, since relatively optimistic new cohorts have been replacing similarly positive early generations. If entering cohorts continue to be relatively confident, future cohort turnover will generate rising confidence as the most pessimistic middle cohorts begin to age out.

We next consider within-cohort trends for the four institutions with the largest cohort reversals. (For full details and all 13 institutions see Smith [2008a].) For banks/finance confidence dropped uniformly within cohorts from 1974 to 1984. It continued to decline for the youngest cohorts from 1984 to 1994, but rose for the older cohorts. From 1994 to 2004 it rose for all cohorts. Also of note is that each entering cohort has more confidence in banks/ finance than the preceding new cohort (rising from 26.6% to 47.0%). The pattern for the military is very similar to that for banks/finance, but with even larger gains within cohorts and across entering cohorts. Confidence in education drops within all cohorts from 1974 to 1984, reverses direction in a couple of cohorts in 1984–1994, and then rises for all but one cohort in 1994– 2004. Confidence in education for entering cohorts, however, changes little over time. For organized religion, the cohort pattern described for education is notably weaker. Declines occur for most cohorts, with only some reversal among the earlier cohorts in 1994–2004.

In contrast to these patterns, each entering cohort has less confidence than the preceding one in the two media institutions. This is a major factor contributing to both the greater depth and the linearity of the media trends.

Correlates of Institutional Confidence

Experiences/Conditions Connected to Specific Institutions

Previous sections established connections between positive and negative societal events and aggregate confidence levels. Such connections also link confidence in institutions and personal experiences with them. Table 7.8 demonstrates these for nine institutions. Party-in-power effects relating to the executive branch and Congress are discussed next; no personal experience or attribute is closely tied to confidence in the Supreme Court. Later discussions of education and the general demographic correlates of confidence connect level of schooling to confidence in education.

Negative economic circumstances are related to lower confidence in both banks/finance and major companies (Lipset and Schneider 1987). Specifically, confidence in banks/finance and in major companies is lower when personal financial satisfaction is low and when recent financial changes have been for

Table 7.8. Confidence in Selected Institutions and Related Experiences, Evaluations, and Attitudes

A. Confidence in banks/finance, by financial satisfaction

	Satisfied	More or less satisfied	Not at all satisfied	
Great deal	37.1	27.2	21.4	
Only some	52.5	60.2	56.2	
Hardly any	10.4	12.6	22.4	$r = .160, p < .001$

B. Confidence in banks/finance, by changes in financial situation

	Better	Same	Worse	
Great deal	33.0	28.1	21.4	
Only some	56.0	57.9	57.2	
Hardly any	11.0	14.0	21.5	$r = .124, p < .0001$

C. Confidence in major companies, by financial satisfaction

	Satisfied	More or less satisfied	Not at all satisfied	
Great deal	27.1	20.8	17.4	
Only some	62.3	64.2	60.1	
Hardly any	10.6	15.1	22.5	$r = .132, p < .0001$

D. Confidence in major companies, by changes in financial satisfaction

	Better	Same	Worse	
Great deal	25.5	21.2	15.8	
Only some	62.6	61.7	63.0	
Hardly any	11.9	22.5	15.8	$r = .122, p < .0001$

E. Confidence in major companies, by job satisfaction

	Very satisfied	Moderately satisfied	A little dissatisfied	Very dissatisfied	
Great deal	25.4	20.2	17.8	10.1	
Only some	62.1	65.5	62.6	64.4	
Hardly any	12.5	14.3	19.5	25.5	$r = .195, p < .0001$

F. Confidence in organized labor, by union membership

	Member	Spouse member	Both member	Neither member	
Great deal	20.4	12.1	8.8	12.4	
Only some	60.9	63.6	63.2	57.7	
Hardly any	18.7	24.3	28.1	29.9	$r = .086, p < .0001$

G. Confidence in medicine, by personal health

	Excellent	Good	Fair	Poor	
Great deal	48.9	39.9	45.8	35.3	
Only some	43.1	51.7	41.3	41.7	
Hardly any	8.0	8.4	12.9	23.0	$r = .080, p < .0001$

Table 7.8. (*continued*)

H. Confidence in television, by TV hours per day

	0	1	2	3	4	5	6–9	10+	
Great deal	2.1	5.5	8.2	8.0	12.1	15.9	11.1	27.2	
Only some	29.9	38.9	47.8	53.3	55.4	49.3	60.1	43.2	
Hardly any	68.0	55.6	44.0	38.8	32.5	34.8	28.8	29.6	$r = .177, p < .0001$

I. Confidence in the press, by newspaper reading

	Every day	Few times a week	Once a week	Less than weekly	Never	
Great deal	10.8	8.4	11.2	6.3	9.6	
Only some	47.7	48.0	46.1	49.0	41.4	
Hardly any	41.6	43.6	42.8	44.7	49.0	$r = .045, p = .069$

J. Confidence in organized religion, by frequency of praying

	Several times a day	Once a day	Several times a week	Once a week	Less than weekly	Never	
Great deal	34.6	29.3	24.5	17.3	11.1	4.6	
Only some	48.2	54.7	58.4	64.6	55.5	45.1	
Hardly any	17.1	17.0	17.1	18.1	33.4	50.3	$r = .260, p < .0001$

K. Confidence in organized religion, by frequency of attending religious services

	Never	Less than yearly	1–2 times yearly	Several times yearly	Once a month	2–3 times monthly	Nearly weekly	Weekly	More than weekly	
Great deal	11.4	16.9	15.9	25.0	25.8	33.0	39.9	37.6	34.4	
Only some	45.1	55.8	59.2	58.2	61.4	56.3	47.5	52.4	51.1	
Hardly any	43.5	27.3	24.8	16.8	12.7	10.8	12.6	9.9	14.5	$r = .304, p < .0001$

L. Confidence in organized religion, by attachment to one's religion

	Strong	Somewhat strong	Not very strong	No religion	
Great deal	37.2	26.5	19.0	8.3	
Only some	49.8	58.3	59.7	42.9	
Hardly any	12.9	15.2	21.3	48.7	$r = .300, p < .0000$

M. Confidence in organized religion, by belief in God

	Don't believe	No way to know	Higher power	Believe sometimes	Believe mostly	Know exists	
Great deal	18.1	7.0	7.4	15.6	18.6	31.3	
Only some	35.1	40.6	50.2	52.8	61.2	52.0	
Hardly any	46.8	52.4	42.4	31.6	20.3	16.8	$r = .262, p < .0001$

(*continued*)

Table 7.8. (*continued*)

N. Confidence in the military, by years in armed forces

	None	Less than 2 years	2–4 years	4+ years	
Great deal	35.0	34.5	36.9	48.5	
Only some	51.7	50.5	49.5	40.7	
Hardly any	13.3	15.0	13.6	10.8	$r = .035, p < .0001$

O. Confidence in the scientific community, by score on science knowledge scale

	0	1	2	3	4	5	6	
Great deal	32.2	40.5	45.7	52.5	63.7	68.1	79.9	
Only some	58.9	51.2	48.6	44.3	34.0	31.9	20.1	
Hardly any	9.0	8.3	5.6	3.2	2.3	0.0	0.0	$r = .194, p < .0001$

Source: GSS, 2000–2006, except for associations involving items no longer measured regularly by the GSS (belief in God and years in armed forces). For the latter, source is most recent years they appeared in GSS.
Note: Values are percentages unless otherwise noted.

the worse. Confidence in major companies is reduced when job satisfaction is low.

As well, positive experiences with institutions generally increase confidence in them. A few exceptions qualify the generality of this relationship, however. Confidence in organized labor is higher among respondents who are union members, but surprisingly not when both the respondent and her or his spouse belong to a union. Confidence in medicine is higher for those with better personal health. Viewing more television is associated with greater confidence in television, but reading newspapers is unrelated to confidence in the press. Confidence in organized religion increases with both religious behaviors and stronger religious beliefs (Hout and Fischer 2002). Confidence in the military is higher among veterans. Confidence in the scientific community increases with level of scientific knowledge (Smith 1997a).

Party-in-Power Effects
Research going back nearly 30 years (Smith, Taylor, and Mathiowetz 1980; Alford 2001; Richardson, Houston, and Hadjiharalambous 2001) shows that confidence in the executive branch of the federal government is closely tied to popular job approval of the president and is thus subject to a party-in-power effect. As Figure 7.1 shows, confidence in the executive branch is greater among the president's political partisans. When the political party controlling the White House switches, partisans reverse their confidence levels: Democrats had more confidence than Republicans during the Carter and Clinton presidencies, while Republicans led during the Nixon, Ford, Reagan, and both Bush administrations. Confidence among independents lies

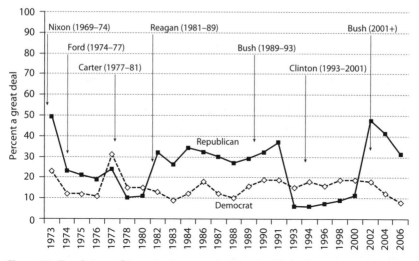

Figure 7.1. Trends in confidence in the executive branch of federal government, by party identification, 1973–2006.

between that of partisans, but is usually closer to those of the out-party than of the in-party. Since the Reagan years, the presidential party-in-power effect has mostly affected Republicans. Their confidence went up sharply under Reagan–G.H.W. Bush, down under Clinton, and back up under G. W. Bush. Democrats fluctuate much less. Overall, the percentage of Democrats with a great deal of confidence in the executive branch is 5.3 percentage points higher when the president is Democratic rather than Republican, while that among Republicans is 22.0 points higher under a Republican president rather than a Democratic leader. A similar pattern also prevails for differences by political ideology.

A party-in-power effect also occurs on Congress. Republicans had more confidence whenever they controlled both houses of Congress, while the Democrats had most confidence when they had congressional majorities. For example, when the Democratic Party controlled both houses from the late 1980s through 1994, confidence in Congress among Democrats exceeded that for Republicans by 5–16 percentage points. During the 1996–2006 period of Republican control, confidence in the legislature among Republicans topped that among Democrats by an average of 4 points. In the early-to-mid-1980s when the Democrats controlled the House of Representatives and the Republicans held the Senate, the pattern was very mixed. Republicans had more confidence in Congress in two years (1984 and 1986), while Democrats had more in two other years (1982 and 1983). In contrast to the party-in-power effect for the executive branch, however, in most years independents rather than out-party affiliates have the least confidence in Congress.

Despite the sensitivity of confidence in these two political institutions to which party controls the White House and Congress, confidence in them is strongly linked even when opposing parties control them. When the same party controls the executive branch and Congress, confidence in them correlates .471; when control of Congress is split, the average correlation is .424; and when opposite parties control the two bodies, the correlation still averages .400. Thus, party-in-power differences only modestly attenuate a strong association between confidence in the two political branches of the federal government.

Education

The association of education with confidence varies greatly across institutions. As Table 7.9 shows, education has a SLC relationship with confidence in each one. For five institutions confidence increases with education. Of these, the association is clear and fairly strong for major companies, the scientific community, and the Supreme Court. For the other two, the executive

Table 7.9. Confidence in Institutions by Highest Educational Degree

	Percentage with a great deal of confidence							
	Less than high school	High school	Some college	Associate's degree	4-year degree	Some graduate	Postgraduate degree	Correlation
Banks/finance	32.1	26.4	25.0	22.2	26.6	25.2	26.0	−.015
Major companies	22.5	23.3	26.4	25.1	34.2	27.8	31.7	.095
Organized religion	35.2	29.9	26.0	24.5	26.2	23.2	24.9	−.046
Education	39.7	30.5	27.4	24.8	25.4	22.8	27.0	−.063
Executive branch	18.7	15.8	17.6	14.7	19.6	18.1	18.0	.015
Organized labor	18.5	12.6	11.0	9.5	7.0	6.2	6.0	−.110
Press	21.9	16.6	15.0	11.6	14.7	14.4	13.2	−.059
Medicine	49.4	48.7	47.7	43.8	49.1	49.2	45.9	.014
Television	21.7	13.6	10.7	10.1	8.5	5.8	6.9	−.143
Supreme Court	29.6	29.6	33.3	34.2	41.2	45.4	45.9	.130
Scientific community	34.1	39.1	46.3	46.7	56.5	61.1	58.4	.185
Congress	17.3	13.3	12.6	11.9	11.8	9.2	11.9	−.029
Military	46.2	39.5	36.9	36.5	32.0	29.9	27.9	−.104

branch and medicine, the association is weak, with dips in confidence among holders of associate's degrees.

For the remaining eight institutions, confidence decreases with education. Negative associations are fairly strong and clear for organized labor, television, and the military. For education, Congress, and organized religion the associations are weak to moderate; confidence is lowest among those who started, but never completed, graduate school. For the press and banks/finance, the association is also weak to moderate, with lowest confidence among those holding associate's degrees. The correlation of education with the 13-item overall scale is weakly negative ($r = -.019$, $p = .002$) because negative associations outnumbered positive ones eight to five.[6]

The mixed associations with education follow some discernable patterns. That confidence in the Supreme Court and the scientific community increases with level of education reflects the association of these institutions with knowledge and higher education. That connection does not work as well for confidence in medicine, however, which rises only weakly with education. Moreover, confidence in education falls with greater education (Klugman and Xu 2008). Associations of education and confidence in economic institutions generally follow a socioeconomic status gradient. Confidence in major companies rises with education, probably reflecting a middle-class orientation, while the decline in confidence in organized labor with educational level reflects the lower socioeconomic status of union workers. Confidence in banks/finance, however, varies little by education and is lowest among those with middle education levels. For media institutions the pattern is also somewhat diverse. The drop of confidence in television with education may denote elite disdain for this mass medium. Confidence in the press also declines with education, but more weakly and with a low point among those with associate's degrees. Relatively high confidence in banks/finance, the military, and the press among those with less than a high school education reflects cohort rather than educational differences.

Misanthropy

Misanthropy—distrust of other people—is arguably linked to confidence because the two constructs share the element of trust. Moreover, misanthropy has shown an upward shift across time (Smith 1997b; Glaeser, Laibson, Scheinkman, and Soutter 2000; Putnam 2000; Robinson and Jackson 2001). The misanthropy scale ranges from 3 (for someone who thinks most people are trustworthy, fair, and helpful) to 9 (for those considering most people to be untrustworthy, trying to take advantage of you, and just looking out for themselves) (Smith 1997b).[7] Table 7.10 shows that confidence in institutions generally is moderately associated with positive evaluations of people (Orren 1997; Newton and Norris 2000; Uslaner 2002). Misanthropy is negatively associated with overall institutional confidence ($r = -.14$ for the 12-item scale, $-.15$ for the 13-item scale). The association varies quite a bit across

Table 7.10. Misanthropy and Confidence in Institutions

	Pearson's r (p value)
12-item scale	−.142 (<.001)
13-item scale	−.146 (<.001)
Scientific community	−.163 (<.001)
Major companies	−.157 (<.001)
Supreme Court	−.141 (<.001)
Executive branch	−.124 (<.001)
Banks/finance	−.102 (<.001)
Organized religion	−.098 (<.001)
Medicine	−.091 (<.001)
Congress	−.078 (<.001)
Education	−.063 (<.001)
Press	−.044 (<.001)
Military	−.012 (.052)
Television	+.027 (<.001)
Organized labor	+.050 (<.001)

Source: GSS, 1973–2006.

institutions, however. It is negative and weak to moderate for 10 institutions and statistically insignificant for confidence in the military. For the remaining 2 institutions, it is weakly positive: people with misanthropic views tend to have greater confidence in television and organized labor than those who judge people positively.

Opinionation

Institutional confidence is also related to opinionation. Those with no opinion on institutional confidence also tend to have no opinion on other matters. People with no opinion on institutional confidence also were much more likely to have high values on a scale counting no-opinion responses to 10 items dealing with government spending priorities, punishing criminals, political ideology, and finances. For example, those rating their confidence in banks/finance gave 0.24 no-opinion responses on the scale, while those responding don't know on banks/finance rating had 1.6 no-opinion responses. Moreover, among those rating institutions, having no opinion on other matters was weakly related to having lower confidence. This association was statistically significant for major companies, medicine, the Supreme Court, the military, and the 13-item overall scale ($r = -.031$, $p \le .0001$).

A General Demographic Model

Table 7.11 summarizes bivariate analyses predicting confidence levels using 12 sociodemographic correlates. It shows that the bivariate background predictors of confidence vary across institutions (Lipset and Schneider 1987; Blendon et al. 1997; Orren 1997; Alesina and La Ferrara 2000; Moy and Pfau 2000; Alford 2001; Cook and Gronke 2001; Richardson et al. 2001; Cook and Gronke 2002; Newton and Norris 2000; King and Karabell 2003). Only two associations—for gender and nativity—are reasonably consistent. First, men have more confidence in nine institutions than women do. Women lead men only in regard to organized religion. Second, those born outside the United States have more confidence than the native born in 10 institutions; there is no difference by nativity for the remaining 3.

Associations of most predictors with confidence differ in direction across institutions. For example, Republicans have the most confidence in eight institutions, and Democrats in five; retired people the most for four and students the most for four; and whites the most for three, nonblacks the most for three, and blacks the most for five, with no difference by race for two. Moreover, most of the associations are rather modest. For most institutions and most demographics, differences involve only a few percentage points. Confidence in the military varies most across subgroups. Previous research indicates that a number of these relationships vary over time (Smith et al. 1980; Pescosolido et al. 2001).

Table 7.11 also indicates that institutions tend to line up as liberal/Democratic (education, organized labor, press, television), conservative/Republican (banks/finance, major companies, military, organized religion), or mixed (Congress, executive branch, medicine, scientific community, Supreme Court). Congress and the executive branch do not line up politically mostly because, as shown earlier, confidence in them shifts with political control. The others are seen as nonpolitical. The liberal/Democratic institutions tend to elicit more confidence from the less educated and minorities, while the college educated and whites are more confident in the conservative/Republican and nonpolitical institutions. This pattern does not hold across all institutions, however.

Apart from an institution's ideological orientation, a second pattern emerges. Those who classify themselves as "extreme" liberals or conservatives have less confidence in all institutions than do liberals or conservatives. This pattern lies principally in the "hardly any confidence" category. When liberals or conservatives tend to be more confident in an institution, one finds a slight reversal of that general tendency in the respective "extreme" category. For example, the percentage with hardly any confidence in organized labor falls monotonically from 49% for extreme conservatives to 25.5% for liberals, but then rises to 27% for extreme liberals. The opposite is true for institutions endorsed by conservatives. For example, the percentage with hardly any confidence in the military declines from 35% for extreme liberals

Table 7.11. Demographic Correlates of Confidence in Institutions

| | Group showing highest confidence for each correlate | | | | | | | | | | | | | |
	Banks/ finance	Major companies	Organized religion	Education	Executive branch	Organized labor	Press	Medicine	TV	Supreme Court	Scientific community	Congress	Military	13-item scale
Degree	LTHS	COL	LTHS	LTHS	—	LTHS	LTHS	Mixed	LTHS	COL	COL	LTHS	LTHS	LTHS
Gender	—	MEN	WOMEN	—	MEN	Mixed	MEN	MEN	MEN	MEN	MEN	MEN	MEN	MEN
Race	WHITE	WHITE	BLACK	BLACK	WHITE	BLACK	—	—	BLACK	NBLK	NBLK	—	NBLK	NBLK
Marital status	WID	MAR	WID	NMAR	NDIV	SING	—	NMAR	NSEP	NMAR	NMAR	WID	WID	NMAR
Region	NWST	—	NWST	SOMW	SO	—	NE	NWST	SO	Mixed	NWST	—	SO	NWST
Community type	RURL	SUBS	RURL	Mixed	NTCC	TCC	TCC	RURL	Mixed	NRURL	SUBS	—	RURL	RURL
# Children	0, 6+	< 5	3+	3+	—	0, 6+	0, 6+	0	0, 6+	0	0	6+	5+	Mixed
Labor force status	RET	RET	RET	RETSC	RETSC	Mixed	UNSC	SCH	Mixed	SCH	SCH	SCH	RET	RETSC
Country of birth	—	—	—	NUSA	NUSA	NUSA	NUSA	—	NUSA	NUSA	NUSA	NUSA	—	NUSA
Income	Mixed	High	Mixed	Low	—	Low	Low	—	Low	High	High	Low	Low	Low
Party identification	REP	REP	REP	DEM	REP	DEM	DEM	REP	DEM	REP	REP	DEM	REP	NIND
Political ideology	CON	CON	CON	LIB	CON	LIB	LIB	NEXT	LIB	NEXT	LIB	Mixed	CON	NEXT

Source: GSS, 1973–2006

Note: Degree: LTHS = less than high school, COL = college; race: NBLK = not black; marital status: WID = widowed, MAR = married, NMAR = not married, NDIV = not divorced, SING = never married, NSEP = not separated; region: NWST = not West, SOMW = South or Midwest, NE = Northeast, SO = South, NEWST = Northeast or West; community type: RURL = rural, SUBS = Suburbs, NTCC = not 12 largest central cities, TCC = 12 largest central cities, NRURL = not rural; labor force: RET = retired, RETSC = retired or in school, UNSC = unemployed or in school, SCH = in school; country of birth: NUSA = not born in United States; party identification: REP = Republican, DEM = Democratic, NIND = not independent; political ideology: CON = conservative, LIB = liberal, NEXT = not extreme liberal or conservative.

— = not statistically significant.

to 8% for conservatives, but then rises to 11% for extreme conservatives. Conversely, when one end of the spectrum lacks confidence, that is amplified for the extreme category. For example, the percentage with hardly any confidence in education is greater among conservatives: it increases by 0.4 percentage points from moderates to slight conservatives, by 4.5 points from slight conservatives to conservatives, and by 8.9 points from conservatives to extreme conservatives. In the other direction, the percentage with hardly any confidence in major companies increases by 0.3 percentage points from moderates to slight liberals, by 4.7 points from slight liberals to liberals, and by 13.9 points from liberals to extreme liberals. Thus, the self-label of "extreme" marks less confidence, either reversing a positive ideological leaning or amplifying a negative one.

Because associations of these demographic variables with confidence are mostly modest in magnitude and vary across institutions, multivariate models for the 12- and 13-item confidence scales yield modest results. No standardized regression coefficient exceeds 0.06 and the coefficients of determination (R^2) reach only .02.

Institutional Confidence's Impact on Government Programs and Other Political Matters

The foregoing analyses examined confidence in institutions as a dependent variable. But institutional confidence can also help to shape people's attitudes and actions toward other components of society (Brooks and Cheng 2001; Chanley, Rudolph, and Rahn 2001). One connection is between institutional confidence and support for government programs and taxes (Smith et al. 1980). Table 7.12 shows that the association is straightforward for the military and the scientific community: the more confidence, the more support for greater spending on defense, scientific research, and space exploration. For education, the Supreme Court, and medicine, the relationship is more complex. The percentage favoring lower spending increases as confidence wanes, but support for more spending does not decline as confidence falls. Instead, support for more spending rises slightly among those with less confidence, while support for unchanged spending falls more sharply. Previous research (Smith et al. 1980) indicates that when people deem an area to be an important priority and support more spending in it (as is clearly the case for education, health care, and crime control—Smith 2007), some support more spending to compensate for the shortcomings of those responsible for that area.

Research also indicates that confidence in the Supreme Court influences political matters such as the acceptance of the decision on the 2000 Bush–Gore election outcome (Gibson et al. 2003a, 2003b; Price and Romantan 2004) and public opinion on gay rights (Stoutenborough, Haider-Markel, and Allen 2006). More generally, Moy and Pfau (2000) argue that confidence in institutions adds to the pool of social capital.

Table 7.12. Confidence in Selected Institutions and Support for Related Governmental Spending and Policies

A. Confidence in the military and defense spending

	More	Same	Less	
Great deal	35.8	44.0	20.2	
Only some	24.3	41.1	34.5	
Hardly any	19.8	19.9	60.3	$r = .232, p < .0001$

B. Confidence in the scientific community and scientific research spending

Great deal	50.7	43.0	6.3	
Only some	35.7	50.1	14.2	
Hardly any	28.7	35.2	36.1	$r = .216, p < .0001$

C. Confidence in the scientific community and space exploration spending

Great deal	19.2	51.6	29.2	
Only some	11.3	46.3	42.4	
Hardly any	6.1	26.0	67.9	$r = .209, p < .0001$

D. Confidence in education and education spending

Great deal	69.4	27.3	3.3	
Only some	77.8	18.2	4.0	
Hardly any	73.2	12.9	13.8	$r = .017, p < .0001$

E. Confidence in the Supreme Court and spending for halting rising crime rate

Great deal	53.2	40.6	6.2	
Only some	57.4	34.9	7.7	
Hardly any	59.8	27.3	12.9	$r = -.007, p < .0001$

F. Confidence in medicine and health spending

Great deal	68.5	25.9	5.6	
Only some	77.6	16.5	5.9	
Hardly any	77.3	13.0	9.7	$r = -.051, p < .001$

Source: GSS, 2000–2006.
Note: Values are percentages unless otherwise noted.

Conclusion

Trends in institutional confidence over the last four decades exhibit a complex pattern. First, trends for most institutions are distinctive. Only for the press and television are declines in confidence similar to one another and largely linear. Second, most individual trends are largely nonlinear. Third, because the trends are distinctive and largely institution specific, they are poorly captured by such general terms as "crisis of confidence/leadership." More limited and nuanced descriptions of the various trends are required.

Episodic positive and negative events are the chief force behind changes in confidence levels. This is well documented for major companies, banks/finance, the executive branch, organized religion, and the military, and probably holds for the others as well. While some findings support the institutional-performance model of confidence (Lipset and Schneider 1987; Blendon et al. 1997; Fan et al. 2001; Newton and Norris 2000; Fried and Harris 2001), this model's focus on institutional outputs is too limited. Institutions are evaluated not merely by their performance but also by relevant events. Several examples illustrate the difference: (1) confidence in the executive branch goes up when a new president is inaugurated, before holding office long enough to be judged on the basis of objective success or failure, (2) confidence in the executive branch and the military soared after the 9/11 attacks, before any gains were achieved, and (3) confidence in major companies suffers during recessions, both those triggered by external shocks like an oil embargo and when corporate shortcomings and missteps were to blame.

The event-based model primarily hinges on examples in which negative events (recessions, scandals, failures) lower confidence, but does include some examples in which positive events (economic recoveries/expansions, inaugurations) boost confidence. Either negative events play a larger role than positive ones or positive developments are less readily identified and studied. This may in part reflect King and Karabell's (2003, p. 84) observation that "[c]onfidence in institutions takes years to build, but far less time to erode. For institutions as for buildings, it is easier to tear down than to construct."

One variant of the event-based model suggests that general, enduring cultural norms and expectations fix the basic confidence position for institutions. Such expectations generate average or expected levels of confidence that unusual events then push upward or downward. Confidence returns to typical levels after the shock of these events wears off.

Because episodic events largely shape confidence ratings, trends described through 2006 do not necessarily project to the future. For example, mid-/late 2008 events in the subprime mortgage market and the economy as a whole probably lowered confidence ratings notably for major companies and banks/finance, and perhaps for the executive branch and Congress. Certainly the event-driven model of confidence would predict such effects.

While confidence trends are definitely a story of individual trees, is a general forest being missed by focusing on the separate institutions? Are Lipset and Schneider (1987, p. 47) right when they contend, "It appears justified to speak of a common confidence trend for the leaders of all institutions"? Several patterns in this chapter's data suggest a general, master confidence trend. First, all confidence items are positively correlated, indicating some commonality. Second, while its pattern is not identical, cohort reversal is a common pattern across almost all institutions. Third, confidence in most institutions declined. Once the important impact of institution-specific events is distilled away, there indeed may be generalized forces weakening confidence in institutions.

Several generalized factors have been proposed. First is a societal-failure model which, consistent with the institutional-performance model, argues that an overall increase in objective problems and system shortcomings lowered confidence. No comprehensive measure of such failures to test this idea is available, but enough counterexamples of improvements and positive developments can be cited to call this explanation into question (e.g., the fall of communism, the drop in the crime rate in the 1990s/2000s, rising life expectancy and real income, the absence of recent political scandals comparable to Watergate).

Second, some argue that leaders have undermined confidence in their own institutions. Fried and Harris (2001) contend that political leaders have exploited distrust and cynicism for political advantage, thereby reducing institutional confidence. Fan et al. (2001, p. 846) find that confidence in the press fell due to an increase in "'self-criticism' of media, perhaps linked to conservative charges of 'liberal media bias.'" Corporate emphasis on short-term profits rather than long-term fundamentals might be another example. But while such examples contain a common thread of leadership shortcomings, it is far from clear that they manifest a broad societal trend.

A third, related, argument is that media negativity about other institutions, and society at large, rose. Moy and Pfau (2000) cite a caustic impact of talk radio on political discourse in general, and on institutional confidence in particular. Shribman (1999) found that media coverage of Congress became more negative over time. These arguments, however, focus only on political institutions. Moreover, they do not clearly establish whether increased negativity reflects real fluctuations in institutional performance or something independent of it.

Fourth, Dalton (2000, p. 261) believes that "legitimacy based on inclusion is replacing legitimacy based on hierarchical authority." This idea is consistent with other societal trends toward greater equality and democratization. He relates this to the rise of postmaterialism. This is thought to undermine confidence both because the transition in the basis of legitimacy is disruptive and because bottom-up confidence is harder to generate and maintain than deferential, top-down confidence.

Fifth, some refer to "rising expectations" as a reason for lower confidence evaluations (Lipset and Schneider 1987). There is no direct evidence that expectations have been on the upswing, however.

Finally, several contend that high institutional confidence should be seen more as the exception than the expectation in American society. Sherman (2001) points out that de Tocqueville wrote that Americans were "suspicious of all authority," and Lipset and Schneider (1987) cite democratic egalitarianism and populism as major themes that question authority. Alford (2001) sees the 1950s and 1960s as a period of atypically high confidence, reflecting American success in World War II and the solidarity generated by the Cold War threat of communism. The Vietnam War and the antiestablishment 1960s burst this bubble of institutional confidence, and since the 1970s traditional American skepticism of authority has reasserted itself. From this perspective, what needs explanation is not why confidence has fallen so low but why it used to be so high. Perhaps the chief reason for questioning this explanation is the cohort-reversal pattern: the return-to-skepticism explanation would seem to indicate that newer generations should have lower and more normal confidence, but instead their confidence is highest. The cohort reversal instead suggests that a Mannheimian negative impact on the middle generations suppressed institutional confidence.[8]

The course of institutional confidence in America since the 1970s is a complex story. Clearly, much change is event driven and institution specific. But there are plausible reasons to expect that more general, interinstitutional factors also are at play. It is unlikely that any single factor drives a decline in confidence: any more general factors are likely to be multifold. The impact of more general societal trends may be better identified, and a fuller understanding of confidence trends achieved, once the effects of specific events on confidence in specific institutions are modeled.

Notes

1. On what people mean by "confidence" in institutions, see Smith (1981, 1991).

2. Percentages expressing a great deal of confidence focus attention on the positive end of the distribution. Also, the percentages in Table 7.4 are calculated using totals that include "don't know" responses, which were excluded when calculating overall confidence scores in Table 7.3.

3. For full annual distributions for trends in all confidence categories, see Smith (2008a) at http://www.norc.org/GSS+Website/Publications/GSS+Reports/Social+Change+Reports/Social+Change+Reports.htm.

4. The impact of the 1980 recession, most severe in the third quarter of 1980, is not detectable because that contraction lasted only six months and the winter 1980 GSS field period fell between the peak of the previous expansion and the trough of the 1980 recession.

5. Responses may have been influenced by questionnaire context (Smith 1981, 1991, 1994). Confidence ratings are affected by both the order in which institutions are presented and the content of prior questions. In the 1970s the order of confidence items changed several times before becoming fixed in 1977 (Smith 1981). It is highly likely that several not-readily-explicable shifts in confidence during this period are due to these context shifts, but no experimental evidence confirms this (Smith 1994). Experimental evidence does indicate that the content of preceding items influences confidence ratings (Smith 1991, 2008b).

6. If education is measured using years of schooling instead of the categories in Table 7.9, the association with the overall scale is marginally stronger ($r = -.023$, $p < .001$). On curvilinear relationships with education and various satisfaction measures see Smith (1982).

7. Question text for the three misanthropy items is as follows: (1) "Would you say that most of the time people try to be helpful or that they are mostly just looking out for themselves?"; (2) "Do you think most people would try to take advantage of you if they got a chance or would they try to be fair?"; and (3) "Generally speaking, would you say that most people can be trusted or that you can't be too careful in dealing with people?"

8. On such cohort effects see Schuman and Scott (1989) or Schuman and Rieger (1992).

References

Alesina, Alberto, and Eliana La Ferrara. 2000. "The Determinants of Trust." Working Paper No. 7621, National Bureau of Economic Research, Cambridge, MA.

Alford, John R. 2001. "We're All in This Together: The Decline of Trust in Government, 1958–1996." In *What Is It about Government That Americans Dislike?*, edited by John R. Hibbing and Elizabeth Theiss-Morse, 28–46. Cambridge: Cambridge University Press.

Bennett, Stephen Earl, Staci L. Rhine, Richard Flickinger, and Linda L. M. Bennett. 1999. "'Video Malaise' Revisited: Public Trust in the Media and Government." *Harvard International Journal of Press/Politics* 4:8–23.

Blendon, Robert J., John M. Febson, Richard Morin, Drew E. Altman, Mollyann Brodie, Mario Brossard, and Matt James. 1997. "Changing Attitudes in America." In *Why People Don't Trust the Government*, edited by Joseph S. Nye, Jr., Philip D. Zelikow, and David G. King, 205–16. Cambridge, MA: Harvard University Press.

Brehm, John, and Wendy Rahn. 1997. "Individual-Level Evidence for the Causes and Consequences of Social Capital." *American Journal of Political Science* 41:999–1023.

Brooks, Clem, and Simon Cheng. 2001. "Declining Government Confidence and Policy Preferences in the U.S.: Devolution, Regime Effects, or Symbolic Change?" *Social Forces* 79:1343–75.

Chanley, Virginia A., Thomas J. Rudolph, and Wendy M. Rahn. 2001. "Public Trust in Government in the Reagan Years and Beyond." In *What Is It about Government That Americans Dislike?*, edited by John R. Hibbing and Elizabeth Theiss-Morse, 59–82. Cambridge: Cambridge University Press.

Cook, Timothy E., and Paul Gronke. 2001. "The Dimensions of Institutional Trust: How Distinct Is Public Confidence in the Media?" Paper presented to the Midwest Political Science Association, Chicago.

———. 2002. "Trust, Distrust, Lack of Confidence: New Evidence of Public Opinion toward Government and Institutions from 2002." Paper presented to the Southern Political Science Association, Savannah, GA.

———. 2005. "The Skeptical American: Revisiting the Meaning of Trust in Government and Confidence in Institutions." *Journal of Politics* 67:784–803.

Cooper, Joseph. 1999. "Trends in Public Trust, 1952–1998." In *Congress and the Decline of Public Trust*, edited by Joseph Cooper, 185–214. Boulder, CO: Westview.

Dalton, Russell J. 2000. "Value Change and Democracy." In *Disaffected Democracies: What's Troubling the Trilateral Countries?*, edited by Susan J. Pharr and Robert D. Putnam, 252–69. Princeton, NJ: Princeton University Press.

DeMint, Jim. 2008. "25 Years after *A Nation at Risk*: Returning to President Reagan's Vision for American Education." Heritage Foundation, Washington, DC.

Edwards, George C. 1990. *Presidential Approval: A Sourcebook*. Baltimore: Johns Hopkins University Press.

Fan, David P., Robert O. Wyatt, and Kathy Keltner. 2001. "How Press Reporting Affects Public Confidence in the Press, the Military, and Organized Religion." *Communication Research* 28:826–52.

Fried, Amy, and Douglas B. Harris. 2001. "On Red Capes and Charging Bulls: How and Why Conservative Politicians and Interest Groups Promoted Public Anger." In *What Is It about Government That Americans Dislike?*, edited by John R. Hibbing and Elizabeth Theiss-Morse, 157–74. Cambridge: Cambridge University Press.

Gibson, James L., Gregory A. Caldeira, and Lester Kenyatta Spence. 2003a. "Measuring Attitudes towards the United States Supreme Court." *American Journal of Political Science* 47:354–67.

———. 2003b. "The Supreme Court and the US Presidential Election of 2000: Wounds, Self-Inflicted or Otherwise?" *British Journal of Political Science* 33:535–56.

Glaeser, Edward L., David I. Laibson, Jose A. Scheinkman, and Christine L. Soutter. 2000. "Measuring Trust." *Quarterly Journal of Economics* 115:811–46.

Gronke, Paul, and Thomas Cook. 2002. "Disdaining the Media in the Post 9/11 World." Paper presented to the American Political Science Association, Boston.

Gronke, Paul, and Timothy E. Cook. 2007. "Disdaining the Media: The American Public's Changing Attitudes toward the News." *Political Communications* 24:259–81.

Gronke, Paul, and Brian Newman. 2000. "FDR to Clinton, Mueller to ??: A 'State of the Discipline' Review of Presidential Approval." Paper presented to the American Political Science Association, Washington, DC.

Hout, Michael, and Claude S. Fischer. 2002. "Why More Americans Have No Religious Preference: Politics and Generations." *American Sociological Review* 67:165–90.

Jiobu, Robert M., and Timothy J. Curry. 2001. "Lack of Confidence in the Federal Government and the Ownership of Firearms." *Social Science Quarterly* 82:77–88.

King, David C., and Zachary Karabell. 2003. *The Generation of Trust: Public Confidence in the U.S. Military since Vietnam*. Washington, DC: AEI Press.

Klugman, Joshua, and Jun Xu. 2008. "Racial Differences in Public Confidence in Education: 1974–2002." *Social Science Quarterly* 89:155–76.

Lipset, Seymour Martin, and William Schneider. 1987. *The Confidence Gap*. Rev. ed. Baltimore: Johns Hopkins University Press.

Mansbridge, Jane. 1997. "Social and Cultural Causes of Dissatisfaction with U.S. Government." In *Why People Don't Trust Government*, edited by Joseph S. Nye, Jr., Philip D. Zelikow, and David G. King, 133–54. Cambridge, MA: Harvard University Press.

Moy, Patricia, and Michael Pfau. 2000. *With Malice toward All? The Media and Public Confidence in Democratic Institutions*. Westport, CT: Greenwood.

Mueller, John E. 1973. *War, Presidents, and Public Opinion*. New York: John Wiley.

National Commission on Excellence in Education. 1983. *A Nation at Risk: The Imperative for Educational Reform*. Washington, DC: Government Printing Office.

Newton, Kenneth, and Pippa Norris. 2000. "Confidence in Public Institutions: Faith, Culture, or Performance?" In *Disaffected Democracies: What's Troubling the Trilateral Countries?*, edited by Susan J. Pharr and Robert D. Putnam, 52–73. Princeton, NJ: Princeton University Press.

Nicholson, Stephen P., and Robert M. Howard. 2003. "Framing Support for the Supreme Court in the Aftermath of Bush v. Gore." *Journal of Politics* 65:676–95.

Orren, Gary. 1997. "Fall from Grace: The Public's Loss of Faith in Government." In *Why People Don't Trust Government*, edited by Joseph S. Nye, Jr., Philip D. Zelikow, and David G. King, 77–107. Cambridge, MA: Harvard University Press.

Pescosolido, Bernice A., Steven A. Tuch, and Jack K. Martin. 2001. "The Profession of Medicine and the Public: Examining Americans' Changing Confidence in Physician Authority from the Beginning of the 'Health Care Crisis' to the Era of Health Care Reform." *Journal of Health and Social Behavior* 42:1–16.

Price, Vincent, and Anca Romantan. 2004. "Confidence in Institutions Before, During, and After 'Indecision 2000.'" *Journal of Politics* 66:939–56.

Putnam, Robert D. 2000. *Bowling Alone: The Collapse and Revival of American Community*. New York: Simon & Schuster.

Rasinski, Kenneth A., Tom W. Smith, Jennifer Berktold, and Bethany Albertson. 2002. "America Recovers: A Follow-Up to a National Study of Public Response to the September 11th Terrorist Attacks." NORC, Chicago.

Richardson, Lilliard E., Jr., David J. Houston, and Chris Sissie Hadjiharalambous. 2001. "Public Confidence in the Leaders of American Government Institutions." In *What Is It about Government That Americans Dislike?*, edited by John R. Hibbing and Elizabeth Theiss-Morse, 83–97. Cambridge: Cambridge University Press.

Robinson, Robert V., and Elton F. Jackson. 2001. "Is Trust in Others Declining in America? An Age-Period-Cohort Analysis." *Social Science Research* 30:117–45.

Rosenthal, S. A., T. L. Pittinsky, D. M. Purvin, and R. M. Montoya. 2007. *National Leadership Index 2007: A National Study of Confidence in Leadership*. Cambridge, MA: Center for Public Leadership, Harvard University.

Schlesinger, Mark. 2002. "A Loss of Faith: The Sources of Reduced Political Legitimacy for the American Medical Profession." *Milbank Quarterly* 80:185–235.

Schuman, Howard, and Cheryl Rieger. 1992. "Historical Analogies, Generational Effects, and Attitudes toward War." *American Sociological Review* 57:315–26.

Schuman, Howard, and Jacqueline Scott. 1989. "Generations and Collective Memories." *American Sociological Review* 54:359–81.

Sherman, Lawrence W. 2001. "Trust and Confidence in Criminal Justice." Unpublished paper, University of Pennsylvania, Philadelphia.

Shribman, David M. 1999. "Insiders with a Crisis from Outside: Congress and the Public Trust." In *Congress and the Decline of Public Trust*, edited by Joseph Cooper, 27–42. Boulder, CO: Westview.

Smith, Tom W. 1981. "Can We Have Confidence in Confidence? Revisited." In *Measurement of Subjective Phenomena*, edited by Denis F. Johnston, 119–89. Washington, DC: Government Printing Office.

———. 1982. "College Dropouts: An Analysis of the Psychological Well-Being and Attitudes of Various Educational Groups." *Social Psychology Quarterly* 45:50–53.

———. 1991. "Context Effects in the General Social Survey." In *Measurement Errors in Surveys*, edited by Paul P. Biemer, Robert M. Groves, Lars E. Lyberg, Nancy A. Mathiowetz, and Seymour Sudman, 57–72. New York: John Wiley.

———. 1992. "Religious Beliefs and Behaviors and the Televangelist Scandals of 1987–1988." *Public Opinion Quarterly* 56:360–80.

———. 1993. "A Comparison of Two Confidence Scales." GSS Methodological Report No. 80, NORC, Chicago.

———. 1994. "Is There Real Opinion Change?" *International Journal of Public Opinion Research* 6:187–203.

———. 1997a. "Does Knowledge in Science Breed Confidence in Science?" Paper presented to the International Conference on the Public Understanding of Science and Technology, Chicago.

———. 1997b. "Factors Relating to Misanthropy in Contemporary American Society." *Social Science Research* 26:170–96.

———. 2007. "Trends in National Spending Priorities, 1973–2006." Unpublished report, NORC, Chicago.

———. 2008a. "Trends in Confidence in Institutions, 1973–2006." GSS Social Change Report No. 54, NORC, Chicago.

———. 2008b. "Trends in Confidence in Institutions, 1973–2006: Methodological Notes." Unpublished report, NORC, Chicago.

Smith, Tom W., Kenneth A. Rasinski, and Marianna Toce. 2001. "America Rebounds: A National Study of Public Response to the September 11th Terrorist Attacks: Preliminary Findings." NORC report, NORC, Chicago.

Smith, Tom W., D. Garth Taylor, and Nancy A. Mathiowetz. 1980. "Public Opinion and Public Regard for the Federal Government." In *Making Bureaucracies Work*, edited by Carol H. Weiss and Allen H. Barton, 37–63. Beverly Hills, CA: Sage.

Stoutenborough, James W., Donald P. Haider-Markel, and Mahalley D. Allen. 2006. "Reassessing the Impact of Supreme Court Decisions on Public Opinion: Gay Civil Rights Cases." *Political Research Quarterly* 59:419–33.

Torres-Reyna, Oscar, and Robert Y. Shapiro. 2002. "Defense and the Military." *Public Opinion Quarterly* 66:279–303.

Uslaner, Eric M. 2002. *The Moral Foundations of Trust*. Cambridge: Cambridge University Press.

Wolfers, Justin. 2003. "Is Business Cycle Volatility Costly? Evidence from Surveys of Subjective Well-Being." *International Finance* 6:1–2.

8

Continuity and Change in American Religion, 1972–2008

Mark Chaves and Shawna Anderson

By world standards, the United States is a religious country. Even when we take into account the considerable overreporting of religious service attendance and uncertainty about what people mean when they say that they pray or believe in God, Americans still are more pious than people in any industrialized country, with the possible exception of Ireland (Baker 2005, pp. 209–11; Greeley 2003). High levels of religious belief and practice have characterized American society from its beginnings.

We cannot say anything definitive about long-term trends in U.S. religious belief or practice since surveys of nationally representative samples of individuals do not exist before the middle of the 20th century. But historical studies of local communities do provide a picture of church attendance rates in some times and places. One prominent historian of American religion who reviewed the available historical evidence concluded that "participation in congregations has probably remained relatively constant." He elaborated, "For most of the past three hundred years, from 35 to 40 percent of the population has probably participated in congregations with some degree of regularity" (Holifield 1994, p. 24). Remarkably, the weekly religious service attendance rate implied by the 2008 General Social Survey is within that range: 37%. This overstates true weekly attendance (Hadaway, Marler, and Chaves 1993; Presser and Chaves 2007), but it probably represents fairly the proportion of Americans who participate in congregations with some degree of regularity.

Considering the continuing high levels of American religiosity, it is tempting to treat any signs of change as mere footnotes to the main story of continuity. We will resist this temptation, however, because the General Social Survey (GSS) does indeed reveal important change since 1972, even if that change is relatively slow. As we will see, several slow-moving—even glacial—trends in American religion have been under way. But slow does not mean unimportant, and long-term, profound social change can occur more slowly than anyone would notice without repeated observation over decades.

This chapter describes eight trends evident in the GSS between 1972 and 2008: increased religious diversity; increased affiliation among Protestants with conservative and evangelical denominations; softening involvement with congregations; reduced belief in an inerrant Bible; reduced confidence in the leaders of religious organizations; reduced tolerance of certain kinds of religious involvement in the public sphere; a tighter connection between religious service attendance and political, social, and religious conservatism; and—the only trend that might be interpreted as an increase in American religiosity—somewhat higher levels of diffusely spiritual attitudes. Some trends are indicated by a single repeated GSS item while others represent our interpretation of a set of similarly trending items. Among the many aspects of religion measured more than once in the GSS, these eight trends stand out.

Some of these trends are well-known.[1] We again document even the well-known trends here in order to provide a stand-alone summary of recent religious change evident in the GSS. Our agenda is descriptive rather than explanatory, and our focus is on aggregate change. Although we occasionally comment on variations across subgroups of Americans or offer explanations of what may underlie these trends, mainly we seek to summarize the aggregate changes in American religion since 1972 that can be seen in the GSS. Readers interested in greater detail may follow our references to literature that explores these trends in more depth.

Continuity in American Religion

We begin by documenting the remarkable continuity in American religious belief and practice between 1972 and 2008. Table 8.1 displays more than two dozen GSS religion items that show no aggregate change over time.[2] The range of beliefs, attitudes, experiences, and practices that show continuity rather than change is impressive. The percentages of Americans who know God exists (64%), who ever had a born-again experience (36%), and who pray at least several times a week (69%) have remained steady from the 1980s to the present. The percentages who read the Bible at least weekly (31%), who watch religious television (28%), who feel extremely close to God (31%), who consider themselves very or extremely religious (26%), and who believe in

Table 8.1. Stable GSS Religion Items, 1972–2008

	Pooled %	N	Years spanned	# surveys
Practice/behavior/experience				
Attended Sunday school most of the time or regularly at 16	71	2,911	1988–1998	2
Watches some religious television each week	28	2,926	1988–1998	2
Reads the Bible at least once a week	31	2,910	1988–1998	2
Prays at least several times/week	69	24,145	1983–2008	16
Has had a "born again" experience	36	10,487	1988–2008	6
Has tried to convince others to accept Jesus Christ	44	7,881	1988–2008	4
Beliefs and attitudes				
Knows God exists and has no doubts	64	12,998	1988–2008	8
Believes in God now and always has	87	4,287	1991–2008	4
Describes self as extremely or very religious	26	3,863	1991–2008	3
Describes self as having strong religious affiliation	38	48,127	1974–2008	25
Attending services regularly is highly important for being a good Christian or Jew	44	2,863	1988–1998	2
Believing in God without doubt is highly important for being a good Christian or Jew	73	2,870	1988–1998	2
Following the teaching of one's church/synagogue is highly important for being a good Christian or Jew	55	2,861	1988–1998	2
Following one's conscience, even if against church/synagogue teachings, is highly important for being a good Christian or Jew	62	2,791	1988–1998	2
Evil in the world has never caused doubts about religious faith	53	2,829	1988–1998	2
Personal suffering has never caused doubts about religious faith	49	2,833	1988–1998	2
Death in the family has strengthened religious faith	68	2,772	1988–1998	2
Birth of a child has strengthened religious faith	75	2,780	1988–1998	2
Probably or definitely believes in heaven	86	3,713	1991–2008	3

Table 8.1. (*continued*)

	Pooled %	N	Years spanned	# surveys
Probably or definitely believes in hell	73	3,657	1991–2008	3
Agrees that God concerns himself with human beings personally	73	3,766	1991–2008	3
Agrees that life is meaningful only because God exists	46	3,754	1991–2008	3
Has had a turning point when made new commitment to religion	43	8,836	1991–2008	5
Feels extremely close to God	31	10,009	1983–1991	7
Thinks that churches and religious organizations have too much power	23	2,267	1991–1998	2

Note: The widest 95% confidence interval for any of these percentages is +/– 2 percentage points.

heaven (86%) or hell (73%) did not change notably during the 7- to 17-year periods over which they were measured.

There is much continuity, then, in the American public's basic religiosity. And it bears repeating that, by world standards, Americans remain remarkably religious in both belief and practice. The trends that we next describe should be seen against the backdrop of these stably high levels of religiosity. This stability cautions us against overstating the amount of change in American religion, but it also makes the trends stand out more than they otherwise might.

Increasing Religious Diversity

Fischer and Hout (2006) emphasize that the United States has become more religiously diverse since the beginning of the 20th century. It is more religiously diverse than it was even in 1972. Figure 8.1 tells the basic story of trends in Americans' self-reported religious affiliations.[3] We call attention to three features of this figure. First, the proportion of Americans who claim no religious affiliation has increased. This increase is most noticeable beginning in the 1990s, when it quickened, but it is a long-term trend. In 1957, 3% of Americans said they had no religious affiliation; by 2008, 17% said so.[4]

Second, there are more Muslims, Buddhists, Hindus, and others who are neither Christian nor Jewish. From one perspective this increase is dramatic, with the number of people claiming a religion other than Christian or Jewish more than doubling from about 1% in the 1970s to between 2.5% and 3% today. The percentage of religious "others" remains very small, however. Though this may seem surprising, recall that a majority of recent immigrants to the United States come from predominantly Christian countries, and

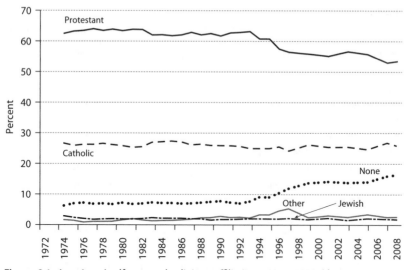

Figure 8.1. Americans' self-reported religious affiliations, 1972–2008 (three-year moving averages).

two-thirds of recent legal immigrants are Christian (Alba and Nee 2003, pp. 181–82; Jasso, Massey, Rosenzweig, and Smith 2003, p. 223). The proportion of self-identified Jews in the United States has remained at about 2% since 1975, and there are about as many Jews in the United States as there are Muslims, Buddhists, and Hindus combined. Still, though the percentage of non-Judeo-Christians in the United States remains small, the proportion of Americans who claim a religious affiliation that is neither Christian nor Jewish has grown, and continues to grow.[5]

Third, the increases in those with no religion and those whose religion is something other than Christian or Jewish have come mainly at the expense of Protestants. The declining proportion of Protestants in the United States is a very long-term trend, and it has continued since 1972. In the early 1970s, approximately 62% of GSS respondents identified with a Protestant church or denomination; by 2008, just over half did. If this continues, as it surely will, the United States soon will not have a Protestant majority for the first time in its history.[6]

The upshot of these trends is that religious diversity increased in the United States over this period.[7] This increasing religious diversity also is evident in friendship circles. In 1988 and 1998, the GSS asked respondents to describe as many as three "good friends they feel close to," not including a spouse.[8] The percentage of friends in the same broad religious category as the respondent (the same five categories in Figure 8.1) declined from 59% in 1988 to 54% in 1998. The percentage of friends who attended the same congregation as the respondent declined from 26% to 22%. Over a longer time span, in 1985 and

2004 the GSS asked respondents to describe as many as five "people with whom you discussed matters important to you." The percentage of nonfamily confidants in the same broad religious category as the respondent declined from 66% in 1985 to 60% in 2004. Though these are not large shifts, their consistency makes them worth noting.

Families as well as friendship circles also are more religiously diverse than they used to be. The overall percentage of people who have married across religious lines is not much different in 2008 than in the 1970s, but increasing religious intermarriage is evident if we look across generations instead of across years. Only about 10% of ever-married people born before 1920 married across one of the five religious categories tracked in Figure 8.1; about 25% of those born after 1970 have married across those lines. Clearly, religious diversity has increased in many people's everyday lives as well as in the society as a whole.

Other data show that Americans also have become more accepting of religious diversity during this period. The percentage of Americans who say they would vote for an otherwise qualified Catholic, Jew, or atheist who was running for president has increased dramatically since the middle of the 20th century, to the point where today almost all say they would vote for a Catholic or Jew and about half say they would vote for an atheist. In Muncie, Indiana, the percentage of high school students who agreed that "Christianity is the one true religion and everyone should be converted to it" dropped from 91% in 1924 to 41% in 1977. Today, three-quarters of Americans say "yes" when asked if they believe there is any religion other than one's own that offers a true path to God.[9] Not only is the United States more religiously diverse than it was several decades ago; Americans appreciate that religious diversity more than they used to.

Increasing Numbers of Conservative Protestants

A second trend is well-known: the center of gravity within American Protestantism has shifted from more liberal, mainline (sometimes now called old line) denominations to more conservative, evangelical denominations. Figure 8.2 shows the trend. Since 1972, the percentage of Americans affiliated with theologically more liberal, mainline denominations has steadily declined while the percentage affiliated with more conservative, evangelical denominations increased slightly until the early 1990s and has remained stable since then. By 2008 there were twice as many individuals affiliated with conservative denominations as with theologically more liberal ones (28% and 14% of GSS respondents in 2008, respectively).[10]

Many attribute this trend to people fleeing liberal denominations for the warmer confines of evangelical churches, but Hout, Greeley, and Wilde (2001) showed that approximately 80% of the shift comes from differential

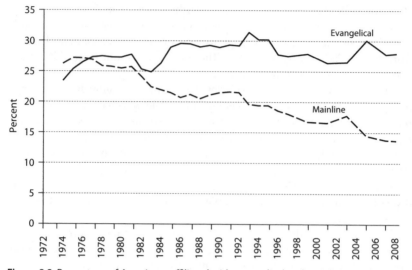

Figure 8.2. Percentage of Americans affiliated with evangelical and mainline Protestant denominations, 1972–2008 (three-year moving averages).

fertility rather than religious switching. In every birth cohort for which we have the relevant data, women affiliated with conservative Protestant denominations have more children than those affiliated with more moderate and liberal denominations. Religious switching is part of the story, but not in the way many people think. The most important trend in religious switching is that conservative denominations now lose fewer people to moderate and liberal denominations than in previous decades, probably because upward social mobility no longer prompts switching from being, say, Baptist to being Presbyterian or Episcopalian. Evangelical denominations and congregations have, with their people, become firmly middle-class, even affluent. Evangelical denominations also lose fewer of their young people to secularity than do more liberal denominations.

In sum, evangelical and conservative denominations have been doing better than more liberal denominations in recent decades, but not because many people have switched from one to the other. The main dynamic is demographic.

Softening Involvement in Religious Congregations

Discussions of religious involvement always begin with attendance at worship services. Figure 8.3 shows trends in the percentage of American adults who attend religious services using two different sources, the GSS and time-use diaries.[11] Note first that the weekly attendance rate implied by the GSS is much

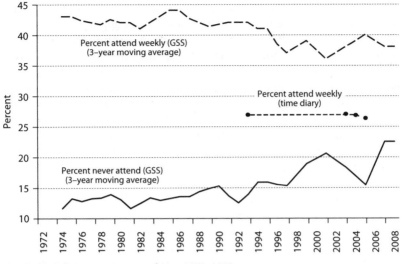

Figure 8.3. Religious service attendance, 1972–2008.

higher than that calculated from time-use studies. Since 1990, the weekly attendance rate implied by the GSS has hovered around 40%, while the four time-diary studies conducted since then all yield weekly rates of about 27%. Time-use studies use an indirect approach by asking respondents to describe what they did on the preceding day. The time-diary numbers in Figure 8.3 represent the percentage of respondents who, when asked to describe what they did on a Sunday, reported attending religious services.[12] The lower numbers are more accurate; they come closer to attendance rates based on direct observation at services (Hadaway et al. 1993).[13]

What about the trend? Since 1990, the GSS shows a modest but statistically significant decline in weekly attendance. The rate of decline in the GSS is very slow—about one-quarter of a percentage point per year since 1990—and the time-use data register no statistically significant decline since 1990. The American National Election Studies also show stability in attendance since 1990. It seems most prudent, then, to conclude that weekly attendance at religious services has been essentially stable since 1990.[14] At the same time, however, Figure 8.3 also shows that the percentage of people who *never* attend religious services, while still relatively small, has increased from 13% in 1990 to 22% in 2008.[15]

Looking at the decades prior to 1990, it is clear that attendance did not increase, but whether it declined or remained stable is a matter of debate. We think attendance did decline between 1960 and 1990. We reach this conclusion for several reasons. First, attendance declined, especially for Catholics, during the 15 or 20 years before the GSS began in 1972, and it seems to have continued its decline, although at a slower pace, since 1970 (Putnam 2000,

p. 71; cf. Fischer and Hout 2006, pp. 203–5). Second, time-use studies indicate a notable decline in weekly attendance, from approximately 40% in 1965 to approximately 27% in 1993 (Presser and Stinson 1998). Third, studies that compare attendance among children and young people at different points in time consistently find that today's young people attend services at lower rates than did comparably aged individuals in earlier decades (Hofferth and Sandberg 2001; Wuthnow 2007, p. 53). Fourth, a different GSS item, asking respondents whether they are members of "church-affiliated groups," also declined from the 1970s to the 1980s and has been stable since then.[16] Overall, then, we conclude that weekly religious service attendance declined in the several decades leading up to 1990 but has remained essentially stable thereafter.

Many people participate in religious activities other than by attending worship services. The GSS occasionally has asked how often people are involved in a religious congregation beyond attendance at services.[17] In all, 17% said they were involved nearly every week or more in the 1990s, declining to 11% in the 2000s. The pattern is the same for people who are regular attenders.

Figure 8.4 extends the discussion of religious involvement by examining trends in childhood religious socialization. Religious involvement in youth is one of the best predictors of religious involvement in adulthood, so trends in the extent to which people are raised in religiously active households can foreshadow future trends in involvement. As with intermarriage, we examine

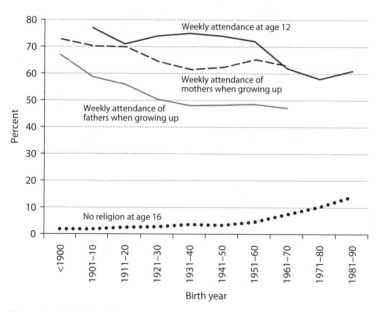

Figure 8.4. Declining religious socialization.

religious socialization by birth year rather than by survey year. Since child-hood religious socialization does not change as an individual ages, in a long-lived population like the United States the percentage of people who were raised in religiously active households will change slowly, even if generational differences in the prevalence of childhood religious socialization are substantial. Limiting our attention to year-by-year change would lead us to overlook the long-term generational change that is afoot.

Generational differences in childhood religious socialization are appreciable. More recently born individuals are increasingly likely to say they had no religion when they were 16 years old, and, beginning with people born after 1940, the percentage increases at a faster rate with each generation. The childhood weekly attendance rate respondents report declines from nearly 80% among people born before 1910 to approximately 60% for those born after 1970. Respondents born in the first part of the 20th century report that, while they were growing up, about 70% of their mothers were weekly attenders, a figure that declines to about 60% for people born in the latter part of the century. Most striking of all is a steady decline in the percentage of people who report growing up with religiously active fathers—from nearly 70% for those born before 1900 to about 45% for those born after 1970. There can be little doubt that Americans are increasingly less likely to grow up in religiously active households.[18]

Putting all of this together, there seems to be softening involvement in American religious congregations over recent decades. Aggregate weekly attendance at worship services is either stable or very slowly declining since 1990, but it declined in the decades before that, and the percentage of people who never attend is steadily increasing. Moreover, each new cohort of individuals attends religious services less than did earlier cohorts at the same age, and each new generation of Americans is less likely to be raised in a religiously active family than were earlier generations.

None of this decline is happening fast, and levels of religious involvement in the United States continue to remain very high by world standards. Calling this a softening rather than a decline in religious involvement strikes an interpretive balance of acknowledging the signs of changing religious involvement while also recognizing the high levels of involvement with American religious organizations evident in the data.

Declining Belief in an Inerrant Bible

Figure 8.5 shows that a gradual but steady decline in belief in an inerrant Bible is under way.[19] Over 30 years, the percentage of people who say they believe that the Bible should be taken literally declined from approximately 40% to just over 30%. This trend appears in two different time series (Gallup polls as well as the GSS), which increases our confidence that this trend is real,

Figure 8.5. Declining belief in inerrant Bible, 1976–2008 (three-year moving averages).

if slow. Much of this change, moreover, is produced by cohort replacement. People do not generally change their minds about the Bible as they get older. Instead, more recently born individuals are less likely to believe in an inerrant Bible than those born longer ago. Almost half of Americans born before 1910 believe that the Bible is the literal word of God; fewer than one-third of those born after 1940 believe that. The overall percentage of inerrantists in American society is declining slowly but surely as older generations are replaced by younger generations with less strict views about the Bible. Social change occurring in this way can be gradual, but still profound.

Connecting this trend with the increase described earlier in tolerance for, and even appreciation of, religions other than one's own, we might say that even in the midst of high levels of religious belief and practice in American society, there is declining confidence in the special status of one's own religion.

Declining Confidence in the Leaders of Organized Religion

Americans are less likely to express a great deal of confidence in leaders of religious institutions than they used to be.[20] Figure 8.6 shows this trend both for all adults and for those who say they attend religious services at least once per month. Between 1975 and 2008, the number of people with a great deal of confidence in religious leaders declined from about 35% to under 25%. Higher percentages of regular attenders express a great deal of confidence in religious leaders, but the trend is the same.

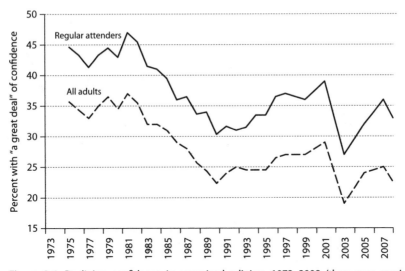

Figure 8.6. Declining confidence in organized religion, 1973–2008 (three-year moving averages).

This declining confidence is not unique to religious organizations. Americans are less confident in the leaders of many kinds of institutions than they were in the 1970s (see Smith, chapter 7 in this volume). Still, confidence in religious leaders has declined faster than confidence in the leaders of other institutions. Between 1973 and 1983, 35% of people, on average, expressed a great deal of confidence in the leaders of religious organizations, compared with only 29%, on average, expressing a great deal of confidence across all of the other institutions about which they were asked. Between 1998 and 2008, only 25% expressed a great deal of confidence in religious organizations—the same percentage expressing a great deal of confidence, on average, in the other kinds of institutions. In the 1970s, religious leaders inspired somewhat greater public confidence than did leaders of other institutions, but their relative position has since declined. People now express as low a degree of confidence in religious leaders as they do, on average, in leaders of other major institutions.[21]

Increasing Disapproval of Religion in the Public Sphere

Americans continue to debate appropriate kinds of public religious expression and appropriate kinds of political involvement for religious leaders. Taken together, several items in the GSS seem to point to increases since the 1970s in disapproval of certain kinds of public expressions of religion. Figure 8.7, for example, shows a rise in the percentage of Americans approving of a

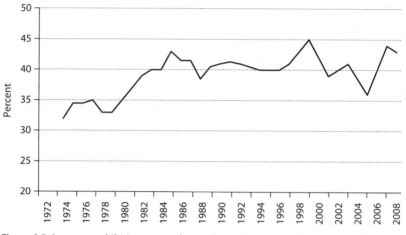

Figure 8.7. Approve prohibition on mandatory Christian prayer in public schools, 1972–2008 (three-year moving average).

Supreme Court prohibition, first articulated in 1962, of mandatory prayer in public schools, from just over 30% in the 1970s to just over 40% in the 1980s. Approval has hovered around 40% since then.[22] The number of people who strongly agreed that "religious leaders should not try to influence how people vote in elections" increased from 30% in 1991 to 37% in 1998, and increased again to 44% in 2008. The number who strongly agreed that "religious leaders should not try to influence government decisions" increased from 22% in 1991 to 31% in 1998, and increased again to 38% in 2008. More recently, according to Gallup polls, the percentage of people who agree that organized religion should have less influence in this nation increased from 22% in 2001 to 34% in 2008 (Blow 2008). Finally, feelings toward both Protestants and Catholics (but not Jews) seem less favorable today than they were in the 1980s.[23]

Was public appreciation of religion dampened by 1990s political activism that was explicitly proclaimed, and sometimes celebrated, as religiously motivated? We cannot be sure about the answer to that question on the basis of these few items. Still, taken together, these mini-trends suggest that over this period the American public became less enamored of at least some kinds of explicit religious involvement in the public sphere.

Tighter Connection between Attendance and Conservatism

We examined correlations between religious service attendance and dozens of other variables to see if the connection between attendance and other beliefs, attitudes, or behaviors might be strengthening or weakening. Religious service attendance is correlated with many beliefs, attitudes, and behaviors,

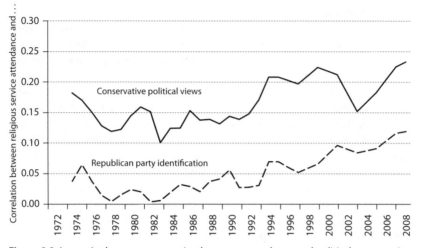

Figure 8.8. Increasingly strong connection between attendance and political conservatism (three-year moving averages).

and many of these correlations have not changed over time. That is, active religious practice does not differentiate Americans on many other individual characteristics any more or less than it did 35 years ago.[24] One major set of attitudes, however, has become more tightly connected with religious service attendance over the last few decades: attitudes indicating political, social, and religious conservatism.[25]

Figure 8.8 shows the trend in the correlation between religious service attendance and two measures of political conservatism: how liberal or conservative a person's political views are and political party identification.[26] Figure 8.8 shows that the correlation between attendance and political conservatism is always positive—throughout this period more religiously active people are also more conservative—but it also shows that this correlation has increased in recent decades. That is, the connection between religiosity and political conservatism has grown tighter. It seems that this correlation became qualitatively stronger after 1992.

Percentages rather than correlations help to convey the magnitude of this trend. In the 1970s, 19% of respondents who attended religious services at least weekly said that their political views were conservative or extremely conservative compared to 13% of less frequent attenders. Across the 2000 through 2008 surveys, 33% of weekly attenders said they are conservative or extremely conservative, compared to only 16% of less frequent attenders. Over recent decades, infrequent religious service attenders have become only slightly more politically conservative while weekly attenders have become much more conservative. The gap between these groups has widened considerably.

The picture is similar for political party identification. In the 1970s, 9% of weekly attenders said that they were strong Republicans, compared to 7% of less frequent attenders. The comparable numbers in the 2000–2008 surveys are 19% and 9%, respectively. Weekly attenders have moved from being nearly indistinguishable from others in their political party affiliations to being nearly twice as likely as others to call themselves strong Republicans. This is a significant change over a 30-year period.[27]

We observe similar trends in several key indicators of social conservatism: attitudes about abortion, sex, and euthanasia. The abortion trend is particularly interesting. The GSS asks respondents whether or not they think it should be possible for a pregnant woman to obtain a legal abortion in seven situations: if there is a strong chance of a serious defect in the baby, if she is married and does not want any more children, if the woman's own health is seriously endangered by the pregnancy, if the family has very low income and cannot afford any more children, if she became pregnant as a result of rape, if she is not married and does not want to marry the man, and if the woman wants it for any reason.[28] Opposing legal abortion in any of these situations is strongly correlated with religious service attendance, but these correlations have become stronger in recent decades for only two of these items: abortion in the case of rape and in the case of serious fetal defect.

Figure 8.9 shows the trend in the correlation between attendance and opposing legal abortion in cases of rape. The correlation has steadily increased since the 1970s, so that being religiously active now is more tightly connected to opposing legal abortion in cases of rape than it was in the 1970s. In the 1970s, 29% of weekly attenders opposed legal abortion in cases of rape, compared with 12% of less frequent attenders. In the 2000–2008 surveys, 43% of weekly attenders opposed legal abortion in this situation, compared to 16% of less frequent attenders. The trend is similar for abortion in cases of seri-

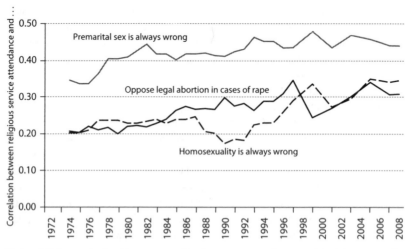

Figure 8.9. Increasingly strong connection between attendance and social conservatism (three-year moving averages).

ous fetal defect. Similar to political conservatism, the attitude gap between weekly and infrequent attenders has widened substantially on these two items because more frequent attenders have become more conservative. None of the other abortion items changes in this way, however. There is no general widening of the gap between attenders and nonattenders in those abortion attitudes. Rather, it seems that the most religiously active people have increased their attitudinal distance from the rest of the population only with respect to the two situations in which support for legal abortion is greatest.[29]

Figure 8.9 also shows the trends in the correlations between attendance and attitudes about premarital sex and homosexuality.[30] Like opposing abortion in cases of rape or serious defect, disapproval of premarital sex and homosexuality both became more tightly connected to religious service attendance in recent decades. There is, however, an important difference between these trends in views about sexuality and those about abortion. For the abortion items, the population at large has grown more conservative, and the correlation with attendance has increased because the most religious people have become especially conservative over time. On the sexuality items the population is trending in a liberal direction, but the most religious people are either resisting liberalization (in the case of premarital sex) or liberalizing more slowly than others (in the case of homosexuality).

Percentages tell the story more clearly. In the 1970s, 53% of weekly religious service attenders said that premarital sex is always wrong, compared to 23% of infrequent attenders; the 2000–2006 numbers are 55% and 16%, respectively. Weekly attenders are about as conservative on premarital sex today as they were in the 1970s, but less frequent attenders have become somewhat less conservative on this issue. Both frequent and infrequent attenders have become more liberal about homosexuality: 85% of 1970s weekly attenders said that homosexuality is always wrong compared to 67% of infrequent attenders, while since 2000 the comparable numbers are 79% and 48%, respectively. On this issue, less religiously active people have liberalized faster.

Attitudes about euthanasia show a similar pattern: the overall trend is in a liberal direction, but the most religiously active people are liberalizing more slowly.[31] In the 1970s, 59% of weekly attenders, compared to 32% of less frequent attenders, opposed legal euthanasia when a terminally ill patient requests it. The comparable numbers from the 2000–2006 surveys are 55% and 25%, respectively.

Turning from political to religious conservatism, Figure 8.10 shows increasingly strong connections between attendance and whether a person believes the Bible is the literal word of God and whether he or she has had a born-again experience.[32] Since the 1980s, the positive correlations of these items with religious service attendance have grown stronger. The increasingly strong connection between attendance and a conservative view of the Bible is especially dramatic because frequent and infrequent attenders are trending in opposite directions. In the 1980s, 48% of weekly religious service

Figure 8.10. Increasingly strong connection between attendance and religious conservatism (three-year moving averages).

attenders said that the Bible is the literal word of God, compared to 31% of less frequent attenders; the comparable 2000–2008 numbers are 53% and 27%, respectively. The "born-again" trend is less dramatic, but similar in shape. Of 1980s weekly attenders, 54% said they were born-again, compared to 30% of infrequent attenders; the comparable 2000–2008 numbers are 61% and 27%, respectively. Not only are the most religiously active people more politically and socially conservative, they also are more *religiously* conservative.[33]

In sum, the connection between frequent religious service attendance and political, social, and religious conservatism is increasingly tight. In some cases, it has grown tighter because the most religiously active people have become more conservative over time. In other cases, the connection has grown tighter because the most religiously active people are liberalizing more slowly than others. It is difficult to avoid the conclusion that the attitudinal distance between the most and least religiously active people in U.S. society has increased in recent decades. The public may not be more polarized on these issues than it was at some point in the past, but differences of opinion now line up with religious differences more than they did previously.[34]

Increasing Diffuse Spirituality

The "spiritual but not religious" phenomenon in American society is now well-known, but it should not be exaggerated. The vast majority of people—approximately 80%—describe themselves as *both* spiritual and religious. Still, a small but growing minority of Americans describe themselves as spiritual but not religious. In 1998, 9% of GSS respondents described themselves as at least moderately spiritual but not more than slightly religious. That number rose to 14% in 2008.[35] Younger people are much more likely than older people to describe themselves in this way. The increase occurred because nonreligious people are more likely to say they are spiritual, not because people are less likely to say that they are religious. In 1998, 24% of people who were slightly or not at all religious said they were at least moderately spiritual; that increased to 35% in 2008. If what people mean when they say they are spiritual but not religious is that they are generally concerned with spiritual matters but are not interested in organized religion, then there seems to be a still small but growing minority of the population whose spiritual inclinations do not lead them to become involved in conventional religious organizations.[36]

There also are small but noticeable increases in the percentage of people who say they believe in life after death, from about 75% in the 1970s to just over 80% in 2008, and in the percentage who definitely believe in miracles, from 46% in 1991 to 55% in 2008.[37] We mention these trends here because we think they are related to the "spiritual-but-not-religious" trend. The largest increases in belief in the afterlife, for example, are among subgroups who have not traditionally emphasized an afterlife. The number of Jews who say they believe in life after death increased from fewer than 20% before the 1970s to 50% in 2006, and among those with no religion the number who believe in life after death increased from fewer than 40% to 60% during that same period.[38] In the 1970s, 90% of weekly attenders said they believe in an afterlife, compared to 71% of less frequent attenders; the comparable 2000–2008 numbers are 91% and 79%, respectively. Here the correlation between religious service attendance and belief in life after death is *weakening* because the gap in belief between the most and least religious people is decreasing.[39]

The increasing number of people saying they are spiritual but not religious comes from increasing interest in spirituality among the nonreligious, and the increase in belief in the afterlife has occurred almost wholly among Jews and the less religious. Hence we see these trends as indicating a small but noticeable increase in a generic and diffuse spirituality rather than an increase in traditional religiosity or piety.

Conclusion

Perhaps the most striking aspect of the eight trends discussed in this chapter is that no indicator of traditional religious belief or practice is going up. There is much continuity, there is some decline, there are shifting fortunes for liberal and conservative Protestant denominations, and there is a tighter connection between religious service attendance and political, social, and religious conservatism. The only upward trend over the last several decades is in a diffuse spirituality. Increasing spirituality may provide a growing market for certain kinds of religious products, such as self-help books with spiritual themes, but even if it continues to rise, it probably will not provide a solid foundation for new kinds of religious institutions or new forms of religious collective action.

The long-term increase in tolerance of, even appreciation for, religions other than one's own is good news for our pluralistic society. The flip side of this increasing tolerance, however, is declining confidence in the special status of one's own religion. The gradual decline in biblical literalism, shaken confidence in institutions in general and religious institutions in particular, and continuing decline in the percentage of children raised in religiously active households together indicate a slow but steady hollowing out of some kinds of traditional religious belief and practice alongside a tentative increase in a generic kind of spirituality that is not tied to any specific religious tradition or institution. These trends pose challenges for U.S. society's religious institutions, despite continuing high levels of religious belief and some kinds of practice. They challenge religious institutions to combine tradition and adaptation in ways that lead people to express their religiosity through face-to-face gatherings and local organizations to the same extent as they have in the past.[40]

We do not believe that the tighter connection between religious service attendance and political, social, and religious conservatism amounts to an increasingly divisive culture war. Recall some of the subtleties of this trend. In a group of 100 regular churchgoers, for example, 33 place themselves on the high end of a political conservative scale and 79 believe that homosexuality is always wrong, while in a group of 100 nonattenders, 16 place themselves high on the conservatism scale and 48 believe that homosexuality is always wrong. These are real differences, but most people in both groups consider themselves politically moderate, liberal, or only slightly conservative, and most (or nearly most) people in both groups still believe that homosexuality is always wrong. Recall also that, when it comes to attitudes about homosexuality, both groups are trending in the liberal direction. On that attitude, the increasingly tight connection between religiosity and conservative attitudes comes about only because one group is liberalizing faster than the other, not because the groups are heading in opposite directions. Indeed, attenders and nonattenders are heading in opposite directions only when it comes to *religious* conservatism. These nuances lead us to refrain from interpreting these trends as indicating dangerously increasing polarization in American society. Still, the attitudinal distance between the most and least religiously active people in U.S. society has increased in recent decades. The public may not be more polarized on these issues than it was previously, but differences of opinion line up with religious differences more in 2008 than they did in the 1970s. This trend should be watched closely in the coming years.

This chapter focused on continuities and changes in American religion that are evident in the GSS, but trends evident in the GSS are not the only important recent trends in American religion. We call attention to one particularly significant shift in the social organization of American religion that is not tracked by the GSS: more and more people are concentrated in the very largest congregations. People always have been concentrated in the largest congregations—today approximately half of all those who attend religious services are in only the largest 10% of congregations—but that concentration began to intensify in the 1970s, and it continues. This can be seen in the increasing number of very large churches across the country, but it goes beyond the stereotypical megachurch. It is occurring in every Protestant denomination on which we have data. It is occurring in large and small denominations, in conservative and liberal denominations, and in growing and declining denominations. Concentration is rising because churchgoers are shifting from small and medium-sized churches into larger ones, not because the very largest churches are attracting the otherwise unchurched.[41]

Increasing concentration helps to answer a question that may arise in response to the trends we have emphasized in this chapter: If the basic story of American religion over the past several decades is one of stability on many fronts and decline on some others, why do many see these decades as a time of increasing public presence, social prominence, and political influence for American religion? Why have some observers even claimed that recent decades are ones of religious revival, awakening, or revitalization?[42]

Part of the answer to this question lies in the increasingly tight connection between religiosity and political and social conservatism. This is the social reality behind, and in part created by, the rise of the religious right in recent decades, a development that has tremendously increased religion's visibility in politics at every level. Another part of the answer, though, is the increasing concentration of churchgoers within very large churches. This shift also increases religion's visibility, and possibly its social and political influence, even in the face of stable or declining religiosity among individuals. One 2,000-person church is more visible than ten 200-person churches; one 2,000-person church presents a more attractive audience for a politician than ten 200-person churches; the pastor of a 2,000-person church gets an appointment with the mayor more easily than the pastors of 200-person churches. Increasing religious concentration, in other words, can create the impression that more people are turning to religion when what is really under way is a change in religion's social organization. Of course, organizational concentration can lead to real increase in the social and political influence of religious congregations and their leaders, if only because it creates more very large congregations and more leaders of very large congregations with which to contend. But we should not mistake this change in social organization for an increase in the underlying levels of religious belief and practice in the society. There is no evidence of such an increase.

We have documented changes in religious belief and behavior, but these changes have not occurred in isolation. Recent waves of immigration obviously contribute to religious diversity and to increased acceptance of that diversity. The century-long movement of the American population from rural areas into cities and suburbs and the decades-long increase in U.S. educational levels also have shaped religious belief and practice. Changes in American family life such as increased divorce rates, declining percentages of two-parent-plus-children households, and the movement of women into the paid labor force all have affected American religious life and institutions. The rapid diffusion of computer technologies across American society is influencing both private and corporate expressions of religion in ways we have only begun to understand. And what we have called softening involvement in religious congregations surely reflects broader trends in civic engagement and involvement in other kinds of voluntary associations. Fully understanding and explaining religious change requires that we attend to these other social changes.

Before we attempt to understand and explain religious change, though, we need to know what kinds of religious change are transpiring. We hope that our distillation of eight trends from the vast reservoir of information about religion available in the GSS clarifies the current state of knowledge about trends in American religion and facilitates ongoing efforts to explore these trends more deeply.

Notes

We thank Jim Davis, Claude Fischer, Jim Lewis, Peter Marsden, Robert Putnam, and Tom Smith for helpful comments on earlier versions of this chapter, and Gary Thompson for help with analyzing data and producing the table and figures.

1. Other discussions of trends in American religion include Greeley (1989), Gallup and Lindsay (1999), Putnam (2000, chap. 4), Fischer and Hout (2006, chap. 8), Putnam and Campbell (2010), and Chaves (2011). Chaves (2011) is an expanded version of this chapter. Unless otherwise noted, all numbers mentioned in this chapter are from the GSS, and all percentage or mean differences to which we call attention are statistically significant at least at the .05 level. We weight the GSS data with the variable WTSSALL, which adjusts for respondents' different household sizes and also for the subsampling design implemented in 2004. We also correct for black over-samples in 1982 and 1987.

2. Given the large sample sizes that result when GSS surveys from different years are combined, some of the cross-year differences behind the pooled percentages in Table 8.1 are statistically significant, but none of them seems substantively important. A few cross-year percentage point differences are greater than 2 or 3 points, but many of these items were measured at only two points in time, and a 5- or 6-percentage-point difference on an isolated item measured at just two points in time seems too flimsy a basis for discerning a trend. We are more comfortable interpreting small-magnitude changes as real trends when several conceptually related items trend in the same direction. Not included in Table 8.1, but also showing no trend over time,

are mean scores on a set of items tracking how people imagine God, for example as father or mother, or as friend or king.

3. These are trends in responses to the item, "What is your religious preference? Is it Protestant, Catholic, Jewish, some other religion, or no religion?"

4. The 1957 number is from the Current Population Survey (U.S. Department of Commerce 1958). This survey included individuals in the civilian population who were at least 14 years old, and in some cases the religion of everyone in a household was reported by a single respondent. Fischer and Hout (2006, pp. 193–94) suggest that the faster pace of this trend after 1990 has political roots: "[T]he increasing identification of churches with conservative politics led political moderates and liberals who were already weakly committed to religion to make the political statement of rejecting a religious identification." See Hout and Fischer (2002) for details.

5. See Sherkat (1999) for a more detailed parsing of the "other" category. See Smith (2002a, 2002b) on the issue of the number of Jews and Muslims in the United States.

6. See Smith and Kim (2005) for more on this trend.

7. Since the GSS began interviewing in Spanish only in 2006, it is not an ideal source for tracking another kind of immigration-related increase in religious diversity over recent decades: the increasing presence of Latinos among American Catholics.

8. In 1998, respondents were asked questions about five friends; in 1988, they were asked about only three friends. To maintain comparability, we use only information about the first three friends in 1998.

9. All of the facts in this paragraph are taken from Fischer and Hout (2006, pp. 192, 200, 341n41). The Muncie numbers are originally from Caplow, Bahr, Chadwick, and Hoover (1983); the other numbers in this paragraph are from Gallup polls. See Wuthnow (2005) for more extensive discussion of religious diversity in the United States.

10. The categories in Figure 8.2 are constructed using a slightly modified version of the classification described by Steensland et al. (2000). The largest group in the mainline category is the United Methodist Church. Other sizable groups in that category include American Baptist Churches in the U.S.A, Episcopal Church, Evangelical Lutheran Church in America, Presbyterian Church in the U.S.A, and United Church of Christ. The largest group in the evangelical category is the Southern Baptist Convention. Other sizable groups in that category include Assemblies of God, Lutheran Church-Missouri Synod, and Seventh-day Adventist. Nondenominational churches also are classified as evangelical.

11. The GSS numbers are from responses to the open-ended question, "How often do you attend religious services?" Responses to this question are coded by interviewers into one of nine categories. We calculate a weekly attendance rate by translating each response category into the following probabilities of attending in any given week: never = 0, less than once a year = .01, about once or twice a year = .02, several times a year = .05, about once a month = .23, two to three times a month = .58, nearly every week = .85, every week = .99, several times a week = .99. The 1993 time-diary number is from the University of Maryland's Time Use Study. The 2002–2004 time-diary numbers are from the American Time Use Study, conducted by the U.S. Bureau of Labor Statistics. See Presser and Chaves (2007) for more information on these time-use studies.

12. Since respondents in these time-diary studies report their activities only for a single day, it is not possible to use those data to adjust the weekly rate to take account of attendance on days other than Sunday. In 1996 and 1998, however, the GSS asked respondents what days they attended. Of those reporting attendance on a day other than Sunday, 80% also attended on Sunday, and only 2% of all respondents reported attending on a day other than Sunday without also attending on Sunday. Hence, even ignoring the overreporting of attendance on days other than Sunday, taking account of attendance on those days would raise the Sunday-based time-diary estimate of weekly attendance by only 2 percentage points.

13. The time-diary studies produce more accurate results because directly asking people how often they attend services leads people who think of themselves as regular (but perhaps not literally weekly) attenders to overstate their attendance. Asking indirectly about attendance, by contrast, seems less likely to evoke an "I'm a churchgoer" identity in respondents' minds, and an indirect approach therefore produces more accurate responses.

14. See Presser and Chaves (2007) for details on attendance trends since 1990.

15. Much of the increase in never attending comes from shifts from very infrequent attendance into nonattendance. Because shifts across these low attendance categories have little effect on the overall weekly attendance rate, the juxtaposition of a stable weekly attendance rate since 1990 and rising "never attend" does not imply that those who attend are attending much more frequently.

16. "Now we would like to know something about the groups or organizations to which individuals belong. Here is a list of various organizations. Could you tell me whether or not you are a member of each type?" This question was asked regularly from 1974 through 1994. After 1994 it was not asked again until 2004. The overall percentage of people who say that they belong to "church-affiliated groups" declines over this period. We hesitate to overemphasize that decline, however, because responses to this item seem to be affected by whether or not respondents already had been asked about their religious affiliation and worship service attendance. The percentage who say "yes" to this item is significantly lower when it is preceded by the standard religion items, perhaps because having already reported their religious affiliation and worship attendance makes people inclined to say "yes" to this question only if they are involved beyond mere affiliation or attendance. When these two contexts are separated, the item declines a bit from the 1970s into the 1980s and then levels off. When the other religion questions precede this item, it is stable from 1980 to 2004.

17. "How often do you take part in the activities and organizations of a church or place of worship other than attending services?"

18. The question about mother's and father's attendance is, "When you were growing up, how often did your mother/father (or mother/father substitute) attend religious services?" Another set of items asked respondents about their parents' attendance "when you were a child." Responses to these items produce similar results, so we used responses to both sets of items to construct Figure 8.4. We compute implied weekly attendance rates in the same manner described in note 11. Respondents who had no father or father substitute present when they were growing up are excluded from these calculations, so the sharp decline in fathers' attendance is not an artifact of increasing divorce or single-mother household rates. Reliability checks reassure us that the trends we report are not produced by people reporting more religious childhoods as they age.

19. In both the GSS and Gallup polls, people are asked, "Which of these state-ments comes closest to describing your feelings about the Bible?" The options are, "The Bible is the actual word of God and is to be taken literally, word for word; The Bible is the inspired word of God but not everything in it should be taken literally, word for word; The Bible is an ancient book of fables, legends, history, and moral precepts recorded by men." Figure 8.5 graphs the percentage choosing the first option.

20. "I am going to name some institutions in this country. As far as the people running these institutions are concerned, would you say you have a great deal of con-fidence, only some confidence, or hardly any confidence at all in them?"

21. There is quite a lot of variation in public confidence in different institutions (see Smith, chapter 7 in this volume). The percentages of people in 2008 who ex-pressed a great deal of confidence in the leaders of various types of institutions are as follows: military (52%), scientific community (40%), medicine (39%), U.S. Supreme Court (32%), education (30%), organized religion (20%), banks and financial insti-tutions (19%), major companies (16%), executive branch of the federal government (11%), organized labor (13%), Congress (11%), press (9%), and TV (9%).

22. "The United States Supreme Court has ruled that no state or local govern-ment may require the reading of the Lord's Prayer or Bible verses in public schools. What are your views on this—do you approve or disapprove of the court ruling?"

23. In 1986, 1988, 1989, and again in 2004, GSS respondents were asked about their feelings toward Protestants, Catholics, and Jews using the following item: "I'd like to get your feelings toward groups that are in the news these days. I will use some-thing we call the feeling thermometer, and here is how it works. I'll read the names of a group and I'd like you to rate that group using the feeling thermometer. Ratings be-tween 50 degrees and 100 degrees mean that you feel favorable and warm toward the group. Ratings between 0 degrees and 50 degrees mean that you don't feel favorable toward the group and that you don't care too much for that group." Combining results from the three 1980s surveys and comparing them to those for 2004, the mean tem-perature rating of Protestants dropped from 69 to 66 degrees, while that for Catholics dropped from 67 to 63 degrees. These drops are small but statistically significant. The rating assigned to Jews was 61 degrees in both periods. Respondents were first asked to rate Muslims in 2004, when they were assigned a mean temperature of 48 degrees. It will be important, of course, to track change in this last number over the coming years.

24. Variables whose correlation with religious service attendance has not changed include measures of economic conservatism, illicit sexual activity, use of computer technology, gender role attitudes, capital punishment attitudes, happiness, and per-ceptions of how much inequality and conflict are present in society.

25. Some of the trends we describe in this section are discussed in more detail in Putnam and Campbell (2010). Putnam and Campbell also emphasize an increasingly positive correlation between religious service attendance and educational attainment, combining it with other evidence to suggest that attendance declined during this pe-riod among the white working class.

26. "We hear a lot of talk these days about liberals and conservatives. I'm going to show you a seven-point scale on which the political views that people might hold are arranged from extremely liberal to extremely conservative. Where would you place yourself on this scale?" And: "Generally speaking, do you usually think of yourself as a Republican, Democrat, Independent, or what?" If Republican or Democrat: "Would

you call yourself a strong (Republican/Democrat) or a not very strong (Republican/Democrat)?" If Independent, no preference, or other: "Do you think of yourself as closer to the Republican or Democratic party?" This set of questions on political party identification produces a 7-point scale ranging from "strong Democrat" to "strong Republican." Figures 8.8, 8.9, and 8.10 report Pearson product–moment correlation coefficients. These coefficients can vary between –1.0 and +1.0, but they are always above zero in these figures, indicating that, throughout this period, more frequent attenders are more conservative than less frequent attenders.

27. This trend is well documented and analyzed by political scientists. See, for example, Green (2007), Fiorina, Abrams, and Pope (2006), and Campbell (2002). It is apparent in the American National Election Studies (ANES) as well as in the GSS, increasing our confidence that it is a real trend. Fiorina et al. (2006, pp. 180–81), using ANES data, also notice a qualitative change in 1992. They suggest that "the common observation that religiosity now is more closely related to party identification may reflect a repositioning of the parties rather than a change in voter attitudes."

28. "Please tell me whether or not you think it should be possible for a pregnant woman to obtain a legal abortion if. . . ."

29. Putnam and Campbell (2010) find that general attitudes about abortion (and homosexuality) are more tightly tied to religiosity among younger generations.

30. "If a man and woman have sexual relations before marriage, do you think it is always wrong, almost always wrong, wrong only sometimes, or not wrong at all?" And: "What about sexual relations between two adults of the same sex. Do you think it is always wrong, almost always wrong, wrong only sometimes, or not wrong at all?" We code these scales so that larger numbers indicate stronger disapproval.

31. "When a person has a disease that cannot be cured, do you think doctors should be allowed by law to end the patient's life by some painless means if the patient and his family request it?"

32. "Would you say you have been 'born again' or have had a 'born again' experience—that is, a turning point in your life when you committed yourself to Christ?" The Bible item is the same item described in note 19.

33. Interestingly, religious service attendance is not increasingly associated with either believing in God or frequency of prayer. Rather than an increasingly tight connection between attendance and general, religiously unspecific belief and practice, we see an increasingly tight connection between religious service attendance and a specific type of conservative evangelical Protestant theology.

34. This discussion brings to mind debates about "culture wars" in American society. For more on this subject see DiMaggio, Evans, and Bryson (1996), Williams (1997), Fiorina et al. (2006), and Fischer and Hout (2006, chap. 9).

35. "To what extent to you consider yourself a religious person? Are you very religious, moderately religious, slightly religious, not religious at all?" And: "To what extent do you consider yourself a spiritual person? Are you. . . ."

36. See Marler and Hadaway (2002) for measurement problems related to the spiritual-but-not-religious phenomenon.

37. "Do you believe there is a life after death?" "Do you believe in miracles?"

38. The numbers in this sentence are from Fischer and Hout (2006, p. 208). See Greeley and Hout (1999) for more detail on trends in belief in an afterlife.

39. The correlation between religious service attendance and frequency of prayer also may have weakened somewhat in recent decades.

40. See Chaves and Anderson (2008) for information about trends within American congregations.

41. See Chaves (2006) for more on this increasing concentration.

42. The *New York Times* columnist David Brooks (2006), for example, referred to "the current religious awakening" as if it were an established fact.

References

Alba, Richard, and Victor Nee. 2003. *Remaking the American Mainstream: Assimilation and Contemporary Immigration*. Cambridge, MA: Harvard University Press.

Baker, Wayne. 2005. *America's Crisis of Values: Reality and Perception*. Princeton, NJ: Princeton University Press.

Blow, Charles M. 2008. "Americans Move to the Middle." *New York Times*, July 26, p. A27.

Brooks, David. 2006. "Ends Without Means" (Op-ed column). *New York Times*, September 14, p. A27.

Campbell, David E. 2002. "The Young and the Realigning: A Test of the Socialization Theory of Realignment." *Public Opinion Quarterly* 66:209–34.

Caplow, Theodore, Howard M. Bahr, Bruce A. Chadwick, and Dwight W. Hoover. 1983. *All Faithful People: Change and Continuity in Middletown's Religion*. Minneapolis: University of Minneapolis Press.

Chaves, Mark. 2006. "All Creatures Great and Small: Megachurches in Context." *Review of Religious Research* 47:329–46.

———. 2011. *American Religion: Contemporary Trends*. Princeton, NJ: Princeton University Press.

Chaves, Mark, and Shawna Anderson. 2008. "Continuity and Change in American Congregations: Introducing the Second Wave of the National Congregations Study." *Sociology of Religion* 69:415–40.

DiMaggio, Paul, John Evans, and Bethany Bryson. 1996. "Have Americans' Social Attitudes Become More Polarized?" *American Journal of Sociology* 102: 690–755.

Fiorina, Morris P., Samuel J. Abrams, and Jeremy C. Pope. 2006. *Culture War? The Myth of a Polarized America*. New York: Pearson Longman.

Fischer, Claude S., and Michael Hout. 2006. *Century of Difference: How America Changed in the Last One Hundred Years*. New York: Russell Sage Foundation.

Gallup, George, Jr., and D. Michael Lindsay. 1999. *Surveying the Religious Landscape: Trends in U.S. Beliefs*. Harrisburg, PA: Morehouse.

Greeley, Andrew M. 1989. *Religious Change in America*. Cambridge, MA: Harvard University Press.

———. 2003. *Religion in Europe at the End of the Second Millennium: A Sociological Profile*. New Brunswick, NJ: Transaction.

Greeley, Andrew M., and Michael Hout. 1999. "Americans' Increasing Belief in Life after Death: Religious Competition and Acculturation." *American Sociological Review* 64:813–35.

Green, John C. 2007. *The Faith Factor: How Religion Influences American Elections*. Westport, CT: Praeger.

Hadaway, C. Kirk, Penny Long Marler, and Mark Chaves. 1993. "What the Polls Don't Show: A Closer Look at U.S. Church Attendance." *American Sociological Review* 58:741–52.

Hofferth, Sandra L., and John F. Sandberg. 2001. "Changes in American Children's Time, 1981–1997." In *Children at the Millennium: Where Have We Come From, Where Are We Going? Advances in Life Course Research*, edited by Timothy Owens and Sandra Hofferth, 193–229. New York: Elsevier.

Holifield, E. Brooks. 1994. "Towards a History of American Congregations." In *American Congregations*. Vol. 2 of *New Perspectives in the Study of Congregations*, edited by James P. Wind and James W. Lewis, 23–53. Chicago: University of Chicago Press.

Hout, Michael, and Claude S. Fischer. 2002. "Why More Americans Have No Religious Preference: Politics and Generations." *American Sociological Review* 67:165–90.

Hout, Michael, Andrew M. Greeley, and Melissa J. Wilde. 2001. "The Demographic Imperative in Religious Change in the United States." *American Journal of Sociology* 107:468–500.

Jasso, Guillermina, Douglas S. Massey, Mark P. Rosenzweig, and James P. Smith. 2003. "Exploring the Religious Preferences of Recent Immigrants to the United States: Evidence from the New Immigrant Survey Pilot." In *Religion and Immigration: Christian, Jewish, and Muslim Experiences in the United States*, edited by Yvonne Yazbeck Haddad, Jane I. Smith, and John L. Esposito, 217–53. Walnut Creek, CA: AltaMira.

Marler, Penny Long, and C. Kirk Hadaway. 2002. " 'Being Religious' or 'Being Spiritual' in America: A Zero-Sum Proposition?" *Journal for the Scientific Study of Religion* 41:289–300.

Presser, Stanley, and Mark Chaves. 2007. "Is Religious Service Attendance Declining?" *Journal for the Scientific Study of Religion* 46:417–23.

Presser, Stanley, and Linda Stinson. 1998. "Data Collection Mode and Social Desirability Bias in Self-Reported Religious Attendance." *American Sociological Review* 63:137–45.

Putnam, Robert D. 2000. *Bowling Alone: The Collapse and Revival of American Community*. New York: Simon & Schuster.

Putnam, Robert D., and David E. Campbell. 2010. *American Grace: How Religion Divides and Unites Us*. New York: Simon & Schuster.

Sherkat, Darren E. 1999. "Tracking the 'Other': Dynamics and Composition of 'Other' Religions in the General Social Survey, 1973–1996." *Journal for the Scientific Study of Religion* 38:551–60.

Smith, Tom W. 2002a. "The Muslim Population in the United States: The Methodology of Estimates." *Public Opinion Quarterly* 66:404–17.

———. 2002b. "Religious Diversity in the America: The Emergence of Muslims, Buddhists, Hindus, and Others." *Journal for the Scientific Study of Religion* 41:577–85.

Smith, Tom W., and Seokho Kim. 2005. "The Vanishing Protestant Majority." *Journal for the Scientific Study of Religion* 44:211–23.

Steensland, Brian, Jerry Z. Park, Mark D. Regnerus, Lynn D. Robinson, W. Bradford Wilcox, and Robert D. Woodberry. 2000. "The Measure of American Religion: Toward Improving the State of the Art." *Social Forces* 79:291–318.

U.S. Department of Commerce, Bureau of the Census. 1958. "Religion Reported by the Civilian Population of the United States: March 1957." *Current Population Reports: Population Characteristics*. Series P-20, no. 79. Released February 2.

Williams, Rhys H., ed. 1997. *Cultural Wars in American Politics: Critical Reviews of a Popular Myth*. New York: Aldine.

Wuthnow, Robert. 2005. *America and the Challenges of Religious Diversity*. Princeton, NJ: Princeton University Press.

———. 2007. *After the Baby Boomers: How Twenty- and Thirty-Somethings Are Shaping the Future of American Religion*. Princeton, NJ: Princeton University Press.

9

Trends in Informal Social Participation, 1974–2008

Peter V. Marsden and Sameer B. Srivastava

Background

Analysts and commentators periodically raise the prospect that large-scale social changes might substantially alter patterns of interpersonal relations, often for the worse. Among putative sources of such disruptions to the social fabric are industrialization, urbanization, and the development and expansion of mass media. Wirth (1938, p. 11), for example, wrote about consequences of a rapid rural–urban transition for modes of life, including declines in kinship bonds, neighborliness, and personal acquaintanceship, and substitution of secondary for primary social ties. Sociological analyses suggested that "mass society" entails a general reduction in the number of communal relationships, together with diminished functionality for those that remain; such atomization, it was feared, would render large numbers of people open to manipulation by elites and susceptible to mass appeals (Kornhauser 1968). Wellman (1979) terms these "community lost" perspectives.

Many mid-20th-century empirical studies suggested that informal social ties were highly resilient to such changes, although few of these studies assessed trends.[1] For example, Bell and Boat (1957) reported that over 60% of men in four varied San Francisco census tracts had informal social contacts at least weekly, while Hunter (1975) found that neighboring in a Rochester, New York, neighborhood was significantly higher in 1974 than in 1949. Residents of a Toronto district maintained numerous intimate relationships with kin and nonkin, many of whom resided elsewhere in the metropolitan area rather than in the immediate locality; nearly a quarter of these ties were with persons outside Toronto. A substantial minority of the relationships were potential sources of everyday and emergency assistance (Wellman 1979). These studies and others like them demonstrated that informal social ties had hardly vanished, notwithstanding the considerable macroscopic changes thought to have threatened them.

While less focused on the spatial aspect of "community" than earlier work, more recent discussions of downward trends in "social capital" raised parallel worries about declining social integration. Informal interpersonal ties are, of course, only one aspect of this multifaceted concept, which can also encompass connections to voluntary groups, social trust, and civic engagement, among other things. Putnam (2000, p. 115) asserts that there has been "a striking diminution of regular contacts with our friends and neighbors." He cites several factors as contributors to reduced connectedness: changing family and household structures; suburbanization, residential mobility, and spatial dispersion; electronic entertainment, especially television; and the replacement of a highly civic cohort born before 1940 by baby boomers and Generation X.

Comparing two GSS samples separated by about 20 years, McPherson, Smith-Lovin, and Brashears (2006) reported a particularly dramatic fall in the number of confiding relationships available to U.S. adults, from a 1985 average of 3.0 to a 2004 figure of 2.1; an estimated 22.6% of the 2004 sample reported no such confidant, compared to 8.0% in 1985—indicating an appreciable rise in isolation from this form of contact.[2] The decline in nonkin confidants was especially notable. Controversy about the validity of these findings has arisen, revolving largely around methodological questions (Fischer 2009; McPherson, Smith-Lovin, and Brashears 2009), but even McPherson et al. (2006) express concern that the findings may overstate the extent of any decline.[3] McPherson et al. (2006, p. 372) also raise the prospect that a falling number of confidants represents part of a trend toward what might be termed "network bifurcation"—contraction of intimate "core" networks, accompanied by growth in the number of weaker, dispersed contacts.[4] They suggest that shifting patterns in employment, spatial dispersion, recreation, and communication technologies might be responsible for this development.

Others outside the academic world make similar observations. Market trend analysts and consultants call attention to "cocooning," a "trend that sees individuals socializing less and retreating into their home more."[5] An increase in cocooning would open opportunities for entrepreneurs who can bring goods and services to consumers in their homes, as opposed to serving them in stores, showrooms, or offices. Some observe that a rise in online socializing accompanies cocooning; the phenomenon would appear to imply a general decline in face-to-face interactions, however.

Continued attention to trends in informal social contact, then, is warranted. This chapter assesses such trends over a 34-year period beginning in

1974, focusing on four forms of informal socializing measured regularly by the GSS. To our knowledge these are the longest available survey time series that include standardized measurements of interpersonal interactions.[6] We introduce the data in the next section, and then describe overall time trends in socializing. Next, we ask whether any changes in socializing might be due to population aging and cohort circulation, and decompose the trends into age-, cohort-, and period-related components. Thereafter, we examine the extent to which the changing composition of the U.S. adult population—in terms of family structure, residential location, education, and other factors—might account for trends in socializing, and briefly examine trends in "never" socializing. In the conclusion, we highlight implications of our analyses for claims that social networks have shrunk or transformed, as well as their limitations.

Measuring Informal Social Contacts

Our analysis focuses on four types of informal socializing measured in 21 GSSs between 1974 and 2008, for just over 30,000 respondents. The survey questions ask about the frequency of informal social contacts with others, not the size or structure of social networks. A broad decline in social integration should, however, imply declines in the frequency of social contact as well as in the number of such contacts.

The GSS measures of socializing we study are the following:

Would you use this card and tell me which answer comes closest to how often you do the following things?
  A. Spend a social evening with relatives
  B. Spend a social evening with friends who live outside the neighborhood
  C. Spend a social evening with someone who lives in your neighborhood
  D. Go to a bar or tavern

Respondents select one of seven frequency levels for each item: almost every day, once or twice a week, several times a month, about once a month, several times a year, about once a year, and never.

Three of these questions refer to spending a "social evening" with relatives, friends outside one's neighborhood, and neighbors, respectively. Most such social evenings, we presume, involve face-to-face contact during shared meals, parties, or joint outings to attend movies, sports events, and the like. Respondents might, however, choose to deem events that are not face-to-face—for instance, sessions in Internet chat rooms—to be "social evenings." Social evenings may—but do not necessarily—involve especially close ties, and they involve sociability—what Krause (2006) calls "companionship" and

Putnam (2000) terms "schmoozing"—rather than flows of social support like counseling or practical aid. The fourth item about socializing in bars or taverns could refer to social interactions in establishments that range from neighborhood taverns to sports bars and upscale cocktail lounges. We conjecture that the others seen in such settings are typically weaker ties than those with whom social evenings are spent. Some who visit bars or taverns, however, do so in order to drink, converse, and relax with an ongoing group of "regulars" found there.

For simplicity in presentation, most of our analyses focus on whether respondents report a given type of socializing "several times a month" or more, as opposed to about once a month or less. Trends in socializing assessed at other thresholds (e.g., "once or twice a week" or more) resemble, in the main, those based on more-than-monthly contact. Toward the end of the chapter, we contribute to discussions of trends in social isolation by briefly assessing trends in nonparticipation in each of the four forms of socializing, distinguishing those who "never" have a form of contact and those reporting some of it.

Overall Socializing Trends

Over the 1974–2008 period, over half (55%) of GSS respondents said that they spent a social evening with relatives more than once per month. More-than-monthly informal social contacts with friends outside the neighborhood (42.3%) or neighbors (35.1%) were less common, while only 16.3% of respondents visited a bar or tavern more than once a month.[7] Just over a fifth of those interviewed (20.5%) said that they do not have more-than-monthly contact with others in any of these four ways.

These forms of socializing are positively, but—at most—moderately, associated with each other. Generally speaking, someone who socializes more than once a month in one way is about 10 percentage points more likely to do so in a second way. Socializing with friends and visiting bars correspond most closely: of those who spend an evening with friends outside the neighborhood more than once a month, an estimated 25.9% also visit a bar or tavern that often, compared to 9.2% of those who socialize with friends once a month or less. Respondents who see relatives more often than monthly, though, are neither more nor less apt to visit bars multiple times per month than those who see their relatives less frequently. Guest and Wierzbicki (1999) report that the correspondence between frequently socializing with friends and often seeing neighbors has weakened over time.

Figure 9.1 depicts over-time trends in informal socializing. Plot symbols show, for each year, estimated proportions of respondents who socialize more often than monthly, while lines illustrate smoothed time trends. Socializing with relatives remained relatively steady between 1974 and 2008. At the

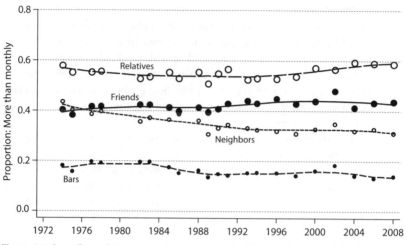

Figure 9.1. Overall socializing trends. Analyses weighted for number of adults in household, sampling phase (after 2002), and oversampling of blacks in 1982.

beginning of the period, nearly 58% of respondents stated that they socialized with relatives more than once a month; this fell to around 52% in the mid-1990s, but rose after that to almost 59% in 2006 and 2008. If anything, the number of people who spent evenings with friends outside the neighborhood more often than monthly increased slightly during these years, from about 40% in the mid-1970s to roughly 43% after 2008.

Socializing with neighbors exhibits the clearest downward trend. In 1974, nearly 44% of GSS respondents said that they spent a social evening with neighbors more than once a month—higher than the percentage that saw friends from outside the neighborhood more than once a month then. This fell to 36% by 1985, 33% by 2000, and just over 31% in 2008. Visiting bars or taverns fell less notably, from about 19% in the mid-1970s and early 1980s to roughly 14% after 2004.

Table 9.1 shows that the downward movements in seeing neighbors and visiting bars or taverns are statistically significant but relatively small, as is the

Table 9.1. Overall Socializing Trends

Form of socializing	Test for overall trend: $X^2(20)$, p value	Logit regression coefficient for linear annual trend (standard error)	Odds ratio	N
Friends	33.8, .028	0.005** (0.002)	1.005	30,077
Relatives	40.3, .005	0.003 (0.002)	1.003	30,097
Neighbors	93.1, < .001	−0.013*** (0.002)	0.987	30,066
Bars	51.3, < .001	−0.011*** (0.003)	0.989	30,043

**p < .01. ***p < .001.

upward trend in socializing with friends. The odds of socializing more often than monthly with a neighbor or at a bar fall by about 1% per year, while those of spending evenings with friends rise by a smaller factor.[8]

Accounts for Changes in Socializing

Analyses contending that social networks have shrunk attribute such contraction to a variety of changes that have taken place during recent years, such as rising media use or suburbanization and the population dispersion attendant to it. We consider some of these accounts below; here we observe that many of them refer to phenomena linked to the periods of time during which network change is thought to have occurred.

Two demographic mechanisms that have received relatively little attention in discussions of network contraction are the aging of the U.S. population and cohort turnover. It is well established that the typical U.S. adult is somewhat older now than in past decades (e.g., Treas and Torrecilha 1995; Meyer 2001). Using one GSS cross section, Marsden (1987) reported that network size fell with age, at an increasing rate, as did Fischer (1982) in a study of Northern Californians. Cornwell, Laumann, and Schumm (2008, p. 186) too found smaller social networks among older adults, citing social disengagement theory—the gradual abandonment of social roles—as one basis for this; Krause (2006) suggests that it might reflect preferences of older people for fewer, but more emotionally meaningful, social ties. One might reasonably conjecture that the frequency of socializing also declines with age. If so, then population aging alone might produce some decline in socializing.

Putnam (2000) suggests that some over-time changes in social capital might be due to the replacement of active cohorts by less active ones. He notes, however, that effects of generational succession are less notable for private "schmoozing" than for other more "public" forms of social capital such as political or civic participation (p. 283). Such a pattern of cohort turnover would yield lower levels of socializing, irrespective of other changes under way. If aging and/or cohort turnover affect socializing, these processes might obscure differences linked to period-related factors.

Because overall trends in socializing might reflect population aging, cohort-related factors, and period-linked differences, we next present an age-period-cohort interpretation of socializing trends, to reveal whether period-related trends are evident after taking these population processes into account. Thereafter, we adjust for several additional period-related changes in population composition.

Age, Cohort, and Period Differences in Socializing

It is widely understood that separating influences of age, period, and cohort on social phenomena requires the introduction of some assumptions that are not subject to empirical verification, owing to the functional interdependence among the three constructs (Fienberg and Mason 1978). The appendix to this chapter outlines and illustrates the methods we use to parse the three. Our principal assumption is that age and cohort effects on socializing are relatively smooth: they do not differ greatly between proximate age groups or birth cohorts. We approximate age- and cohort-related trends by equating coefficients within sets of adjacent age and cohort groups and then conduct successive tests that ask whether disaggregating these groupings into narrower intervals would improve model fit; this procedure yields different sets of age and cohort groupings for each form of socializing. We do not constrain period differences because they are of central interest in this chapter.

We present the results of our analyses graphically. Figures 9.2–9.4 present estimated proportions socializing more often than monthly by age, cohort, and year, respectively. Each figure displays proportions calculated while holding the other two factors at average levels: those in Figure 9.2, for example, give the estimated fractions of adults in each age group who socialize more than monthly, for an average year and an average cohort. Smoothed trend lines run through each set of adjusted proportions to illustrate the general pattern of age, cohort, and year differences for each of the four forms of socializing.

Table 9.2 displays results of statistical tests for age, period, and cohort differences. High test statistics and low p values offer strong evidence against the hypothesis of no age differences for all four forms of socializing. Cohort differences are detectable at the conventional .05 significance level for three of the four forms of socializing, relatively modest evidence given the large sample

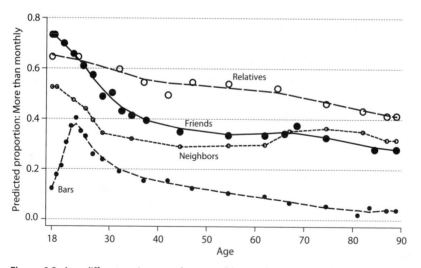

Figure 9.2. Age differences in more-than-monthly socializing. Proportions calculated for persons in an "average" cohort in an "average" year.

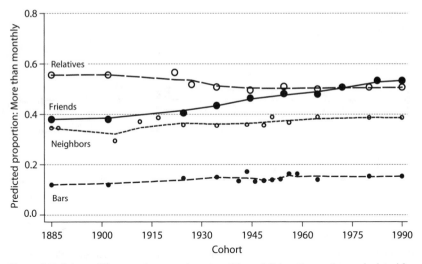

Figure 9.3. Cohort differences in more-than-monthly socializing. Proportions calculated for persons of an "average" age in an "average" year.

size. Adjusting for age and cohort differences, socializing with relatives and socializing with neighbors also appear to vary by year, as does visiting bars. We do not detect significant year-related differences in spending social evenings with friends outside the neighborhood, however.

Age Differences

Age differences in socializing appear substantial, as illustrated by the adjusted proportions for age groups shown in Figure 9.2. Plot symbols show the estimated proportion at the midpoint of each age group. The adjusted proportion of adults who spend social evenings more than once a month with relatives falls steadily with age. Socializing with friends declines rapidly among the young and middle-aged; beyond the early 40s it continues to fall with age, but much more gently.

Socializing with neighbors more often than monthly also declines with age among the young, but levels off among adults in their 40s and 50s. Mirroring a finding of Cornwell et al. (2008, p. 197), however, spending more than one social evening per month with neighbors rises somewhat after age 60, after which it falls off slightly. Among those over age 70, socializing with neighbors is a little more common than with friends. These patterns may reflect age-related factors such as retirement, widowhood, and reduced mobility.

Socializing in bars is highly concentrated among the young. The adjusted proportion visiting a bar or tavern more than once a month rises rapidly with age among young adults, peaking among 23-year-olds, just above the legal U.S. drinking age (21). It then falls rapidly until the early 30s, and more gently but steadily thereafter.

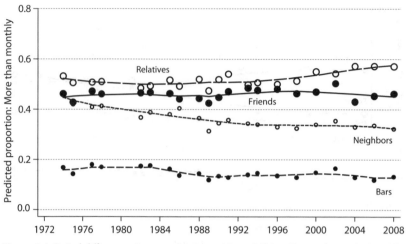

Figure 9.4. Period differences in more-than-monthly socializing. Proportions calculated for persons of an "average" age in an "average" cohort.

Taken together, age differences in socializing seem appreciable. To the extent that demographic processes have shifted greater fractions of U.S. adults into older age groups, these differences imply downward over-time movement in all four forms of socializing.

Cohort Differences

By comparison, differences in socializing across birth cohorts appear quite modest, though detectable (Table 9.2). Figure 9.3 depicts them. What movement in socializing there is across cohorts seems to be generally upward, with the exception of socializing with relatives. Cohort differences in seeing friends appear most pronounced: the adjusted proportion doing so more often than monthly rises visibly in Figure 9.3 across the cohort groups we distinguish. The proportion seeing neighbors more often than monthly also rises slightly for more recent cohorts, as does that for visiting bars or taverns. More-than-monthly socializing with relatives appears to be somewhat less common in later cohorts.

The direction of these cohort differences, apart from those for relatives, would imply increases, not decreases, in socializing. Because their magnitude is generally small, however, their implications for overall trends are also modest.

Period (Year) Differences

Figure 9.4 displays the period-related differences in socializing. These are, in essence, adjusted versions of the overall trends in Figure 9.1 that take differences we have attributed to aging and cohort turnover into account. By

Table 9.2. Wald Tests for Age, Period, and Cohort Differences in More-Than-Monthly Socializing

Effect	Form of socializing			
	Friends	Relatives	Neighbors	Bars
Age	$X^2(16) = 336.1, p < .001$	$X^2(9) = 109.9, p < .001$	$X^2(12) = 231.3, p < .001$	$X^2(20) = 213.7, p < .001$
Cohort	$X^2(7) = 14.4, p = .044$	$X^2(7) = 13.8, p = .054$	$X^2(11) = 25.0, p = .009$	$X^2(12) = 21.4, p = .044$
Period	$X^2(20) = 27.2, p = .129$	$X^2(20) = 37.2, p = .011$	$X^2(20) = 56.2, p < .001$	$X^2(20) = 37.4, p = .010$
N	29,974	29,994	29,963	29,939

and large, the patterns shown in Figure 9.4 resemble those in Figure 9.1. One difference is that the slightly upward-sloping year-related trend line for contact with friends seen in Figure 9.1 flattens: the adjusted proportion of adults who socialize with friends more often than monthly stays relatively steady throughout this period, with no statistically detectable differences across years (Table 9.2). The flattening evidently reflects adjustment for somewhat greater socializing with friends on the part of younger cohorts (Figure 9.3).

Socializing with relatives falls slightly during the first half of the period, before rising slightly in the most recent GSSs. Steadier downward trends across years are evident for socializing with neighbors and in bars/taverns. Variation across years in these patterns is slightly less than that shown in Figure 9.1, reflecting the fact that portions of the overall trends can be attributed to aging and age differences in socializing (Figure 9.2).

Net of aging and cohort change, then, period-related differences in socializing largely resemble the overall patterns. Taken together, they do not suggest dramatic change in informal social contact. The clearest downward movement is in neighboring, but even that is modest. Contact with friends has remained steady, while the fraction spending evenings with relatives more often than monthly seems to have risen slightly since the early 1990s.

Compositional Change and Socializing

"Demographic explanations" hold that change within a population in a phenomenon such as socializing is partially or entirely attributable to changes in the population's composition in terms of characteristics associated with the phenomenon (Davis 2001). Accounts that suggest recent declines in informal social contacts call attention to several such compositional features. This section reassesses socializing trends after making statistical adjustments for features of population composition that the GSS has measured regularly. We note at the outset that the four forms of socializing examined here may be related to such features in different ways.

Fischer (2011) inventories several types of accounts that have been put forward as bases for anticipating network decline and transformation, including technological, demographic, economic, and cultural sources of change; he notes that few empirical indicators for the cultural category are readily available. Technological accounts stress the use of media that either compete with interpersonal relationships (e.g., television, video games) or facilitate their formation (e.g., social networking websites). Among these, only television viewing is consistently measured over time in the GSS.[9]

Many changes in demographic factors alter family and household structures. Among these are falling rates of entry into marriage, increases in divorce and separation, and decreased childbearing, which have served to reduce family size (Spain and Bianchi 1996; Elliott and Umberson 2004). As well, increases in life spans make it increasingly likely that people will live alone as widows or widowers for some years (Fischer and Hout 2006). Reduced family sizes and smaller households reduce opportunities for socializing with relatives, and perhaps make people more apt to spend time with unrelated others (Putnam 2000). Our measures reflecting family size and structure include marital status (currently married, formerly married, never married), number of children, and number of siblings.

Allied to demographic factors is residential location. Fischer and Hout (2006) highlight suburbanization as the principal recent trend in U.S. residential patterns; Putnam (2000) includes suburbanization, sprawl, and commuting among the factors that increase time pressures on adults and may limit their engagement with others. In urban settings, the others one may prefer to see may be more readily accessible, while in dispersed suburban locations neighbors may be less apt to encounter one another. Our analysis distinguishes respondents who live in urban, suburban, and rural settings.

The primary economic factor we consider is employment status, on the reasoning that work commitments make it less likely that people will socialize with others. Putnam (2000) notes this as one of several factors related to recent increases in time and financial pressures, especially on women (see also Jacobs and Gerson 2004).

Our analyses also adjust for three additional sociodemographic factors: sex, race (white, black, neither black nor white), and years of education. We included all of these compositional measures together with age, cohort, and period differences in logistic regression analyses. Odds ratios for compositional explanatory variables are displayed in Table 9.3; Figure 9.5 presents, for each year, adjusted proportions of respondents who socialize more often than monthly.[10]

More-than-monthly socializing with relatives is linked to family status: it is more common among currently married adults than those never married, and especially common among the formerly married. It is also greater among those with larger numbers of children or siblings. Compositional changes due to declining marriage rates and smaller families should thus reduce monthly socializing with relatives. Those never married and those with fewer children are more apt to socialize with friends, with neighbors, and in bars; over-time compositional changes in family status should promote increases in these forms of informal social contact.

Table 9.3. Odds Ratios for Compositional Predictors of Socializing

		Friends	Relatives	Neighbors	Bars
Residential location	Urban	1.180*** (0.031)	0.930** (0.024)	0.884*** (0.020)	1.154* (0.080)
	Suburban	1.150*** (0.046)	0.935 (0.038)	0.806*** (0.033)	1.074 (0.087)
	Rural	0.737*** (0.042)	1.149* (0.065)	1.404*** (0.076)	0.806 (0.114)
Marital status	Married	0.748*** (0.013)	0.998 (0.017)	0.824*** (0.014)	0.631*** (0.016)
	Never married	1.489*** (0.064)	0.788*** (0.036)	1.384*** (0.061)	2.051*** (0.110)
	Formerly married	0.898* (0.043)	1.272*** (0.065)	0.877** (0.044)	0.773*** (0.048)
Family size	Number of siblings	0.995 (0.005)	1.012* (0.005)	1.009 (0.005)	0.991 (0.007)
	Number of children	0.930*** (0.009)	1.049*** (0.010)	0.978* (0.009)	0.973 (0.015)
Education	Years of education	1.040*** (0.006)	0.963*** (0.005)	0.998 (0.005)	1.018* (0.008)
Race	Black	0.969 (0.021)	1.121*** (0.025)	1.084*** (0.024)	0.799*** (0.025)
	Nonblack, nonwhite	0.911 (0.059)	0.991 (0.079)	0.835* (0.063)	0.661*** (0.065)
	White	1.132 (0.072)	0.900 (0.068)	1.105 (0.084)	1.895*** (0.187)
Gender	Female	0.981 (0.014)	1.133*** (0.015)	0.924*** (0.013)	0.652*** (0.013)
	Male	1.019 (0.015)	0.883*** (0.012)	1.082*** (0.016)	1.534*** (0.030)
Employment status	Employed	1.005 (0.016)	1.011 (0.015)	0.835*** (0.013)	1.112*** (0.027)
	Not employed	0.995 (0.016)	0.989 (0.015)	1.197*** (0.018)	0.900*** (0.022)
	N	29,756	29,773	29,744	29,722

Note: Standard errors in parentheses. Categorical predictors (rural/urban residence, marital status, race, sex, employment) are effect coded; we report odds ratios for all categories, but they are constrained such that their product across categories is 1.0 and interpreted as differences from an average across the categories. Analyses also include contrasts for age, period, and cohort groupings.

$*p < .05. **p < .01. ***p < .001.$

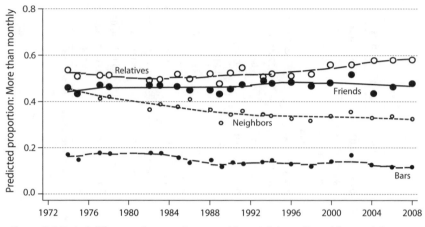

Figure 9.5. Period differences in more-than-monthly socializing, adjusted for trends in compositional variables. Calculated for persons of an "average" age in an "average" cohort, with predictors in Table 9.3 set at "average" levels.

Urban and suburban residents tend to socialize with friends and in bars more often than adults who live in rural areas. Those living outside of metropolitan regions, on the other hand, are more apt to see both relatives and neighbors socially than are residents of cities or suburbs. These findings are consistent with what Fischer (1982) reports based on his much more extensive study of the social networks of Northern Californians. Other things being equal, neighboring is lowest in suburban settings. Trends in settlement patterns that concentrate people in metropolitan areas (Fischer and Hout 2006), then, imply upward movements in socializing with friends and at bars, and downward ones in the other two forms.

Employment is linked to less frequent socializing with neighbors, but also to visiting bars and taverns somewhat more often—perhaps as an after-work leisure activity, or in connection with after-hours work obligations. Employed adults are neither more nor less likely than those outside the labor force to socialize with friends and relatives.

We found no statistically significant differences in socializing by television viewing, adjusting for the other compositional factors considered.[11] Moreover, the average number of hours of television viewing reported by GSS respondents has remained relatively steady at around three hours over the past three decades. Perhaps using other communication media (not measured in the GSS) competes with interpersonal socializing. Our admittedly limited analyses on this point yield no evidence suggesting an influence of technological factors, however.

None of the compositional factors we introduce has a consistent association with all four forms of socializing. More educated adults tend to spend more social time with friends and in bars or taverns, but a little less with relatives. Black adults are slightly more apt than nonblacks to see relatives and neighbors, while whites report more visits to bars and taverns than comparable nonwhites. Consistent with an image of women as "kin-keepers" (Moore 1990), women are more apt than comparable men to report more-than-monthly socializing with relatives, but less so to say that they see neighbors or (especially) visit bars.

If trends in these compositional measures could account entirely for over-time differences in socializing, then the trend lines shown in Figure 9.4 would flatten after adjustments for compositional change. Figure 9.5 presents differences in socializing by year, net of age differences, cohort differences, and compositional trends. Considered jointly, the compositional factors in Table 9.3 made socializing with friends and in bars a little more likely during the period of time covered here. Changes such as movement toward metropolitan areas, smaller families, and more never-married people imply some reduction in socializing with relatives. Adjusting for compositional factors alters trends in socializing with neighbors only negligibly.

The aggregate implications of compositional change are not large, however, so the adjusted trend lines in Figure 9.5 are generally similar to the respective lines in Figure 9.4, which adjust only for age and cohort differences. The recent upward movement in socializing with relatives appears somewhat more pronounced in Figure 9.5, since the downward influence of compositional change on this form of socializing has been removed. There is a hint, then, that factors not measured in our analyses have made adults somewhat more disposed to see their relatives socially than they were two decades ago.

A Note on Trends in Nonsocializing

Much of the discussion that ensued after McPherson et al. (2006) reported a dramatic contraction in the size of confiding networks focused on the especially large rise between 1985 and 2004 in the percentage of U.S. adults saying that they do not discuss important matters with anyone (McPherson, Smith-Lovin, and Brashears 2008b; Fischer 2009). This section describes the comparable trends in the GSS data on socializing, asking whether "never" socializing has risen notably since 1974. We note that relationships with confidants are generally stronger than those with others one sees socially, so these data do not bear directly on the issue of whether confiding networks per se have grown smaller. If, however, a more general rise in social disconnectedness is under way, we would expect trends in "never" socializing to parallel those in the absence of confidants. Indeed, if nonsocializing with comparatively weak ties is on the rise, it might be viewed as especially worrisome because such activities may involve only modest interpersonal commitment.

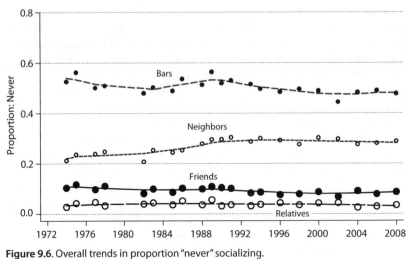

Figure 9.6. Overall trends in proportion "never" socializing.

Across the 1974–2008 period, estimates based on the GSS data indicate that just under 4% of adults do not ever see relatives, and that fewer than 10% never socialize with friends. The percentage who never spend a social evening with neighbors is larger (just under 27%), while about half of adults say that they never visit bars or taverns. Only 1% of respondents report that they never engage in any of these four forms of socializing. By this standard, utter isolation from informal social contact is quite rare.

Figure 9.6 depicts overall trends in the proportion "never" socializing across the period. For relatives, the trend line is level at around 0.04. Likewise, there is little movement in nonsocializing with friends: if anything, the proportion of respondents reporting that they never see friends fell slightly during this interval, from between 0.10 and 0.11 in the 1970s to under 0.09 by the middle 2000s. Consistent with our earlier findings for more-than-monthly socializing, the proportion of adults who never see their neighbors socially rose, from just over 0.20 in the 1970s to nearly 0.30 in the 2000s. More adults than in the 1970s, however, now visit bars or taverns at least occasionally: the proportion never doing so fell from above 0.55 to around 0.47 during this interval.[12]

We asked whether the patterns shown in Figure 9.6 would be notably altered by the adjustments made in our above analyses focused on more-than-monthly socializing—for age and cohort differences, as well as trends in population composition. Introducing such statistical controls modifies some details of the trend lines in nonsocializing but does not alter the main conclusions we reach. Taken together, our analyses suggest no dramatic change in extreme social disconnectedness. They do indicate a fall in neighboring, but this may well be made up by increasing social contact in other venues. We do not wish to downplay the negative consequences of social isolation in its different aspects (e.g., Wilson 1987; Cacioppo and Hawkley 2003), but these data on nonsocializing do not suggest a sharp increase in isolation during recent years.

Conclusion

This chapter contributes to recent debates about possible social network contraction by analyzing trends in items that measure the frequency of informal socializing in 21 GSS surveys spanning a 35-year period. We identify some modest overall trends in socializing since the 1970s, but these are neither large nor consistent in direction. The lower frequency of contact with neighbors reported here and by others (Guest and Wierzbicki 1999; Putnam 2000) provides the clearest evidence of shrinkage. This is balanced to some extent by a discernable rise in social contact with relatives since the 1990s, and tempered by stable or slightly increasing levels of contact with friends outside one's neighborhood (Figure 9.1).

We examined the contributions of aging and cohort turnover to socializing trends. Spending social evenings with others and visiting bars and taverns prove to be considerably more common among the young (Figure 9.2), perhaps to a greater extent than other types of social ties such as confiding. Adjustments for population aging and cohort turnover do not substantially alter our conclusions about over-time trends in informal social participation, however (Figure 9.4). Nor does taking other important compositional shifts that have taken place in recent decades—especially in family structures and residential location—into account (Figure 9.5).

While these data are not consistent with a hypothesis of general social network shrinkage, they do offer at least suggestive evidence of "network reconfiguration" since tendencies to socialize with different types of others seem to have shifted in different directions. We note Guest and Wierzbicki's (1999) finding that tendencies to socialize with friends and with neighbors have grown increasingly independent of one another over time. That neighbors are seen less frequently, and friends perhaps more often, may mark a rise in the extent to which one's associates are chosen rather than constrained by availability (Wellman 1979; Fischer 1982).

The recent rise in socializing with relatives, on the other hand, resonates with the notion of network bifurcation suggested by McPherson et al. (2006), involving an intensification of contact with a small number of very close associates, accompanied by a proliferation of weaker narrow-purpose ties. The rise in seeing relatives is of special interest in that it has taken place while families have been growing smaller and the fraction of married adults has been falling—compositional trends that decrease the availability of relatives.

Our analyses are subject to a number of limitations that should be considered when assessing their bearing on debates surrounding declines in social connectedness. First, we study only informal socializing, an important but far from comprehensive indicator of social ties. It is possible that over-time trends in other types of interpersonal relationships—such as those that offer counseling support or tangible interpersonal assistance—might differ from those observed here.[13] Notably, our analyses do not incorporate possible expansion in social relationships facilitated by electronically mediated communication and cellular telephones, which vastly reduce the costs of forming and maintaining ties with others (see Wang and Wellman 2010). Our data refer to socializing in predominantly face-to-face settings.

As well, the GSS measurements of socializing are based on respondent reports on the frequency of socializing with different types of others. They differ from the "name generator" methods for measuring social network size on which the McPherson et al. (2006) findings are based. Our measurements do not capture trends in important dimensions of social networks such as the number of contacts, the intensity of ties, the breadth of relationships, or closure and clustering. And, of course, our efforts to adjust estimated time trends for cohort turnover and population aging are conditional on the assumptions we introduced in doing so, as all efforts to separate age-, period-, and cohort-related elements of change are.

Implications of these findings for arguments about declining social capital should be drawn with even greater caution. Informal social networks represent only one facet of social capital, though one that many (e.g., Lin 2001) regard as vital. Even so, the socializing on which we have focused seems more likely to represent what Putnam (2000) terms "bonding" social capital, which undergirds relationships with similar others, than "bridging" social capital, which facilitates ties with dissimilar others. Our data do not reflect on trends in the latter.

Notwithstanding these limitations, the findings presented in this chapter, taken together, suggest that the informal social participation levels of U.S. adults have undergone limited change, at most, during recent decades. An earlier wave of research suggested that urbanization transformed social networks, rather than diminishing them. Perhaps investigations into the effects of more contemporary social changes on social connectedness will reach a similar conclusion.

Appendix: Tactics for Separating Age, Period, and Cohort Influences on Socializing

We construct an age, period, and cohort interpretation of trends in socializing using a variation on Fienberg and Mason's (1978) fixed-effect approach to separating age, period, and cohort (APC) components of change in repeated cross-sectional survey data. The essence of the APC identification problem resides in the interdependency among the linear components of APC effects (Fienberg and Mason 1978, p. 23).

The fixed-effect approach estimates a regression model of the form,

$$f(Y_{ijk}) = b_0 \ \square \ a_i \ \square \ p_j \ \square \ c_k \ \square \ e_{ijk}$$

where Y_{ijk} is a response measured for a respondent of age i, period (year) j, and birth cohort k, b_0 is a constant term, a_i, p_j, and c_k are (respectively) coefficients for age i, period j, and cohort k, and e_{ijk} is a stochastic error. Let there be A distinct ages, P distinct periods, and C distinct cohorts. It is common to set one each of the $\{a_i\}$, $\{p_j\}$, and $\{c_k\}$ to 0, or to constrain the sum of each set of coefficients to 0 (e.g., $\sum_{i=1}^{A} a_i = 0$); even so, one of the remaining C-1 cohort contrasts is an exact linear function of the A-1 age contrasts and P-1 period contrasts. One approach to breaking this linear determinacy is to constrain a single pair of adjacent APC coefficients to be equal (e.g., Fienberg and Mason 1978, p. 24); this yields a just-identified model. Glenn (2005), however, shows that estimates thus obtained can vary widely, depending on which of the many possible such constraints an analyst selects.

APC analyses of repeated cross-sectional data often group observed ages, periods, and cohorts into ranges, for example, by combining persons age 18–29 or those born during a given decade. Data sometimes are available only in aggregated form (e.g., Fienberg and Mason 1978, p. 44), but such categorization is also common when age, period, and cohort are measured to the year (as, e.g., in Yang and Land's 2008 analyses of GSS data). When measurements to the year are available, using broad categories constrains the effects of those ages, periods, and cohorts grouped together to be equal, thereby imposing multiple equality constraints that serve to resolve the APC identification problem. Such grouping models APC effects as step functions, and usually results in a substantially overidentified model.

The analyses we present in this chapter also group adjacent ages and cohorts, assuming that these effects are locally similar to one another; we leave period (year) disaggregated because of that dimension's central interest here. Rather than assuming groupings ex ante, however, we begin with broad groupings and disaggregate them, guided by Wald tests of the equality constraints they imply. If model fit improves by splitting a broad grouping into two narrower ones, we tentatively accept the narrower groupings and in turn ask if additional splitting can further improve model fit. We stop narrowing groupings when Wald tests indicate that further disaggregation does not further improve model fit.[14]

Our procedure fits step functions to the data, none of which is exactly collinear with the linear component of age or cohort effects. It adjusts the groupings to patterns in the data, including any nonlinearities that may be present, and usually results in groupings having unequal width. The groupings reached differ for the four different forms of socializing we study. Our search procedure does not necessarily locate the unique sets of groupings that best fit the data. Imposing multiple equality constraints simultaneously rather than relying on only one, however, makes our estimates less subject to chance fluctuations in particular data sets. By testing to see if fit can be improved by relaxing the equality constraints implied by our groupings, we ensure that they do not unduly distort the data.

Example: Monthly Socializing with Friends

We illustrate our model selection procedure for studying APC differences with an analysis of more-than-monthly socializing with friends outside the neighborhood, using logistic regression to model the dichotomous response. Table 9.A.1 presents some statistics from these analyses.

Because period (year) differences are of principal interest here, we chose not to group years. Model 1 includes highly aggregated age and cohort groups: seven 10-year-width age groupings (18–29, 30–39, . . . 80–89) and seven 10-year-width birth cohort groupings (pre-1920, 1930s, . . . post-1970). Model 2 disaggregates these into 5-year intervals.

Table 9.A.1. Comparison of Fit of Model 1 (~10-year groupings) and Model 2 (~5-year groupings) for More-Than-Monthly Socializing with Friends

	Wald $X^2(df)$	p value
Age effects equated in model 2	62.7 (1)	<.0001
< 25 and 25–29		
30–34 and 35–39	12.8 (1)	<.0001
40–44 and 45–49	0.2 (1)	.67
50–54 and 55–59	3.3 (1)	.07
60–64 and 65–69	0.5 (1)	.50
70–74 and 75–79	0.0 (1)	.93
80–84 and 85+	0.0 (1)	.95
10-year groupings vs. 5-year groupings	73.3 (7)	<.0001
Cohort contrasts equated in model 2		
<1900 and 1900–1919	0.7 (1)	.40
1920–1924 and 1925–1929	1.1 (1)	.29
1930–1934 and 1935–1939	1.9 (1)	.17
1940–1944 and 1945–1949	0.0 (1)	.94
1950–1954 and 1955–1959	0.2 (1)	.68
1960–1964 and 1965–1969	0.0 (1)	.98
1970–1974 and > 1974	2.0 (1)	.16
10-year groupings vs. 5-year groupings	5.4 (7)	.61

Note: Analyses weighted for number of adults in household, sampling phase (after 2002), and oversampling of blacks in 1982, with robust standard errors. Both models include 20 contrasts for year.

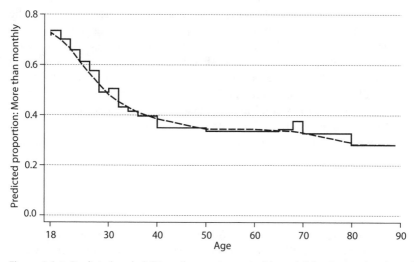

Figure 9.A.1. Predicted probabilities of more-than-monthly socializing by age in selected model. Predicted probabilities calculated for persons in an "average" cohort and an "average" year. Solid line shows step function fit by model; dashed line is a running-mean smoother.

Table 9.A.1 presents Wald tests comparing the goodness of fit for these two models. Each 10-year grouping in model 1 constrains the coefficients corresponding to two 5-year groupings in model 2 to equal one another. The test statistics in the top panel of Table 9.A.1 examine whether loosening each of the constraints on the age differences by disaggregating the 10-year groups into 5-year groups significantly improves model fit. We see that it does so for the younger age groups (where the p values for the Wald statistics are very small), but not for the older ones, where 5-year groupings do not appear to improve fit over 10-year ones. The last line of the top panel shows that taken together, the 5-year age intervals yield a better fit to the data than do the 10-year ones ($X^2 = 73.30$, 7 df, $p > .0001$). The bottom panel shows, in contrast, that disaggregating 10-year birth cohort intervals into shorter ones does not appear to improve the fit of the model ($X^2 = 5.40$, 7 df, $p = .61$).

We considered further disaggregation of the intervals by specifying still shorter (2–3 years) age and cohort intervals, and made similar comparisons of model fit. These indicated that 10-year intervals appeared sufficient for grouping cohorts, whereas age groupings required considerable disaggregation into unequal-length intervals: shorter at younger ages, longer at older ones. Based on these comparisons, we selected a model that includes the seven 10-year cohort groups and 17 unequal-interval age groups (18–19, 20–21, 22–23, 24–25, 26–27, 28–29, 30–31, 32–33, 34–35, 36–39, 40–49, 50–59, 60–64, 65–67, 68–69, 70–79, 80+). Results presented in Figure 9.2 are based on this model.

Figure 9.A.1 depicts the age effects in the selected model graphically. The solid line displays the step function fit by the model, showing predicted probabilities of monthly socializing by age calculated for persons in an "average" year and an "average" cohort. The dashed line overlaid on this is a running mean smoother.[15] Both lines show a relatively rapid decline between youth and middle age in the predicted probability of more-than-monthly socializing with friends, from over 0.7 among persons in their late teens to about 0.4 among those in their late 30s. Thereafter, socializing with friends continues to decline with age, but at a gentler rate.

Notes

1. See, however, Fischer (2011).

2. These figures differ in detail from those that appear in McPherson, Smith-Lovin, and Brashears (2006) because they take account of a data error discovered after that article was published; see McPherson, Smith-Lovin, and Brashears (2008a).

3. Data from a 2008 telephone survey reported by Hampton, Sessions, and Her (2011) suggest a decline in the size of core networks by comparison to the 1985 GSS estimate, but no change in social isolation. Hampton et al. conjecture that social media have increased the specialization of close ties.

4. See also Dunkelman (2011), who suggests that recent changes have given rise to a "cluster-networked system" with more "inner-ring" and "outer-ring" relationships and fewer "middle-ring" ones.

5. "Cocooning—A Steady Trend" (http://www.predictivedomaining.com/2009/01/26/cocooning-a-steady-trend/).

6. Prior studies have examined one or more of these series over shorter intervals, including Putnam (2000), for 1974–1998; Paxton (1999), for 1974–1994; and Guest and Wierzbicki (1999), for 1974–1996. See also Fischer (2011).

7. All statistics presented in this chapter are weighted for the number of adults in the household, sampling phase (after 2002), and oversampling of black respondents in 1982 (the 1987 GSS, which also includes a black oversample, did not measure the socializing items).

The socializing items were first administered in a nationally representative survey on anti-Semitism in the United States conducted by NORC in 1964. In that study, an estimated 53% of respondents said that they spent social evenings with relatives more than once per month, while 41% and 36% did so with friends and neighbors, respectively. About 15% of the 1964 respondents said that they visited a bar or tavern more often than monthly. These figures are quite close to the average levels during the GSS years, though the level of neighboring is somewhat lower than that measured in early GSSs. They suggest relatively little change in socializing levels between the mid-1960s and mid-1970s.

8. The linear trend in socializing with relatives is statistically insignificant, as shown in Table 9.1, but a polynomial regression (not reported) indicates that this form of socializing was significantly less common midperiod.

9. Extended GSS topical modules on the "Information Society" in 2000, 2002, and 2004 measured Internet, electronic mail, and computer use (including participa-

tion in chat rooms), and asked about acquaintances first met online. Use of social networking websites became widespread after the last of these modules was administered. See Wang and Wellman (2010) for a discussion of Internet use and friendship network size between 2002 and 2007.

10. Age and cohort patterns in the analyses that include compositional indicators closely resemble those in Figures 9.3 and 9.4, so we do not reiterate them here.

11. Because the GSS did not begin measuring it until 1975, we do not report odds ratios for television viewing in Table 9.3. They are statistically negligible in parallel analyses that cover the 1975–2008 period. Bivariate analyses show that watching more television is inversely related to socializing with friends and in bars, but directly associated with seeing relatives and neighbors. This suggests that some social evenings with relatives and neighbors might be spent watching television.

12. The declining number of adults who never visit establishments that serve alcohol does not reflect a downward trend in abstention from alcohol use. The GSS does not measure use of alcohol after 1994, but Gallup polls indicate that the percentage of U.S. adults classified as "total abstainers" rose from about 30% in the mid-1970s to 36% in 2009 (Saad 2009).

13. See, however, Fischer's (2011) assessment of available over-time data on a variety of interpersonal ties, which suggest that few notable changes in connectedness have taken place.

14. We rely on Wald tests because we use weights to take the GSS sample design into account. Were weighting not necessary, we could further establish the plausibility of our groupings by comparing our final, overidentified model to a just-identified model using a likelihood ratio test, the Akaike information criterion (AIC), or other indicators of model fit.

15. To limit clutter, the figures in the text present only dots indicating the midpoint of each step of the step function and the smoothed trend.

References

Bell, Wendell, and Marion D. Boat. 1957. "Urban Neighborhoods and Informal Social Relations." *American Journal of Sociology* 62 (4): 391–98.

Cacioppo, John T., and Louise C. Hawkley. 2003. "Social Isolation and Health, with an Emphasis on Underlying Mechanisms." *Biology and Medicine* 46 (3, suppl.): S39–S52.

Cornwell, Benjamin, Edward O. Laumann, and L. Philip Schumm. 2008. "The Social Connectedness of Older Adults: A National Profile." *American Sociological Review* 73 (2): 185–203.

Davis, James A. 2001. "Testing the Demographic Explanation of Attitude Trends: Secular Trends in Attitudes among U.S. Householders, 1972–1996." *Social Science Research* 30 (3): 363–85.

Dunkelman, Marc. 2011. "The Transformation of American Community." *National Affairs* 8:135–51.

Elliott, Sinikka, and Debra Umberson. 2004. "Recent Demographic Trends in the US and Implications for Well-Being." In *The Blackwell Companion to the Sociology of Families*, edited by Jacqueline Scott, Judith Treas, and Martin Richards, 34–53. Oxford: Blackwell.

Fienberg, Stephen E., and William M. Mason. 1978. "Identification and Estimation of Age-Period-Cohort Models in the Analysis of Discrete Archival Data." In *Sociological Methodology 1979*, edited by Karl F. Schuessler, 1–67. San Francisco: Jossey-Bass.

Fischer, Claude S. 1982. *To Dwell among Friends: Personal Networks in Town and City*. Chicago: University of Chicago Press.

———. 2009. "The 2004 GSS Finding of Shrunken Social Networks: An Artifact?" *American Sociological Review* 74 (4): 657–69.

———. 2011. *Still Connected: Family and Friends in America since 1970*. New York: Russell Sage Foundation.

Fischer, Claude S., and Michael Hout. 2006. *Century of Difference: How America Changed in the Last One Hundred Years*. New York: Russell Sage Foundation.

Glenn, Norval D. 2005. "Age, Period, and Cohort Effects." In *Encyclopedia of Social Measurement*, edited by Kimberly Kempf-Leonard, 27–32. Oxford: Elsevier.

Guest, Avery M., and Susan K. Wierzbicki. 1999. "Social Ties at the Neighborhood Level: Two Decades of GSS Evidence." *Urban Affairs Review* 35 (1): 92–111.

Hampton, Keith N., Lauren F. Sessions, and Eun Ja Her. 2011. "Core Networks, Social Isolation, and New Media." *Information, Communication & Society* 14 (1): 130–55.

Hunter, Albert. 1975. "The Loss of Community: An Empirical Test through Replication." *American Sociological Review* 40 (5): 537–52.

Jacobs, Jerry A., and Kathleen Gerson. 2004. "Understanding Changes in American Working Time: A Synthesis." In *Fighting for Time: Shifting Boundaries of Work and Social Life*, edited by Cynthia Fuchs Epstein and Arne L. Kalleberg, 25–45. New York: Russell Sage Foundation.

Kornhauser, William. 1968. "Mass Society." In *International Encyclopedia of the Social Sciences*, edited by David L. Sills, 58–64. New York: Macmillan.

Krause, Neal. 2006. "Social Relationships in Late Life." In *Handbook of Aging and the Social Sciences*, 6th ed., edited by Robert H. Binstock and Linda K. George, 181–200. New York: Academic Press.

Lin, Nan. 2001. *Social Capital: A Theory of Social Structure and Action*. New York: Cambridge University Press.

Marsden, Peter V. 1987. "Core Discussion Networks of Americans." *American Sociological Review* 52 (1): 122–31.

McPherson, Miller, Lynn Smith-Lovin, and Matthew E. Brashears. 2006. "Social Isolation in America: Changes in Core Discussion Networks over Two Decades." *American Sociological Review* 71 (3): 353–75.

———. 2008a. "Erratum: Social Isolation in America: Changes in Core Discussion Networks over Two Decades." *American Sociological Review* 73 (6): 1022.

———. 2008b. "The Ties That Bind Are Fraying." *Contexts* 7 (3): 32–36.

———. 2009. "Models and Marginals: Using Survey Evidence to Study Social Networks." *American Sociological Review* 74 (4): 670–81.

Meyer, Julie. 2001. "Age: 2000." *Census 2000 Brief C2KFR/01-12*. http://www.census.gov/prod/2001pubs/c2kbr01-12.pdf.

Moore, Gwen. 1990. "Structural Determinants of Men's and Women's Personal Networks." *American Sociological Review* 55 (5): 726–35.

Paxton, Pamela. 1999. "Is Social Capital Declining in the United States? A Multiple Indicator Assessment." *American Journal of Sociology* 105 (1): 88–127.

Putnam, Robert D. 2000. *Bowling Alone: The Collapse and Revival of American Community*. New York: Simon & Schuster.

Saad, Lydia. 2009. "Drinking Habits Steady amid Recession." http://www.gallup.com/poll/121277/Drinking-Habits-Steady-Amid-Recession.aspx.

Spain, Daphne, and Suzanne M. Bianchi. 1996. *Balancing Act: Motherhood, Marriage, and Employment among American Women*. New York: Russell Sage Foundation.

Treas, Judith, and Ramon Torrecilha. 1995. "The Older Population." In *State of the Union: America in the 1990s, Volume Two: Social Trends*, edited by Reynolds Farley, 47–92. New York: Russell Sage Foundation.

Wang, Hua, and Barry Wellman. 2010. "Social Connectivity in America: Changes in Adult Friendship Network Size from 2002 to 2007." *American Behavioral Scientist* 53:1148–69.

Wellman, Barry. 1979. "The Community Question: The Intimate Networks of East Yorkers." *American Journal of Sociology* 84 (5): 1201–31.

Wilson, William Julius. 1987. *The Truly Disadvantaged: The Inner City, the Underclass, and Public Policy*. Chicago: University of Chicago Press.

Wirth, Louis. 1938. "Urbanism as a Way of Life." *American Journal of Sociology* 44 (1): 1–24.

Yang, Yang, and Kenneth C. Land. 2008. "Age-Period-Cohort Analysis of Repeated Cross-Section Surveys: Fixed or Random Effects?" *Sociological Methods and Research* 36 (3): 297–326.

Stability and Flux in Social Indicators

10

Income, Age, and Happiness in America

Glenn Firebaugh and Laura Tach

Richer Americans tend to be happier, and incomes generally increase over the working life cycle, peaking in the years just before retirement and declining thereafter. After taking the nonincome determinants of happiness into account, then, we would expect the age-happiness trajectory for a typical American to mimic the familiar hump-shaped or inverted-U pattern of the age-income trajectory, with happiness peaking in the preretirement years when incomes tend to be highest. In other words, if people are happier when they have more income, then we expect happiness to covary with age in the same way that income does, rising with age at a decreasing rate and then starting to decline a few years before retirement.

Yet prior studies do not find such an inverted-U pattern when they adjust for the nonincome determinants of happiness. Yang (2008, Figure 2) finds that happiness in the United States either rises linearly with age or is J-shaped, depending on the controls. Blanchflower and Oswald (2007) find that the age-happiness pattern is U-shaped. For women as well as men, in Europe as well as in the United States, Blanchflower and Oswald (2007) conclude that people who are in their mid- to late 40s—close to their peak earning years—tend to be somewhat *less* happy than people who are younger or older, again controlling for nonincome determinants of happiness.

Why does the age-happiness trajectory not follow the age-income trajectory? This is the puzzle we address in this chapter. We proceed in two stages.

First, we show that overall trends in happiness in the United States are not what we would expect if the effect of income on happiness were entirely a matter of absolute income (the more money we have, the more things we can purchase and consume, and the happier we are). It appears, instead, that the income effect is also relative: the rich are happier in part because they are richer than others are (Layard 2005; Luttmer 2005; Veblen 1899/2001).

After discovering trends that suggest the existence of relative income effects, we turn to a more targeted analysis focusing on income, age, and happiness in the United States. The underlying question is why, for Americans, happiness does not rise along with the general increase in income over the working life cycle. An important part of the answer, we suggest, is that the incomes of one's age peers also rise. In other words, a particular type of relative income effect is at work—a relative income effect where the peer group is *age based*.[1] The idea is that young adults, whose age peers generally have more modest incomes, are happier at lower income levels than older adults, who have higher-income age peers, would be. If so, then the average income of one's age group should have a negative effect on one's happiness, controlling for one's own income. The existence of age-based relative income effects would help explain why rising income over much of the life course fails to produce greater satisfaction for many Americans.

Income, Age, and Happiness in the General Social Survey

Since the first survey in 1972, the General Social Survey (GSS) has asked this question about happiness:

> Taken all together, how would you say things are these days—would you say that you are very happy, pretty happy, or not too happy?

In every survey, richer people tend to be happier. Figure 10.1, for example, depicts the association between happiness and family income in the 2006 GSS. The percentage "very happy" increases monotonically with income while the percentage "not too happy" declines monotonically with income. Those in the poorest category—with annual family incomes below $20,000—were more likely to report being "not too happy" than being "very happy." In sharp contrast, those at the other end of the income distribution—with family incomes of $150,000 or greater—were *13 times* more likely to report being "very happy" rather than "not too happy."

Other surveys, in the United States and elsewhere, show similar cross-sectional associations of income and happiness. In his review of 30 cross-sectional studies within countries, for example, Easterlin (1974) found that in every study wealthier persons tended to be happier than poorer persons. Subsequent studies confirm this result (e.g., Di Tella, MacCulloch, and Oswald 2001; Easterlin 2001, table 1; Graham and Pettinato 2002, tables 4-1 and 4-5).

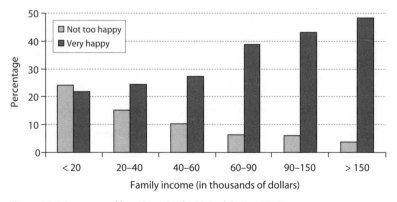

Figure 10.1. Income and happiness in the United States, 2006.

If the rich are happier at any point in time, then we might expect Americans as a whole to be happier now than in 1972, since Americans on average are richer now (Figure 10.2). Yet, as Figure 10.2 shows, Americans' average reported happiness has *declined* slightly over the last three decades.[2]

The significance of Figure 10.2 lies not in the magnitude of the decline, since Table 10.1 shows that the change is barely perceptible, though statistically significant. Rather, the significance lies in the fact that happiness in America is declining at all. With rising prosperity, we would expect an increase in happiness. Importantly, the decline in happiness appears even when we restrict our analysis to those ages 20–64, the prime working ages in America.

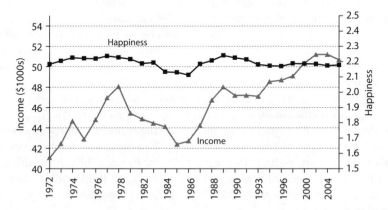

Figure 10.2. Average family income and average happiness in America, 1972–2006. *Source*: Happiness: 1972–2006 GSS, where happiness is coded "not too happy" = 1, "pretty happy" = 2, and "very happy" = 3. (Sample is adjusted for black oversamples in 1982 and 1987.) Average family income: 1972–2006 GSS, adjusted to 2000 real dollars using the Consumer Price Index. Values for income and happiness are three year moving averages.

Table 10.1. Trend in Happiness among U.S. Adults, 1972–2006

Average annual change (slope)		Implied total change, 1972–2006	
All adults	Ages 20–64	All adults	Ages 20–64
–0.00086**	–0.00102**	–0.029	–0.035
(0.00029)	(0.00032)		

 Data: Cumulative GSS, 1972–2006 (Davis, Smith, and Marsden 2006), adjusted for black oversamples in 1982 and 1987.

 Note: Results are based on OLS regression of self-reported happiness on year of survey, where happiness is coded *not too happy* = 1, *pretty happy* = 2, and *very happy* = 3. Logistic regression yields the same trends. Standard errors are in parentheses.

 **$p < .01$.

Those are the ages where we might expect happiness to rise the fastest, as wages increase with work experience.

The issue we face, then, is why, during a period of rising incomes, happiness has not risen for Americans.[3] Because the GSS is not a panel, we cannot follow individuals over time, but we can track birth cohorts over time. As a first step, we use linear decomposition (Firebaugh 2008, chap. 6) to determine whether the fall in overall happiness is due to declining happiness within birth cohorts or to declining happiness across birth cohorts (as older, happier cohorts are replaced by younger, less happy ones). We do not expect to find net decreases in happiness over time within cohorts since prior research indicates that, controlling for cohort effects, those in their 60s and older are at least as happy as those in their 20s (Yang 2008). By default, then, we expect the decline in happiness to be due to different starting points for successive cohorts: Americans born later in the 20th century tend to be somewhat less happy than Americans born earlier in the 20th century.

The coefficients for the linear decomposition in Table 10.2 are consistent with these expectations. Linear decomposition regresses a focal outcome variable on two other variables: *cohort*, which refers to year of birth, and *year*, which refers to year of survey. The coefficient for *cohort* reflects the weighted-average change in happiness across cohorts, holding *year* constant. Hence the negative coefficient for *cohort* in Table 10.2 indicates that, at a given point in time, those with higher values on *cohort* (the younger cohorts, who were born later) tend to be somewhat less happy than those with lower values on *cohort* (those born earlier). This result holds for those in the prime working-age population, ages 20–64, as well as for all adults; it also holds whether we use ordinary least squares (OLS) or logistic regression to decompose the trend in happiness.

What do these two trends—a negative trend across cohorts (lower happiness among later-born cohorts) and no net change over time within cohorts (the coefficient for *year* is not significant)—suggest about why Americans are somewhat less happy than they were three decades ago? Consider several ex-

Table 10.2. Decomposition of Trend in Happiness among U.S. Adults, 1972–2006

Variable	All adults	Ages 20–64
Cohort	−0.00117**	−0.00124**
	(0.00017)	(0.00027)
Year	0.00022	0.00017
	(0.00033)	(0.00041)

Data: Cumulative GSS, 1972–2006 (Davis, Smith, and Marsden 2006), adjusted for black oversamples in 1982 and 1987.

Note: OLS coefficients, based on self-reported happiness coded *not too happy* = 1, *pretty happy* = 2, and *very happy* = 3. Logistic regression gives the same results. "Cohort" is year of birth, and "year" is year of survey. Standard errors are in parentheses.

**p < .01.

planations. One is rising income inequality (Stevenson and Wolfers 2008), which has, among other things, increased the proportion of Americans whose income falls below the mean (Hout 2003). Another possibility is that rising family income has come at the cost of longer work days and more income earners per family (Fischer 2008), reducing the amount of time Americans have to spend with family and friends—an important determinant of happiness (Frank 2007). Or perhaps other countervailing trends, such as rising divorce rates over some of the period, trumped the positive effect of rising incomes. Importantly, the findings in Table 10.2 identify declining happiness across cohorts as the proximate source of the overall decline in happiness in the United States, so the explanations listed above would be more convincing if they could be linked to differences across birth cohorts. We might ask, for example, whether rising inequality, declining family time, and rising divorce rates have been more pronounced among later-born cohorts. We do not pursue those issues here since the aim of our analysis is to explain why there was no net within-cohort change in happiness from 1972–2006 (why is the coefficient for *year* not positive?), rather than explaining the decline in happiness across cohorts (why is the coefficient for *cohort* negative?).

The central issue for this chapter, then, is to account for why happiness did not increase over time within cohorts. We know that real incomes rose significantly within cohorts over this period. Given the association between income and happiness observed in Figure 10.1, why did happiness not follow suit? An important part of the answer, we hypothesize, is that Americans desire not just to be rich, but to be richer than others like them. Who are those "others"? We posit that they include other Americans at a similar stage in the life course—which could account for our finding that individuals in birth cohorts do not become happier as they become richer. The remainder of this chapter investigates this possibility by estimating models that determine if the income of age peers has a depressing effect on happiness, independent of own income.

Relative Income as Key

A natural explanation for the positive association between income and happiness (Figure 10.1) is that the rich are more satisfied with life because they enjoy a higher material standard of living. This is called an *absolute income effect*. As Tibor Scitovsky (1976, pp. 133–34) observes, economists often view absolute income effects on happiness as virtually self-evident because "the higher one's income, the more one can spend, and the more one spends, the more satisfied one should be."

Because it is difficult to be happy under conditions of physical discomfort, we expect substantial absolute income effects in the world's most impoverished regions, where rising income means relief from chronic hunger, danger, and exposure to the elements. But once basic needs are met, the importance of money might turn from how much we have to how much we have relative to others. Thorstein Veblen (1899/2001, p. 492) made that case more than a century ago in his classic book *The Theory of the Leisure Class*:

> The desire for wealth can scarcely be satiated in any individual instance. . . . However widely, or equally, or "fairly," it may be distributed, no general increase of the community's wealth can make any approach to satiating this need, the ground of which is the desire of everyone to excel everyone else in the accumulation of goods.

To appreciate the significance of relative income effects in today's wealthy societies, consider Paul Krugman's (1996, p. 1) observation about American families in the second half of the 20th century:

> Imagine that a mad scientist went back to 1950 and offered to transport the median family to the wondrous world of the 1990s, and to place them at, say, the 25th percentile level. The 25th percentile of 1996 is a clear material improvement over the median of 1950. Would they accept his offer? Almost surely not—because in 1950 they were middle class, while in 1996 they would be poor, even if they lived better in material terms. People don't just care about their absolute material level— they care about their level compared with others.[4]

Krugman's observation resonates with classic sociological literature on the effect of reference groups (Merton and Rossi 1950; Stouffer et al. 1949). If the observation is correct, rising income does not necessarily boost happiness if peers' incomes are rising just as fast or faster. Individuals no doubt use multiple peer groups for income comparisons—neighbors (Luttmer 2005; Firebaugh and Schroeder 2009), fellow workers, or brothers-in-law, to name a few. To provide a defensible relative income account of why, within birth cohorts, Americans' happiness has not grown along with their income, not just any peer group will do—we must identify groups whose income has ratcheted upward over time. To understand why, suppose Americans compared themselves only to groups with declining incomes. Then, even if Americans' incomes failed to rise, they should nonetheless become happier over time according to the tenets of relative income theory.

We use age-based peer groups, which have two features that distinguish them from other reference groups. First, Americans are conditioned to compare themselves to age peers by the age-graded character of the educational system. Second, age peers provide a rising income target over the course of most of one's working life.[5] Other reference groups might or might not provide rising income targets (rich and poor neighbors, for example, come and go; and we might ourselves move to a richer or poorer neighborhood). It is not surprising, then, that an income level that many Americans consider to be satisfactory at age 25 is no longer considered satisfactory at age 45 or 55.[6]

We turn now to the second stage of our analysis. Our aim is to estimate age-based relative income effects more directly using GSS data. In the analysis most similar to ours, McBride (2001) finds a negative coefficient for mean income of age peers (defined as those within five years of one's own age), controlling for one's own income and a few other variables. The McBride study uses a sample of only 324 GSS respondents in a single year (1994); moreover, its coefficient for mean income of age peers does not reach statistical significance in one of two models and is barely significant (at the .05 level) in the other. We follow up on McBride's suggestive findings by using the full GSS time span (thus expanding the sample size from 324 to over 20,000), by increasing the number of age-peer contexts, and by adding a fuller set of control variables to rule out alternative explanations.

Estimating Relative Income Effects with Individual-Level Data

The estimation of relative income effects with individual-level survey data involves three steps. The first step is to place individuals in peer groups (here, age groups at each point in time). The second step is to estimate the income standard μ_j set by those peer groups for the $j = 1, 2, \ldots J$ peer groups.

The final step is to estimate the effect of those income standards on happiness, independent of the effect of individual's income and nonincome control variables,

$$H_{ij} = \beta_0 + \beta_1 X_{ij} + \beta_2 \mu_j + \sum_q \gamma_q Z_{qij} + \varepsilon_{ij} \tag{1}$$

where H_{ij} is happiness for the ith person in the jth peer group, X_{ij} is income for the ith person in the jth peer group, μ_j is the income standard for the jth peer group (we use mean income), Z_q is the qth control variable, γ_q is the effect of the qth control variable, and ε is a random error term.

The parameter β_2 in equation 1 provides the critical test for a relative income effect, since the telltale mark of such an effect is a *negative sign for peer income* ($\beta_2 < 0$) Alternatively, peer income could have no effect on happiness ($\beta_2 = 0$), or peer income could have a positive contextual effect ($\beta_2 > 0$). A positive contextual effect is unlikely here since that would suggest that your happiness increases when your peers receive raises and you do not.[7]

We restrict our analysis to those in the prime working ages of 20–64. For respondents 65 years of age and older, very often income is less important than wealth; likewise, income is likely to be a less important consideration for students and beginning workers ages 18–19 than it is for those in the prime working-age population. With exclusions,[8] there are 27,088 respondents ages 20–64 with nonmissing data on age, income, and happiness, and 20,410 with complete data on all control variables as well.

Measurement of Key Variables

Happiness

As noted earlier, we measure happiness using the standard GSS question employed since 1972: "Taken all together, how would you say things are these days . . . ?" The preliminary statement "Taken all together . . ." invites respondents to think of happiness as a durable trait rather than as a temporary emotion or mood. Over 99% of respondents have answered this question in the GSS, so people appear to have little difficulty answering the question.

Although this question and similar questions have been widely used to study happiness in sociology, economics, and other fields,[9] some may doubt whether individuals can accurately assess their "true" happiness. That issue has been addressed in various ways. In a longitudinal study, Koivumaa et al. (2001) find that self-reported happy people are less likely to commit suicide decades later. In addition, self-reported happiness or subjective well-being has positive and generally high correlations with reports of spouses, with recall of positive and negative life events, with the duration of authentic smiles, with heart rate and blood pressure measures of responses to stress, and with skin resistance measures of responses to stress (Konow and Earley 2008, note 1). Apparently self-reports of happiness do effectively reflect one's true state.

Note also that the GSS question asks about happiness in general, not about happiness with one's income itself. The focus on the association between overall happiness and income (we might call this *happiness from income*) distinguishes the relative income literature from the distributive justice literature (e.g., Alwin 1987; Jasso 1978), which focuses on *happiness with income* (i.e., on whether our income is fair). We might find stronger income effects if we used satisfaction with income as the dependent variable; but that is a different issue, better treated from a distributive justice perspective, where satisfaction is conceptualized as a function of inputs (such as effort) as well as of rewards (such as income).

Income

The GSS measures both family income and personal earnings. Firebaugh and Schroeder (2009) find that family income has the greater effect on happiness. This makes sense: if money is consequential primarily because of what it can do for you—in terms of either consumption or relative family status— then who earns the money or the way it is earned is less relevant than *how much* money is earned. Consistent with this reasoning we find that employment status has little independent effect on happiness: full-time workers, part-time workers, housekeepers, retirees, and students are all about equally happy or unhappy (the exception is the unemployed, who are notably unhappier). In our analysis we use family income and control for involuntary unemployment.

The GSS asks the same income question in every survey: "In which of these groups did your total *family* income, from *all* sources, fall last year—before taxes, that is?" Income response categories in the GSS have been adjusted over time because of inflation; to permit comparison over time we adjust all the income figures to year 2000 dollars using the Consumer Price Index (CPI) provided by the Bureau of Labor Statistics (http://www.bls.gov/cpi). We follow standard research practice by assigning respondents the midpoint dollar value of the category they selected. The greatest potential for measurement error occurs in the top income category, where there is no upper bound (for respondents selecting the highest category we assign an income 1.5 times the lower limit of that category). Imputing incomes from income categories is less than ideal, and a likely result is that our estimates understate the true income effect. This problem is diminished, however, by our use of logged income.

Income Contexts

Empirically, our objective in this analysis is to determine whether the income of age peers affects happiness independent of own income. We must, then, construct age-peer groups. We define an age-peer group as consisting of all those who are the same age (in years) and whose incomes are measured using the same GSS income response categories. Response categories in the GSS changed in 1977, 1982, 1986, 1991, 1998, and 2006, so each age, ages 20–64, in the surveys 1972–1976, 1977–1981, 1982–1985, 1986–1990, 1991–1996, 1998–2004, and 2006 is defined as a peer group, resulting in $45 \times 7 = 315$ groups. In keeping with the focus on GSS data in this volume, we use GSS income data to calculate mean incomes for the 315 age-peer groups. With a total sample size of about 27,000, the average group size is about 85.

Because the effect of the peer group income mean (μ_j) is the key, our relatively large number of age-peer contexts permits a reasonable test for age-based income context effects. Note that the income of one's age peers is related both to one's age and to the period of measurement. For example, in the initial year of the GSS the age peers for someone age 25 consisted of others who were age 25 in 1972; 30 years later, the age peers of 25-year-olds consisted of a different group, those who were 25 in 2002. In other words, we use *age-peer groups*, not *age groups*; we assume that individuals make income comparisons with those who are the same age at the same period in history. Because rising income has affected all birth cohorts, we would not expect the mean income of those age 25 in 2002 to be the same as the mean income of those age 25 in 1972 (because we adjust income for inflation, we are able to compare incomes in 1972 and 2002). And of course by using 315 groups instead of 45 groups we have a more powerful test for the effect of the μ_j.

The next step is to specify the functional form of relative income effects. In comparing their income to others' income, do individuals focus on income differences or on income ratios? (See Fischer and Hout [2006, pp. 260–61].) If the answer is income differences, then relative incomes remain constant when $100 is added to everyone's income. This conceptualization assumes, however, that a $100 raise has the same utility for the rich and the poor, and prior research (e.g., Graham and Pettinato 2002, figure 2-2) finds that the income-happiness curve for individuals flattens out at higher levels of income, indicating diminishing utility of additional income. This suggests that we should think of relative incomes as remaining constant when everyone's income increases at the same rate, and measure reference income accordingly, as logged income.

Estimated Effects of Income and Income Context on Happiness

Our conclusions hinge on the sign of the coefficient for income context (here, age-peer groups). A negative coefficient for β_2 in equation 1 would be consistent with the relative income notion that your happiness is depressed by increases in the income of your peers.

Because income and income contexts are not randomly assigned, it is important to consider and rule out alternative explanations for a negative coefficient for income context. Endogeneity bias—a common problem in observational analysis—can probably be ruled out in this case. Our analysis centers on the effect of *others' income* on an individual's happiness. Although your happiness might well affect your own income—so our estimate of β_1 might be affected by reverse causation—your happiness is not likely to affect the income of your age peers, so our estimate of β_2 should not be affected by endogeneity bias.

There are nonetheless other threats to our interpretation of a negative μ_j effect as a relative income effect. Two plausible alternative explanations are the following:

- *Health effect*. Self-reported physical health is the best single predictor of happiness in the GSS, and physical health declines with age (although less so for ages 20–64 than for the full age range). Because the peer income means (the μ_j) are positively correlated with age, a negative coefficient for μ_j could be picking up the negative effect of declining health as people age.
- *Education effect*. More educated people tend to be somewhat happier, and educational attainment increased rapidly in the 20th century (Fischer and Hout 2006). As a result, education, like health, declines as we move from young to old peer groups. Because the μ_j s are positively correlated with age, a negative coefficient for μ_j could be picking up the negative correlation of age with education.[10]

Thus we add control variables for health and education to our model. We also include age as a regressor (to control for unmeasured aging effects not captured by health and education) as well as marital status, race, unemployment, and gender. From prior studies of happiness using the GSS data (e.g., Blanchflower and Oswald 2004), as well as our own preliminary analysis, we know that Americans who are unmarried, nonwhite, and unemployed tend to be less happy than Americans who are married, white, and not experiencing a spell of unemployment.

Before turning to the regression results, it is useful to look briefly at the major correlates of happiness in the United States (Table 10.3). Americans on the whole are fairly happy; about seven of eight rate themselves as "very" or "pretty" happy. We might expect this happiness to be closely tied to income, especially in a consumerist society such as the United States. Yet as Table 10.3 suggests, income is by no means the only—or even the most important— determinant of Americans' happiness. Health and marital status are at least as important as income is. Being in excellent health, for example, appears to "buy" the same level of happiness as a family income of $75,000 or more (in 2000 dollars). On the other end of the scale, poor health appears to matter more than income poverty does: among those who rate their health as poor, 39% rate themselves as "not too happy"; of those with family incomes less than $15,000, a much lower percentage (24%) so rate themselves. In that sense, then, it is better to be healthy than to be rich.

Along the same vein, the difference in happiness between the married and the unmarried is almost as large as the difference between those who are poor (family income less than $15,000) and those who are five times richer ($75,000+). The size of the marriage difference relative to the income difference is noteworthy in view of likely major differences in the quality of

Table 10.3. Correlates of Happiness in the United States, 1972–2006 ($N = 20{,}410$)

	Very happy (%)	Pretty happy (%)	Not too happy (%)
Family income			
<$15,000	20	56	24
$75,000 and above	44	51	5
Health			
Excellent	45	49	6
Good	26	63	10
Fair	18	59	23
Poor	15	45	39
Education			
<High school degree	25	54	21
High school degree	29	59	12
Some college	30	60	10
College or above	37	55	8
Marital status			
Married	40	53	7
Not married	20	62	18
Race			
White	32	57	11
Nonwhite	24	57	19
Work status			
Working full-time	31	59	10
Working part-time	28	60	12
Temporarily not working	29	56	15
Retired	36	50	14
Student	30	57	13
Keeping house	34	52	15
Unemployed	17	54	29
Other	20	51	29
Gender			
Male	30	59	12
Female	31	56	12
Overall	30.6	57.3	12.1

Data: 1972–2006 GSS respondents ages 20–64 using listwise deletion of missing data (so the percentages above are all based on the same sample of respondents). Results are similar using pairwise deletion.

marriage across couples. As Table 10.3 indicates, money is associated with happiness, but it is not as important as some other things.

Results for Ordered Logit Models

We first regress happiness on family income and the age-based income means with no control variables to determine simply whether individuals in high-income contexts tend to be less happy than individuals with the same income but poorer age peers. Because our dependent variable is categorical, we estimate coefficients using the generalized ordered logit model.[11]

Table 10.4 reports results for all working-age respondents (ages 20–64) with data on happiness, age, and income in the cumulative GSS, 1972–2006. Because we use generalized ordered logit regression, there are two sets of coefficients to report, one set for "very happy" versus "pretty happy" or "not too happy" (first column of coefficients) and one set for "very happy" or "pretty happy" versus "not too happy" (second column of coefficients). In both columns a positive coefficient indicates a greater level of happiness: In the first column a positive sign indicates an increase in the likelihood of being "very happy," and in the second column a positive sign indicates a reduction in the likelihood of being "not too happy."

The results indicate that family income has a positive effect on happiness and that the average income of age peers has a negative effect. The first finding is well documented. The news here is the second finding, the negative coefficient for age peers' income.

Table 10.4. Estimated Effects of Family Income and Peer Income on Happiness: No Control Variables ($N = 27,088$)

	Very happy versus pretty happy or not too happy (logit)	Very happy or pretty happy versus not too happy (logit)
Family income	0.401**	0.582**
	(0.016)	(0.019)
Income mean of age peers	−0.237**	−0.428**
	(0.053)	(0.073)

Data: 1972–2006 GSS respondents ages 20–64 with data on happiness and income, excluding oversamples of African Americans in 1982 and 1987, and GSS forms where the question on general happiness was preceded by a similar question about the respondent's marriage.

Note: Coefficients are estimated using generalized ordered logistic regression in Stata. Standard errors are in parentheses. Reported results are for logged income. Results are the same when income is not logged. Adding the control variables reduces the sample to $N = 20,410$ (Table 10.5), but the coefficients are substantially the same when we apply the model without control variables to the reduced sample of 20,410. The estimated effect (logit) of mean income of age peers changes from −.237 (above) to −.216 for very happy versus pretty happy or not too happy, and from −.428 to −.379 for very happy or pretty happy versus not too happy.

**p < .01.

Although a negative coefficient for age peers' income is consistent with age-based relative income effects, there are other possible explanations, as noted earlier. Next we control for health and education, two variables that might account for the negative μ_j effect. We also control for age, marital status, race, gender, and unemployment. The results are reported in Table 10.5.

Adding the control variables reduces the estimated effect of family income by more than half for both coefficients. In other words, independent of the income of their age peers, richer people are happier in large part because they tend to be healthier, are more likely to be married, tend to have more education, and so on.[12] Much of the observed positive association of income and happiness in the United States can be accounted for by the association of income with health, education, age, marital status, unemployment, and race.

The estimated effect of *peer income*, by contrast, is *not* reduced when the control variables are added. Thus the negative effect of age-peer income on happiness cannot be readily dismissed as spuriously due to the fact that the income of one's age peers is associated with one's age, education, health, marital status, unemployment status, gender, or race. These results provide evidence for an age-based relative income effect.

Results for the control variables for the most part are in line with expectations. In general terms happiness is positively related to age, marriage, education, and health. Nonwhites tend to be less happy than whites. The unemployed are also an unhappy group.

There are nonetheless a few unexpected results. We were not expecting gender differences, yet (other things being equal) women are more likely than men to report being "very happy" (first column in Table 10.5). There is no gender difference in being *unhappy*, however (last column in Table 10.5). The effect of race has the opposite pattern: Removing the effect of variables such as income and education that mediate the race effect, there is no difference between whites and nonwhites with respect to "very happy," but nonwhites are more likely to report being "not too happy" (as indicated by the negative sign in the last column). Education follows the same pattern as race: Level of education has little effect on the likelihood that a person is "very happy" but a large effect on the likelihood of being "not too happy" (those lacking a high school diploma are unhappier). Most surprising of all, the independent effect of health is not monotonic: Individuals who report being in excellent or good health are significantly happier than those in fair or poor health, but those in poor health are *more* likely to report being "very happy" than comparable others in fair health.

We can now summarize. First, richer Americans tend to be happier (as we already knew). Second—and critically—the income of age peers matters. For Americans at a given level of income, those whose age peers enjoy higher incomes tend to be less happy than those whose age peers are poorer. This is the case (1) when we suppose that peer income comparisons are based on income proportions, and use logged income to capture the effect; (2) when

Table 10.5. Estimated Effects of Family Income and Peer Income on Happiness: Control Variables Added ($N = 20{,}410$)

	Very happy versus pretty happy or not too happy		Very happy or pretty happy versus not too happy	
	Logit	*SE*	*Logit*	*SE*
Family income	0.141**	(0.022)	0.262**	(0.025)
Income mean of age peers	−0.506**	(0.065)	−0.401**	(0.085)
Age	0.010***	(0.001)	0.001	(0.002)
Female	0.148***	(0.032)	0.085	(0.046)
Married	0.902***	(0.036)	0.859***	(0.052)
Nonwhite	−0.083	(0.045)	−0.344***	(0.053)
Education (reference: <high school)				
High school	−0.063	(0.052)	0.267***	(0.062)
Some college	0.013	(0.054)	0.429***	(0.066)
College or higher	0.127*	(0.056)	0.492***	(0.075)
Health (reference: poor health)				
Fair	−0.307***	(0.074)	−0.084	(0.073)
Good	0.147*	(0.061)	0.699***	(0.069)
Excellent	0.943***	(0.063)	1.072***	(0.080)
Unemployed	−0.250**	(0.085)	−0.589***	(0.078)
Constant	1.610*	(0.643)	2.302**	(0.848)

Data: See note to Table 10.4.

Note: Coefficients are estimated using generalized ordered logistic regression in Stata. Standard errors are in parentheses.

*$p < .05$. **$p < .01$. ***$p < .001$.

we suppose that income comparisons are based on income differences, and use metric income to capture the effect (not shown); (3) when we use income ratios to measure the relative income effect (not shown); and (4) when we use separate variables for family and peer income. In every instance the peer effects remain after we control for the other major determinants of happiness. Taken together our results suggest that the income of your age peers does matter: *richer peers tend to reduce your happiness.*

It is important, however, not to exaggerate the effect of age-peer income. The mean income of age peers is associated with happiness, but other factors such as health, marital status, and race are more consequential. Figure 10.3 compares, for several key variables, the predicted probability of being "very happy" derived from the coefficients in Table 10.5 for married, high-school-educated, employed men in good health (with values set at their sample means for continuous predictor variables). Whites, for example, have a predicted probability of .31 of reporting that they are very happy, compared to

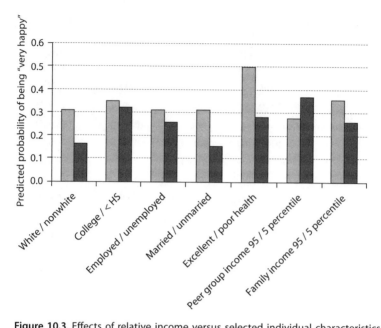

Figure 10.3. Effects of relative income versus selected individual characteristics on predicted probability of being "very happy." Predicted probabilities are derived from column 1 of Table 10.5. Variables are set to their sample means for continuous variables and to married, high-school-educated, employed men in good health for the categorical variables.

.16 for nonwhites. The likelihood of being very happy is reduced among individuals who have poor health, are unmarried, or are unemployed. With regard to the size of the peer income effect, individuals with average incomes are about 10 percentage points less likely to say they are very happy when they are members of age groups at the 95th percentile (i.e., richer groups) than when they are members of age groups at the 5th percentile. Interestingly, as Figure 10.3 shows, the effect of *age peer income* on happiness is comparable in size, but opposite in direction, to the effect of *family income* when we use the same metric (percentiles) to compare their effects.

Conclusion

In poor societies where individuals lack the necessary income to provide for their basic needs for food, shelter, and freedom from danger, an increase in income is likely to make people happier no matter how much their neighbors' incomes also rise. But once income becomes largely a status marker, we might expect that relative income will also matter for one's happiness.

America over the past one-third of a century provides a useful test case for the notion that relative income is consequential for individuals' happiness. Rich Americans tend to be happier than poor Americans, yet the average American is no happier now than three decades ago, when incomes were lower. Nor does happiness tend to rise notably with age in the United States, despite the relatively rapid rise in income experienced by many Americans in their early and middle careers. Together these patterns suggest that happiness might be affected by the incomes of age peers: unless one's income keeps pace, happiness tends to decline for an individual as the incomes of similar others rise.

For a given level of family income, we find that the higher the income of others in one's age group, the lower one's happiness, with and without controls for age, health, education, marital status, and other correlates of happiness. Since real incomes tend to increase over most of one's working life, this finding implies that working-age families must earn more and more over time to maintain a constant level of happiness. This is an example of what Brickman and Campbell (1971) called a "hedonic treadmill"—individuals must run faster and faster to maintain a constant status. Families whose income earners are in jobs with flat income trajectories are likely to become less happy over time. Thus the relative income effect observed here implies adverse effects for some individuals over the working years of their lives.

This is the case because competition for status is a zero-sum game. If income serves as a marker of relative status, some individuals will always have low status on the basis of their income, lowering their subjective well-being. Moreover, because we exhibit our status through consumption (Veblen 1899/2001), effects for society could be perverse as well: as a society, we could end up consuming more than is socially optimal if we individually work to raise our relative status, engaging in what Frank (1997) calls a "consumption arms race" akin to a military arms race.

Notes

This work was supported by NSF Grant # 0549718 to Firebaugh. We thank Richard Felson, Christopher Jencks, Erzo Luttmer, Peter Marsden, and R. Salvador Oropesa for comments and suggestions, and absolve them from responsibility for the way we used their input.

1. Note that over most of one's working life rising incomes are necessary to "keep up with the Joneses" where the Joneses are others the same age—so, as we elaborate later, age-based relative income effects may result in a treadmill where individuals need to run faster just to maintain their relative status.

2. The United States might not be unique in this respect. Quoting Richard Layard (2003), "People in the West have got no happier in the last 50 years. They have become much richer, they work much less, they have longer holidays, they travel more,

and they are healthier. But they are not happier. This shocking fact should be the starting point for much of our social science." For a contrary view, see Stevenson and Wolfers (2008), who argue that in most Western societies happiness has risen with income (the United States being the notable exception).

3. Black Americans, whose happiness has risen over recent decades (not shown), are an exception. The rise in happiness among blacks is not large enough to offset the decline in happiness in Table 10.1 among other Americans. Because this chapter examines the overall trend in happiness for Americans, we do not report separate analyses by race. In our subsequent regression analyses, however, we do control for the additive effect of race, since blacks report significantly lower levels of happiness.

4. Krugman (1996, p. 1) points out that many Americans in 1950 did not have telephones or cars, very few had televisions, and about one-third lacked full indoor plumbing. Today an American family "at the 12th percentile (that is, right at the poverty line) surely has a flushing toilet, a working shower, and a telephone with direct-dial long-distance service; probably has a color television; and may well even have a car. . . . [Thus] it does not seem at all absurd to say that the material standard of living of that poverty-level family in 1996 is as good or better than that of the median family in 1950."

5. Consider, for example, the breakdown of 1999 income for all households in the United States by age of householder (from the 2000 U.S. census, summary file 3, P56): a median income of $22,679 for those under age 25, $41,414 for those ages 25 to 34, $50,654 for those ages 35 to 44, $56,300 for those ages 45 to 54, and $47,447 for those ages 55 to 64. We see the same income profile when we follow birth cohorts over time (e.g., Gourinchas and Parker 2002).

6. Of course, additional income is needed for many Americans over much of the life course as households grow with the addition of children. To help disentangle income comparison effects from income demand effects—both of which are age related—we measure income comparison on the basis of the actual income of age peers, not on their needed income.

7. Alternatively, we could use a ratio variable to specify the relative income effect:

$$H_{ij} = \phi_0 + \phi_1 (X_{ij} / \mu_j) + \sum_q Z_{qij} + \varepsilon_{ij} \qquad (2)$$

Here $\phi_1 > 0$ indicates a relative income effect. We prefer Equation 1 because Equation 2 fails to provide a separate estimate of the effect of own income. Our conclusions are the same using either equation.

8. In some surveys the question on general happiness was preceded by a similar question about the respondent's happiness with his or her marriage, and Smith (1990) warns that the question order may have influenced responses to the general happiness question. We exclude these cases, as well as the 1982 and 1987 GSS oversamples of African Americans. Although we report results only for the more restricted sample recommended by Smith, our conclusions are the same with or without the problematic cases.

9. Surging interest in the "new science of happiness" is reflected in a spate of popular books (e.g., Layard 2005; Gilbert 2006), a new specialty journal (*Journal of Happiness Studies*), a growing literature in academic journals (Veenhoven's *Bibliography of Happiness* lists more than 3,000 scholarly publications on happiness), and

a recent article on happiness in the *American Sociological Review* (Yang 2008). For an introduction to psychological research on happiness, see Diener, Suh, Lucas, and Smith (1999) and Kahneman, Diener, and Schwarz (1999); for research in economics, see Frey and Stutzer (2002) and Di Tella and MacCulloch (2006).

10. A third possibility is that a negative coefficient for age-peer income captures the effect of increasing income *demands* over most of the working life span (e.g., adolescent children create greater income demands than younger children). But the income demand hypothesis is difficult to reconcile with the decline in happiness across cohorts because the demand hypothesis implies that, income fixed, happiness should rise as income demands decline. But the average American household has been getting richer while shrinking in size (U.S. Census Bureau 2002, appendix table 13)—completed family size for GSS respondents ages 45 and older declined from over 3.0 children on average for the 1930s birth cohorts to just over 2.0 children for those in the 1950s cohorts. The income needed for sustenance, then, did not shoot up for younger GSS cohorts from 1972 to 2006. To be sure, "income demand" in the sense of a socially expected income—the income needed to buy a normatively expected basket of goods (e.g., cell phones, more dining out)—no doubt has risen across cohorts. Arguably, though, the rise in normative expectations itself was largely driven by everyone's desire to keep up with the Joneses—which is the essence of an income comparison effect, not an income demand effect.

11. Conventional ordered logistic regression is appropriate if a change in income would have the same effect on the odds of answering "very happy" or "pretty happy" versus "not too happy" as it would for the odds of answering "very happy" versus "pretty happy" or "not too happy." We tested this assumption using a chi-square likelihood-ratio test (Long 1997). The test was statistically significant in every model we estimated, indicating that the constant effect assumption is inappropriate. Hence we use the generalized ordered logit model, which allows effects to differ across outcomes.

12. The reduction in the effect of family income on happiness is not due to the loss of cases due to missing data (see note to Table 10.4).

References

Alwin, Duane. 1987. "Distributive Justice and Satisfaction with Material Well-Being." *American Sociological Review* 52:83–95.

Blanchflower, David G., and Andrew J. Oswald. 2004. "Money, Sex and Happiness: An Empirical Study." *Scandinavian Journal of Economics* 106:393–415.

———. 2007. "Is Well-Being U-Shaped over the Life Cycle?" Working Paper 12935, National Bureau of Economic Research, Cambridge, MA.

Brickman, Philip, and D. T. Campbell. 1971. "Hedonic Relativism and Planning the Good Society." In *Adaptation-Level Theory: A Symposium*, edited by M. H. Appley, 287–302. New York: Academic Press.

Davis, James A., Tom W. Smith, and Peter V. Marsden. 2006. *General Social Surveys, 1972–2006* [Machine-readable cumulative file]. Chicago: NORC (producer). Storrs, CT: Roper Center for Public Opinion Research, University of Connecticut (distributor).

Diener, Edward, Eunkook M. Suh, Richard E. Lucas, and Heidi L. Smith. 1999. "Subjective Well-Being: Three Decades of Progress." *Psychological Bulletin* 125:276–303.

Di Tella, Rafael, and Robert MacCulloch. 2006. "Some Uses of Happiness Data in Economics." *Journal of Economic Perspectives* 20:25–46.

Di Tella, Rafael, Robert J. MacCulloch, and Andrew J. Oswald. 2001. "Preferences over Inflation and Unemployment: Evidence from Surveys of Happiness." *American Economic Review* 91:335–41.

Easterlin, Richard A. 1974. "Does Economic Growth Improve the Human Lot?" In *Nations and Households in Economic Growth: Essays in Honour of Moses Abramovitz*, edited by P. A. David and M. W. Reder, 89–125. New York: Academic Press.

———. 2001. "Income and Happiness: Towards a Unified Theory." *Economic Journal* 111:465–84.

Firebaugh, Glenn. 2008. *Seven Rules for Social Research*. Princeton, NJ: Princeton University Press.

Firebaugh, Glenn, and Matthew B. Schroeder. 2009. "Does Your Neighbor's Income Affect Your Happiness?" *American Journal of Sociology* 115:805–31.

Fischer, Claude. 2008. "What Wealth-Happiness Paradox? A Short Note on the American Case." *Journal of Happiness Studies* 9:219–26.

Fischer, Claude, and Michael Hout. 2006. *Century of Difference: How America Changed in the Last One Hundred Years*. New York: Russell Sage Foundation.

Frank, Robert H. 1997. "The Frame of Reference as a Public Good." *Economic Journal* 107:1832–47.

———. 2007. *Falling Behind: How Rising Inequality Harms the Middle Class*. Berkeley: University of California Press.

Frey, Bruno S., and Alois Stutzer. 2002. "What Can Economists Learn from Happiness Research?" *Journal of Economic Literature* 40:402–35.

Gilbert, Daniel. 2006. *Stumbling on Happiness*. New York: Knopf.

Gourinchas, Pierre-Olivier, and Jonathan A. Parker. 2002. "Consumption over the Life Cycle." *Econometrica* 70:47–89.

Graham, Carol, and Stefano Pettinato. 2002. *Happiness and Hardship: Opportunity and Security in New Market Economies*. Washington, DC: Brookings Institution.

Hout, Michael. 2003. "Money and Morale: What Growing Inequality Is Doing to Americans' Views of Themselves and Others." Working paper, University of California, Berkeley, Survey Research Center.

Jasso, Guillermina. 1978. "On the Justice of Earnings: A New Specification of the Justice Evaluation Function." *American Journal of Sociology* 83:1398–1419.

Kahneman, Daniel, Edward Diener, and Norbert Schwarz, eds. 1999. *Well-Being: The Foundations of Hedonic Psychology*. New York: Russell Sage Foundation.

Koivumaa, Honkanen Heli, Risto Honkanen, Heimo Viinamaki, Kauko Heikkila, Jaakko Kaprio, and Markku Koskenvuo. 2001. "Life Satisfaction and Suicide: A 20-Year Follow-Up Study." *American Journal of Psychiatry* 158:433–39.

Konow, James, and Joseph Earley. 2008. "The Hedonistic Paradox: Is *Homo Economicus* Happier?" *Journal of Public Economics* 1–2:1–33.

Krugman, Paul. 1996. "The CPI and the Rat Race: New Evidence on the Old Question of Whether Money Buys Happiness." *Slate*. www.slate.com/id/1915/.

Layard, Richard. 2003. "Happiness: Has Social Science Got a Clue?" Lionel Robbins Memorial Lectures, London School of Economics. http://cep.lse.ac.uk/events/lectures/layard/RL030303.pdf.

———. 2005. *Happiness: Lessons from a New Science*. New York: Penguin.

Long, J. Scott. 1997. *Regression Models for Categorical and Limited Dependent Variables*. Thousands Oaks, CA: Sage.

Luttmer, Erzo F. P. 2005. "Neighbors as Negatives: Relative Earnings and Well-Being." *Quarterly Journal of Economics* 120:963–1002.

McBride, Michael. 2001. "Relative-Income Effects on Subjective Well-Being in the Cross-Section." *Journal of Economic Behavior and Organization* 45:251–78.

Merton, Robert K., and Alice K. Rossi. 1950. "Contributions to the Theory of Reference Group Behavior." In *Continuities in Social Research*, edited by Robert K. Merton and Paul F. Lazarsfeld, 40–115. New York: Free Press.

Scitovsky, Tibor. 1976. *The Joyless Economy*. New York: Oxford University Press.

Smith, Tom W. 1990. "Timely Artifacts: A Review of Measurement Variation in the 1972–1989 GSS." GSS Methodological Report No. 56, NORC, Chicago.

Stevenson, Betsey, and Justin Wolfers. 2008. "Economic Growth and Subjective Well-Being: Reassessing the Easterlin Paradox." Draft, Wharton School, University of Pennsylvania, Philadelphia.

Stouffer, Samuel, Arthur A. Lumsdaine, Marion Harper, Robin Williams, Brewster M. Smith, Irving L. Janis, Shirley A. Star, and Leonard S. Cottrell. 1949. *The American Soldier: Adjustment during Army Life*. Princeton, NJ: Princeton University Press.

U.S. Census Bureau. 2002. *Demographic Trends in the 20th Century*. Washington, DC: U.S. Census Bureau.

Veblen, Thorstein. 1899/2001. "Excerpts from 'The Theory of the Leisure Class.'" In *Social Stratification*, 2nd ed., edited by David Grusky, 491–98. Boulder, CO: Westview.

Yang, Yang. 2008. "Social Inequalities in Happiness in the United States, 1972 to 2004: An Age-Period-Cohort Analysis." *American Sociological Review* 73: 204–26.

11

Religion and Happiness

Michael Hout and Andrew Greeley

Morale and happiness were staple interests among the early proponents of a project to develop "social indicators" (Duncan 1970, 1975; Easterlin 1974; Andrews and Withey 1976; T. W. Smith 1979). They had the noble idea that the nation's mental health was not only the absence of mental illness but also the maintenance of positive mental outlooks among Americans. No one had a specific recipe for instilling or maintaining morale, but social scientists could contribute reliable measurements of the state of affairs from time to time. These interests melded with others to provide the rationale and content for the original General Social Survey (GSS) in 1972.

Interest in morale is no longer tied to the social indicators agenda, but research continues with more academic motivations. Kahneman (1999) has used people's answers to questions about their happiness as grist for his ongoing inquiry into the foundations of economic theory. Answers to questions about happiness help clarify what people think they are achieving when they choose one activity (or object) over another. Economists and sociologists have discovered an empirical puzzle: happiness does not change when the economy improves, even though the income–happiness connection is strong at the individual level (Davis 1984; Easterlin 1996; Frey and Stutzer 2002; Frank 2006; Firebaugh and Tach, chapter 10 in this volume). Hout (2003) and Fischer (2008) link this puzzle to economic inequality. In particular they note that growth on average does not imply more income for all; recent U.S.

experience certainly fits with that generalization as steadily rising GDP in the United States has led to only occasional increases in family and personal incomes (Fischer and Hout 2006, pp. 140–47). As the economic gap between the poor and the affluent widened in the 1980s and early 1990s, the poor became less happy and the affluent happier than they used to be (Hout 2003).

Neglected in this largely utilitarian literature is the morale-building potential of religious affiliation and participation. The meaning and sense of belonging long associated with religious attachment (e.g., Greeley 1969, 1972, 1994; Wuthnow 1993; C. Smith 1998) seems a likely source of feelings of well-being, personal efficacy, and, dare we say it, happiness. Our hypotheses extrapolate from the "meaning and belonging" tradition within the sociology of religion:

Hypothesis 1: People with a religious preference will be happier than people with none.

Hypothesis 2: Among people with religious preferences, those who more frequently participate in religious services will be happier than those who never participate.

Hypothesis 2a: People who have a religion but do not participate in it will not be happier than people who have no religion.

Hypothesis 3: People who are religiously active will be "inoculated" against the general downward trend in the morale of American adults.

These hypotheses stem from the theory developed over many years, initially in *The Denominational Society* (Greeley 1972) and most recently in *Religion as Poetry* (Greeley 1994). The key idea is that the religious stories engender a sense of transcendent reality that becomes, in turn, an important resource for identity and attachment in plural mass society. Overlaid upon these psychic resources are the positive feelings and associations that come from participation in practices that are, at once, local and world historical. The first hypothesis refers to the mere fact of belonging. If we find that people with a religious affiliation are indeed happier than those who have none, we will have to discern whether the relationship reflects religious content or just something else that correlates with religion but is not substantively religion. Thus, the second hypothesis further specifies that attending religious services explains, in the statistical sense, the association between affiliation and happiness. Finally, when we look at trend data, we hypothesize that the overall trend toward slightly less happiness among Americans is limited to the unaffiliated and the inactive affiliates. All three hypotheses are confirmed by the GSS data.

The theory is a perfectly general statement, meant to apply to any complex society and certainly not intended as a specific theory of American religion. *Religion as Poetry* (Greeley 1994), *Catholic Imagination* (Greeley 2000), and *Religion in Europe* (Greeley 2003) all include data from Europe. We also examine the association between religion and happiness outside the United States using data from the International Social Survey Programme, an international collaborative survey to which the GSS contributes the American data.

Measures

The GSS happiness question is, "Taken altogether, how would you say things are these days—would you say that you are very happy, pretty happy, or not too happy?" (Davis, Smith, and Marsden 2006). This simple item correlates well with more elaborate scales of morale and psychological functioning—gammas range from .5 to .8 (T. W. Smith 1979).[1]

The religion item asks, "What is your current religious preference? Is it Protestant, Catholic, Jewish, no religion, or something else?" A follow-up question ascertains specific denominations for Protestants and Jews. We differentiated among Protestants, creating "conservative" and "mainline" categories using the protocol developed by T. W. Smith (1990b). "Conservative Protestants" belong to denominations that emphasize a literal reading of the Bible, personal conversion through a "born-again" experience, and mission to convert non-Christians, while "mainline Protestants" belong to moderate or liberal denominations under Smith's scheme.[2]

The GSS question on church attendance classifies people into nine categories of attendance (ranging from 0 for "never" to 8 for "more than once a week").[3] So prior to using this variable in our analysis we must settle on the mathematical function that simply but accurately expresses the relationship between attendance and happiness. Exploratory analyses led us to conclude that the scores assigned by the GSS provide the optimal coding for the relationship between attendance and happiness.[4]

As our analysis progresses, we will need some substantive details about the content of religious people's beliefs in order to test key hypotheses. The 1998 GSS included a question about belief in God that has often been part of the GSS and some one-time-only questions measuring religious feelings shown in the appendix to this chapter. We constructed an additive index from these religious feelings items; they perform well as a scale.[5]

The hypothesis that competes with the religious one is a "sociability" hypothesis. Our measure for testing that hypothesis is the GSS "social evening with friends" question: "Which answer comes closest to how often you do the following things? Spend a social evening with friends who live outside the neighborhood: 1) almost every day, 2) once or twice a week, 3) several times a week, 4) about once a month, 5) several times a year, 6) about once a year, 7) never." We reversed the scoring of this item (0 indicates "never" and 6 indicates "almost every day"), so we expect that the regression coefficient of happiness on sociability will be positive.

Throughout our analysis of the relationship between happiness and religion, we restrict our working sample to adults 25–74 years old. For people under 25 and over 75, significant transfers of money from family members and government agencies obscure the link between income and standard of living. In addition, many seniors live off savings, further distancing standard of living from income.

Statistical Models

We tailor our statistical tests to the order among the happiness response categories by using the stereotype ordered logit regression model (Anderson 1984; DiPrete 1990). Using the more conventional ordered logit model requires a "parallel logits" assumption that religion has the same effect on the odds of a more positive response versus a less positive response, regardless of how "more positive" and "less positive" are defined (Long 1997). Brant's (1990) test rejected the parallel logits assumption for our data. The stereotype ordered regression (SOR) model is a parsimonious alternative.

The general form of the SOR model, following Anderson (1984) and DiPrete (1990), is

$$y_{ij} = \ln\left(\frac{p_{ij}}{p_{iJ}}\right) = (\theta_j - \theta_J) + \sum_{k=1}^{K} (\phi_j - \phi_J)\beta_k X_{ki} \tag{1}$$

where $i = 1, \ldots, N$ indexes people, $j = 1, \ldots, J$ indexes responses, $k = 1, \ldots, K$ indexes the independent variables, y_{ij} is the logit for response j relative to a reference response J, the θs are intercepts, the βs are slopes, and the ϕs alter the slopes.[6] The model is underidentified without restrictions on the θs and ϕs. It is conventional to specify $\theta_J = \phi_J = 0$ and $\phi_1 = 1$. The ϕs between ϕ_1 and ϕ_J will usually fall between 0 and 1 so they can usefully be thought of as proportions, that is, how large the slope in question is compared with the slope for the extreme contrast between categories 1 and J.

With the conventional identifying restrictions applied to the GSS happiness question with its three responses, (1) very happy, (2) pretty happy, and (3) not too happy, we get this model:

$$\ln\left(\frac{p_{ij}}{p_{i3}}\right) = \begin{cases} \theta_1 + \sum \beta_k X_{ki} & \text{for } j = 1, \text{and} \\ \theta_2 + \phi_2 \sum \beta_k X_{ki} & \text{for } j = 2. \end{cases} \tag{2}$$

Readers comfortable with logit regression results can view the SOR results the same way with one important emendation: The ϕ_2 parameter modifies each of the β_k proportionally. So if, for example, $\beta_1 = .75$ and $\phi_2 = .60$, we would say that a one point increase in X_1 raises the log odds on being very happy instead of not too happy by .75 and raises the log odds on being pretty happy instead of not too happy by $.60 \cdot .75 = .45$.

Regression results have useful properties as descriptions of data, but they are not the straightforward evidence of causal relationships they were once thought to be (see, e.g., Morgan and Winship 2007, pp. 10–13). In social life people do things, at least in part, because they expect rewards. Regression-based techniques compare people who have an attribute to those who do not have it. If the people who have an attribute have it, in part, because they find it rewarding while others lack the attribute because they do not expect it to be rewarding for them, regression-based comparisons will misstate—usually overstate—the actual causal effects. The "treatment," so to speak, likely has a bigger effect on those who select it than on those who do not. There are likely at least two causal effects underlying the regression coefficient (if we have the causal order right): the big effect on those who sought out the "treatment"—religious affiliation in this case—and the small (potentially zero) effect on those who avoided it.

This way of thinking goes under the general heading of "counterfactual analysis." Instead of averaging the whole population together we ask the more pointed questions: "What would the average happiness be for people who have a religious affiliation—the 'treated'—if we reversed their personal choice and removed their affiliation?" and "What would the average happiness be for people who lack an affiliation—the 'untreated'—if we reversed their personal choice and gave them a religious affiliation?" Modern tools of counterfactual analysis yield estimates of both of these average effects: the average effect of the treatment on the treated and the average effect of the treatment on the untreated. If we think of having a religious affiliation as the treatment, those who chose to have one as the treated and those who chose not to have one as the untreated, the effect of the treatment on the treated estimates how much happier the affiliated are than they would have been if they lacked an affiliation and the effect of the treatment on the untreated estimates how much happier the unaffiliated would be if they were to have an affiliation. When there is "positive selection" into a treatment group, the average effect of the treatment on the treated exceeds the average effect of the treatment on the untreated.

In this chapter we engage in some counterfactual thinking about religion and happiness. When we observe that people who have a religion are happier than people who do not have a religion, we cannot immediately conclude that acquiring a religion would make the unchurched happier. What we seek are estimates of how much happier the unchurched would be if they had a religion, and how much less happy those with an affiliation would be if they were suddenly unchurched. A standard analysis would compare the average religious person with the average unchurched person and see which group is happier. In the counterfactual analysis we first estimate how likely each person in the data set is to have a religion; this is known as the person's "propensity score." Then we compare people who do and do not have a religion among the subset who are equally likely (or unlikely) to have a religion.

Specifically we follow the propensity score weighting methods laid out by Morgan and Todd (2008). We use the sociodemographic model of Hout and Fischer (2002) to estimate the probability $\hat{p}_i$ that person i has a religion. To estimate the effect of having a religion on the happiness of the religious—the effect of the treatment on the treated—we fit the SOR model with every person who has a religion weighted 1.0 and every person without a religion weighted by $\hat{p}_i/(1-\hat{p}_i)$. To estimate the effect of having a religion on the happiness of the unchurched—the effect of the treatment on the untreated group—we fit the SOR model with every person who has no religion weighted 1.0 and every person with a religion weighted by $(1-\hat{p}_i)/\hat{p}_i$. The first estimate tells us how much less happy a person with a religion would be if she or he were to drop her or his religion, while the second tells us how much happier a person without a religion would be if she or he acquired a religious identity. These two estimates will be equal only under some pretty atypical circumstances (Morgan and Winship 2007, chap. 5).

Religion and Happiness in the United States in the 2000s

We begin with a cross-sectional analysis of recent data from the 2000–2006 GSSs. Then we will turn to the longer time span. We pool three GSSs together for this part of the analysis because the number of Jewish people in any GSS is small.[7]

In these recent data, about one-third of American adults were very happy, one-tenth were not too happy, and the majority (56%) were in between ("pretty happy"). Religious people were slightly above the national norm in happiness and below the national norm in unhappiness (see Table 11.1). People who had no religion were significantly less happy than average; only 26% were very happy (compared to 35% of the religious), 61% were pretty happy (compared to 55% of the religious), and 13% were not too happy (compared to 10% of the religious). The difference between the happiness of religious Americans and those who had no religion was statistically significant and accounted for much of the total association between religion and happiness.[8] Further analysis shows that although Afro-American Protestants are significantly less happy than other Christians, the important distinction is between having or not having a religion. Hypothesis 1 is confirmed.

Establishing a statistical relationship is just the first step in thinking about how religion might affect happiness; it does not establish religion as a cause. There is always the possibility that happy people are more likely to take up religion and that unhappy people lose their religion. Or there might be a common cause that boosts both religiosity and happiness without the two actually being connected. Our survey data cannot resolve the issue of causal order. We can use our data to address the question of whether there are variables associated with having a religion that could be the underlying factor in

Table 11.1. Happiness by Religion

| | Happiness (%) | | | | |
| | Not too | Pretty | Very | | |
Religion	happy	happy	happy	Total	N
Conservative Protestant	10	53	37	100	1,798
Afro-American Protestant	14	55	31	100	462
Mainline Protestant	8	55	36	100	1,574
Catholic	10	56	34	100	1,689
Jewish	15	53	32	100	128
Other religion	14	54	32	100	226
No religion	13	61	26	100	1,020
Total	10	56	34	100	6,897

Source: Persons 25–74 years old, GSS, 2000–2006.
Note: Percentages were calculated using sampling and design weights; Ns are unweighted counts of valid cases.

happiness. For example, Waite and Gallagher (2000) argue that marriage makes people happy. Married people are also more likely to have a religion than single people are (Hout and Fischer 2002). So, arguably, the relationship we see in Table 11.1 might just reflect the higher marriage rate among religious people compared with marriage among those who have no religion. Similar arguments could be made about regional subcultures affecting both religious affiliation and happiness, or socioeconomic differences associated with having more or less education or more or less money, being a woman or a man, having one racial or ethnic ancestry instead of another, and being born in one decade rather than another (Yang 2008).

To test whether differences in happiness are somehow spurious due to the influence of these sociodemographic factors, we compare the gross effects of religion with the results we obtain in a model that includes all of these variables along with religious preference. The results are in Table 11.2. The first column shows the coefficients and standard errors for each religious denomination in a model that is the stereotype ordered logit equivalent of Table 11.1; it has year dummies as the only control variables so we refer to it as the "gross differences" model. The second column shows the results after controlling for the sociodemographic variables. (See Table 11.A.1 in the appendix to this chapter for all the coefficients in the sociodemographic model.)

The results of this more or less standard analysis are clear: religion differences in happiness do not, for the most part, reflect the social and demographic composition of religious denominations. A Wald test shows that the association between religious preference and happiness controlling for sociodemographic variables is statistically significant at conventional levels. After adjustment for socioeconomic differences, the diverse "other religions" category stands out; people outside the Judeo-Christian tradition are less

Table 11.2. Happiness by Religion: Stereotype-Ordered Regression Results by Model

	Model		
Coefficient	Gross	SD	Attendance
Religion			
Conservative Protestant	0.72* (0.15)	0.64* (0.16)	0.07 (0.17)
Afro-American Protestant	0.22 (0.23)	0.69* (0.28)	0.18 (0.29)
Mainline Protestant	0.84* (0.14)	⊛ 0.50* (0.16)	0.09 (0.17)
Catholic	0.61* (0.14)	0.50* (0.16)	0.01 (0.17)
Jewish	0.07 (0.44)	0.61 (0.47)	0.80 (0.46)
Other religion	0.16 (0.34)	–0.14 (0.34)	–0.43 (0.34)
No religion	0.00 (—)	0.00 (—)	0.00 (—)
Wald chi-square test (*df* = 6)	44.05*	26.58*	6.63
Frequency of attendance	—	—	0.18* (0.02)
Slope adjustments			
Very happy	1.00 (—)	1.00 (—)	1.00 (—)
Pretty happy	0.50* (0.13)	0.55* (0.03)	0.54* (0.03)
Not too happy	0.00 (—)	0.00 (—)	0.00 (—)
Additional variables in the model	Year	SD	SD
Observations	6,309	6,309	6,309

Source: Authors' calculations from the GSS, 2000–2006.
Note: Standard errors in parentheses. SD = sociodemographic.
*$p < .05$.

happy than we would expect given their social and demographic characteristics (though not significantly less happy than people with no religion).

Counterfactual Analysis
We now know that the difference between the average outcomes of people who do and do not have some attribute—and regression-adjusted variants of that difference—only rarely give us an accurate image of the underlying causal process (Morgan and Winship 2007, pp. 46–50). That is because, in real life, people choose the "treatments" that benefit them most. Formally, we need to think of statistical differences as reflecting at least two causal effects— the larger effect of the treatment on those who have chosen it and the smaller (possibly null) effect of the treatment on those who have chosen not to have it. In this case, religion is the "treatment," so we are interested in the realized effect of religion on the happiness of religious people and the potential effect of religion on the happiness of people who have no religion. Consistent with the logic of counterfactual analysis more generally, we start with the hypothesis that religious people benefit more from having a religion than people who have no religion would if they suddenly joined one. So the number we

Table 11.3. Happiness by Religion: Stereotype-Ordered Regression Estimates of Average Treatment Effects

	Weighted to estimate effect on the		
Coefficient	Unweighted	Treated	Untreated
Estimate	0.49* (0.14)	0.55* (0.15)	0.33* (0.14)
Slope adjustments			
Very happy	1.00 (—)	1.00 (—)	1.00 (—)
Pretty happy	0.54* (0.13)	0.50* (0.05)	0.51* (0.05)
Not too happy	0.00 (—)	0.00 (—)	0.00 (—)
Additional variables in the model	SD	SD	SD
Observations	6,309	6,309	6,309

Source: Authors' calculations from the GSS, 2000–2006.
Note: Standard errors in parentheses. SD = sociodemographic.
*p < .05.

get as our regression coefficient is somewhere in between the bigger impact religion has had on the religious and the smaller potential impact it might have on the people who have no religion.

Table 11.3 shows the overall difference, as estimated by conventional analysis, and these two counterfactual effects, as estimated by propensity score weighting regressions (Morgan and Todd 2008). The effect of religion on the happiness of the religious (the average effect of the treatment on the treated) is more than half again as big as the potential effect of religion on the happiness of people who do not already have a religion (the average effect of the treatment on the untreated)—.55 compared to .33.[9] Each estimate lies just outside the 95% confidence interval of the other, so the difference is statistically as well as substantively significant. Finding a religion would not boost the happiness of the unchurched up to the level of those who already have a religion, but it would make them happier. Taking away the religions of the already religious would reduce their happiness well below that of those who do not currently have a religion. For them the religious treatment has been instrumental to their happiness.

Do the Religious Have to Practice Their Religion to Be Happier?
So religion makes people happier. The next step is to discern whether the relationship has religious content. To make the substantive link between religion and happiness, we need evidence that a variable with religious content explains the gross differences among religions in how happy their members are. Beliefs are not useful in this context because some religions dispute beliefs that are central to others. We need an aspect of religiosity not only that differentiates the religious from the nonreligious but also that does not divide the religious of one denomination from the religious of another. Attendance

at religious services is precisely that kind of general factor. Active participation in religious rituals exposes people to whatever benefits religion might confer, regardless of the practice or expression that the rituals themselves entail. Formally, we deduce that if the effect of religion on happiness is substantively religious, then we should see that people who attend frequently are happier than those who seldom participate in religious services and that people who never attend religious services are no happier than people who have no religion.

When we add frequency of attendance to the sociodemographic model of happiness, the differences between people with and without a religion disappear (up to the limited precision of a sample of 6,309 individuals), as do the differences among the five denominations and the residual "other religions" category. This is substantively meaningful. It shows that to get the happiness benefit of religion, a person has to practice her or his religion. The more she or he practices, the happier she or he gets. Without practice, she or he gets no benefit.

We obtain this result whether we ignore or include the sociodemographic variables in the model and whether or not we use the propensity score weighting to estimate treatment effects on the treated and untreated. Returning to Table 11.2, the last column shows the results we get from the full model that includes religion, the sociodemographic variables, and religious attendance. In the gross differences model, all six coefficients are positive and the coefficients for the three largest denominations are statistically significant. In the third model, the coefficient for other religions has a negative sign and none of the six is statistically significant. On that basis it is accurate to say that attendance accounts for nearly all of the difference in happiness between religious and nonreligious Americans.

Frequent attenders are substantively as well as statistically happier than infrequent attenders. The coefficient for attendance is 0.18 (with a standard error of 0.02); in percentage terms 0.18 translates to a 3- to 5-point increase in the expected percentage very happy for each upward tick on the GSS scale of frequency of attendance.[10] For example, the percentage very happy among otherwise average Catholics rises from 23% to 34% to 42% as attendance rises from never to monthly to weekly. The greater happiness of an otherwise average person who attends religious services weekly compared with one who attends once a month is equivalent to (1) 1.2 times the difference between a white and an African American, (2) the difference between a person with an advanced degree and a high school dropout, and (3) 1.6 times the difference between a southerner and a midwesterner.[11] However it is only one-third the difference between a married and a single person.

These results go a long way toward confirming hypotheses 2 and 2a. That is, to this point we have shown evidence that, on average, people who attend religious services more often are happier and that people who have a religion but do not attend services are no happier than people who have no religion.

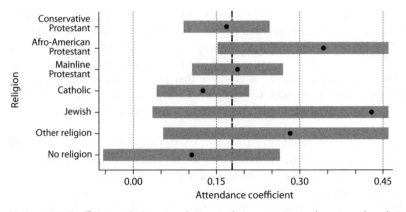

Figure 11.1. Coefficients relating attendance at religious services to happiness by religion. *Source*: Authors' calculations from GSS, 2000–2006. Dashed vertical line shows the average within-religion coefficient.

However, we have not yet attempted to measure differences among denominations in the strength of association between attendance and happiness. It is pretty much impossible to get the results we have if attendance is not important for the large denominations, but it could be that we are overgeneralizing. Nothing in the results so far can rule out the possibility that attendance matters a great deal for happiness within some denominations but not at all in others. If attendance is inconsequential in any denomination, it will temper our conclusions.

Toward that end we fit our third model—the one with the sociodemographic variables and attendance—for each denomination and for people who have no religion. We show our results graphically in Figure 11.1. The circles indicate the effect of attendance on happiness for each religion category. The gray lines emanating out from each circle indicate the 95% confidence interval for that coefficient. The vertical line at 0.18 is the attendance coefficient from Table 11.2. These calculations strongly support hypothesis 2 and the conclusions we drew from Table 11.2. In particular, the coefficient for each category except "no religion" is statistically significant (note how the lower bound of each confidence interval is greater than zero). More importantly, each confidence interval includes the average within-denomination coefficient (0.18)—even the confidence interval for no religion. Thus we conclude that the effect is the same in all denominations. The results for people with no religion imply some ambivalence. On the one hand, we cannot reject the null hypothesis of no attendance effect for them; on the other hand, their coefficient is actually closer to the average within-denomination effect than to zero. So the evidence slightly favors the conclusion that attendance (rare as it is) has a positive effect on people with no religion.[12]

We now ask the same question about attendance that we asked about denomination. Could it be something nonreligious about attending religious services that is making people happy? One possibility is socializing. After all, the religious content of religious services might have no effect on morale; it might be bound up in the chance to see other people at services. It seems reasonable to think, for example, that people who lack other opportunities to socialize might compensate by attending religious services and that the social element of attendance, not its religious content, is the source of happiness. The GSS routinely asks people how often they spend a social evening with friends. If sociability, not religiosity, is the reason why attending services makes people happy, then adding frequency of social evenings with friends to the model should show that it—and not frequency of religious attendance—is the significant influence on happiness or that attendance affects only people who do not have social evenings with friends. As Table 11.4 shows, neither is

Table 11.4. Happiness by Frequency of Attendance at Religious Services, Socializing with Friends, and Marital Status

Independent variable	Main effects	Interaction effects	
		Socialize with friends	Marital status
Frequency of attendance	0.18* (0.02)	0.18* (0.05)	0.13* (0.05)
Socialize with friends	0.14* (0.04)	0.13 (0.07)	0.14* (0.04)
Marital status			
Married	1.40* (0.18)	1.40* (0.18)	1.14* (0.27)
Widowed	0.11 (0.30)	0.11 (0.30)	−0.36 (0.46)
Divorced or separated	0.01 (0.20)	0.01 (0.20)	−0.08 (0.30)
Never married	0.00 (—)	0.00 (—)	0.00 (—)
Interaction: Attendance by			
Socialize with friends	—	0.00 (0.02)	—
Marital status			
Married	—	—	0.08 (0.06)
Widowed	—	—	0.13 (0.09)
Divorced or separated	—	—	−0.02 (0.07)
Never married	—	—	0.00 (—)
Slope adjustments			
Very happy	1.00 (—)	1.00 (—)	1.00 (—)
Pretty happy	0.50* (0.03)	0.50* (0.03)	0.51* (0.03)
Not too happy	0.00 (—)	0.00 (—)	0.00 (—)
Additional variables in the model	SD	SD	SD
Observations	4,190	4,190	4,190

Source: Authors' calculations from the GSS, 2000–2006.

Note: Standard errors in parentheses. SD = sociodemographic.

*p < .05.

the case. People who spend social evenings with friends are happier, just as people who attend religious services are happier. But the efficacy of attending services does not depend on the friends factor. Formally, there is no statistical interaction between socializing with friends and attending services, indicating that attendance increases the happiness of those who socialize frequently just as much as it affects those who seldom socialize. There is no evidence that church attendance increases happiness by displacing loneliness.

As a further check on our social relations hypothesis, we compare the coefficient on attendance for married and single people. The gap between those who attend frequently and rarely turns out to be a little bigger for the married (the interaction is .08), but the difference is not statistically significant.

We should have some positive evidence of the religious content of attendance as well as ruling out the competing hypotheses. For that we turn to the special module of the 1998 GSS that ascertained people's religious beliefs and practices in some detail. Adding these two items to the model (see Table 11.5) refines our sense that attendance at religious services has real religious content. First, the coefficient for attendance after controlling for belief in God and religious feelings is less than half as large as its coefficient without controlling these substantive religious variables, and is statistically insignificant in this reduced sample. Second, religious feelings increase happiness, but belief in God has no effect.[13] We interpret this pattern of association (and nonassociation) as evidence that religion fosters happiness not through socializing but through the emotional response to religious services.

Table 11.5. Happiness by Frequency of Attendance at Religious Services, Socializing with Friends, Marital Status, and Religious Beliefs

Independent variable	Attendance and social life	Religious Feelings
Frequency of attendance	0.16* (0.07)	0.06 (0.07)
Socialize with friends	0.23* (0.11)	0.24* (0.11)
Marital status		
Married	1.99* (0.48)	1.88* (0.47)
Widowed	−0.17 (1.07)	0.00 (1.07)
Divorced or separated	−0.16 (0.51).	−0.19 (0.52)
Never married	0.00 (—)	0.00 (—)
Belief in God	—	0.07 (0.17)
Religious feelings	—	0.64* (0.31)
Additional variables in the model	SD	SD
Observations	653	653

Source: Authors' calculations from the GSS, 1998.
Note: Standard errors in parentheses. SD = sociodemographic.
*$p < .05$.

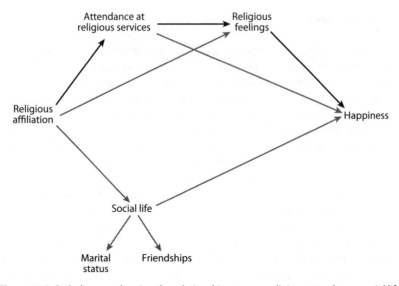

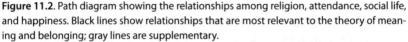

Figure 11.2. Path diagram showing the relationships among religion, attendance, social life, and happiness. Black lines show relationships that are most relevant to the theory of meaning and belonging; gray lines are supplementary.

Belief is not enough to engender high morale on its own. Praying alone at home is a private religious devotion. It has much in common with communal religious experience in content but is outside the communal context. A multivariate analysis that substituted the frequency of prayer—which could be private or part of a religious service—for frequency of attendance as a predictor failed to account for all the difference between the happiness of religious people and the unchurched. Religion, to be effective, must be social. Neither socializing without religious affect nor praying without social context is sufficient for gaining a religious boost to happiness. Attending religious services makes people happy when the service brings about a sense of closeness to God—"an aura of factuality" in Geertz's (1973, p. 90) phrasing. This is the deep core of the "meaning and belonging" theory. People might derive meaning from a private spirituality, but if they practice in private they miss out on belonging and forego the "collective effervescence" of communal practices (Greeley 1994). The complement is just as true: belonging without believing misses out on meaning. Religion affects social life through the conjunction of meaning and belonging; neither by itself is sufficient.

Figure 11.2 summarizes our findings so far. Having a religious affiliation increases happiness indirectly through attendance at religious services. And attendance increases happiness mostly through the emotional attachment to God and denomination. Social life is an important contributor to happiness, but it is complementary to, not competing with, religion in making people happy.

Happiness Trends

The 1990s was, by some measures, a decade of polarizing religion (e.g., Hout and Fischer 2002). The relationship between religion and happiness we have documented to this point could, conceivably, be a by-product of polarizing trends. Theory that stresses meaning and belonging says no. Meaning and belonging reach back to the unknown dawn of organized religion according to the theory. Thus it would be a complication for this theory if the association between religion and happiness emerged only recently. On the other hand, evidence of a persistent relationship would strengthen the theory. We look at trends two ways: by denomination and by attendance.

Figure 11.3 shows the trends—smoothed by the loess method in Cleveland (1994)—in being "very happy" for each denomination except the residual "other religions." Overall, there was a modest but statistically significant decrease in the percentage very happy between the mid-1970s and the mid-1990s—from roughly 36% to 33%; the trend leveled off in this decade. Could the trend toward having no religion (Hout and Fischer 2002) have contributed to the erosion of happiness? If there was no trend in happiness within denominations while the proportion in the least happy religious category—no religion—grew, then we could say "yes" the changing religious combination explains the modest drop-off in happiness. If the trends within denominations echo the national trend, then the explanation must lie elsewhere.

The happiness of Protestants and Jews fell in concert with national trend. Catholics and people with no religion were about as happy in 2006 as they had been 33 years earlier. These trends led to a modest convergence in the

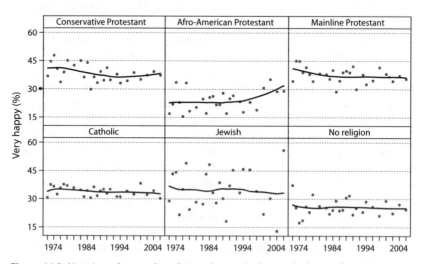

Figure 11.3. Happiness by year by religion. *Source*: Authors' calculations from GSS, 1972–2006. Data smoothed using locally estimated (loess) regression.

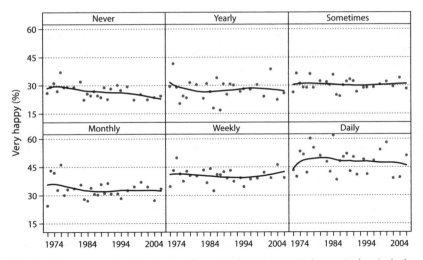

Figure 11.4. Happiness by year by attendance at religious services. *Source*: Authors' calculations from GSS, 1972–2006. Data smoothed using locally estimated (loess) regression.

happiness of different religious groups. Denominational differences diminished and religious people got ever so slightly closer to the level of happiness among nonreligious people.

Our main concern here is whether religious differences in happiness were peculiar to this decade. Clearly not. People with religious preferences have been happier than people without religion throughout the period covered by the GSS. Only Afro-American Protestants were as unhappy as people with no religion in the period from 1972–1998, and our multivariate analysis makes clear that African Americans in every denomination were less happy than the whites in that denomination during those years. Among people in larger denominations, the percentage very happy never fell below 30%; among people with no religion, the percentage very happy never got above 30%.[14] If the relationship between religion and happiness has changed at all, it may have decreased very slightly (none of the models we considered yielded a statistically significant increase). Conservative and mainline Protestants, in particular, became significantly less happy over time. Change over time is not statistically significant for any other religion category. With two of the three happiest groups decreasing while the others held steady or increased, the association between religion and happiness decreased slightly.

We now shift our attention to attendance at religious services. Figure 11.4 shows trends in happiness for six categories of attendance. Among people who never attend religious services (despite their nominal affiliation), happiness fell from 30% to 23% very happy between 1973 and 2006.[15] People who attend services monthly became less happy, too; the percentage very happy was about 5 points lower in 1988 than in 1973. Weekly attenders and the most religiously active people were equally happy throughout the 34-year period.

These trends confirm hypothesis 3: frequent attendance at religious services offset the factors that made less active Americans less happy over time. The small decline in the nation's morale was concentrated among those who seldom or never attended religious services.

International Comparisons

"American exceptionalism" is a perennial cry whenever U.S. data show that religion improves social life in some way, despite mounting evidence that religion matters in Europe as well (Greeley 2003). Happiness questions have appeared in several internationally comparative surveys. Here we present the results from the 1998 religion module from the International Social Survey Programme (ISSP), of which the 1998 GSS was the U.S. component (see www .issp.org). The ISSP's happiness question differs slightly from the question we have been analyzing; in particular, it has four answers instead of three: "If you were to consider your life in general these days, how happy or unhappy would you say you are, on the whole: (1) Very happy, (2) Fairly happy, (3) Not very happy, (4) Not at all happy, (8) Can't choose." The answers given by Americans who responded to both questions in 1998 match very well, despite their different response categories; the gamma measure of ordinal association between the two answers is .85.[16]

We have data on 30 national populations to add to our data on the United States.[17] Figure 11.5 shows the percentage very happy by religion in each nation. People with a religion get a solid circle; people with no religion get an open circle. We grouped the nations into language groups because the cross-national variation in answers seems too large to be purely a matter of morale. The Slavic nations were, of course, undergoing trying economic times as they made the transition from central planning to market-based economies throughout the 1990s. Nonetheless, their happiness readings of less than 10% suggest to us that the vague term "fairly happy" is difficult to translate and may carry different connotations in different languages. Within language groups, we ranked countries according to overall percentage very happy (marked X).

Religious people are significantly happier than nonreligious people in 9 nations, and significantly less happy in only 1 nation; in the other 20 nations the difference between religious and nonreligious people is not statistically significant.[18] The gap in happiness between religious and nonreligious people is greatest in the United States and Ireland (19 and 16 percentage points, respectively), followed by Chile (13 percentage points). Within language groups, there appears to be no relationship between the prevalence of religion and the overall level of happiness or the gap between religious and nonreligious people.

In the United States, attendance at religious services explains the relationship between religion and happiness, so it is important to consider participa-

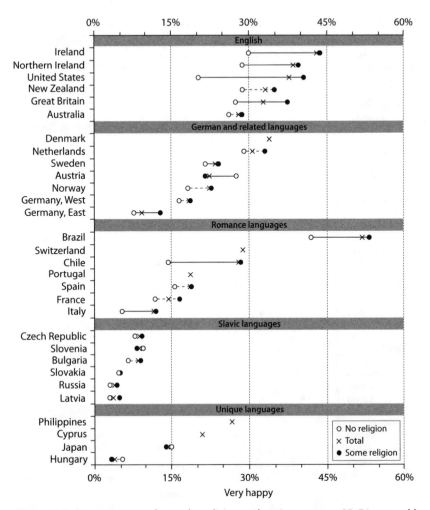

Figure 11.5. Percentage very happy by religion and nation, persons 25–74 years old, circa 1998. Within language groups, the nations are ranked from highest to lowest percentage having a religion. Horizontal lines show the differences by religion; solid lines indicate significant differences ($p < .05$); and dashed lines indicate statistically insignificant differences. Percentages based on fewer than 10 cases (persons with no religion in Cyprus and the Philippines) are not shown. The difference by religion is significant in Slovenia despite the difference of 1 percentage point because 54% of people with no religion chose "fairly happy" while only 41% of people with a religion chose that response; the "not very happy" responses show a corresponding difference in the opposite direction. In Denmark, Switzerland, Portugal, and Slovakia, the difference between people with and without a religion was so small that only the X for the total sample shows.

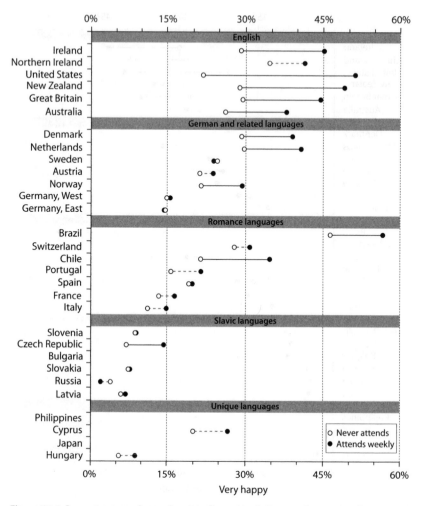

Figure 11.6. Percentage very happy by attendance at religious services and nation, persons 25–74 years old, circa 1998. Within language groups, the nations are ranked from highest to lowest overall happiness. Horizontal lines show the differences by attendance; solid lines indicate significant differences ($p < .05$); and dashed lines indicate statistically insignificant differences.

tion as well as affiliation in our cross-national comparisons. The ISSP provides data on religious participation in all but three countries (researchers in Bulgaria, the Philippines, and Japan did not ask about attending religious services). Attendance is reported in six categories in most ISSP countries, though there are some differences.[19] We have distilled the relationship between attendance and happiness down to the contrast between people who never attend and those who attend weekly, and arrayed the results in Figure 11.6. This simple contrast captures the essence of the full relationship in all but one nation. In Figure 11.6 the solid circles show the percentage very happy among weekly attenders; the open circles show the percentage very happy among adults who never attend religious services.[20] The solid horizontal lines indicate statistically significant differences (at the .05 level).

Attendance at religious services increases happiness significantly in 11 countries, including five of the six English-speaking countries. In 11 more countries the weekly attenders are happier than the nonattenders, but not by a statistically significant amount. In no country are nonattenders happier than regular attenders by a statistically significant amount and in only two countries are nonattenders more than two percentage points happier than frequent attenders. While the overall pattern supports the hypothesis that attending services increases happiness, it is also worth noting that in this respect as well, the relationship is stronger in the United States than anywhere else.

Thus the cross-national data show that religious people, especially religiously active people, are happier in most countries. But nowhere is the gap between religious and nonreligious as great as it is in the United States. Having a religion and practicing it produce slightly different patterns. Only in Ireland, Britain, Brazil, Chile, and the United States do both dimensions of religiosity show significant effects. In four nations religious people are happier than nonreligious, but frequent attenders are not (significantly) happier than nonattenders; in six others members and nonmembers differ little, but frequent attenders are happier than those who do not attend services. In one form or another we replicated the U.S. result in 14 other nations. In 12 other nations—most of them in Southern Europe or formerly communist nations—we found no significant relationship between religion and happiness. These include 9 of the 10 least-happy nations in the ISSP data. Thus the appropriate conclusion from this cross-national analysis is that religion increases happiness where happiness is found.

Conclusion

Religious people are happier than others. We think the relationship is causal—that religion makes people happy—and the preponderance of the evidence is consistent with our conclusion. Cross-sectional data cannot prove causality, but every analysis is consistent with the patterns we would see if religion literally made people happier. Modern methods of counterfactual analysis do indicate substantial selectivity—people who have a religion are the ones most likely to benefit from religion's positive effects—but also show a significant positive potential effect for religion on the "untreated"—people who have no religion could, on average, expect to be happier if they found a religion, though not as much as simple correlations or even multivariate regression coefficients suggest they might.

Theories of meaning and belonging in pluralist society predict these results (see Greeley 1969, 1994, 2000). The GSS data confirm three hypotheses and a corollary derived from the theory. In particular we have found that Americans who belong to a religion are happier than those who have no religion. Initially we confined our analysis to recent data, but when we elaborated it to span the entire 30 years of the GSS we found that religion increased happiness in each year. More importantly, the source of greater happiness is active participation in the religion of one's choice. People who frequently attend religious services are the ones who are happier; people who do not participate do not differ from those who have no religion. Other features of social life make people happier too, but the effect of attendance is just as large for sociable people as it is for lonely people. Attendance appears to improve morale, in part, by engendering emotional feelings of closeness to God and church. Thus we conclude that though each piece of evidence has a weakness, the accumulated evidence implies that religion per se is the causal factor in religious people's greater happiness; it cannot be sloughed off as a consequence of correlated but substantively irrelevant factors.

Comparative data from 30 nations show that these relationships are stronger in the United States than they are elsewhere, but Americans are by no means unique. In nearly every country, people who identify with a religion and attend religious services are happier than those who do not, although the relationships are statistically insignificant in about half of the nations.[21] For the most part religious people were as happy or less happy than nonreligious people only in nations that had both low levels of religiosity and very low overall happiness. They are also predominantly former communist or Southern European nations.[22] We conclude that religion boosts happiness where happiness is found.

Active and affective religiosity are catalysts for happiness. Passive belief has no effect. Nor does private prayer that is not accompanied by attending services. Attendance accounts for the relationship between affiliation and happiness in the United States (and most other countries where there is a significant relationship between affiliation and happiness). Feeling close to God and finding strength and comfort in one's religion explain about half of the relationship between attendance and happiness. Altogether this pattern of relationships adds support to the meaning and belonging perspective on religion.

Appendix: The Religious Feelings Scale and Belief in God Item

Religious Feelings Scale

The following questions deal with possible daily spiritual experiences. To what extent can you say you experience the following:

	Many times a day	Every day	Most days	Some days	Once in a while	Never	Don't know
A. I feel God's presence	1	2	3	4	5	6	8
B. I find strength and comfort in my religion	1	2	3	4	5	6	8
C. I feel deep inner peace or harmony	1	2	3	4	5	6	8
D. I desire to be closer to or in union with God	1	2	3	4	5	6	8
E. I feel God's love for me, directly or through others	1	2	3	4	5	6	8
F. I am spiritually touched by the beauty of creation	1	2	3	4	5	6	8

Note: Cronbachs' α for scale is .91.

Belief in God Item

Which of these statements comes closest to your beliefs about God?

I don't believe in God.
I don't know whether there is a God and I don't believe there is any way to find out.
I don't believe in a personal God, but I do believe in a Higher Power of some kind.
I find myself believing in God some of the time but not at others.
While I have doubts, I do feel I believe in God.
I know God really exists, and I have no doubts about it.
I don't know.

Table 11.A.1. Details of Sociodemographic Model in Table 11.2, and Estimates of Treatment Effects in Table 11.3, Coefficients for Religion and Adjustment Variables by Quantity of Interest

	Unweighted		Propensity score weighted for	
	Religion	Any-religion		
Independent variable	dummies	dummy	Treated	Untreated
Religion				
Conservative Protestant	0.636* (0.160)	—	—	—
Afro-American Protestant	0.692* (0.279)	—	—	—
Mainline Protestant	0.500* (0.160)	—	—	—
Catholic	0.501* (0.162)	—	—	—
				(continued)

Table 11.A.1. (*continued*)

Independent variable	Unweighted		Propensity score weighted for	
	Religion dummies	Any-religion dummy	Treated	Untreated
Jewish	−0.607 (0.466)	—	—	—
Other religion	−0.136 (0.345)	—	—	—
No religion	0.000 (—)	0.000 (—)	0.000 (—)	0.000 (—)
Any religion	—	0.489* (0.135)	0.554* (0.150)	0.329* (0.144)
Woman	−0.007 (0.101)	0.009 (0.100)	0.328* (0.150)	0.362* (0.148)
African American	−0.238 (0.199)	−0.138 (0.154)	0.081 (0.217)	0.121 (0.236)
Latino	−0.610* (0.178)	−0.592* (0.170)	−0.802* (0.258)	−0.481 (0.253)
Marital status				
Married	1.538* (0.145)	1.559* (0.145)	1.188* (0.188)	1.334* (0.191)
Widowed	0.132 (0.242)	0.087 (0.242)	0.698 (0.401)	0.322 (0.382)
Divorced or separated	−0.153 (0.156)	−0.124 (0.155)	−0.435* (0.208)	−0.317 (0.210)
Never married	0.000 (—)	0.000 (—)	0.000 (—)	0.000 (—)
Education				
High school dropout	−0.751* (0.239)	−0.646* (0.236)	−0.478 (0.365)	−0.667* (0.328)
High school graduate	−0.525* (0.199)	−0.425* (0.195)	−0.568 (0.302)	−0.539* (0.265)
Some college	−0.135 (0.196)	−0.046 (0.192)	−0.236 (0.296)	−0.196 (0.249)
College graduate	0.134 (0.208)	0.167 (0.206)	0.079 (0.315)	0.052 (0.273)
Advanced degree	0.000 (—)	0.000 (—)	0.000 (—)	0.000 (—)
Family income (ratio scale)	0.600* (0.084)	0.596* (0.084)	0.647* (0.119)	0.592* (0.115)
Region				
Northeast	0.000 (—)	0.000 (—)	0.000 (—)	0.000 (—)
Midwest	−0.145 (0.152)	−0.089 (0.152)	0.137 (0.222)	0.001 (0.215)
South	0.191 (0.149)	0.265 (0.144)	0.535* (0.217)	0.309 (0.202)
Mountain	0.301 (0.217)	0.345 (0.215)	0.588* (0.297)	0.554 (0.293)
Pacific	−0.117 (0.177)	−0.084 (0.176)	0.202 (0.248)	0.004 (0.255)
Decade of Birth				
Before 1940	0.000 (—)	0.000 (—)	0.000 (—)	0.000 (—)
1940s	−0.678* (0.196)	−0.663* (0.194)	−0.767* (0.317)	−0.642* (0.322)
1950s	−1.001* (0.188)	−1.003* (0.185)	−0.750* (0.295)	−0.748* (0.301)
1960s	−0.669* (0.187)	−0.663* (0.185)	−0.615* (0.298)	−0.603* (0.298)
1970s	−0.451* (0.199)	−0.454* (0.197)	−0.443 (0.308)	−0.361 (0.312)
1980s	0.004 (0.421)	0.005 (0.415)	0.017 (0.538)	0.275 (0.586)
Slope adjustments				
Very happy	1.00 (—)	1.00 (—)	1.00 (—)	1.00 (—)
Pretty happy	0.549* (0.026)	0.543* (0.027)	0.504* (0.046)	0.514* (0.048)
Not too happy	0.00 (—)	0.00 (—)	0.00 (—)	0.00 (—)

Table 11.A.1. (*continued*)

Independent variable	Unweighted		Propensity score weighted for	
	Religion dummies	Any-religion dummy	Treated	Untreated
Intercepts				
Very happy	0.00 (—)	0.00 (—)	0.00 (—)	0.00 (—)
Pretty happy	0.370 (0.216)	0.302 (0.216)	0.276 (0.343)	0.418 (0.297)
Not too happy	−1.513* (0.255)	−1.681* (0.254)	−1.938* (0.693)	−1.716* (0.604)
Year dummies	Yes	Yes	Yes	Yes
N	6,309	6,309	6,309	6,309

Source: Authors' calculations from the GSS, 2000–2006.
Note: Family incomes adjusted for inflation.
*p < .05.

Notes

We presented a very preliminary version of this chapter at the annual meeting of the American Sociological Association, August 16–19, 2003, and published some of the results in *The Truth about Conservative Christians* (University of Chicago Press, 2006). We are grateful to the Russell Sage Foundation and the University of California, Berkeley Survey Research Center for their financial support and to Aliya Saperstein for her research assistance.

1. Some context and switching problems interfere with accurate measurements of the time trend in happiness. T. W. Smith (1990a) has identified these problems, and we follow his recommendation to drop some forms in a few years and to leave the 1972 and 1985 data out of the time series.

2. We modified the GSS variable FUND in light of the critiques by Steensland et al. (2000). Our "conservative Protestants" belong to denominations coded "evangelical" under their "reltrad" scheme. We modified the Afro-American category (see Greeley and Hout 2006, pp. 6–9); we use "Afro-American" to distinguish this category of Protestant denominations from people of any denomination who have African American ancestry. Our "mainline Protestants" are all other Protestants, that is, those whose denomination is moderate, liberal, or unknown and not part of the Afro-American category.

3. There is considerable controversy over the accuracy of these reports (see, e.g., T. W. Smith 1998; Presser and Stinson 1998). Our estimates of the relationship between attendance and happiness will be attenuated by random measurement errors to the extent to which they lead us to rank order respondents incorrectly. Random measurement errors can also lead us to underestimate the degree to which attendance explains the relationship between religion and happiness (see Duncan 1975).

4. We refer to this scale as "frequency of attendance."

5. The Cronbach's alpha for the simple additive scale was .91.

6. In the original article, Anderson (1984, equation 7) wrote the model as ($s = 1, \ldots, k; \beta_{0k} = \phi_k = 0$). The minus sign in front of ϕs makes interpretation unnecessarily confusing, so we write the model with a plus sign in front of the ϕs. Stata estimates the model as Anderson wrote it, so we reverse the signs of the β coefficients produced by Stata.

7. For this analysis we have 128 Jewish respondents between the ages of 25 and 74 years who answered the question about happiness; 19 of them have missing data on one or more of the other variables we use, so most of the analyses of the 2000–2006 data include just 109 Jewish respondents.

8. The adjusted Wald test for the contrast between any religion and no religion was 12.64 with 2 and 353 degrees of freedom. The adjusted Wald test is necessary because the complexities of the GSS sampling frame rule out the more familiar chi-square tests.

9. The difference between these two coefficients would be much harder to interpret if the slope adjustments for the treated and untreated were significantly different from one another. But the ϕ_2 estimates of .50 and .51 turn out to be virtually identical, rendering our interpretation of the difference between the effect of the treatment on the treated and untreated straightforward.

10. Recall that the stereotype ordered regression model, like all logit models, is nonlinear.

11. In each pair we list the happier group first.

12. A critic asks us, "How can attendance without belief be efficacious?" The question wrongly assumes that people with no religion do not believe. In fact, the majority of American adults with no religion are "unchurched believers" who hold a variety of conventional religious attitudes, most importantly a belief in God and life after death (Hout and Fischer 2002).

13. We tried several expressions for this relationship. The zero-order relationship between belief in God and happiness is significant but not linear. People who believe sometimes but not other times are less happy than believers, agnostics, and atheists.

14. Our discussion refers to the trend lines that remove sampling fluctuations that occasionally yield observed percentages at odds with our generalizations. We trust the smoothed data because they, by design, are less prone to random changes over time.

15. As before we base our conclusions on smoothed percentages to guard against drawing inappropriate conclusions from the raw data.

16. The hypothetical range of the measure is from 0 to 1; .85 represents a very high correspondence.

17. The German project oversampled the former East Germany, and the United Kingdom project oversampled Northern Ireland. We tabulated those two special oversamples as separate nations.

18. In Cyprus, no one reported not having a religion; in the Philippines, only three people did.

19. ISSP practice requires strict comparability in the topical questions for each year's module but allows for some variation, in deference to previously established common practice and other local factors, in the measurement of background variables. Attendance at religious services is a mandatory background measure for all ISSP members, but, as noted, researchers in three nations failed to ask the question in 1998.

20. In Ireland there were too few people who said they never attended, so we combined "never" with the "once a year or less" category.

21. Affiliation had a significant positive association with happiness in 9 nations, and religious attendance significantly increased happiness in 11 nations.

22. Further research could look into the cultural roots of Slavic melancholy and the linguistic implications of trying to gauge it with terms and concepts that may not exactly translate into Slavic languages. The greater happiness of the Chileans and Brazilians compared with Spaniards and Portuguese suggests that there is more than just language differences involved, though.

References

Anderson, J. A. 1984. "Regression and Ordered Categorical Variables." *Journal of the Royal Statistical Society, Series B* 46:1–30.

Andrews, Frank M., and Stephen B. Withey. 1976. *Social Indicators of Well-Being.* New York: Plenum.

Brant, Rollin. 1990. "Assessing Proportionality in the Proportional Odds Model for Ordinal Logistic Regression." *Biometrics* 46:1171–78.

Cleveland, William S. 1994. *The Elements of Graphing Data.* Murray Hill, NJ: AT&T Bell Laboratories.

Davis, James A. 1984. "New Money, an Old Man/Lady, and 'Two's Company': Subjective Welfare in the GSS, 1972–1982." *Social Indicators Research* 15:319–50.

Davis, James A., Tom W. Smith, and Peter V. Marsden. 2006. *General Social Surveys, 1972–2006: Cumulative Codebook* [Machine-readable data file]. Chicago: NORC (producer). Storrs, CT: Roper Center for Public Opinion Research, University of Connecticut (distributor).

DiPrete, Thomas A. 1990. "Adding Covariates to Loglinear Models." *American Sociological Review* 55:757–73.

Duncan, Otis Dudley. 1970. *Toward Social Reporting: Next Steps.* New York: Russell Sage Foundation.

———. 1975. "Does Money Buy Satisfaction?" *Social Indicators Research* 2:267–74.

Easterlin, Richard A. 1974. "Does Economic Growth Improve the Human Lot? Some Empirical Evidence." In *Nations and Households in Economic Growth*, edited by P. A. David and M. W. Reder, 89–125. New York: Academic Press.

———. 1996. *Growth Triumphant: The Twenty-First Century in Historical Perspective.* Ann Arbor: University of Michigan Press.

Fischer, Claude S. 2008. "What Wealth-Happiness Paradox? A Short Note on the American Case." *Journal of Happiness Studies* 9:219–26.

Fischer, Claude S., and Michael Hout. 2006. *Century of Difference: How America Changed over the Last One Hundred Years.* New York: Russell Sage Foundation.

Frank, Robert H. 2006. *Falling Behind: How Rising Inequality Harms the Middle Class.* Berkeley: University of California Press.

Frey, Bruno S., and Alois Stutzer. 2002. *Happiness and Economics: How the Economy and Institutions Affect Well-Being.* Princeton, NJ: Princeton University Press.

Geertz, Clifford. 1973. "Religion as a Cultural System." In *The Interpretation of Cultures: Selected Essays*, edited by Clifford Geertz, 87–125. New York: Fontana.

Greeley, Andrew M. 1969. *Religion in the Year 2000*. New York: Sheed and Ward.

———. 1972. *The Denominational Society*. Glenview, IL: Scott Foresman.

———. 1994. *Religion as Poetry*. New Brunswick, NJ: Transaction.

———. 2000. *Catholic Imagination*. Berkeley: University of California Press.

———. 2003. *Religion in Europe at the Start of the Third Millennium*. New Brunswick, NJ: Transaction.

Greeley, Andrew M., and Michael Hout. 2006. *The Truth about Conservative Christians*. Chicago: University of Chicago Press.

Hout, Michael. 2003. "Money and Morale: What Growing Inequality Is Doing to What Americans Think of Themselves." Working paper, Russell Sage Foundation, New York.

Hout, Michael, and Claude S. Fischer. 2002. "Why More Americans Have No Religion: Generations and Politics." *American Sociological Review* 67:165–90.

Kahneman, Daniel. 1999. "Objective Happiness." In *Well-Being: The Foundations of Hedonic Psychology*, edited by D. Kahneman, E. Diener, and N. Schwartz, 3–26. New York: Russell Sage Foundation.

Long, J. Scott. 1997. *Regression Models for Categorical and Limited Dependent Variables*. Thousand Oaks, CA: Sage.

Morgan, Stephen L., and Jennifer J. Todd. 2008. "A Diagnostic Routine for the Detection of Consequential Heterogeneity of Causal Effects." *Sociological Methodology* 38:231–81.

Morgan, Stephen L., and Christopher Winship. 2007. *Counterfactuals and Causal Inference*. New York: Cambridge University Press.

Presser, Stanley, and L. Stinson. 1998. "Data Collection Mode and Social Desirability Bias in Self-Reported Religious Attendance." *American Sociological Review* 63:137–45.

Smith, Christian. 1998. *American Evangelicalism: Embattled and Thriving*. Chicago: University of Chicago Press.

Smith, Tom W. 1979. "Happiness: Time Trends, Seasonal Variations, Intersurvey Differences, and Other Mysteries." *Social Psychology Quarterly* 42:18–30.

———. 1990a. "Timely Artifacts: A Review of Measurement Variation in the 1972–1989 GSS." GSS Methodological Report No. 56, NORC, Chicago.

———. 1990b. "Classifying Protestant Denominations." *Review of Religious Research* 31:225–45.

———. 1998. "A Review of Church Attendance Measures." *American Sociological Review* 63:131–36.

Steensland, Brian, Jerry Z. Park, Mark D. Regnerus, Lynn D. Robinson, W. Bradford Wilcox, and Robert D. Woodberry. 2000. "The Measure of American Religion: Toward Improving the State of the Art." *Social Forces* 79:291–318.

Waite, Linda J., and Maggie Gallagher. 2000. *The Case for Marriage: Why Married People Are Happier, Healthier, and Better Off Financially*. New York: Doubleday.

Wuthnow, Robert. 1993. *Christianity in the 21st Century*. New York: Oxford University Press.

Yang, Yang. 2008. "Social Inequalities in Happiness in the United States, 1972–2004: An Age-Period-Cohort Analysis." *American Sociological Review* 73:204–26.

12

Labor Force Insecurity and U.S. Work Attitudes, 1970s–2006

Arne L. Kalleberg and Peter V. Marsden

Social, economic, and political forces in operation for several decades in the United States and the rest of the world have produced major changes in the nature of employment relations. Prominent among these is a growth in *precarious work*: work that is insecure and uncertain, and in which the worker—rather than the employer or the government—bears most risks associated with employment. The growth of precarious work since the 1970s contrasts with the relative security that characterized the U.S. labor force during the three decades following World War II, and has emerged as a core contemporary concern.

This chapter examines the consequences of these macrostructural changes for trends in U.S. workers' assessments of their job security, their economic standing, and their job satisfaction, as measured by the General Social Survey (GSS) since the mid-1970s. Consistent with a narrative of how U.S. employment relations have become more precarious (Kalleberg 2009, 2011), we show that net of overall employment levels, perceived job and economic insecurity has grown. The overall quality of work as reflected in job satisfaction has not changed very much, however.

The Growth of Precarious Work in the United States since the 1970s

The three decades following World War II were marked by sustained growth and prosperity.[1] During this postwar boom, economic compensation generally increased for most people, and job security was relatively high. The establishment of a new social contract between business and labor beginning in the 1930s solidified the growing security and economic gains of this period. The employment relationship became more regulated over time, enforced by labor laws and the diffusion of norms of employer conduct. Combined with the full blooming of Fordist production techniques and U.S. dominance in world markets, this ushered in an era of relatively full employment, security, and sustained economic growth (Ruggie 1982).

Some workers benefited more than others during this period of prosperity, however. The concept of a dual labor market was used to describe this situation, with relatively high wage, secure jobs located in the primary market, and more precarious, unstable, and uncertain jobs concentrated in a secondary labor market (for a review, see Kalleberg and Sørensen 1979). The degree of precarity and insecurity was a key characteristic used to distinguish jobs in the primary and secondary labor market segments.

Cracks in the social contract began to appear in the 1950s as the percentage of the U.S. nonagricultural labor force belonging to unions started to decline. Growing employer resistance to unionization, coupled with a growing U.S. culture of individualism, a shift to a white-collar, service-providing "knowledge" economy, and growing diversity of the labor force (especially the increase in women workers) all contributed to a steady decline in union members, though the patterns of change in union membership differed for various groups within the labor force (e.g., public-sector unionism has grown in the past thirty years—Cornfield 1991; Farber 2006; Burawoy 2008).

The most recent era of precarious work in the United States is generally agreed to have begun in the mid- to late 1970s.[2] The years 1974–1975 marked the onset of macroeconomic changes (such as the first oil shock) that contributed to an increase in global price competition. U.S. manufacturers were challenged initially by companies from Japan and South Korea in the automobile and steel industries, respectively. The process that came to be known as neoliberal globalization intensified economic integration, increased the competition that companies faced, provided greater opportunities for employers to outsource work to lower-wage countries, and—through immigration—introduced new sources of workers into the U.S. labor market. Technological advances both forced companies to become more competitive globally and enabled them to do so.

Changes in legal and other institutions accompanied and mediated the impacts of globalization and technology on work and employment relations. Unions continued their decline that began in the 1950s, weakening a traditional source of institutional protections for workers and severing the postwar business–labor social contract. Government regulations that set minimum acceptable standards in the labor market eroded, as did rules that governed competition in product markets. Union decline and deregulation reduced countervailing forces that had enabled workers to share in returns to productivity gains, and the balance of power shifted from workers to employers.

The pervasive political changes associated with President Ronald Reagan's election in 1980 accelerated both business ascendancy and labor decline, increasing the freedom of firms and capitalists to pursue their interests. Deregulation and reorganization of employment relations allowed for the massive accumulation of capital. Political and social policies in the United States—such as the replacement of welfare by workfare programs in the mid-1990s—made it essential for people to participate in paid employment, often forcing them into low-wage jobs.

Ideological changes toward greater individualism and personal responsibility for work and life supported these structural changes; the slogan "you're on your own" replaced the notion of "we're all in this together" (Bernstein 2006). The neoliberal revolution spread throughout the world, emphasizing the centrality of markets and market-driven solutions, privatization of government resources, and reduction of government protections in many countries.

Work also changed during this period. Increases in knowledge-intensive work accompanied the accelerated pace of technological innovation. Service industries continued to expand as the principal sources of jobs, as the U.S. economy shifted from manufacturing industries and mass production toward information-based industries organized around flexible production. The percentage of the U.S. labor force in service industries rose from 52% in 1950 to over 75% in 2000 (Hodson and Sullivan 2002).

These macro-level changes led employers to seek greater flexibility in their relations with workers. Market forces came to play a greater role within the workplace, mirroring the neoliberal idea at the societal level. This eroded the bureaucratic organizational model of a standard employment relationship, in which workers are employed full-time by a particular employer at the employer's workplace, often progressing upward on job ladders within internal labor markets (Cappelli 1999). Management efforts to increase flexibility led to various types of corporate restructuring and downsizing, notably affecting white-collar as well as blue-collar workers. These transformed the employment relationship (Osterman 1999) and increased the precarity of work. This, in turn, had—and continues to have—far-reaching effects on all of society.

In tandem with these structural changes, the labor force became more diverse: the numbers of female, nonwhite and immigrant workers, as well as older workers, increased markedly. Rises in immigration—due to globalization and lowered barriers to the movement of people across national borders—led to greater labor surpluses. Gaps in earnings and other indicators of labor market success between people with different amounts of education grew (e.g., Mishel, Bernstein, and Allegretto 2007; Goldin and Katz 2008).

Evidence of the Growth of Precarious Work

While it is widely agreed that work and employment relations have changed in important ways since the 1970s, less consensus exists on the specifics of these changes. Part of the reason for this is that little systematic longitudinal data on employment relations and organizational practices are available, so it is difficult to evaluate just how much change has really occurred.

For example, the U.S. government often collects data on phenomena only after they are deemed to be problematic. The Bureau of Labor Statistics began to count displaced workers only in the early 1980s and did not collect information on nonstandard work arrangements and contingent work until 1995. The Current Population Survey's measure of employer tenure changed in 1983, so assessing trends in job stability using this measure is challenging. Few have assembled over-time data on organizations and employees that shed light on mechanisms producing precarity and other changes in employment relations.

Nevertheless, several pieces of evidence gleaned from "objective" sources suggest that precarious work has indeed increased in the United States since the 1970s. One indicator is the average length of time a person spends with his or her employer (employer tenure). The question of whether employer tenure has increased or decreased has been examined extensively by labor economists, and much of the earlier research on this topic yielded mixed results (e.g., Neumark 2000). More recent analyses, however, indicate that employer tenure has declined for men in the private sector. The patterns of change in employer tenure vary across labor force subgroups: women's employer tenure has increased, while men's has decreased (though private-sector tenure levels for women remain substantially lower than those for men). The decline in employer tenure is especially pronounced among older white men, the group formerly most protected by internal labor markets (Farber 2008).

Second, the proportion of workers who are long-term unemployed (i.e., jobless for six months or more) has grown. Nearly a quarter of those unemployed after the 2001 recession were long-term jobless, approaching the long-term unemployment levels observed during the severe recession of the early 1980s. The large proportion of long-term unemployed after the 2001 recession is likely due to both low rates of job growth and challenges faced by displaced workers in industries such as manufacturing (Mishel et al. 2007).

Third, nonstandard work arrangements such as contracting and temporary work have expanded. Data from a representative sample of U.S. establishments collected in the mid-1990s indicated that over half of them purchased goods or services from other organizations (Kalleberg and Marsden 2005).

The key point about outsourcing is the threat that virtually all jobs can be outsourced (except perhaps those that require personal contact such as home health care and food preparation), including high-wage white-collar jobs that were once seen as safe. The temporary help agency sector grew at an annual rate of over 11% from 1972 to the late 1990s; its share of U.S. employment rose from 0.3% in 1972 to 2.5% in 1998 (Kalleberg 2000). Temporary workers remain a relatively small proportion of the overall labor force, but the institutionalization of the temporary help industry increases precarity since it reminds all employees that they are potentially replaceable by temporary workers.

The shifting of risk from employers to employees (see Hacker 2006) is a final indicator of the growth of precarious work. Some writers see this as the key feature of precarity (Jacoby 2001). Trends toward defined contribution pension and health insurance plans (in which employers pay a fixed premium and employees assume the remaining risk) and away from defined benefit plans (in which the employer guarantees a certain level of benefits) (see Mishel et al. 2007) vividly illustrate risk shifting from employers to employees.

Consequences of Precarious Work

Job and Economic Insecurity

Increased job insecurity for individuals is a counterpart to increased flexibility for employers. The growth of precarious work clearly should have consequences for perceived job insecurity and assessments of one's economic standing (e.g., Jacobs and Newman 2008). Precarity is intimately related to perceived job insecurity, which should increase as employer tenure declines, outsourcing and offshoring of jobs rise, and downsizing, restructuring, plant closings, and mass layoffs become commonplace. Though individuals differ in their perceptions of insecurity and risk, we anticipate that over time these phenomena will lead people to be increasingly worried about job loss. To a large extent, this is because many phenomena that increase precarity also increase the negative consequences of losing one's job. In contrast to job losses related to ordinary business cycle downturns, those linked to structural dislocations such as technological change, offshoring, and restructuring are often quasi-permanent. Hence it is reasonable to anticipate that precarity will decrease people's expectations of locating jobs of comparable quality in the event of job loss.

Rises in precarious work are also associated with greater economic inequality, insecurity, and instability. The growth of economic inequality in the United States since the 1980s is well documented (Levy and Murnane 1992; Morris and Western 1999; Mishel et al. 2007). Earnings have also become more volatile and unstable (Hacker 2006). Real incomes for families have increased, but primarily because most families now have two earners in the labor market rather than one. Poverty and low-wage work persist, and the economic security of the middle class is declining (Mishel et al. 2007).

Results of these changes include growing pessimism and decreased satisfaction with standards of living, as proportionately more income must be spent on necessities such as medical care and housing and as debt and bankruptcies rise (Sullivan, Warren, and Westbrook 2001). In April 2008, the University of Michigan's consumer sentiment index showed more economic pessimism than Americans had expressed for over a quarter century (Krugman 2008).[3] This is due to both objective economic conditions and somewhat reduced confidence in economic institutions such as banks and major companies (see Smith, chapter 7 in this volume). We anticipate that over time these factors will contribute to lower financial satisfaction and subjective assessments of economic well-being.

Job Dissatisfaction

The effects of increasing precarity—and the accompanying job and economic insecurity—on trends in job satisfaction are less easily anticipated. On the one hand, we might expect that by raising insecurity, precarity increases uncertainty about future job rewards, in turn leading workers to grow more dissatisfied with their jobs. It has been well established that job insecurity is a stressor linked to poor mental and physical health outcomes, as well as to lower job satisfaction (De Witte 1999; Uchitelle 2006).

On the other hand, there are also theoretical reasons to expect relatively little change in average job satisfaction over time. Psychological theories maintain that individuals adjust their expectations rapidly to changes in the environment and the economy. Constancy in job satisfaction would also be consistent with economists' claims that the labor market efficiently sorts individuals into jobs.

Moreover, assessments of satisfaction are arguably sensitive to the comparison standards people assume (Hodson 1989; Jasso 1990) and often adapt to worker circumstances (Gruenberg 1980). Easterlin (1980), for example, argues that one's economic fortunes are shaped by the size of one's birth cohort as well as by the experience of different cohorts with dissimilar "slices of history." He presents evidence (Easterlin 1995) indicating that happiness (subjective well-being) varies directly with one's own income and inversely with the incomes of others. Clark and Oswald (1996; see also Clark, Fiijters, and Shields 2008) also provide evidence for such a model of interdependent preferences, showing that people with higher incomes are on the average happier within a country at a given time, though changes in happiness are dependent on changes in comparison incomes over time (see also Firebaugh and Tach, chapter 10 in this volume). Such reference groups may also help explain why workers' assessments of "how good" their job security is may remain unchanged despite objective increases in insecurity, since standards for judging the "goodness" of security may be lowered over time. If reduced job security comes to be viewed as a typical feature of a job, then expectations decline together with job quality, and levels of satisfaction remain steady. According to such logic, workers who have jobs at all during times of growing precarity might consider themselves to be relatively fortunate and hence satisfied. Likewise, if workers perceive their peers' jobs to be no more secure than their own, they may also be satisfied with their jobs. The way in which rising precarity alters trends in job satisfaction thus depends on the difference between its effects on actual job quality and its effects on worker expectations of jobs.

Differential Vulnerability to Precarious Work
A distinctive feature of the current era of precarious work is its wider scope: virtually the entire labor force is now vulnerable. As we discussed above, unstable and uncertain jobs in the past were generally found in a secondary segment of a dual labor market. Phenomena such as eliminating layers of middle management, using contractors to provide professional services, and offshoring of work in service (as well as manufacturing) industries make precarious work much more pervasive and generalized, spreading it into all sectors of the economy and all occupational groups. Blue-collar work has long been precarious, but professional and managerial jobs now experience precarity also. Since those at the top of the labor market have experienced faster recent growth in job and economic precariousness while those at the bottom have long confronted such conditions, we may find greater recent growth in job and economic insecurity at upper socioeconomic levels.

Measures and Methods

This section introduces the indicators that we use to examine trends in perceived job insecurity, economic well-being, and job dissatisfaction since the 1970s. These analyses reveal the extent to which people are experiencing precarity in their everyday lives and are worried about the consequences of the macrostructural changes discussed above. We score our measures such that higher values reflect more negative outlooks: more job insecurity, less optimistic assessments of economic standing, and dissatisfaction with one's job.

Perceived Job Insecurity
The GSS regularly measures two subjective aspects of job insecurity (scores assigned to responses appear in brackets):

1. *Likelihood of losing current job* (see also Fullerton and Wallace 2005): "Thinking about the next 12 months, how likely do you think it is that you will lose your job or be laid off?" Possible answers are very likely [4], fairly likely [3], not too likely [2], and not at all likely [1].

2. *Difficulty of finding a comparable job* (see also Anderson and Pontusson 2007): "About how easy would it be for you to find a job with another employer with approximately the same income and fringe benefits you now have? Would you say: very easy [1], somewhat easy [2], or not easy at all [3]?"

The first indicator reflects insecurity in one's current position, while the second measures a more general concern about employability security.

We also combine these two indicators into a summary measure developed by Schmidt (1999). Reflecting the simultaneous presence of these two aspects of insecurity, it is coded 1 if a respondent thinks it is very or fairly likely that he or she will lose his or her current job *and* that it would be not easy at all to find another comparable job; otherwise it is coded 0. Those scored 1 perceive themselves at risk of a "costly job loss."

The GSS began measuring job insecurity only in 1977, so our analyses of trends in job insecurity cover the period 1977–2006.

Perceived Economic Standing

Each GSS since 1972 has measured three indicators of a respondent's subjective financial standing. We assume that more pessimistic assessments indicate greater economic insecurity. The indicators are as follows:

1. *Dissatisfaction with finances*: "We are interested in how people are getting along financially these days. So far as you and your family are concerned, would you say that you are pretty well satisfied with your present financial situation [1], more or less satisfied [2]) or not satisfied at all [3]?"
2. *Change in financial situation*: "During the last few years, has your financial situation been getting better [1], worse [3], or has it stayed the same [2]?"
3. *Assessment of relative family income*: "Compared with American families in general, would you say your family income is far below average [4], below average [3], above average [2], or far above average [1]?"

Those dissatisfied with their financial situation, perceiving their situation as worsening, or viewing their family income as below average are expressing a more general economic insecurity, as distinct from job insecurity. As a summary index of pessimism regarding economic standing, we use a scale that adds these three indicators (standardized) (Cronbach's alpha = .61).

Job Dissatisfaction

We measure job dissatisfaction using the common "direct" indicator: "On the whole, how satisfied are you with the work you do—would you say you are very satisfied [1], moderately satisfied [2], a little dissatisfied [3], or very dissatisfied [4]?" This measure too is available in all 26 GSSs conducted between 1972 and 2006.

Explanatory Variables

We begin by examining over-time trends in insecurity and job dissatisfaction. We link these trends to general labor market conditions using annual U.S. unemployment rates (see http://www.bls.gov/cps/cpsaat01.pdf).

We then consider the possibility that trends in economic orientations may reflect changing labor force composition. We therefore introduce controls for age (years), education (years), sex (indicator variable identifying women), race (indicator variables identifying black respondents and those of races other than black or white), occupation (indicator variables identifying specific occupational groups), real family income (measured in thousands of 1986 dollars), and employment status (indicator variable identifying full-time workers).

Statistical Models

Our analyses use regression techniques suitable for our measures of insecurity and dissatisfaction. Most apply ordinal logistic regression. Analyses of the dichotomous "costly loss" job insecurity measure use logistic regression, while those of the summary scale of economic standing rely on ordinary least squares.[4]

Analytic Sample

The analyses that follow include those GSS respondents currently in the labor force, excluding persons who are in school, keeping house, retired, or unemployed. To estimate trends within the pre-2006 GSS target population of English-speaking adults residing in households, we exclude Spanish monolingual respondents to the 2006 GSS. Because not all indicators appear in every GSS, the numbers of observations in our analyses vary, from a low of 15,992 (risk of costly job loss) to a high of 28,771 (job dissatisfaction).

Precarious Work and Job Insecurity

Our discussion of consequences of the growth of precarious work since the 1970s suggested that we should observe rises in both job and economic insecurity during this period. We begin with the first of these claims, focusing on trends in job insecurity for the years 1977–2006.

Indicators of perceived job insecurity are intimately linked to general labor market conditions. Figure 12.1 demonstrates this point for the dichotomous summary indicator of job insecurity (see also Schmidt 1999; Fischer and Hout 2006). Variations in the overall average percentage of GSS respondents

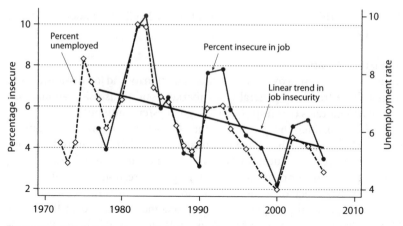

Figure 12.1. Trends in job insecurity and unemployment.

perceiving themselves at risk of a costly job loss track the unemployment rate closely. Notably, the trend in unemployment was downward between the peak in the recession of the early 1980s and 2006. For this reason, the trend line for job insecurity in Figure 12.1 is likewise downward, with notable variations around it corresponding to business cycles.

To assess our first hypothesis, we control for labor market conditions as reflected in the unemployment rate, to reveal structural trends in job insecurity net of cyclical employment levels. We expect to find rising concern about job insecurity once we hold constant the overall risk of unemployment.

Table 12.1 presents estimates of trends in job insecurity. For each of our three insecurity indicators, the regression coefficient for "year" in column 1 estimates the unadjusted annual trend, while that in column 2 displays the yearly trend adjusted for unemployment. Unemployment levels themselves are closely associated with perceived insecurity: a one-percentage-point rise in the unemployment rate is linked to a 13% increase in the odds of perceiving greater risk of job loss, an 18% rise in the odds of perceiving greater difficulty in obtaining comparable work, and a 33% rise in the odds of perceiving oneself at risk of costly job loss.

Unadjusted per-year trends in these measures suggest declines in insecurity over time (Table 12.1, column 1), but these trends turn positive when the unemployment rate is held constant. Controlling for the unemployment rate, the odds of perceiving greater risk of job loss grow by an estimated 1.5% per year between 1977 and 2006, while the odds of being at risk of a costly job loss grow by nearly 2% per year. The adjusted annual trend indicates no statistically significant change in the perceived difficulty of locating comparable employment, but this coefficient too becomes more positive when labor market conditions are held constant. These results confirm our hypothesis of an upward trend in perceived job insecurity net of the unemployment rate. Our

Table 12.1. Linear Trends in Job Insecurity

Explanatory variable	Likelihood of losing job		Difficulty of finding comparable job		At risk of costly job loss	
	(1)	(2)	(1)	(2)	(1)	(2)
Year	−0.001	0.015**	−0.017**	0.005	−0.023**	0.018*
	(0.003)	(0.003)	(0.002)	(0.003)	(0.005)	(0.007)
Unemployment Rate		0.120**		0.169**		0.284**
		(0.017)		(0.017)		(0.030)
(N)	(16,302)		(16,210)		(15,992)	

Note: We report ordinal logistic regression coefficients for likelihood of losing job and difficulty of finding comparable job, and logistic regression coefficients for costly job loss. Standard errors in parentheses.
$*p < .01. **p < .001.$

interpretation is that this increased insecurity reflects the impact of macro-structural conditions that have increased precarity.

We next ask how the estimated growth in job insecurity over time in Table 12.1 is affected by changes in labor force composition since the 1970s. During this period, average education rose, while higher-level professional and managerial occupations expanded; because upper-SES workers have historically been more secure, we might anticipate that these shifts would decrease insecurity levels. Demographically, the labor force has come to include more women, nonwhites, and older workers; the increased proportion of nonwhites might raise perceived insecurity, while greater numbers of older workers might decrease it.

The regressions in Table 12.2 add measures of seven individual-level sociodemographic variables (age, education, sex, race, occupation, real family income, and employment status) to the analyses in Table 12.1. The estimated annual trends in insecurity are substantively unchanged after we adjust for changing labor force composition. Indeed, all three estimates are somewhat more positive after this adjustment. This suggests that the structural forces contributing to the growth in precarious work in the United States during this period led to greater perceived job insecurity, notwithstanding changes in labor force composition that might have been expected to alter such perceptions. Figure 12.2 illustrates this result for the summary insecurity indicator (risk of costly job loss). The upward-sloping dashed line shows the estimated annual trend in perceived insecurity after adjusting for the unemployment rate and sociodemographic labor force characteristics. Holding the unemployment rate constant at about 6% (its average annual level for this period) and setting all sociodemographic variables at their mean levels, we see a rise in the predicted percentage insecure from around 3% in 1977 to nearly 5% by 2006.

The estimates in Table 12.2 show which individual characteristics make people more or less vulnerable to job insecurity, controlling for the others.

Table 12.2. Predictors of Job Insecurity, 1977–2006

Explanatory variable	Likelihood of losing job	Difficulty of finding comparable job	At risk of costly job loss
Year	0.019** (0.003)	0.005 (0.003)	0.023* (0.007)
Unemployment Rate	0.135** (0.018)	0.175** (0.017)	0.301** (0.032)
Age (years)	−0.007** (0.001)	0.027** (0.002)	0.007 (0.003)
Education (years)	−0.018 (0.008)	−0.047** (0.007)	−0.055** (0.016)
Sex (female)	0.052 (0.040)	0.027 (0.040)	0.102 (0.100)
Race			
Black	0.405** (0.060)	0.213** (0.056)	0.777** (0.097)
Other	0.226 (0.101)	0.172 (0.076)	0.342 (0.169)
White-collar occupation	−0.431** (0.052)	−0.260** (0.047)	−0.768** (0.102)
Real family income ($1,000s)	−0.007** (0.001)	−0.001 (0.001)	−0.010** (0.002)
Employed full-time	−0.275** (0.051)	0.280** (0.043)	−0.244 (0.103)
(pseudo) R^2	.023	.029	.069
N	14,920	14,858	14,679

Note: We report ordinal logistic regression coefficients for likelihood of losing job and difficulty of finding comparable job, and logistic regression coefficients for costly job loss. Standard errors in parentheses.
    *$p < .01$. **$p < .001$.

Workers of greater socioeconomic status (those with higher education, in white-collar occupations, or with greater family income) express less job insecurity. Nonwhite workers, especially blacks, say they are more insecure in their jobs than whites. Older and full-time workers perceive themselves at lower risk of losing their current jobs, but are more apt to expect that it would be difficult to find a job of comparable quality. Perceived job insecurity levels for men and women do not differ significantly.

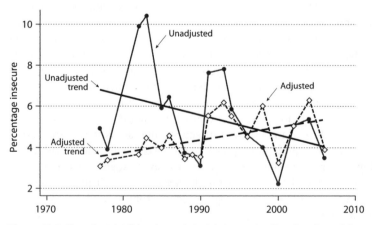

Figure 12.2. Overall and adjusted trends in job insecurity. Trends adjusted for unemployment and labor force characteristics. From Kalleberg 2011, fig. 5.2.

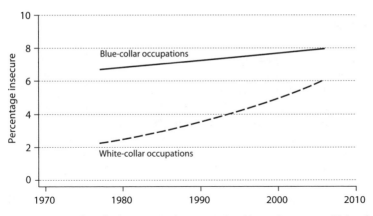

Figure 12.3. Predicted job insecurity, by occupation. Unemployment and labor force characteristics at average levels.

Finally, we ask if trends in job insecurity vary among types of workers. In particular, we examine differences in annual trends across groups of workers differing on the sociodemographic characteristics shown in Table 12.2. Unevenness in recent exposure to precarity would be indicated if the annual increase in perceived insecurity were more rapid in certain labor market segments. In particular, our argument that precarity has broadened beyond secondary labor markets would predict faster growth in insecurity among more educated workers and/or those in upper-SES occupations.

To investigate, we added interaction terms involving year and each of the seven individual labor force characteristics to the models estimated in Table 12.2. Almost all coefficients of these terms were statistically negligible, indicating that estimated annual rises in insecurity apply across all labor force segments. This suggests that effects of increased precarity are rather general.

We did detect a significant difference in annual trends toward greater insecurity in one important case, however. This trend appears to be somewhat stronger among those in white-collar occupations.[5] Figure 12.3 illustrates this by plotting predicted percentages at risk of costly job loss separately for blue- and white-collar occupations, assuming an average unemployment rate and average levels of labor force characteristics other than occupation. We see a slight growth in predicted insecurity for blue-collar workers, from about 7% in 1977 to 8% as of 2006. Though predicted insecurity for white-collar workers is always lower than that in the blue-collar group, the growth in their predicted insecurity is much more rapid, so that the blue-collar/white-collar difference is appreciably smaller at the end of the period studied than at its beginning. The predicted risk of costly job loss among white-collar workers was only about 2% in 1977, but it tripled to about 6% by 2006. This result is consistent with our suggestion that precarity grew to encompass formerly secure portions of the labor force during these years.

Economic Standing

....

We turn next to trends in perceived economic standing, which we regard as indicative of a perceived general economic/financial insecurity. We suggested that increased precarity is associated with growing economic insecurity. We examine that claim here, and estimate the extent to which economic security reflects the heightened job insecurity documented above.

Table 12.3 presents regressions of the indicators of economic standing, including the summary economic standing scale, on year and the unemployment rate. In general, trends in perceived economic standing are weaker than those in perceived job insecurity. Only one unadjusted linear trend is statistically significant ($p < .05$): people grew somewhat less likely to feel that their economic situation was deteriorating during this period.

Economic conditions reflected in the unemployment rate are linked to greater financial dissatisfaction, worsening financial situations, and generally more pessimistic economic outlooks (summary scale). After adjusting for over-time variations in unemployment, we found growing financial dissatisfaction across years, but no significant annual trend toward perceiving a worsening financial situation or a lower relative income.

Some changes in labor force composition since the 1970s—especially growth in education and in professional and managerial positions—increased the number of workers who might be expected to hold positive economic outlooks. Table 12.4 presents estimates for regressions that add the seven sociodemographic characteristics, as well as the composite measure of job insecurity, to the models in Table 12.3.[6] Upper-income and higher-SES persons generally have less pessimistic economic outlooks, as do nonblacks and full-time workers. Women appear somewhat more pessimistic than men, es-

Table 12.3. Linear Trends in Subjective Economic Pessimism, 1972–2006

Explanatory variable	Financial dissatisfaction		Worsening in financial situation		Subjectively lower income		Subjective economic standing scale	
	(1)	(2)	(1)	(2)	(1)	(2)	(1)	(2)
Year	0.003	0.006**	−0.006**	0.002	0.000	0.001	−0.001	0.002
	(0.002)	(0.002)	(0.002)	(0.002)	(0.002)	(0.002)	(0.001)	(0.001)
Unemployment Rate		0.031*		0.099**		0.013		0.026**
		(0.010)		(0.011)		(0.012)		(0.005)
N	28,568		28,490		28,452		28,619	

Note: We report ordinal logistic regression coefficients for financial dissatisfaction, worsening in financial situation, and subjective income, and ordinary regression coefficients for the scale of subjective economic standing. Standard errors in parentheses.

*$p < .01$. **$p < .001$.

Table 12.4. Predictors of Subjective Economic Pessimism, 1977–2006

Explanatory variable	Financial dissatisfaction	Worsening in financial situation	Subjectively lower income	Subjective economic standing scale
Year	0.009* (0.003)	0.008 (0.003)	0.011** (0.003)	0.004** (0.001)
Unemployment rate	0.032 (0.015)	0.112** (0.017)	0.014 (0.015)	0.026** (0.006)
Age (years)	−0.009** (0.001)	0.026** (0.001)	−0.005* (0.002)	0.002** (0.001)
Education (years)	0.015 (0.008)	−0.006 (0.008)	−0.088** (0.007)	−0.010** (0.003)
Sex (female)	0.035 (0.035)	0.050 (0.036)	0.223** (0.033)	0.045** (0.012)
Race				
Black	0.329** (0.060)	−0.002 (0.056)	0.272** (0.062)	0.097** (0.022)
Other	0.042 (0.094)	0.085 (0.088)	0.258* (0.081)	0.054 (0.031)
Professional or managerial occupation	−0.170** (0.044)	−0.253** (0.046)	−0.290** (0.047)	−0.108** (0.016)
Real family income ($1,000s)	−0.021** (0.001)	−0.013** (0.001)	−0.036** (0.001)	−0.010** (0.000)
Employed full-time	0.026 (0.050)	−0.356** (0.044)	−0.185** (0.047)	−0.086** (0.016)
Risk of costly job loss	0.641** (0.079)	0.727** (0.079)	0.425** (0.078)	0.302** (0.029)
(pseudo) R^2	.059	.044	.140	.214
N	14,372	14,346	14,333	14,385

Note: We report ordinal logistic regression coefficients for financial dissatisfaction, worsening in financial situation, and subjective income, and ordinary regression coefficients for the scale of subjective economic standing. Standard errors in parentheses.
*$p < .01$. **$p < .001$.

pecially as to their relative family incomes. Older workers are less apt to be financially dissatisfied or to view their incomes as lower than average, but more likely to perceive their situations as worsening. Job insecurity is strongly and positively related to economic outlooks: workers perceiving themselves at risk of costly job loss are much more apt to express pessimism.

After adjusting for these labor force characteristics and perceived job insecurity, we find positive time trends for two of the three indicators of subjective economic standing (financial dissatisfaction and perceptions that one's income is below average) as well as for the overall scale. This is in keeping with our view that labor market precarity has led not only to greater job insecurity, but also to a more general increase in economic insecurity. That these trends appear only after adjustments for changing labor force composition and perceived job insecurity indicates that they run counter to the changes one would anticipate based on labor force trends such as the rise in well-educated workers or increased real family income.

Finally, we examined the possibility that trends in economic outlooks vary across labor force groups, by adding interactions between year and our explanatory variables to the models in Table 12.4. Once again, the only detectable differences in trends involved occupation: we found a steeper trend

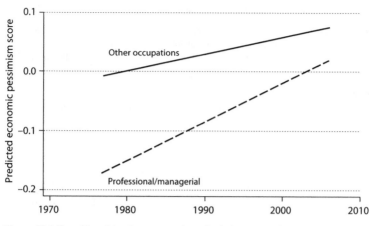

Figure 12.4. Trend in subjective economic outlook, by occupation.

toward economic pessimism among upper white-collar (professional and managerial) workers. Figure 12.4 illustrates this for the summary economic outlook scale. Professional and managerial workers always exhibit more optimism than do workers in other occupations, but they grew more pessimistic at a faster rate during the period covered by the GSS.

Job Dissatisfaction

Precarious work, job insecurity, and economic insecurity are all likely to affect the quality of jobs experienced by workers. It is arguable that such differences in job quality will in turn affect reported job satisfaction, so that rises in job dissatisfaction might accompany the net annual trends toward greater job and economic insecurity we have documented. As noted above, though, job satisfaction judgments depend on how workers perceive job quality, the comparison standards (such as reference groups) they adopt, the weights they assign to different job attributes, and their conceptions of what a satisfactory job should be. Hence it is difficult to predict just how increases in precarity and insecurity will affect trends in job satisfaction.

We began by estimating overall trends in job dissatisfaction; estimates appear in Table 12.5. Coefficients reported in columns 1 and 2 there indicate no significant trend toward greater or lower dissatisfaction over the period covered by the GSS. Notably, the coefficient for the unemployment rate is statistically insignificant: its negative sign, however, suggests that workers may view their jobs slightly more positively when jobs are scarcer.

There are nonetheless some systematic over-time regularities in dissatisfaction. Column 3 of Table 12.5 reports a linear decomposition of the nontrend in job dissatisfaction, following Firebaugh (1997; Firebaugh and Harley

Table 12.5. Linear Trends in Job Dissatisfaction, 1972–2006

Explanatory variable	(1)	(2)	(3)
Year	0.002 (0.001)	0.001 (0.002)	–0.024** (0.002)
Unemployment Rate		–0.010 (0.010)	–0.019 (0.010)
Cohort			0.026** (0.001)
N	28,771	28,771	28,688

Note: Ordinal logistic regression coefficients. Standard errors in parentheses.
**$p < .001$.

1995). This reveals countervailing movements in job satisfaction since the early 1970s that are attributable to cohort turnover (intercohort change) and individual-level change within cohorts. The positive and significant coefficient for cohort indicates that circulation in the labor force—the departure of older workers in earlier birth cohorts in favor of younger ones from later cohorts—serves to increase dissatisfaction. Workers entering the labor force typically are less satisfied than those they replace. Once people enter the labor force, however, their dissatisfaction tends to decline as they age and time advances. This pattern is evident in the significant negative coefficient for year, which here estimates the extent of intracohort change.[7] These inter- and intracohort coefficients are of opposite signs but nearly identical magnitude, resulting in the negligible overall annual trends shown in columns 1 and 2.

Table 12.6 elaborates the linear decomposition by estimating a regression of job dissatisfaction adding sociodemographic characteristics and the composite measures of job insecurity and economic insecurity as predictors.[8] The cohort replacement (cohort) and intracohort change (year) coefficients are virtually unchanged, but the negative coefficient of the unemployment rate is now statistically significant, suggesting perhaps that workers value their jobs more, or lower their standards for satisfaction, when jobs are in short supply.

Workers who perceive themselves at risk of job loss tend to be more dissatisfied with their jobs, as do those having more pessimistic economic outlooks. Such conditions indicate that their jobs provide fewer rewards, so it is not surprising that their dissatisfaction would rise.

Estimated coefficients for sociodemographic variables are consistent with those reported by previous studies of job satisfaction. Holding other predictors constant, more educated people express greater job dissatisfaction, presumably because their expectations are higher (Gruenberg 1980). Women tend to be more satisfied with their jobs than men; Hodson (1989) reasons that such gender differences reflect the different reference groups that men and women use when assessing their jobs. Dissatisfaction among blacks tends to be higher, undoubtedly a result of the lower quality of their jobs. Differences in satisfaction by occupation generally follow an SES gradient: those in all occupational groups tend to be less dissatisfied than laborers (the reference category), though the difference between operatives and laborers is not

Table 12.6. Predictors of Job Dissatisfaction, 1977–2006

Explanatory variable	Ordinal logistic regression coefficient
Year	−0.024** (0.003)
Unemployment rate	−0.048* (0.015)
Cohort	0.024** (0.002)
Education (years)	0.032** (0.009)
Sex (female)	−0.185** (0.043)
Race	
Black	0.273** (0.057)
Other	0.177 (0.083)
Occupation	
Professional	−0.821** (0.120)
Managerial	−0.692** (0.116)
Sales	−0.389* (0.123)
Clerical	−0.348* (0.111)
Crafts	−0.678** (0.105)
Operative	−0.182 (0.115)
Farm	−1.015** (0.182)
Service	−0.456** (0.115)
Real family income ($1,000s)	−0.002 (0.001)
Employed full-time	−0.101 (0.047)
Risk of costly job loss	0.484** (0.086)
Subjective economic insecurity scale	0.561** (0.028)
(pseudo) R^2	.046
N	14,319

Note: Standard errors in parentheses. Reference category for occupation consists of laborers.
*$p < .01$. **$p < .001$.

statistically significant. Dissatisfaction is especially low among professionals and those in farming. Neither family income nor full-time employment status is significantly associated with job dissatisfaction.

It is possible that these relatively stable levels of overall job satisfaction in the United States since the early 1970s might reflect, in part, offsetting changes in labor force composition. Increases in the number of women and higher-level occupational positions (especially professionals and managers) are likely to raise satisfaction levels, but these may be countered by negative compositional effects associated with increased educational attainment as well as the net rises in insecurity previously discussed. Over-time changes in the importance people assign to specific aspects of work may also be involved, as may changes in comparison standards; we are unable to separate out these factors with the GSS data.

We investigated the possibility that trends in job satisfaction differ among labor force groups, but found few notable patterns.[9] There was some indication that the within-cohort movement toward lower dissatisfaction was weakest among laborers and strongest among farm and service workers, and that it was weaker among those with higher family incomes.

A Note on Unions

Notwithstanding the substantial declines in union membership since the 1970s, especially in the private sector (Farber 2006), it is an important characteristic shaping work orientations. Supplementary analyses (not reported here) added union membership to the sets of predictors included in Tables 12.2, 12.4, and 12.6.[10] These analyses found that union members perceive greater job insecurity than do nonmembers. This may reflect unions' weakened ability to exercise collective voice and effectively represent their members during the last several decades, concessions that unions were forced to make to precarious companies, and unions' experience with relocations of work sites to unorganized regions of the United States or overseas. The rise in job insecurity documented in Table 12.2, however, appears to be less rapid among union members, echoing the pattern of occupational differences displayed in Figure 12.3. Union members do not differ significantly from nonmembers in their perceived economic standing.

Union members are also significantly more apt than nonmembers to express dissatisfaction with their jobs. This finding is well established (e.g., Freeman and Medoff 1984), underscoring the role of unions in mobilizing discontent by providing members with a voice option as an alternative to exiting the workplace.

Summary and Conclusion

This chapter examined trends in three key work-related attitudes—perceived job insecurity, subjective financial and economic standing, and job satisfaction—for the U.S. workforce from the 1970s to the present. The analyses were framed within an argument that macrostructural changes have increased the precarity of work and employment relations (Kalleberg 2009, 2011).

We found that perceptions of job insecurity—both the likelihood of losing one's current job and the difficulty of finding a comparably good one—increased during this period, after we adjust for the cyclical variations in unemployment that are closely linked to perceived insecurity. This growth in perceived job insecurity appears to be fairly widespread within the labor force, supporting the view that precarious work has become more pervasive; but we did find some evidence indicating that job insecurity grew more rapidly among those occupations that had previously been relatively secure (white-collar workers) and that economic insecurity increased the most in higher-level (managerial and professional) occupational groups. Job insecurity is strongly associated with economic insecurity, which also increased since the 1970s net of labor market conditions and labor force characteristics.

We found no strong overall trends in job satisfaction since the 1970s, though modest year-to-year variations are evident. A linear decomposition revealed offsetting changes attributable to cohort replacement and to within-cohort change. Growing job and economic insecurity should presage greater job dissatisfaction, but some changes in labor force composition that enhance job satisfaction—such as growing numbers of women and professional/managerial workers—introduced compensating changes toward higher satisfaction levels.

Our findings are consistent with our argument that work has become more precarious in the United States since the 1970s. Our analyses are limited in that we could not measure increases in precarity directly, however. Instead, we interpret the time trends represented by "year" as reflecting unmeasured macrostructural changes in the organization of work and employment relations. It is certainly possible that other large-scale changes since the 1970s might also have contributed to the increases in insecurity that we have observed. For example, rising international terrorism in the 2000s could well have made people feel less secure about their jobs and economic situations, though the pattern of rising insecurity was already fairly well established before 2001. More precise conclusions could be drawn using direct (though unfortunately rare) data on the changing nature of organizations, employment relations, and many critical features of jobs.

We finally emphasize that the trends we detect became evident only after we adjusted for labor market conditions embodied in unemployment rates. Unadjusted trends in insecurity, economic standing, and job dissatisfaction are flat, or even downward. It is important to control for cyclical effects on insecurity and economic standing since business cycles and labor market conditions represented by unemployment rates are an important context shaping these work orientations, and may mask the effects of macrostructural effects related to precarious work. Adjusting for these cyclical effects reveals the structural consequences of the vast changes toward greater uncertainty in the world of work that have taken place during this period, and we believe that we can safely conclude that these are the primary explanations of the net trends toward greater insecurity and more pessimistic outlooks we have found.

The growth of precarious work—and its consequences for job and economic insecurity, along with a variety of other individual, family, and community outcomes—constitutes a challenge for social policy in the United States, as well as in other industrial countries. Social indicators such as those measured by the GSS offer a valuable source of information for tracking changes in these correlates of precarity.

Notes

We thank Glenn Firebaugh for his comments on an earlier version of this chapter.

1. This section draws on the argument presented in Kalleberg (2009, 2011).

2. The previous period of precarious work in the United States ended with the establishment of social protections and the social contract between business and labor in the 1930s (see Kalleberg 2009, 2011).

3. The October 2008 index fell sharply from its September reading, the sharpest monthly decline on record. This drop undoubtedly reflects the large decline in the stock market and other indicators of the financial crisis that began then.

4. All analyses are weighted for the number of adults in the household, sampling phase in 2004 and 2006, and oversampling of black respondents in 1982 and 1987 (see the appendix to this book). Standard errors are adjusted for clustering in the GSS area probability sampling design.

5. We defined white-collar occupations to include professional, managerial, sales, service, farm, and clerical categories. Blue-collar occupations include crafts-people, operatives, and laborers.

6. The analysis in Table 12.4 covers only 1977–2006, rather than 1972–2006 as in Table 12.3, because the job insecurity indicator is among the predictor variables.

7. The cohort coefficient combines, but does not distinguish, effects of birth cohorts and aging. Likewise, the year coefficient for intracohort change combines effects of period differences and aging. The linear decomposition does not separate age, period, and cohort effects.

8. This analysis covers 1977–2006, rather than 1972–2006 as in Table 12.5, because job insecurity is among the predictors.

9. Fischer and Hout (2006, p. 132) report a widening gap in job satisfaction between more and less educated workers. Their analyses measure education in terms of credentials (highest degree earned), rather than years of education, and do not adjust for other predictors of job satisfaction.

10. We did not include union membership in the primary analyses we report because the GSS measures it and some other variables in our analyses on different "ballots" (see the appendix to this book). Including it reduces our working sample sizes—particularly for analyses involving job insecurity—by nearly 50%.

References

Anderson, Christopher J., and Jonas Pontusson. 2007. "Workers, Worries and Welfare States: Social Protection and Job Insecurity in 15 OECD Countries." *European Journal of Political Research* 46 (2): 211–35.

Bernstein, Jared. 2006. *All Together Now: Common Sense for a New Economy*. San Francisco: Berrett-Koehler.

Burawoy, Michael. 2008. "The Public Turn: From Labor Process to Labor Movement." *Work and Occupations* 35 (4): 371–87.

Cappelli, Peter. 1999. *The New Deal at Work: Managing the Market-Driven Workforce*. Boston: Harvard Business School Press.

Clark, Andrew E., Paul Fiijters, and Michael A. Shields. 2008. "Relative Income, Happiness, and Utility: An Explanation for the Easterlin Paradox and Other Puzzles." *Journal of Economic Literature* 46 (1): 95–144.

Clark, Andrew E., and Andrew J. Oswald. 1996. "Satisfaction and Comparison Income." *Journal of Public Economics* 61:359–81.

Cornfield, Daniel B. 1991. "The U.S. Labor Movement: Its Development and Impact on Social Inequality and Politics." *Annual Review of Sociology* 17:27–49.

De Witte, Hans. 1999. "Job Insecurity and Psychological Well-Being: Review of the Literature and Exploration of Some Unresolved Issues." *European Journal of Work and Organizational Psychology* 8 (2): 155–77.

Easterlin, Richard A. 1980. *Birth and Fortune: The Impacts of Numbers on Personal Welfare*. New York: Basic Books.

———. 1995. "Will Raising the Incomes of All Increase the Happiness of All? *Journal of Economic Behavior and Organization* 27:35–47.

Farber, Henry S. 2006. "Union Membership in the United States: The Divergence Between the Public and Private Sectors." In *Collective Bargaining in Education: Negotiating Change in Today's Schools*, edited by Jane Hannaway and Andrew J. Rotherham, 27–52. Cambridge, MA: Harvard Education Press.

———. 2008. "Shorter Shrift: The Decline in Worker-Firm Attachment in the United States." In *Laid Off, Laid Low: Political and Economic Consequences of Employment Insecurity*, edited by Katherine S. Newman, 10–37. New York: Columbia University Press and Social Science Research Council.

Firebaugh, Glenn. 1997. *Analyzing Repeated Surveys*. Sage University Paper Series on Quantitative Applications in the Social Sciences, no. 07–115. Thousand Oaks, CA: Sage.

Firebaugh, Glenn, and Brian Harley. 1995. "Trends in Job Satisfaction in the United States by Race, Gender, and Type of Occupation." In *The Meaning of Work*. Vol. 5 of *Research in the Sociology of Work*, edited by Richard L. and Ida H. Simpson, 87–104. Greenwich, CT: JAI.

Fischer, Claude S., and Michael Hout. 2006. *Century of Difference: How America Changed in the Last One Hundred Years*. New York: Russell Sage Foundation.

Freeman, Richard B., and James L. Medoff. 1984. *What Do Unions Do?* New York: Basic Books.

Fullerton, Andrew S., and Michael Wallace. 2005. "Traversing the Flexible Turn: U.S. Workers' Perceptions of Job Security, 1977–2002." *Social Science Research* 36:201–21.

Goldin, Claudia, and Lawrence F. Katz. 2008. *The Race between Education and Technology*. Cambridge, MA: Harvard University Press.

Gruenberg, Barry. 1980. "The Happy Worker: An Analysis of Educational and Occupational Differences in Determinants of Job Satisfaction." *American Journal of Sociology* 86:247–71.

Hacker, Jacob. 2006. *The Great Risk Shift*. New York: Oxford University Press.

Hodson, Randy. 1989. "Gender Differences in Job Satisfaction: Why Aren't Women Workers More Dissatisfied?" *Sociological Quarterly* 30 (3): 385–99.

Hodson, Randy, and Teresa A. Sullivan. 2002. *The Social Organization of Work*. 3rd ed. Belmont, CA: Wadsworth.

Jacobs, Elisabeth, and Katherine S. Newman. 2008. "Rising Angst? Change and Stability in Perceptions of Economic Insecurity." In *Laid Off, Laid Low: Political and Economic Consequences of Employment Insecurity*, edited by Katherine S. Newman, 74–101. New York: Columbia University Press and Social Science Research Council.

Jacoby, Sanford M. 2001. "Risk and the Labor Market: Societal Past as Economic Prologue." In *Sourcebook of Labor Markets: Evolving Structures and Processes*, edited by Ivar Berg and Arne L. Kalleberg, 31–60. New York: Kluwer /Plenum.

Jasso, Guillermina. 1990. "Methods for the Theoretical and Empirical Analysis of Comparison Processes." In *Sociological Methodology 1980*, edited by Clifford C. Clogg, 369–419. Cambridge, MA: Basil Blackwell.

Kalleberg, Arne L. 2000. "Nonstandard Employment Relations: Part-Time, Temporary, and Contract Work." *Annual Review of Sociology* 26:341–65.

———. 2009. "Precarious Work, Insecure Workers: Employment Relations in Transition." *American Sociological Review* 74:1–22.

———. 2011. *Good Jobs, Bad Jobs: The Rise of Polarized and Precarious Employment Systems in the United States, 1970s to 2000s*. New York: Russell Sage Foundation.

Kalleberg, Arne L., and Peter V. Marsden. 2005. "Externalizing Organizational Activities: Where and How U.S. Establishments Use Employment Intermediaries." *Socio-Economic Review* 3:389–416.

Kalleberg, Arne L., and Aage B. Sørensen. 1979. "Sociology of Labor Markets." *Annual Review of Sociology* 5:351–79.

Krugman, Paul. 2008. "Crisis of Confidence." *New York Times*, April 14, p. A27.

Levy, Frank, and Richard J. Murnane. 1992. "U.S. Earnings Levels and Earnings Inequality: A Review of Recent Trends and Proposed Explanations." *Journal of Economic Literature* 30 (3): 1333–81.

Mishel, Lawrence, Jared Bernstein, and Sylvia Allegretto. 2007. *The State of Working America, 2006/2007*. Ithaca, NY: ILR Press.

Morris, Martina, and Bruce Western. 1999. "Inequality in Earnings at the Close of the Twentieth Century." *Annual Review of Sociology* 25:623–57.

Neumark, David, ed. 2000. *On the Job: Is Long-Term Employment a Thing of the Past?* New York: Russell Sage Foundation.

Osterman, Paul. 1999. *Securing Prosperity: How the American Labor Market Has Changed and What to Do about It*. Princeton, NJ: Princeton University Press.

Ruggie, John Gerard. 1982. "International Regimes, Transactions, and Change: Embedded Liberalism in the Postwar Economic Order." *International Organization* 362:379–415.

Schmidt, Stefanie R. 1999. "Long-Run Trends in Workers' Beliefs about Their Own Job Security: Evidence from the General Social Survey." *Journal of Labor Economics* 17:S127–41.

Sullivan, Teresa A., Elizabeth Warren, and Jay Lawrence Westbrook. 2001. *The Fragile Middle Class: Americans in Debt*. New Haven, CT: Yale University Press.

Uchitelle, Louis. 2006. *The Disposable American: Layoffs and Their Consequences*. New York: Knopf.

13

Population Trends in Verbal Intelligence in the

United States

Duane F. Alwin and Julianna Pacheco

Social trends in cognitive resources, for example, changes in average intelligence test scores, have received a great deal of scholarly attention in recent years. The psychological sciences refer to historical rises in scores on standardized intelligence tests from one generation to another as the *Flynn Effect* (Neisser 1997, 1998), for James Flynn, a political scientist at the University of Otago in New Zealand, who discovered it and quantified its pervasiveness (Flynn 1984, 1987, 1998, 1999). Under a framework consistent with the Flynn Effect (referenced here as the "progress model"), several researchers report generally higher test scores among more recent cohorts across a range of cognitive measures (e.g., Schaie 2005, 2008, Schaie, Willis, and Pennack 2005; for a recent review of this work, see Alwin 2009a). Such results square with expectations that increasing levels of education bring about better intellectual performance in a population.

Using a measure of verbal knowledge ("WORDSUM") administered in 18 General Social Surveys (GSSs) spanning nearly 35 years (from 1974 to 2008), as well as in a small 1941 Gallup survey that served as the benchmark for the GSS measure, this chapter examines population trends in verbal intelligence in the United States, with primary attention to trends over time and their components. We place trends in the GSS measure in the context of the 1941 survey (designed by Robert L. Thorndike in collaboration with George Gallup of the American Institute of Public Opinion) partly to confirm the nature and direction of the population trends, but also to evaluate the psychometric properties of the items in the WORDSUM measure. We conclude that the WORDSUM score was an excellent instrument for measuring the underlying trait at the time of its creation: its component items varied significantly in difficulty and discriminated well between higher- and lower-ability subjects.

Because of concerns about the dimensionality of the measure, however, we examine the individual items comprising WORDSUM as well as the total score itself. The chapter assesses the evidence for several interpretations advanced for trends observed in the GSS data, specifically hypotheses concerning (1) the persistence of intercohort patterns of decline in WORDSUM scores to the present, (2) the increasing difficulty of the WORDSUM items, and (3) cohort aging as an account for patterns of within-cohort change in WORDSUM scores. We find strong and very consistent support for intercohort variation at the item-specific level, no support for the notion that these patterns are due to increasing item difficulty, and no support for the hypothesis that cohort differences reflect patterns of cognitive aging with respect to verbal knowledge.

Background

Recent analyses of GSS data on vocabulary knowledge—specifically the items that make up the WORDSUM score—do not conform to the patterns suggested by the progress model. Rather than favoring the later-born birth cohorts, the reverse is evident— WORDSUM scores are generally higher among those from earlier-born cohorts (Alwin 1991, 2009a; Alwin and McCammon 1999, 2001; Glenn 1994, 1999; Yang and Land 2006, 2008).

Indeed, test scores have not always risen over time, nor have they risen in all domains. During the 1960s and 1970s, analysts expressed serious concern about declining performance by the young on measures of verbal ability. Average verbal scores on standardized assessments like the Scholastic Aptitude Test (SAT) and the American College Testing Service (ACT) tests (see Wirtz and Howe 1977) fell systematically from the mid-1960s through the mid-1980s. Interpreting changing college admissions test scores as if they reflect true changes in the verbal and quantitative skills of high school students is highly problematic, of course, given the changing composition of the test-taking population. Most observers nonetheless conceded that the test score decline was real, net of these compositional shifts (e.g., Blake 1989; Alwin 1991).

Alwin (1991) tested for test score declines using nine GSS probability samples representative of the U.S. population between 1974 and 1990, finding systematic education-adjusted differences in vocabulary knowledge among cohorts, with a notable drop beginning with those born after 1945. From Alwin's (1991) original publication of these patterns to more recent analyses that report the same finding (Alwin and McCammon 1999, 2001), the conclusion

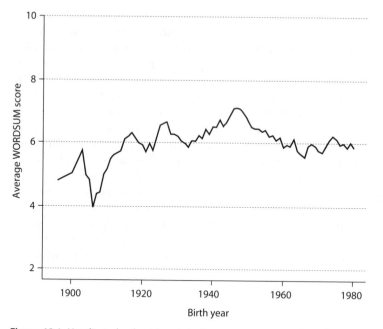

Figure 13.1. Unadjusted cohort trends in the WORDSUM measure, based on the 1974–2008 GSSs.

that systematic intercohort declines in vocabulary knowledge began with post–World War II (baby boom) birth cohorts and continued through the cohorts that reached maturity in the 1970s and 1980s has met with little objection (see Alwin 2009a; Alwin and McCammon 1999, 2001; Glenn 1994, 1999; Hauser and Huang 1997; Wilson and Gove 1999; Yang and Land 2008). Figure 13.1 presents unadjusted cohort trends in the WORDSUM measure based on the 1974–2008 GSSs. Intercohort declines in vocabulary knowledge after the mid-1940s are evident using these most recent data.

Owing to problems such as mortality selection, however, interpreting these intercohort differences is not straightforward (see, e.g., Alwin 2009a, 2009b). Some contend that intercohort trends in the GSS data derive from "word obsolescence"—drift in the meaning of words in the United States and changing fashions in the use of words. This argument suggests that lower WORDSUM scores for more recent cohorts reflect increased difficulty and unfamiliarity of the words in the vocabulary test (e.g., Alwin 1991, p. 628).[1] This interpretation coincides with Hauser and Huang's (1997) detailed analysis of English-language lexicons over much of the 20th century. They conclude that "WORDSUM has become somewhat more difficult across time, independent of any other change in verbal ability in the general population" (Hauser and Huang 1997, pp. 344–45). Based on their study of word frequency counts and ranks for English words in dictionaries for 1921, 1931, 1944, and 1967 (see Thorndike 1921, 1931; Thorndike and Lorge 1944; Kučera and Francis 1967), they state that this tendency "occurs to some degree across the lists of 1921, 1931, and 1944, and it appears strongly when we include the 1967 list in the comparison" (Hauser and Huang 1997, p. 345).

Others attribute the intercohort trends found by Alwin (1991) partially or wholly to processes of aging, suggesting that they cannot be traced to differences in cohort experiences (see Wilson and Gove 1999). This hypothesis bears investigation because much evidence suggests general cognitive declines in older age (see Hofer and Alwin 2008). In fact, however, very little evidence for an aging interpretation of these intercohort patterns exists, especially because crystallized abilities such as vocabulary knowledge show little decline until relatively advanced ages (Alwin and McCammon 2001; Bowles, Grimm, and McArdle 2005; Park et al. 1996; Schaie 2005; Verhaeghen 2003).[2] While most cognitive abilities peak in early adulthood and then decline with age, vocabulary knowledge is among the few skill sets that remain relatively intact over the adult life span, reaching a high around ages 50–60, and then falling only slowly, if at all, in old age.

We begin by briefly reviewing the conceptual issues involved in assessing population trends using survey data, including both potential shifts due to cohort replacement and intracohort changes resulting from aging and period influences. We then introduce the Gallup and GSS surveys and describe trends in verbal intelligence (i.e., word knowledge) in these data. Next, we assess interpretations for these patterns advanced in the recent research literature, focusing on the persistence of intercohort patterns of decline, the hypothesized rise in difficulty of the WORDSUM items, and patterns of within-cohort change that potentially reflect cohort aging. This chapter analyzes variation in both the WORDSUM score itself and the individual items comprising it, employing item response theory (IRT) models and logistic regression techniques.

Research Problem

It is generally recognized that three general sets of factors can contribute to trends in vocabulary measures—(1) those due to cohort experiences (or generational influences), that is, *cohort effects* (Alwin 1991; Alwin and McCammon 1999; Schaie 2008; Schaie et al. 2005);[3] (2) those linked to the period studied and the possible effects of historical factors on a population, that is, *period effects* (Hauser and Huang 1997; Wilson and Gove 1999; Yang and Land 2008); and (3) those reflecting changes that occur within cohorts due to *life cycle and/or aging effects* (Alwin and McCammon 2001; Austad 1997; Baltes 1997). The following discussion briefly reviews what is known about how each of these sets of factors influences verbal skills.

Cohort experiences can affect cognitive scores, for example, verbal and quantitative abilities, through several mechanisms. Childhood and youth are periods for learning vast amounts of new information that becomes a resource for further development. The distinctiveness of cohort experiences may affect such knowledge. Formal schooling is a major mechanism for transmitting knowledge, so it is reasonable to expect that greater time in school should be related to acquiring more knowledge across a wide range of domains. More recently born cohorts' greater schooling should better prepare them for adult life, compared to earlier-born cohorts.

As noted earlier, psychometricians have long known that standardized test scores tend to rise from one generation to another. Flynn (1984) found increasing raw scores on every major test, in every age range and in every modern industrialized country, although increases were smallest on the tests most closely linked to school content (see review by Neisser 1997, pp. 441–42; Flynn 1998, p. 61). Flynn (1984, p. 48) argued that increased educational levels accounted for much, but far from all, of these IQ gains. Test scores continued to rise even after cohort-specific levels of schooling peaked among those born in 1945 and after. Continued rises in scores in the United States after the mid-1960s could not be due to increasing aggregate levels of schooling in the population.

The pattern found under the Flynn argument (e.g., Flynn 1998, 1999) is most apparent for measures that are highly loaded in fluid abilities (the capacity for insight into complex relations independent of the sensory or cultural area in which tests are expressed). Somewhat surprisingly, it is least evident in measures of crystallized abilities (abilities that result from investing fluid abilities in particular higher-level cultural skills). Fewer or no gains were found for acculturated skills acquired through schooling, that is, crystallized learning. If cohort factors were producing Flynn's effect, though, one would expect his patterns to be even *more* apparent for crystallized abilities. Flynn (1998, p. 61) wrote the following about cohort and period effects in intelligence test scores:

> Gains may be age specific, but this has not yet been established and they certainly persist into adulthood. The fact that gains are fully present in young children means that causal factors are present in early childhood but not necessarily that they are more potent in young children than among older children or adults.

Thus, it is not clear whether Flynn considered the effect exclusively a cohort phenomenon or something that also involved period factors (see also Flynn 1999).

In their recent commentary on Flynn's (1984, 1999) work, Schaie et al. (2005) argue that Flynn found cohort effects, that is, that the macro-level changes he observed primarily reflect differences in cohort experiences. Moreover, the largest gains, as suggested by their Seattle Longitudinal Study (SLS) data, were for cohorts born in the early part of the 20th century. This argument is consistent with a "progress" view of the consequences of expanded education, namely cognitive and intellectual improvement (see also Schaie 2005, 2008). Schaie's work on cohort effects generally suggests that more recent birth cohorts have higher levels of cognitive performance compared to earlier ones observed at the same age (see esp. Schaie 2005, 2008; Schaie et al. 2005).

Yang and Land's (2008) recent reanalysis of trends in the WORDSUM score bears out Alwin's earlier finding of cohort effects, reporting a systematic decline in verbal test scores for the post-1945 cohorts, and also aging and period effects (see also Alwin 1991; Alwin and McCammon 1999; Glenn 1994, 1999). Their findings bolster those in past research concerning the relative role of aging and cohort factors in producing variation in vocabulary scores (e.g., Alwin and McCammon 2001, pp. S151–61). Once cohort differences in cognitive performance are statistically controlled, the residual effect of aging-related processes contributes only very slightly to variation in verbal knowledge (Alwin and McCammon 2001, pp. S156–59). This is in keeping with our earlier suggestion that scores on tests that measure crystallized intelligence, such as vocabulary knowledge, decline less with age than those on tests assessing fluid abilities like speed of processing or memory performance (Alwin and McCammon 2001; Park et al. 1996; Verhaeghen 2003; Schaie 2005). Bowles et al. (2005) suggest that aging effects differ depending on the difficulty of words—specifically, that "basic vocabulary knowledge" (e.g., the easier words in WORDSUM) peaks around age 30, declining systematically thereafter, whereas "advanced vocabulary knowledge" (e.g., the difficult WORDSUM words) is unrelated to age between the ages of 35 and 70.

Yang and Land (2008) also report period effects on the WORDSUM score, specifically a decline in vocabulary knowledge during the 1980s that reached a nadir in 1988. They do not suggest any account of what might be responsible for these effects, however. Apart from this drop in the 1980s, only negligible differences are associated with year of survey, in contrast to the notable cohort differences. It is difficult to imagine what constellation of conditions would raise or lower an entire population's verbal skills for a few years, and then abruptly reverse the pattern, except possibly some technical factor (e.g., sample frame selection, or systematic sampling bias). Social change in vocabulary knowledge is much more likely a result of cohort mechanisms (e.g., Ryder 1965) because it involves a trait acquired by the young, principally through education. Processes producing a period effect (and its reversal) would have to operate on the entire population, not just the young. Moreover, without the assumption that period effects (i.e., effects tied to survey year) are negligible in the short term, disentangling the effects of aging and cohort is difficult (see Alwin and McCammon 1999; Alwin 2009a).

Data Sources and Methods

This chapter examines trends in verbal intelligence using two data sources—a 1941 Gallup survey employing a 20-item test of vocabulary knowledge and the 1974–2008 GSS series known as WORDSUM that includes a 10-item subscale drawn from the original Gallup items.[4] The WORDSUM measure is an indicator of verbal intelligence. Nearly 100 published articles and chapters have used it in recent decades (see the review by Malhotra, Krosnick, and Haertel 2007). WORDSUM includes a subset of the vocabulary items from Thorndike's early article on developing short screening tests of verbal abilities (Thorndike 1942, p. 129). Thorndike chose test words from the vocabulary section of the Institute for Educational Research (IER) intelligence scale, CAVD (see Thorndike 1942, p. 129). The actual words that comprise the WORDSUM score originated from Form A of Thorndike's test (see Table 13.1; also Miner 1957, pp. 28–31; Hauser and Huang 1997, p. 341);[5] we do not identify them here.

Our Measures of Vocabulary Knowledge

Measures of vocabulary knowledge correlate highly with tests of general intelligence—usually at .7, .8, or higher (see Miner 1957, pp. 28–31)—and are considered good indicators of scores on the verbal component of standard tests of general intelligence (see also Wolfle 1980; Hauser and Huang 1997). Thorndike and Gallup (1944, pp. 78–79) described the vocabulary measure administered in the 1941 survey as a "test of verbal intelligence . . . [assessing] the nature of past learnings and not the ability to make novel adaptations." Interviewers introduced the word test by reading the following instructions to the respondent:

> Here are some words which may be included on a quiz program, depending upon how many people understand their meaning. We are trying to find out now how familiar these words are to people. Will you please look at this card (*hand card to respondent*) and give me the number of the word that seems to be closest to each word in capital letters.

The card handed to the respondent included instructions as follows:

> Please look first at the word in capital letters on each line. Then look at the other words in smaller type on the same line and tell me which one of these words comes closest in meaning to the one in capital letters.

> EXAMPLE

> BEAST   1. Afraid   2. Words   3. Large   4. Animal   5. Bird

> The correct answer in this example is No. 4 since the word "animal" comes closer to "beast" than any of the other words.

The data we present in the following analysis are from the Form A ballot of the 1941 Gallup survey. This form includes four groups of items that span the range of difficulty: group A is the easiest set, group D is the most difficult.

The GSS protocol is very similar, although its instructions do not refer to the "quiz program" as the 1941 survey did. This introduction precedes the WORDSUM series:

> We would like to know something about how people go about guessing words they do not know. On this card are listed some words—you may know some of them, and you may not know quite a few of them.
>
> On each line the first word is in capital letters—like BEAST. Then there are five other words. Tell me the number of the word that comes closest to the meaning of the word in capital letters. For example, if the word in capital letters is BEAST, you would say "4" since "animal" comes closer to BEAST than any of the other words. If you wish, I will read the words to you. These words are difficult for almost everyone—just give me your best guess if you are not sure of the answer.

We present these details about the administration of these verbal tests to properly document the survey context for the questions, not because we believe that these differences notably alter the answers respondents give. Recall, however, that the 10 GSS WORDSUM items were originally embedded in the 20-item Gallup Form A test. It is possible that answers to the Gallup and GSS items may differ because of order effects: responses to earlier items may affect the items that follow.

Samples

The data from the 1941 Gallup survey were described by Thorndike and Gallup (1944, pp. 77–81). The sample was "the standard voting sample of the Institute [the American Institute of Public Opinion] . . . who were eligible to vote . . ."; it was interviewed about a range of topics, including knowledge of vocabulary. By today's standards, this sample is somewhat suspect: it was a quota sample limited to eligible voters. Additionally, a common concern with data from the 1940s that claim to represent the entire English-speaking population is that they may represent African Americans inadequately. These features of the sample must be considered by any interpretation of these data, particularly when comparing the 1941 survey to more recent ones. We nonetheless explore them because they were the source of the GSS vocabulary measure. We base no conclusions on these data alone, employing them solely to supplement our conclusions from the GSS studies.[6]

Our principal data source is the 18 nationally representative GSS surveys conducted between 1974 and 2008 that include the 10-item measure of verbal ability known as WORDSUM.[7] See the appendix to this book for details on GSS sampling methods. In early surveys, roughly 1,500 respondents answered the verbal test; in later ones it was administered to a randomly selected

Table 13.1. Univariate Distributions for the WORDSUM Items: Native-Born Respondents, Age 24 years and Older, 1978–2008 GSSs ($N = 19,027$)

	% right	% wrong	% don't know
Word A	78.8	14.6	6.6
Word B	88.9	4.8	6.3
Word C	21.4	53.9	24.7
Word D	90.1	3.9	6.1
Word E	73.7	15.8	10.5
Word F	76.2	14.4	9.4
Word G	33.1	53.6	13.4
Word H	28.0	25.2	46.8
Word I	73.5	20.1	6.4
Word J	22.5	66.4	11.0

Note: Limited to 1978–2008 GSSs because the foreign-born question was not asked in 1974 or 1976. Weighted for household size and oversampling of African Americans.

two-thirds of each GSS sample. We employ weights for household size and oversampling of African Americans in analyzing GSS samples. Where possible, we limit our analysis samples to the native English-speaking subpopulation aged 24 and older, residing in households in the United States.[8]

Table 13.1 displays the frequency distribution of right, wrong, and "don't know" (DK) answers for each of the 10 words in the vocabulary test for U.S.-born respondents to the 1978–2008 GSSs aged 24 and older who validly answered at least one of the word items. About 19,000 respondents attempted each word. DK answers were most frequent for the most difficult words (those answered correctly by small proportions of the sample) and lowest for the easiest words. The highest DK percentages were found for word C (24.7%) and word H (46.8%), while those for word B (6.3%) and word D (6.1%) were lowest.[9] Like others who study these data (e.g., Alwin and McCammon 2001; Malhotra et al. 2007), we consider DKs to be "wrong" answers in all further analyses.

As noted, we restrict our analyses to native-born, English-speaking respondents in the GSS household samples. Table 13.2 presents justification for excluding nonnatives from our analysis samples, reporting differences in means for WORDSUM and several other variables between respondents born in the United States and those born elsewhere. Although the education levels of foreign-born and U.S.-born respondents are similar, the foreign born are significantly more likely to give DK answers on the vocabulary test, and also significantly more likely to identify words incorrectly. Hence they have a lower mean WORDSUM score than native-born respondents, by about one word. This is no doubt because the foreign born are less likely to use English as their primary language; they are also more likely to be male, white, and young. These results, together with precedents set in previous research (see

Table 13.2. Means for WORDSUM and Selected Variables, Native- and Foreign-Born Respondents, Age 24 Years and Older, 1978–2008 GSSs (N = 19,484)

Variable	Foreign born (N = 1,443)	Born in United States (N = 18,041)	p value, difference in means
WORDSUM score	5.19	6.13	.00
Number of don't know responses	1.51	0.83	.00
Percentage black	11.70	14.70	.00
Years of schooling	13.07	13.05	.85
Percentage female	54.80	57.50	.04
Age at interview	44.46	47.38	.00
Birth year	1950.77	1945.43	.00

Note: Limited to 1978–2008 GSSs because the foreign-born question was not asked in 1974 or 1976.

Alwin 1991; Alwin and McCammon 1999, 2001), are our basis for excluding foreign-born respondents from our trend analyses.[10] We restrict the analysis sample to those aged 24 or older because household samples like that employed by the GSS do not interview on college campuses or military reservations, so they typically do not represent the lower adult age ranges well (see Alwin 1991, p. 628).

Psychometric Properties of the GSS WORDSUM Items

To verify that WORDSUM was a good test for measuring verbal intelligence when first developed, we investigated the psychometric properties of the ten GSS items using the 1941 data and IRT methods (see Embretson and Reise 2000). We estimated a three-parameter IRT model, including a "guessing" parameter because of the multiple-choice format of the items.

Table 13.3 presents estimated difficulty, discrimination, and guessing parameters for this analysis. These indicate that the GSS WORDSUM items constitute an excellent instrument for measuring the underlying verbal knowledge trait: the words included vary significantly in difficulty (i.e., some are answered correctly by most respondents, others only by high-knowledge respondents) and have high discrimination values (i.e., they distinguish well between respondents with knowledge levels just below and above an item's difficulty). Except for some of the more difficult words (e.g., words H and J), estimated guessing levels for the 1941 survey are negligible.[11]

Despite these results, the literature about the GSS WORDSUM items expresses some concern that they do not have good scale properties because they are not unidimensional (Bowles et al. 2005; Malhotra et al. 2007). Exploratory factor analyses routinely suggest that the items reflect two underlying common factors rather than just one, calling the legitimacy of using the WORDSUM score into question. Pooling GSS WORDSUM data from 1974

Table 13.3. Estimated Item Parameters for Three-Parameter Item Response Model, 1941 Gallup Survey ($N = 477$)

	Difficulty parameter	Discrimination parameter	Guessing parameter
Word A	−1.24***	2.39***	0.0001
	(0.12)	(0.35)	(0.003)
Word B	−1.19***	2.98***	0.0003
	(0.11)	(0.50)	(0.01)
Word C	0.68***	1.86	0.01
	(0.21)	(1.16)	(0.14)
Word D	−0.67***	3.25***	0.00
	(0.07)	(0.48)	(0.001)
Word E	−0.16*	2.33***	0.001
	(0.08)	(0.30)	(0.03)
Word F	−0.60***	2.67***	0.00
	(0.08)	(0.40)	(0.001)
Word G	0.56	2.07	0.04
	(0.42)	(2.35)	(0.27)
Word H	0.21***	5.73***	0.10***
	(0.08)	(1.76)	(0.03)
Word I	−0.44***	1.82***	0.0001
	(0.09)	(0.24)	(0.003)
Word J	0.83***	4.89	0.14***
	(0.08)	(3.55)	(0.03)
Log likelihood	−2238		
AIC	4536		
BIC	4661		

Note: Standard errors in parentheses.
*$p < .05$. ***$p < .001$ (two-tailed test).

to 2000, Bowles et al. (2005, p. P237) conclude that two factors that "were directly related to difficulty" account for the correlations among the GSS items. One consisted of the easy items, which they labeled as "Basic Vocabulary," the other of the difficult items, called "Advanced Vocabulary." Bowles et al. (2005, p. P237) report a "congruence coefficient between the factor loadings on the first factor and difficulty as indicated by the proportion correct was .96, whereas the congruence coefficient between the second factor and one minus difficulty was .97." Despite the clear confounding of item-specific difficulties with the substantive concept of vocabulary knowledge, they concluded that "a two-factor solution best describes the GSS vocabulary test" (Bowles et al. 2005, p. P237), citing previous studies that found two underlying difficulty-related vocabulary factors in other intelligence tests (Bailey and Federman 1979; Beck et al. 1989; Gustafsson and Holmberg 1992). Malhotra et al.'s (2007) independent analysis of the GSS WORDSUM items echoed this conclusion.

Both Bowles et al. (2005, p. P239) and Malhotra et al. (2007) recognize that factors related to the difficulty of the items create a complexity that has no straightforward resolution, something well-known in the psychometric literature—especially when analyses involve dichotomous items (e.g., Mc-Donald and Ahlawat 1974). It is entirely possible that the GSS WORDSUM data reflect two underlying factors, one a substantively interpretable factor representing vocabulary knowledge independent of item difficulty, the second reflecting an artifact of measurement having to do with the difficulty of the items. In practice, however, separating these dimensions may not be possible. Bowles et al. (2005, p. P239) concede that "research into the sources of difficulty factors has not yielded definitive means of addressing potential artifactuality," and admit that "it is not possible to assess to what degree we were successful in eliminating the potential for artifactual multidimensionality." They propose that "a conclusion of actual multidimensionality may be justified" if the factors have different relationships with external criterion variables, suggesting that age differences may be critical in determining the "validity of the bidimensionality of the GSS vocabulary test" (Bowles et al. 2005, p. P239).

Modeling Strategy

We follow an essentially descriptive approach to the GSS and Gallup data. Because of the ambiguity about their factorial complexity just discussed, we separately analyze trends in answers about each individual word comprising WORDSUM, as well as in the composite WORDSUM score itself. We examine the component items of WORDSUM score using logistic regression models, employing standard likelihood ratio tests for choosing between alternative models (see Hosmer and Lemeshow 2000, pp. 6–7, 116–28). We use ordinary least squares (OLS) regression techniques to study the composite WORDSUM scores.

Our analysis focuses on two main components of trends in the WORD-SUM data, those occurring between cohorts and those taking place within cohorts. Following Firebaugh's (1989, 1992) framework for studying social change using repeated cross-sectional data, we note that within-cohort variation over time can be due either to period effects on verbal scores linked to historical time and/or to life-cycle/aging variation linked to biographical time. Likewise, cross-sectional (point-in-time) differences between cohorts can be due to the differences in cohort experiences usually known as "cohort effects" and/or differences in the age composition of the cohorts. While we acknowledge the possibility that period effects may be operating, our analysis reveals that they are at most trivial. Hence, we essentially assume that within-cohort trends in WORDSUM scores are primarily due to biographical (aging/life-cycle) factors, while between-cohort variations—what Firebaugh terms "cohort replacement"—are due to cohort effects.

Time Trends

This section examines temporal patterns in verbal intelligence by comparing the 1941 Gallup survey to the more recent GSS data. We are principally interested in over-time differences in the proportions of these samples that identify words correctly, both between the 1941 and the GSS surveys, and within the GSS series itself. These results bear particularly on assertions that "word obsolescence" contributes to recent declines in measured English vocabulary knowledge. The WORDSUM measure is based on the same 10 words between 1941 and 2008. If particular words gradually move in and out of fashion, using a constant list of words makes it possible that changing scores reflect the changing availability of the words in the American lexicon rather than genuine changes in verbal ability (e.g., Wilson and Gove 1999; Hauser and Huang 1997, p. 345).

Changing Word Difficulty? Word Knowledge in the 1941
Gallup Survey vs. Recent GSSs

We place the GSS time trends in some historical perspective by presenting information about verbal knowledge among U.S. adults from the Gallup survey of 1941. The first column of Table 13.4 presents the proportions of the 1941 sample that correctly identified the 10 words that were later included in the GSS WORDSUM instrument. The remaining columns present proportions correct for the same words for the combined GSSs of 1974–1978, 1982–1987, 1988–1993, 1994–1998, and 2000–2008. For some words (e.g., words D and I), notably higher proportions of GSS respondents than 1941 respondents answered correctly; for others (e.g., words H and J), the proportions correct are

Table 13.4. Proportion Correct Answers for 10 Items in GSS WORDSUM Score, 1941 Gallup Survey and 1974–2008 GSSs ($N \sim 20,500$)

	Gallup 1941	GSS 1974–1978	GSS 1982–1987	GSS 1988–1993	GSS 1994–1998	GSS 2000–2008
Word A	.85	.82	.82	.83	.87	.86
Word B	.86	.95	.94	.95	.96	.95
Word C	.32	.29	.31	.31	.29	.27
Word D	.73	.94	.94	.96	.97	.97
Word E	.56	.76	.79	.82	.84	.86
Word F	.70	.83	.81	.85	.85	.85
Word G	.36	.41	.38	.40	.37	.38
Word H	.48	.42	.36	.39	.39	.39
Word I	.64	.82	.77	.79	.79	.77
Word J	.32	.25	.23	.26	.27	.27

Note: GSS estimates for respondents age 24 and older; foreign-born respondents excluded after 1976.

Table 13.5. Logistic Regression Models Assessing Linear Trends in Correct Responses to
WORDSUM Items, 1974–2008 GSSs ($N \sim 20{,}500$): Native-Born GSS Respondents, 24 Years
of Age and Older in the 1974–2008 Surveys

	β_Year	Odds ratio	Δ prob. from min to max (%)	Intercept
Word A	.1078***	1.1139	5	1.4734***
	(.0273)	(0.0304)		(0.0567)
Word B	.0397	1.0405	n/a	2.8250***
	(.0551)	(0.0573)		(0.1184)
Word C	−.0689**	0.9334	−5	−0.8002***
	(.0249)	(0.0233)		(0.0526)
Word D	.2538***	1.2889	4	2.6502***
	(.0508)	(0.0654)		(0.0967)
Word E	.2807***	1.3240	14	0.9701***
	(.0276)	(0.0365)		(0.0576)
Word F	.0992**	1.1043	5	1.4586***
	(.0287)	(0.0316)		(0.0592)
Word G	−.0649**	0.9372	−5	−0.3549***
	(.0217)	(0.0204)		(0.0468)
Word H	−.0410	0.9598	n/a	−0.4197***
	(.0229)	(0.0220)		(0.0488)
Word I	−.0324	0.9681	n/a	1.3631***
	(.0254)	(0.0246)		(0.0563)
Word J	.0813**	1.0846	5	−1.2472***
	(.0242)	(0.0263)		(0.0521)
WORDSUM[a]	.0700***			5.9800***
	(.0200)			(0.0500)

Note: Estimates are weighted for household size and oversampling of African Americans. Standard errors in
parentheses. Estimates for respondents age 24 and older; foreign-born respondents excluded after 1976. n/a =
not calculated due to insignificance of trend coefficient.

[a]OLS regression estimates.

**p < .01. ***p < .001 (two-tailed test).

somewhat lower among GSS respondents, suggesting that these words might
have become more difficult.

Table 13.5 presents results of an analysis of within-GSS trends. For each
specific word, we estimated the logistic regression of a dichotomous variable
distinguishing correct and incorrect answers on survey year (scored in decades).[12] For five words (words A, D, E, F, and J), the odds of responding
correctly increase with time between 1974 and 2008 (suggesting that these
words became easier). The amount of change over that time span is small,
however, 5 percentage points or less for all words except word E. For three
words (words C, G, and I), downward changes were observed: the proportion
giving correct answers declined slightly, no more than 5 percentage points.

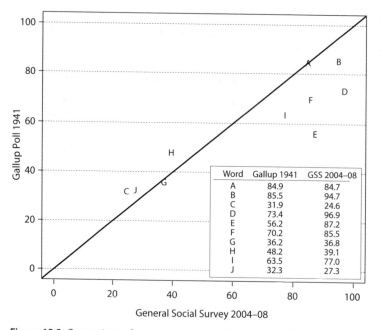

Figure 13.2. Comparison of percentages correct for the 10 individual words in WORDSUM, 1941 Gallup survey and 2004–2008 GSSs.

On the basis of these results, a case could be made that many words comprising WORDSUM became *easier* during the course of the GSS; a smaller number became more difficult, but only slightly so.

The results in Tables 13.4 and 13.5 demonstrate considerable, though not complete, convergence between the 1941 Gallup results and within-GSS trends in vocabulary knowledge. Both studies show that words such as D, E, and F appear to have grown easier beginning in the 1940s. The within-GSS trends indicate that additional words, including A and J, became easier beginning in the 1970s. On the other hand, the two sources of evidence show that at least one word (C) became slightly but steadily more difficult beginning in the 1940s; additionally, the GSS data suggest systematic downward movement in the proportion correct for words G and I.

Summarizing the above, Figure 13.2 directly compares percentages correct for the 10 words in the 1941 Gallup data and in the three most recent GSS surveys (of 2004, 2006, and 2008). The diagonal reference line shows where the two percentages would be equal. Words above it were more often answered correctly in the 1941 survey (hence becoming more difficult over time). Words beneath the diagonal became easier, as their proportions correct are higher in recent GSSs. Figure 13.2 depicts a bifurcation of changes in word difficulty over time: words that were comparatively easy in 1941 became easier, while those that were then difficult grew more challenging. These results are nearly opposite to Hauser and Huang's (1997, p. 345) conclusion that the WORDSUM items had "become more difficult across time, independent of any other change in verbal ability in the general population." Our analysis indicates that some words in WORDSUM are getting easier, some are getting harder, but none have changed substantially; the predominant pattern is toward decreasing rather than rising item difficulty.

Inter- and Intracohort Components of the GSS Trends in Word Knowledge

Table 13.6 uses Firebaugh's (1989) linear decomposition technique to separate the over-time trends in word knowledge into within-cohort and cohort replacement components. It presents logistic regression coefficients (as well as odds ratios) for predicting the probability of correctly identifying each word from survey year (the intracohort component) and birth year (the cohort replacement component), adjusted for years of schooling completed. To ensure that the constant term has substantive meaning, we centered survey year on 1972 and birth year around its overall mean (1945); both were then divided by 10 to ease interpretation. Years of schooling was centered at 12.[13]

Table 13.6 shows that most within-cohort change is positive, that is, toward improved word knowledge over time, but a few notable changes in the negative direction (words C and I) occur consistent with our observations above. By contrast, most change due to cohort replacement is negative, clearly reflecting a tendency for more recent birth cohorts to score lower on verbal intelligence, net of survey year and schooling. Cohort replacement effects are negative for 8 out of the 10 words. Words A and I, with small positive cohort replacement effects and negative within-cohort trends, are the primary exceptions to the general pattern. Most of the positive intracohort trends are counteracted by negative cohort replacement effects, so that there is little net overall shift in verbal ability, as seen in Tables 13.4 and 13.5. In sum, notwithstanding the fact that verbal knowledge appears to be lower among those born more recently, upward within-cohort trends indicate that most words in WORDSUM got easier over time, after controlling for cohort differences and education.

As noted, some researchers contend that the generally positive within-cohort trends (net of schooling) shown in Table 13.6 represent period effects on the WORDSUM measure (e.g., Wilson and Gove 1999; Yang and Land 2008), but they provide little or no substantive account for such effects. Aside from the possibility of beyond-chance levels of sampling error, we can think of no reason for year-to-year fluctuations in the population's knowledge of vocabulary. Such findings beg for an interpretation that has not been forthcoming in the literature (e.g., see also Yang et al. 2008; Yang and Land 2006). In the absence of an account that substantiates a period effect interpretation, we would attribute the within-cohort trends associated with survey year in Table 13.6 to life-cycle processes and/or aging.

Table 13.6. Cohort-Replacement and Intracohort Components of Temporal Trends in Vocabulary Knowledge, Controlling for Level of Schooling, 1974–2008 GSSs (N~20,500)

	Intracohort change			Cohort replacement			Schooling			
	β_Year	Odds ratio	Δ prob. from min to max (%)	β_Cohort	Odds ratio	Δ prob. from min to max (%)	β_Educ	Odds ratio	Δ prob. from min to max (%)	Intercept
Word A	-.0484	0.9527	n/a	.0452*	1.0463	6	.1680***	1.1830	55	1.6897***
	(.0320)	(0.0304)		(.0192)	(0.0201)		(.0104)	(0.0123)		(0.0673)
Word B	.0344	1.0350	n/a	-.1708***	0.8430	-6	.2583***	1.2947	54	2.8089***
	(.0703)	(0.0727)		(.0383)	(0.0323)		(.0203)	(0.0263)		(0.1598)
Word C	-.0748*	0.9279	-5	-.1488***	0.8618	-30	.2407***	1.2722	63	-1.1818***
	(.0298)	(0.0277)		(.0164)	(0.0141)		(.0105)	(0.0133)		(0.0626)
Word D	.1516*	1.1637	2	-.0971**	0.9075	-3	.2902***	1.3367	58	2.8567***
	(.0621)	(0.0723)		(.0351)	(0.0319)		(.0184)	(0.0246)		(0.1255)
Word E	.3361***	1.3994	15	-.2340***	0.7913	-27	.3277***	1.3878	91	0.7252***
	(.0343)	(0.0480)		(.0197)	(0.0156)		(.0124)	(0.0173)		(0.0691)
Word F	.0898*	1.0939	3	-.1923***	0.8251	-20	.3157***	1.3713	89	1.3689***
	(.0362)	(0.0396)		(.0206)	(0.0170)		(.0137)	(0.0188)		(0.0731)
Word G	.0557*	1.0572	4	-.2776***	0.7576	-59	.2178***	1.2434	70	-0.8792***
	(.0260)	(0.0275)		(.0148)	(0.0112)		(.0087)	(0.0108)		(0.0553)
Word H	.0884**	1.0924	7	-.3207***	0.7256	-66	.2741***	1.3153	77	-1.0624***
	(.0281)	(0.0307)		(.0163)	(0.0189)		(.0095)	(0.0125)		(0.0589)
Word I	-.1700***	0.8436	-10	.0468**	1.0479	8	.1384***	1.1484	52	1.5352***
	(.0296)	(0.0250)		(.0158)	(0.0165)		(.0091)	(0.0105)		(0.0654)
Word J	-.0025	0.9975	n/a	-.0971***	0.9075	-17	.3164***	1.3722	72	-1.5892***
	(.0294)	(0.0293)		(.0164)	(0.0149)		(.0101)	(0.0139)		(0.0629)
WORDSUM[a]	-.0100			-.1800***			.3900***			5.7700***
	(.0200)			(.0100)			(.0100)			(0.0500)

Note: Estimates weighted for household size and oversampling of African-Americans. Standard errors in parentheses. Estimates for respondents age 24 and older; foreign-born respondents excluded after 1976. n/a = not calculated due to insignificance of trend coefficient.

[a] OLS regression estimates.

*p < .05. **p < .01. ***p < .001 (two-tailed test).

The linear term for survey year in Table 13.6 does not adequately represent age effects, however. Vocabulary knowledge typically grows from young adulthood through midlife, peaks around ages 50–60, and then gradually declines into older age. In other words, age has a curvilinear relationship with vocabulary knowledge (Alwin and McCammon 2001; Bowles et al. 2005). We examine aging effects on knowledge of the components of WORDSUM next.

Aging and Verbal Intelligence

Here we test for aging effects by predicting the probability of correctly identifying each word in WORDSUM, as well as the aggregate WORDSUM score, representing age differences using linear and quadratic terms. Although the functional form of this relationship might be specified more precisely (e.g., Goldberger 1964, pp. 214–15), this form fits the general pattern in the data quite well (see Alwin and McCammon 2001, p. S155). We centered age at 24 years due to our definition of the sample, so that intercepts in our regression models represent the predicted verbal knowledge levels for the youngest age group in our sample. Our models include two additional variables: birth cohort (represented by 85 dummy variables representing 86 cohort categories, with the 1947 cohort as the reference category)[14] and schooling (measured as number of years completed, centered at 12 years as above).

Table 13.7 assesses the magnitude of age effects on the total WORDSUM score by presenting the coefficients of determination (R^2) from regressions including effects of aging. The actual coefficients for two models, as well as those from logistic regressions examining specific words, are shown in Table 13.8.

Table 13.7. Coefficients of Determination (R^2) for Assessing Effects of Aging on the Total WORDSUM Score, Net of Schooling and Cohort Differences, 1974–2008 GSSs ($N \sim 20,500$).

Model	Terms included	R^2
1	Age, Age^2	.0080
2	Age, Age^2, Cohorts, Schooling	.2911
3	Age, Age^2, Schooling	.2763
4	Cohorts	.0202
5	Age, Age^2, Cohorts	.0240
6	Schooling	.2598
7	Schooling, Cohorts	.2895
Model comparison		**R^2 increment**
2 vs. 7		.0017***
3 vs. 6		.0168***
5 vs. 4		.0038***
7 vs. 6		.0301***

Note: Estimates weighted for household size and oversampling of African Americans. Standard errors in parentheses. Estimates for respondents age 24 and older; foreign-born respondents excluded after 1976.

***$p < .001$ (two-tailed test).

Table 13.8. Sample Estimates of the Item-Specific Curvilinear Effects of Aging, Controlling for the Effects of Cohort and Level of Schooling: Native-Born GSS Respondents, 24 Years of Age and Older in the 1974–2008 Surveys ($N \sim 20,500$)

	Model 1: Age only				Model 2: Age, cohort, and schooling					
	β_Age	β_Age^2	Intercept	Wald x^2 (2 df)	β_Age	β_Age^2	β_Educ	Intercept	Wald x^2 (87 df)	Test of aging effect[a]
Word A	.0039 (.0063)	-.0003** (.0001)	1.8177*** (.0735)	70.35***	.0057 (.0078)	-.0001 (.0001)	.1648*** (.0103)	1.7724*** (.1953)	498.01***	1.0550
Word B	.0470*** (.0113)	-.0009*** (.0001)	2.4985*** (.1320)	22.19***	.0456** (.0148)	-.0080*** (.0002)	.2610*** (.0200)	1.8737*** (.5008)	387.17***	6.4919**
Word C	.0355*** (.0056)	-.0058*** (.0001)	-1.2922*** (.0642)	40.07***	.0082 (.0068)	-.0003* (.0001)	.2392*** (.0103)	-1.1950*** (.1612)	727.78***	13.3252***
Word D	.0272** (.0104)	-.0006*** (.0001)	2.9617*** (.1275)	28.73***	.0394*** (.0135)	-.0005* (.0002)	.2912*** (.0184)	2.7204*** (.3763)	513.40***	8.3163***
Word E	.0410*** (.0059)	-.0007*** (.0001)	1.0573*** (.0622)	48.34***	.0588*** (.0077)	-.0005*** (.0001)	.3295*** (.0124)	.6210* (.2487)	1043.79***	96.7824***
Word F	.0202** (.0061)	-.0003* (.0001)	1.4385*** (.0705)	11.07**	.0194* (.0083)	-.0003 (.0001)	.3209*** (.0139)	1.4872*** (.3108)	696.44***	6.1206**
Word G	.0455*** (.0049)	-.0005*** (.0001)	-1.1005*** (.0558)	186.49***	.0204* (.0060)	-.0002* (.0001)	.2148*** (.0086)	-.8821*** (.1442)	946.23***	16.0580***
Word H	.0411*** (.0052)	-.0004*** (.0001)	-1.0980*** (.0583)	180.53***	.0169* (.0067)	-.0001 (.0001)	.2734*** (.0095)	-1.0169*** (.1576)	1156.26***	17.4752***
Word I	-.0063 (.0055)	-.00009 (.0001)	1.5164*** (.0642)	61.91***	-.0216** (.0068)	.0001 (.0001)	.1396*** (.0092)	1.4079*** (.2174)	418.30***	46.4620***
Word J	.0032 (.0052)	-.0001 (.0001)	-1.1065*** (.0588)	2.16	.0038 (.0065)	-.0001 (.0001)	.3216*** (.0102)	-1.7005*** (.1620)	1121.28***	5.1414**
WORDSUM[a]	.0374** (.0046)	-.0001*** (.0001)	5.8167*** (.0508)		.0213*** (.0051)	-.0004*** (.0001)	.3842*** (.0063)	5.6569*** (.1594)		

Note: Estimates are weighted. Foreign-born respondents were included prior to 1978 because this question was not asked in 1974 or 1976. Standard errors in parentheses.

[a]Log likelihood test for the difference between model 2 and a model that excludes Age and Age².

*p < .05. **p < .01. ***p < .001.

Table 13.7 displays R^2 values for seven regressions predicting the total WORDSUM score.[15] Model 1 assesses the gross association between age and vocabulary knowledge by predicting WORDSUM from Age and Age^2 only. Model 2 adds the set of 85 dummy variables for cohort and centered years of schooling, while model 3 includes Age, Age^2, and schooling, but not the dummy variables representing cohort differences. Model 4 contains *only* the dummy variables for cohort, and model 5 age and cohort differences, but not schooling. The sixth model represents effects of schooling alone, while the last predicts WORDSUM from cohort and schooling, but not the terms for aging. We evaluate the relative power of aging, cohort, and schooling for predicting vocabulary knowledge by comparing R^2 values for selected pairs of these models; we later display selected regression coefficients for the first and second models both numerically (Table 13.8) and graphically (Figures 13.3 and 13.4).

The results in Table 13.7 estimate aging effects on the total WORDSUM score. They show, first, that by itself the quadratic age function (i.e., the Age and Age^2 terms) accounts for very little variance in the total WORDSUM score—see the R^2 value of less than .01 in model 1. This modest explanatory power is reduced by half—to less than half of 1% of the variance—after controlling for cohort differences (see the increment to R^2 for comparing models 4 and 5). If one controls for *both* cohort differences and schooling, Age and Age^2 explain less than two-tenths of 1% of the variance of WORDSUM (see the increment to R^2 for comparing models 2 and 7). In other words, given schooling, *within-cohort* processes of aging account for virtually none of the variance in vocabulary knowledge—a finding completely consistent with existing literature on the role of aging in vocabulary knowledge (see, e.g., Verhaeghen 2003).

By contrast, as one would expect, level of schooling is the most powerful predictor of aggregate WORDSUM scores. On its own, schooling accounts for some 26% of the variance in WORDSUM (see model 6). We do not dwell on this except to underscore the fact that differences in schooling levels between age groups account for about one-half of the gross association between vocabulary knowledge and Age and Age^2. When one further takes cohort differences into account, the contribution of Age and Age^2 to variation in the aggregate WORDSUM score virtually vanishes. This conclusion about the role of age-related factors could, of course, differ across the individual words that comprise WORDSUM, which we examine below.

Before assessing the contributions of Age and Age^2 on a word-specific basis, we note that cohort differences in the total WORDSUM score appear substantially greater than differences related to aging (compare, e.g., the R^2 values for models 1 and 4). Indeed, because schooling serves to suppress cohort differences (those born more recently generally have higher schooling), cohort differences net of schooling are even greater—accounting for about 3% of the variance (see the increment to R^2 for comparing models 6 and 7).

For each word in WORDSUM, Table 13.8 presents estimates of logistic regression models that follow the first and second specifications in Table 13.7.

As well, for comparison purposes we report estimates under both models for the total WORDSUM score. The first model, including Age and Age^2, assesses the gross association between aging and vocabulary knowledge. The second one includes the two terms in aging, the set of 85 dummy variables representing cohort differences, and centered years of schooling, though Table 13.8 does not report the coefficients for the 85 dummy variables for cohort.

We focus here on (1) the importance of Age and Age^2 in predicting correct identification of the meaning of words comprising WORDSUM; (2) differences in the size and direction of the Age and Age^2 coefficients across items, particularly any systematic differences having to do with differences in item difficulty; and (3) the relative importance of these patterns after controlling for cohort and schooling differences. Recall that Bowles et al. (2005) suggested that aging effects vary by word difficulty—specifically, that "basic vocabulary knowledge" (e.g., the easiest WORDSUM items) is highest around age 30, thereafter falling systematically with age, whereas "advanced vocabulary knowledge" (e.g., the difficult WORDSUM items) varies little between the ages of 35 and 70. We further noted that Bowles et al. (2005, p. P239) proposed that finding such an interaction between item difficulty and aging effects could address the potential artifactuality of their assertion that two difficulty-related factors (one for the easy items, the other for the difficult ones) underlie the WORDSUM score. They admitted that their analysis may confuse item difficulty with substantive dimensions of vocabulary knowledge but proposed that a conclusion of bidimensionality might be justified if external criterion variables such as age have different relationships with the factors (Bowles et al. 2005, p. P239).

The results in Table 13.8 provide virtually no support for the hypothesis that the association between age and vocabulary knowledge differs by word difficulty. Estimates for model 2 show, for all words except word I, that knowledge either rises until at least middle age or bears little relationship to age at all. Figure 13.3 depicts the estimated age-related patterns for each word under this model, showing how the predicted probability of correctly answering a word varies with age, adjusted for schooling and cohort differences.[16] Only 2 words among the 10—words C and I—show any systematic decline with age. The proportion correctly identifying word C begins to fall after age 30, while that correctly answering word I falls steadily with age. Word C is relatively difficult, while word I is comparatively easy. Four other words (A, B, G, and J) show very slight declines in old age; two of these are easy and two are difficult. We find no evidence here of the systematic relationship between age effects and word difficulty hypothesized by Bowles et al. (2005).

With the exception of words I and C, there is hardly any support here for an age-related decline in vocabulary knowledge. Indeed, knowledge of a significant minority of the words (E, G, and H) continues to grow even into old age. The relationship of age to knowledge is very flat for the remaining items, though a few do show very slight declines in old age. Even these patterns

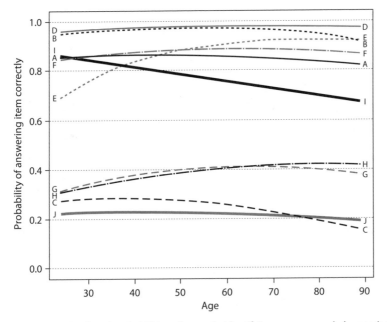

Figure 13.3. Predicted probabilities of correctly identifying WORDSUM words, by age (adjusted for cohort and schooling), under model 2, Table 13.8.

are absolutely unrelated to item difficulty, however. Moreover, most findings reported for model 2 also apply to the gross age patterns (not adjusted for schooling or cohort differences) estimated under model 1 in Table 13.8, leading us to further question the Bowles et al. (2005) hypothesis.

Cohort Differences in Patterns of Verbal Knowledge

This final section analyzes cohort differences in knowledge of the GSS words, controlling for age and schooling. We rely on the coefficients for cohort dummy variables estimated under model 2 of Table 13.7 for the total WORD-SUM score, adjusting for age and schooling. The patterns in these results are rather surprising if one assumes the progress model is correct: after adjusting for age and schooling levels, composite WORDSUM scores are systematically higher for the *earlier-born* cohorts. The dashed line in Figure 13.4 presents these results, with two additional patterns superimposed. The dotted line plots the mean WORDSUM scores for birth cohorts ranging from before the 1900s to the late 1970s, without controlling for age and schooling. The solid line represents the theoretical expectations of the progress model, in which cohorts systematically rise in cognitive resources over time.

The results displayed in Figure 13.4 highlight the departure of the GSS results from those theoretically anticipated under the theoretical progress model. The decline in vocabulary test scores from the 1945 cohort onward

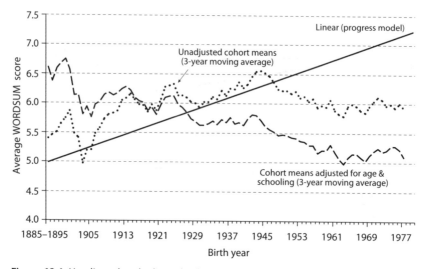

Figure 13.4. Unadjusted and adjusted cohort means on the WORDSUM score. *Source:* 1974–2008 GSSs; estimates based on model 2, Table 13.7.

is particularly notable. These cohort patterns here are, however, completely consistent with the cohort interpretation given for the "verbal meaning" score in Schaie's (2005) analyses. Possible explanations for the differences in adjusted cohort means seen in Figure 13.4 include (1) historical effects on socialization, learning, or cognitive development and/or (2) mortality selection favoring the earlier born cohorts, such that the most cognitively fit persons in earlier-born cohorts are differentially likely to survive and have a comparative advantage relative to those in later-born cohorts. Clearly more than one explanation may account for the trends in Figure 13.4; quite possibly, different explanations for cohort disparities apply at different points. For example, the school and extracurricular experiences of the 1960s birth cohorts may have systematically lowered their vocabulary knowledge, but this would not explain the relatively higher scores in the earliest-born cohorts. Compositional phenomena linked to mortality selection discussed at length elsewhere (Alwin, McCammon, Wray, and Rodgers 2008) are possible bases for the latter.

This chapter does not attempt a thorough interpretation of these cohort differences, but we note that arguments about cohort experiences advanced to account for other intercohort declines, for example, the 1960s–1970s fall in test scores, may also apply to understanding these patterns (see Alwin 1991; Alwin and McCammon 2001). Jencks (1979, p. 13), for example, suggested that schools and parents failed to instill proper academic values in children during this period, concluding that students "lost respect for the values of reason." Others proposed different mechanisms generally related to the same theme—

that children of the 1960s and 1970s were exposed to a different climate for learning—with less motivation and fewer hours spent in homework (Winter 1977; Menard 1988), increased time spent watching television, and less reading (Wirtz and Howe 1977; Schramm 1977; Glenn 1994, 1999; Morgan 1986). Some also suggested that drug and alcohol use by high school students may have contributed to test score declines during the 1960s and 1970s, but few suggest this as a principal explanation (Wirtz and Howe 1977). Finally, educational researchers offered other explanations for test score declines involving school composition and curriculum—one involving the "dumbing down" of learning materials in schools, another an overall tendency toward declining complexity in schooling content (e.g., Chall and Conard 1991; Hayes, Wolfer, and Wolfe 1996; Stedman 1996).

Conclusions

This chapter investigated population trends in the verbal intelligence in the United States using GSS data on verbal knowledge from 18 national surveys that span nearly 35 years (from 1974 to 2008). We placed these findings in context and evaluated the psychometric properties of the GSS vocabulary items by analyzing a small 1941 Gallup survey, which administered the items some 30 years prior to the GSS. We focused on over-time trends in verbal intelligence (and their components) both within the GSS time frame and between 1941 and the GSS era.

We focused on trends in identifying individual words because of concerns raised about the WORDSUM measure's dimensionality, but also examined change in the total WORDSUM score itself. We assessed several interpretations advanced for patterns observed in the GSS data. Our most affirmative conclusion is that intercohort variation proved to be strong and consistent at the word-specific level. Our analyses generally indicate that net of schooling, verbal knowledge is lower among more recently born cohorts, though some exceptions exist. We found little or no evidence consistent with claims that these intercohort trends reflect increased difficulty of the words comprising WORDSUM, or that they are due to cohort aging.

Schaie's work on cohort effects, the best longitudinal research on cognitive abilities, generally suggests the opposite conclusion, that is, that levels of cognitive performance are higher among more recent birth cohorts observed at the same age as older ones. This suggests that the GSS WORDSUM results require some other explanation (see esp. Schaie 2005, 2008; and Schaie et al. 2005). Several observations about the results of Schaie and his colleagues should be made before accepting such findings uncritically, however. First, although the available trends exhibit a great deal of uniformity across measures, supporting the conclusion that intercohort trends involve systematic and substantial positive advances, some inconsistencies are evident. Indeed, some trends that are downward, and others change direction at points along the birth cohort continuum. Cohort differences for verbal ability show inter-cohort gains from 1889 to 1952, but those scores decline following the 1952 birth cohort (see Schaie et al. 2005, p. 50). Other examples include a decline in number fluency beginning with the 1910 cohort. Second, although most attention to "massive IQ gains" has focused on the post–World War II co-horts, Schaie and colleagues presented data revealing an intercohort pattern that extends back to birth cohorts of the early 1900s, arguing that trends are generally positive over the past century (Schaie et al. 2005). They argue that one of the major reasons for this is that sociocultural factors were working to ensure that advances in educational attainment and shifts in the occupational structure resulted in protective factors, what is often called *cognitive reserve*, that compensate for the cognitive health risks linked to neurobiological dis-eases that accompany longevity (Stern 2007).

Consistent with some of Schaie's findings, we observe that test scores have not always risen, nor have they done so in all domains. The analyses in this chapter, responding in part to the need for information about verbal abil-ity based on national probability samples, show that systematic education-adjusted cohort differences in the GSS vocabulary test score began with those born after 1946. We suggested that these differences reflected the same social processes responsible for the test score declines of the 1960s and 1970s. An ar-gument that cohort differences in levels of schooling might account for these differences in cognitive test performance does not seem applicable to the present case because the cognitive performance data here conform to a pat-tern in which earlier-born cohorts have *higher* performance than later-born ones. These differences are accentuated rather than reduced when intercohort differences in the schooling level are controlled. Overall, the results point to the conclusion that despite their higher levels of schooling, post–World War II cohorts have scored systematically lower on cognitive tests compared to those born earlier. Our recent research based on Health and Retirement Study data (see Alwin et al. 2008) also identified this pattern. Though these results are puzzling, and even potentially alarming, hopefully they will chal-lenge researchers to further explore and understand the patterns observed here.

While virtually all of our analyses revealed evidence of intercohort vari-ation at the item-specific level, they yielded little or no indication of sub-stantial intracohort changes in the WORDSUM items, due either to temporal influences affecting the entire U.S. adult population or to effects of cognitive aging. Moreover, we addressed the assertion put forward in recent years that declining American vocabulary knowledge reflects "word obsolescence"—reduced familiarity with particular words due to changing fashions within the American lexicon (e.g., Hauser and Huang 1997, p. 345). Rather than the widespread increase in difficulty suggested by this line of argument, we found a general rise in correct identification of WORDSUM words over time.

Comparisons between the most recent data and earlier results from the 1941 Gallup survey reinforced these broad trends toward decreasing item difficulty. They also revealed an evident bifurcation: relatively easy words in 1941 became easier while difficult ones grew more difficult.

Finally, this chapter's analyses do not support the hypothesis that cognitive aging accounts for intracohort differences in verbal knowledge. This finding is not new because most available evidence has long suggested that crystallized abilities such as vocabulary knowledge decline little if at all in functional capacities until people reach quite advanced ages. For example, Alwin and McCammon (2001) previously documented this finding using the GSS WORDSUM score. What is new here is that we demonstrate the applicability of this finding at the item-specific level. Despite some puzzling exceptions, the general pattern of our results shows that vocabulary knowledge declines little with age: knowledge of most words in WORDSUM varies little over the life span, rises relatively steadily with age, or rises steadily before declining among the very oldest adults. These age-related patterns are unrelated to item difficulty, contrary to the hypothesis proposed by Bowles et al. (2005). Future research should further examine the structure of the WORDSUM score and disentangle the factors contributing to changing verbal ability in populations of interest, over both biographical and historical time.

Notes

This research was supported in part by a grant from the National Institute on Aging (R01-AG021203-06) and funds from the McCourtney endowment, College of the Liberal Arts, Pennsylvania State University. The authors acknowledge the assistance of Alyson Otto.

1. This chapter uses the term "difficulty" in two related but distinct ways. First, we describe words as "easy" or "hard" according to the proportion of a sample that correctly identifies a word's meaning. The second usage refers to the difficulty parameter in item response theory (IRT), the theoretical point along a latent "ability" continuum at which half of a population correctly identifies the meaning of an item. We rely on the context of the discussion to distinguish the concept to which our usage of "difficulty" refers.

2. We follow convention in distinguishing between *fluid* and *crystallized* abilities. Fluid abilities refer to capacities for insight into complex relations independent of the sensory or cultural area involved in a test, while crystallized ones refer to capacities that result from applying fluid abilities in particular higher-level cultural domains, for example, educational experiences (see Cattell 1971).

3. Cohort effects are conceptually distinct from cohort replacement. In the latter, members of later-born cohorts (e.g., younger citizens) replace members of early-born cohorts (e.g., older citizens) as they exit society. The cohort replacement component of aggregate change reflects the simultaneous operation of cohort and aging "effects." Cohort effects refer to specific events or environmental factors that occur to members of the same cohort at a particularly important developmental period.

4. We employ the concept of "verbal intelligence" to interpret this measure, following Thorndike's (1942, p. 128) early work. To some, that interpretation goes beyond WORDSUM's actual content, which is clearly "vocabulary knowledge." One resolution of the terminological debate is that WORDSUM measures one indicator of verbal intelligence, namely vocabulary knowledge, which—along with other indicators—tells something about a population's level of verbal intelligence.

5. See note 9.

6. We know of at least two additional sources that collected data on the Thorndike measures. Miner's (1957) Ph.D. dissertation at Princeton University used a Gallup survey conducted in December 1953 and January 1954, which is directly comparable to a subset of the data obtained in the 1941 Gallup survey. While these data were available to Miner, to our knowledge they no longer exist. Second, a NORC survey conducted in 1967 included the 10 GSS items, plus the 10 other items in Form A of the Thorndike–Gallup data. The 1967 NORC survey interviewed only people born after 1920, that is, who were then roughly age 45 or over (Tom W. Smith, personal correspondence, January 4, 1991), so we do not examine the 1967 NORC data here.

7. Data exist on the verbal measure in 1974, 1976, 1978, 1982, 1984, 1987, 1988, 1989, 1990, 1991, 1993, 1994, 1996, 1998, 2000, 2004, 2006, and 2008.

8. No questions about nativity were asked in the 1941 Gallup survey or in the GSS prior to 1978, so analyses using these surveys do not exclude foreign-born respondents.

9. We identify the individual items in the WORDSUM score using the mnemonics WORDA, WORDB, . . . WORDJ in keeping with the GSS's request that we not publicize the actual words. Miner (1957, p. 53) gives representative content from the Thorndike (1942) vocabulary test. For further information about the content of the WORDSUM score and the meaning of its words, contact Tom W. Smith, Director of the General Social Survey, NORC, Chicago, Illinois.

10. Because we are unable to identify foreign-born respondents in the 1974 and 1976 GSSs, we include foreign-born cases for those years.

11. We also explored the item properties of the words using the GSS data. We do not present these estimates here, given the challenges in "equating" tests across different populations. The important issue of whether item properties have changed over time is beyond the scope of this chapter.

12. We also estimated trends using a set of dummy variables to represent survey year, permitting nonlinear changes in the proportion correct for words (results not shown here), but these did not detect any substantively significant departures from linearity.

13. We estimate these linear decompositions using logistic regressions (see Brooks 2000) rather than the ordinary least squares (OLS) techniques used by Firebaugh (1989) because our dependent variables are dichotomous.

14. Because of small sample sizes in some earlier- and later-born cohorts, we combined persons born in 1885–1895, 1896–1897, 1898–1899, and 1981–1984. Cohorts from 1900 to 1980 consist of respondents born in that particular year.

15. The coefficient estimates themselves are available from the authors on request.

16. Probabilities graphed in Figure 13.3 were calculated by setting schooling and cohort dummy variables at their mean levels.

References

Alwin, Duane F. 1991. "Family of Origin and Cohort Differences in Verbal Ability." *American Sociological Review* 56:625–38.

———. 2008. "Social Structure and Cognitive Aging." In *Handbook of Cognitive Aging: Interdisciplinary Perspectives*, edited by Scott M. Hofer and Duane F. Alwin, 418–44. Thousand Oaks, CA: Sage.

———. 2009a. "History, Cohorts, and Patterns of Cognitive Ageing." In *Aging and Cognition: Research Methodologies and Empirical Advances*, edited by Hayden B. Bosworth and Christopher Hertzog, 9–38. Washington, DC: American Psychological Association.

———. 2009b. "Social Structure, Cognition, and Ageing." In *International Handbook of Social Gerontology*, edited by Dale Dannefer and Chris Phillipson, 265–79. London: Sage.

Alwin, Duane F., and Scott M. Hofer. 2008. "Opportunities and Challenges for Interdisciplinary Research." In *Handbook of Cognitive Aging: Interdisciplinary Perspectives*, edited by Scott M. Hofer and Duane F. Alwin, 2–31. Thousand Oaks, CA: Sage.

Alwin, Duane F., and Ryan J. McCammon. 1999. "Aging vs. Cohort Interpretations of Inter-cohort Differences in GSS Verbal Scores." *American Sociological Review* 64:272–86.

———. 2001. "Aging, Cohorts, and Verbal Ability." *Journal of Gerontology: Social Sciences* 56B:S151–61.

Alwin, Duane F., Ryan J. McCammon, Linda A. Wray, and Willard L. Rodgers. 2008. "Population Processes and Cognitive Aging." In *Handbook of Cognitive Aging: Interdisciplinary Perspectives*, edited by Scott M. Hofer and Duane F. Alwin, 69–89. Thousand Oaks, CA: Sage.

Austad, Steven N. 1997. *Why We Age—What Science Is Discovering about the Body's Journey through Life.* New York: John Wiley.

Bailey, Kent G., and Edward J. Federman. 1979. "Factor Analysis of Breadth and Depth Dimensions on Wechsler's Similarities and Vocabulary Subscales." *Journal of Clinical Psychology* 35:341–45.

Baltes, Paul B. 1997. "On the Incomplete Architecture of Human Ontogeny." *American Psychologist* 52:366–80.

Beck, Niels C., David Tucker, Robert Frank, Jerry Parker, Rebecca Lake, Susan Thomas, Wemara Lichty, Ellen Horwitz, Bruce Horwitz, and Frank Merritt. 1989. "The Latent Factor Structure of the WAIS-R: A Factor Analysis of Individual Item Responses." *Journal of Clinical Psychology* 45:281–93.

Blake, Judith. 1989. *Family Size and Achievement.* Berkeley: University of California Press.

Bowles, Ryan P., Kevin J. Grimm, and John J. McArdle. 2005. "A Structural Factor Analysis of Vocabulary Knowledge and Relations to Age." *Journal of Gerontology: Psychological Sciences* 60B:P234–41.

Brooks, Clem. 2000. "Civil Rights Liberalism and the Suppression of a Republican Political Realignment in the United States, 1972–1996." *American Sociological Review* 65:483–505.

Cattell, Raymond B. 1971. *Abilities: Their Structure, Growth and Action*. Boston: Houghton Mifflin.

Chall, Jeanne S., and Sue S. Conard. 1991. *Should Textbooks Challenge Students? The Case for Easier or Harder Books*. New York: Teachers College Press.

Davis, James A., Tom W. Smith, and Peter V. Marsden. 2008. *General Social Surveys, 1972–2008: Cumulative Codebook* [Machine-readable data file]. Chicago: NORC (producer). Storrs, CT: Roper Center for Public Opinion Research, University of Connecticut (distributor).

Embretson, Susan E., and Steven P. Reise. 2000. *Item Response Theory for Psychologists*. Mahwah, NJ: Lawrence Erlbaum.

Firebaugh, Glenn. 1989. "Methods for Estimating Cohort Replacement Effects." *Sociological Methodology* 19:243–62.

———. 1992. "Where Does Social Change Come From? Estimating the Relative Contributions of Individual Change and Population Turnover." *Population Research and Policy Review* 11:1–20.

Flynn, James R. 1984. "The Mean IQ of Americans: Massive Gains." *Psychological Bulletin* 95:29–51.

———. 1987. "Massive IQ Gains in 14 Nations: What IQ Tests Really Measure." *Psychological Bulletin* 101:171–91.

———. 1998. "IQ Gains over Time: Toward Finding the Causes." In *The Rising Curve: Long-Term Gains in IQ and Related Measures*, edited by Ulric Neisser, 25–66. Washington, DC: American Psychological Association.

———. 1999. "Searching for Justice: The Discovery of IQ Gains over Time." *American Psychologist* 54:5–20.

Glenn, Norval D. 1994. "Television Watching, Newspaper Reading, and Cohort Differences in Verbal Ability." *Sociology of Education* 67:216–30.

———. 1999. "Further Discussion of the Evidence for an Inter-cohort Decline in Education-Adjusted Vocabulary." *American Sociological Review* 64:267–71.

Goldberger, Arthur S. 1964. *Econometric Theory*. New York: John Wiley.

Gustafsson, Jan-Eric, and Lena M. Holmberg. 1992. "Psychometric Properties of Vocabulary Test Items as a Function of Word Characteristics." *Scandinavian Journal of Educational Research* 36:191–210.

Hauser, Robert M., and Min-Hsiung Huang. 1997. "Verbal Ability and Socioeconomic Success: A Trend Analysis." *Social Science Research* 26:331–76.

Hayes, Donald, Loreen Wolfer, and Michael Wolfe. 1996. "Textbook Simplification and Its Relation to the Decline in SAT-Verbal Scores." *American Educational Research Journal* 33:489–508.

Hofer, Scott M., and Duane F. Alwin, eds. 2008. *Handbook of Cognitive Aging: Interdisciplinary Perspectives*. Thousand Oaks, CA: Sage.

Hosmer, David W., and Stanley Lemeshow. 2000. *Applied Logistic Regression*. 2nd ed. New York: John Wiley.

Jencks, Christopher. 1979. "Why Students Aren't Learning." *The Center Magazine* July/August:12–14.

Kučera, Henry, and W. Nelson Francis. 1967. *Computational Analysis of Present-Day American English*. Providence, RI: Brown University Press.

Malhotra, Neil, Jon A. Krosnick, and Edward Haertel. 2007. "The Psychometric Properties of the GSS WORDSUM Vocabulary Test." GSS Methodological Report 111, NORC, Chicago.

McDonald, Roderick P. 1981. "The Dimensionality of Tests and Items." *British Journal of Mathematical and Statistical Psychology* 34:100–117.

McDonald, Roderick P., and K. S. Ahlawat. 1974. "Difficulty Factors in Binary Data." *British Journal of Mathematical and Statistical Psychology* 27:82–99.

Menard, Scott. 1988. "Going Down, Going Up: Explaining the Turnaround in SAT Scores." *Youth and Society* 20:3–28.

Miner, John B. 1957. *Intelligence in the United States*. New York: Springer.

Morgan, Michael. 1986. "Television and Adults' Verbal Intelligence." *Journalism Quarterly* 63:537–41.

Muthén, Linda K., and Bengt O. Muthén. 2004. *Mplus: The Comprehensive Modeling Program for Applied Researchers. User's guide*. Version 3.1. Los Angeles: Muthén and Muthén.

Neisser, Ulric. 1997. "Rising Scores on Intelligence Tests." *American Scientist* 85:440–47.

———. 1998. *The Rising Curve: Long Term Gains in IQ and Related Measures*. Washington, DC: American Psychological Association.

Park, Denise C., Anderson D. Smith, Gary Lautenschlager, Julie L. Earles, David Frieske, Melissa Zwahr, and Christine L. Gaines. 1996. "Mediators of Long Term Memory Performance across the Life Span." *Psychology of Aging* 11:621–37.

Ryder, Norman B. 1965. "The Cohort as a Concept in the Study of Social Change." *American Sociological Review* 30:843–61.

Schaie, K. Warner. 2005. *Developmental Influences on Adult Intelligence: The Seattle Longitudinal Study*. Oxford: Oxford University Press.

———. 2008. "Historical Patterns and Processes of Cognitive Aging." In *Handbook of Cognitive Aging: Interdisciplinary Perspectives*, edited by Scott M. Hofer and Duane F. Alwin, 368–83. Thousand Oaks, CA: Sage.

Schaie, K. Warner, Sherry L. Willis, and Sara Pennak. 2005. "A Historical Framework for Cohort Differences in Intelligence." *Research in Human Development* 2:43–67.

Schramm, Walter. 1977. *Television and the Test Scores*. Princeton, NJ: College Entrance Examination Board.

Stedman, Lawrence C. 1996. "An Assessment of Literacy Trends, Past and Present." *Research in the Teaching of English* 30:283–302.

Stern, Yaakov, ed. 2007. *Cognitive Reserve: Theory and Applications*. New York: Taylor and Francis.

Thorndike, Robert L. 1921. *The Teacher's Word Book*. New York: Teachers College, Columbia University.

———. 1931. *The Teacher's Word Book of the Twenty Thousand Words Found Most Frequently and Widely in General Reading for Children and Young People*. New York: Teachers College, Columbia University.

———. 1942. "Two Screening Tests of Verbal Intelligence." *Journal of Applied Psychology* 26:128–35.

Thorndike, Robert L., and George H. Gallup. 1944. "Verbal Intelligence of the American Adult." *Journal of General Psychology* 30:75–85.

Thorndike, Robert L., and Irving Lorge. 1944. *The Teacher's Word Book of 30,000 Words*. New York: Teacher's College, Columbia University.

Verhaeghen, Paul. 2003. "Aging and Vocabulary Score: A Meta-Analysis." *Psychology and Aging* 18:332–39.

Wilson, James, and Walter Gove. 1999. "The Inter-cohort Decline in Verbal Ability: Does It Exist?" *American Sociological Review* 64:253–66.

Winter, David G. 1977. *Motivational Factors in the SAT Score Decline.* Princeton, NJ: College Entrance Examination Board.

Wirtz, Willard, and Harold Howe II (Committee Chairs). 1977. *On Further Examination: Report of the Advisory Panel on the Scholastic Aptitude Test Score Decline.* New York: College Entrance Examination Board.

Wolfle, Lee M. 1980. "The Enduring Effects of Education on Verbal Skills." *Sociology of Education* 53:104–14.

Yang, Yang, and Kenneth C. Land. 2006. "A Mixed Models Approach to the Age-Period-Cohort Analysis of Repeated Cross-Section Surveys, with an Application to Data on Trends in Verbal Test Scores." *Sociological Methodology* 36:75–97.

———. 2008. "Age-Period-Cohort Analysis of Repeated Cross-Section Surveys: Fixed or Random Effects?" *Sociological Methods and Research* 36:297–326.

Yang, Yang, Sam Schulhofer-Wohl, Wenjiang J. Fu, and Kenneth C. Land. 2008. "The Intrinsic Estimator for Age-Period-Cohort Analysis: What It Is and How to Use It." *American Journal of Sociology* 113:1697–1736.

Appendix

The General Social Survey Project

Peter V. Marsden and Tom W. Smith

The studies of U.S. social trends in this book all draw on data assembled by the General Social Survey (GSS) project, which began in 1972. This appendix presents a general overview of the project, its research methods, and its content, omitting many nuances. Davis and Smith (1992) provide a more extended guide to the GSS through 1990. Individual chapters of this book provide details of special importance to their analyses, such as question wording for key items.

The GSS is the principal data collection activity of the National Data Program for the Social Sciences (NDPSS). Primary objectives of NDPSS include (1) assembling high-quality, nationally representative survey data on societal trends in the United States, (2) developing databases permitting comparisons of the United States to other societies, and (3) making these data easily accessible to scholars, students, and the public with minimal delay. The GSS pursues its first objective through regular measurement of a "replicating core" set of survey questions. It addresses the second via its participation in the International Social Survey Programme (ISSP). To meet the third, NDPSS disseminates data via numerous channels, notably a dedicated website (http://www .norc.org/GSS+Website/). As of mid-2011, more than 17,000 books, articles, chapters, and other research publications had drawn on GSS data.

The National Science Foundation provides ongoing core financial support for NDPSS. Numerous other agencies and foundations also support the project, primarily through funding innovative modules on particular topics that ordinarily appear in only one GSS. NORC at the University of Chicago conducts GSS sampling, fieldwork, and data preparation.

James A. Davis originated the GSS concept and was a principal investigator of the project from 1972 until 2009, at which point he became its senior advisor. As the project continued and grew, the set of principal investigators expanded to include Tom W. Smith (in 1980), Peter V. Marsden (in 1997), and Michael Hout (in 2009). A Board of Overseers of outstanding scholars in the social sciences also guides the GSS.[1]

Study Design

The GSS is designed principally as a repeated cross-sectional survey that draws a new random sample of respondents each time it is conducted. Such a design is optimal for measuring aggregate change within a population. From 1972 until 1993, GSSs were conducted almost annually. Beginning in 1994, GSSs have been done biennially, with larger samples.[2]

A repeated cross-sectional design does not measure change at the level of individuals, however. Beginning in 2006, the GSS added a panel component to its basic design. It now reinterviews each year's respondents in each of the two subsequent GSSs, producing three-wave, two-year-interval panels that can distinguish true change and unreliability. The first GSS panel covers the period 2006–2010, the next will cover 2008–2012, and so on. Because data collection for the 2006–2010 panel was not complete when chapters in this book were prepared, none of them makes use of the panel feature. Some chapters include data from the new cross-sectional sample drawn in 2008 (the baseline measurement for the 2008–2012 panel), but not data from the 2008 reinterviews of respondents first sampled and interviewed in 2006.[3]

Target Population

The GSS targets the adult (age 18 and older) household population of the United States. Adults living outside of households—in dormitories, military quarters, nursing homes, prisons, or other group quarters—are not represented by the survey. As of 2000, the U.S. Census Bureau reported that about 96.4% of U.S. adults reside in households.[4]

Until 2006, only English-speaking adults were part of the GSS target population. In the mid-1980s, more than 98% of the adult household population was English speaking. As of 2007, the U.S. Census Bureau estimated that 1.5% of U.S. adults did not speak English "at all," while an additional 3.1% of adults spoke English "not well."[5] Beginning in 2006, the GSS expanded its target population to include Spanish-speaking adults.[6] Recent U.S. Census Bureau estimates for 2007 indicate that 82.3% of U.S. residents age five or older who do not speak English at all are Spanish speaking and that 70.4% of U.S. residents age 5 and over who speak English "not well" are Spanish speaking (Shin and Kominski 2010). Adults who do not speak English or (after 2004) Spanish are not represented by the survey.

Sampling Methods

For each GSS, NORC draws a nationally representative sample of U.S. households. Details of its sampling methods have changed somewhat over time, but they always begin by sampling successively smaller geographic areas in several stages. Such multistage designs are commonly employed when drawing cluster samples for large-scale studies that rely on in-person interviews for data collection. Early GSSs (1972–1974) employed quota sampling (with quotas for sex, age, and employment status) at the block level. GSSs beginning in 1975 shifted to a full probability design, enumerating and then sampling households within blocks. Until 2002, households within blocks were listed via traditional field-listing techniques. Since 2004, much household listing has relied on U.S. Postal Service Delivery Sequence Files.[7] One adult per sampled household is randomly selected as the interviewee from a list of eligible adults within that household.

Beginning in 2004, the GSS added a "two-phase" or "subsampling of non-respondents" component to its sampling design. This maintains a nationally representative sample while limiting the high field costs incurred in pursuing difficult-to-interview cases at the end of the survey's field period (see Hansen and Hurwitz 1946). During the first phase, interviewers attempt to secure interviews with respondents from all sampled households. Nonrespondents at the end of phase 1 are then randomly subsampled: no further attempts are made to contact some, while intensive efforts are made to complete interviews with others. Such subsampling potentially reduces both nonresponse error and nonresponse bias.[8]

Weights

The basic GSS sampling design assigns equal probabilities of selection to all eligible U.S. households, so at the household level (for measures of household characteristics such as the number of resident adults or whether the housing unit is rented or owned) the sample is "self-weighting." Several features of the sample design can require that weights be used, however.

First, most analyses of GSS data seek to estimate characteristics of the adult population, not characteristics of the population of households. Since it includes only one adult per household, the GSS sample underrepresents adults living in larger households. Weighting observations proportionally to the number of adults residing in a household can adjust for this. Second, the subsampling-of-nonrespondents feature of post-2002 GSS samples means that they include a disproportionate number of first-phase respondents, so weights based on sampling phase are necessary. Third, the 1982 and 1987 GSSs included supplementary oversamples of black adults to allow improved estimates for this subgroup, and hence observations should be weighted accordingly when calculating estimates for the adult population in those years.[9]

Interview Mode and Field Methods

After households are sampled, interviewers contact them in person. They begin by enumerating the composition of the household and determining which household members are within the target population and therefore eligible as GSS respondents. One eligible adult is then randomly chosen as the designated interviewee for that household.

The in-person interview is the preferred data collection mode for the GSS, and the vast majority of GSS data are collected via personal interviews. Until the 2000 GSS, interviewers used traditional paper-and-pencil techniques relying on printed questionnaires. Beginning in 2002, interviewers used computer-assisted personal interview (CAPI) techniques; physical questionnaires no longer exist, though visual aids such as show cards are still printed and used. Most questions are administered by the interviewer, but some data—notably questions about sexual behavior and (in some years) ISSP modules—are collected using self-administered instruments. In some instances when it proves impossible to arrange an in-person interview, GSS interviews are conducted by telephone.

The GSS and NORC assign high priority to quality control and pursue it in several ways. Interviewers are extensively trained on topics including their role and responsibilities, the importance of confidentiality and data security, methods of household listing and respondent selection, approaches to obtaining respondent cooperation, asking questions and recording answers, and neutral probing of answers. They also undergo project-specific training about the GSS per se. Supervisors monitor the work of interviewers closely and regularly. After interviewers submit data, NORC recontacts 20% of respondents to verify that interviews took place.

Response Rates

As part of its emphasis on data quality, the GSS devotes considerable effort to maintaining representativeness by securing the cooperation of respondents at high rates. To do so, NORC uses tactics including highly experienced interviewers, multiple attempts to contact respondents (at different times of day), offers to conduct interviews in locations other than the respondent's household, and (sometimes) offers of cash or noncash incentives. Highly skilled "converter" interviewers are employed in attempts to secure interviews with reluctant respondents. In the subsampling-of-nonrespondents design introduced beginning in 2004, the reduced interviewing staff in the second phase is composed of those interviewers who proved to be most productive during the first phase.

Prior to 2000, the GSS response rate—that is, the percentage of eligible respondents who completed interviews—varied around 75–77%, with a high of 82.4% in 1993 and a low of 73.5% in 1978. Since 2000, response rates have fallen somewhat, averaging just over 70%.[10] Nonetheless, GSS response rates remain very high by standards of the survey industry (Dixon and Tucker 2010).

Data Preparation, Coding, and Postfield Processing

Data from completed interviews are promptly and carefully edited for completeness, clarity, and proper use of coding conventions. This includes, for example, consistency checks and checks for missing data on crucial questions, especially basic demographic items. Codes to identify cases with missing data are also supplied at this stage.

The GSS distinguishes three standard types of missing data: "don't know," for answers indicating that the respondent is uncertain or ambivalent; "no answer," for cases in which data are unavailable as a result of interviewer error or respondent refusal to answer;[11] and "not applicable," for respondents who were intentionally not asked a question for one reason or another. A question may be "not applicable" because the respondent is screened out (e.g., never-married respondents are not asked about marital happiness), because he or she was not randomly designated to answer a particular ballot or experimental form, or because a question (e.g., from a one-time topical or cross-national module) was not part of the GSS in the year when the respondent was sampled.

The vast majority of GSS questions are closed-ended items with predesignated sets of response alternatives. Some open-ended items are used, however, notably for measuring industry and occupation. These are coded according to well-established standard protocols. Supervisors direct and monitor the work of coders for these operations.

For the most part, NDPSS leaves recoding and scale construction to users, rather than constructing scales and indexes based on batteries of related items on topics such as intergroup relations or gender role attitudes. It makes occasional exceptions to this practice, supplying recodes of occupation into prestige and socioeconomic index scores (Nakao and Treas 1994) and a recode of religious denomination into three categories spanning a fundamentalist–liberal continuum (Smith 1990).

Overview of Content

The substantive content of the GSS consists of three major components: the replicating core, topical modules, and cross-national (ISSP) modules. The replicating core consists of questions included regularly. It is the principal resource for studies of social trends like those reported in this book and is discussed in more depth in the next section of this appendix.

Topical modules introduce innovative content and depth into the GSS, providing data on topics not previously investigated or more detailed coverage of topics already included in the replicating core. Most topical modules appear in only a single GSS, but some—notably one including measures of sexual behavior—have been included repeatedly. Items from topical modules are sometimes later added to the replicating core. Through 2010, over 80 topical modules on a wide range of subjects—including immigration, intergroup relations, medical care, political participation, religion, social networks, work, and many more—had appeared as part of the GSS.

Cross-national modules are developed collaboratively by the GSS with other members of ISSP and are administered as part of ongoing surveys such as the GSS in all member nations. These modules support the comparative study of important societal domains by examining differences across societies and across time.[12] The topics of ISSP modules rotate over time, now on roughly a 10-year cycle. Such modules mix replication and innovation, typically including about 60 questions—40 drawn from previous ISSP modules on the given topic and 20 new items. Modules are developed over a two-year period that begins when a topic is selected at an annual ISSP plenary session. A drafting group proposes a set of questions, which is then pretested and revised. All member nations subsequently have the opportunity to comment on the draft, and individual questions are eventually approved one by one at a later plenary session. ISSP questions are proposed and discussed in British English; upon adoption, modules are translated into the local language(s) of member countries.

Between 1985 and 2010, the GSS collected U.S. data for 26 separate ISSP modules on 10 distinct topics, including citizenship, the environment, leisure time and sports, national identity, the role of government, religion, social inequality, social networks and social support, women and work, and work orientations. To facilitate comparative analysis, all member nations collect data on a standard set of sociodemographic variables.

Within both the replicating core and topical modules, the GSS regularly conducts randomized experiments that assess effects of variations in question wording and other aspects of the survey process. A long-running (since 1984) experiment within the core involves the wording of items about national spending priorities (Rasinski 1989; Smith 2006b). Several topical modules— e.g., on attitudes toward poor families or the stigma associated with mental illness—have used factorial vignette designs (Rossi and Nock 1982; Pescoso- lido, Monahan, Link, Stueve, and Kikuzawa 1999).

Content of the Replicating Core

The GSS replicating core supports the study of societal trends by measuring a wide range of attitudes, behaviors, and individual characteristics regularly over time. It emphasizes literal replication of question wordings over time, on the oft-repeated reasoning that change is most readily measured if measures themselves remain intact (Smith 2005).[13] The trend studies reported in this book draw extensively on the replicating core.[14]

The primary components of the core measure sociodemographic and "background" characteristics of respondents and their households, and a broad range of social and political attitudes and behaviors. The core includes an unusually large set of sociodemographic items, including such standard measures as age, education, family income, family/marital status, race, and sex, as well as less common ones such as ethnic origins, political party af- filiation, and religious affiliation. It measures features of work/employment including employment status, annual earnings, occupation and industry, and supervisory responsibilities. Also included are proxy reports about the spouse (e.g., education, religious affiliation) and extensive information about the re- spondent's social origins, such as family type, parental education and occupa- tion, and religious background.

Most, though not all, core items measuring attitudes and behaviors are administered as part of a split-ballot structure, such that usually a random two-thirds of GSS respondents answer each item in any given year. This de- vice permits the survey to track a larger number of attitudes and behaviors within the available interview time and also to estimate associations between all pairs of core items. Major categories of attitudes and behaviors measured include abortion views, civil liberties, class identification/economic well- being, confidence in institutions, attitudes about crime and criminal justice, views about family and children, gender role attitudes, intergroup attitudes, political orientations, national spending priorities, religious attitudes and be- haviors, sexual attitudes, socializing, subjective well-being, verbal ability, vot- ing and voting preferences, and work orientations.

Apart from the series generated by items within the replicating core per se, GSS time series arise when cross-national (ISSP) modules repeat items. For example, the GSS measured several items in ISSP role of government mod- ules four times between 1985 and 2006.

Documentation and Resources

The *GSS Cumulative Codebook* (Smith, Marsden, and Hout 2011) provides the most comprehensive documentation for the GSS, including detail on its sampling design, the question wording for all items, details on fieldwork procedures and interviewer specifications, and extensive information on coding and recoding of items. The *Codebook* may be viewed at the official GSS project website (http://www.norc.org/GSS+Website/), among other locations.

The website offers numerous other resources of interest to GSS users. These include a guide to more than 275 GSS reports—almost all of which are available via the site—organized into topical, social change, international, methodological, and project report series. Also available is a searchable GSS project bibliography listing uses of the GSS known to NDPSS. The project website permits users to download data, including customized data sets, and allows them to conduct basic statistical analyses.

NDPSS seeks to make the GSS widely available and easy to use. It encourages others to prepare special-purpose GSS data sets for use in teaching and other applications. Hundreds of versions of GSS data exist. Apart from the official NORC project website, GSS data are available through—among many other sources—the Roper Center for Public Opinion Research (http://www.ropercenter.uconn.edu/), the Inter-University Consortium for Political and Social Research (http://www.icpsr.umich.edu/), and the Survey Data Archive at the University of California, Berkeley (http://sda.berkeley.edu/).

Notes

1. More than 80 scholars representing many fields from over 60 universities and research institutes have served on the Board of Overseers. Many authors of chapters in this book—including Alwin, Bobo, Campbell, Charles, Chaves, Firebaugh, Hout, Kalleberg, Krysan, Manza, Marsden, and Wright—have served on the board. Additionally, numerous researchers—from a dozen disciplines and more than 100 institutions—have participated in the design of GSS topical modules.

2. Due to funding shortages, no GSSs took place in 1979, 1981, or 1992. The 1994 shift to biennial administration was a cost-saving measure.

3. Because a new cross-sectional sample is drawn in each GSS year, the panel design preserves the GSS's basic repeating cross-sectional design. Data on repeated items from reinterviews two and four years after a respondent is sampled can also contribute to estimating trends in such items, if suitably weighted for attrition and adjusted for within-respondent correlation.

4. See http://www.census.gov/population/www/cen2000/briefs/phc-t7/tables/grpqtr01.pdf.

5. See http://www.census.gov/population/www/cen2000/briefs/phc-t20/tables/tab03.pdf.

6. Because of this change in the GSS target population, trend studies involving GSSs after 2004 must take measures to ensure that their working samples are comparable across years. This is not straightforward because bilingual respondents who elect to be interviewed in Spanish after 2004 could nonetheless complete the interview in English, and hence would have been within the pre-2006 target population. Smith (2007) assesses language-related differences in responses in the 2006 GSS and suggests that Spanish monolinguals (i.e., those Spanish-speaking respondents who would not have been in the pre-2006 target population) can be identified using respondent self-assessments of whether they could have completed an interview in English (mnemonic SPANSELF) and interviewer assessments of the same (mnemonic SPANINT).

7. See Harter, Eckman, English, and O'Muircheartaigh (2010) for an informative discussion of multistage area probability designs in general, and the sample design for recent GSSs in particular.

8. Smith (2006a) gives details about the implementation of the subsampling-of-nonrespondents design within the GSS.

9. Mnemonics for available GSS weighting variables include ADULTS (to adjust for undersampling of adults in larger households), PHASE (to distinguish first- and second-phase respondents in the two-stage sampling design), and OVERSAMP (to adjust for oversampling of blacks in 1982 and 1987). For the 2004 and later GSSs, the variable WTSS adjusts for both number of adults and phase, while the variable WTSSNR includes an additional adjustment for differential nonresponse across areas. WTSSALL adjusts for household size until 2002, and for both household size and phase thereafter. WTSS, WTSSNR, and WTSSALL do not compensate for the oversampling of black respondents in 1982 and 1987, so special weighting factors must be introduced in those years. One may adjust for the oversampling of black adults in 1982 and 1987 by excluding the oversampled cases (values 4, 5, and 7 on the variable SAMPLE) or weighting by OVERSAMP. Appendix A in Smith, Marsden, and Hout (2011) lists some other special situations that require other weights.

10. Since the introduction of the subsampling-of-nonrespondents design in 2004, response rates reported are weighted rates that give extra weight to responses by second-phase (post-subsampling) respondents.

11. Explicit "refused" codes are used for a few items, such as income and presidential vote.

12. As of 2011, the ISSP included some 48 member nations. European and North American countries are well represented among these, as are Australia, New Zealand, and—increasingly—East Asian countries. Fewer countries in Africa, South America, and South or Central Asia are currently members, though the number of members from such regions has grown.

13. Notwithstanding this vital principle, both the substantive content of the core and the wording of core items do occasionally change. Many new time series have been initiated—sometimes by incorporating items from topical modules—and many existing ones have been terminated. To properly assess the effect of changes in question wording on measured trends, the GSS ideal is to phase in wording changes by conducting split-sample experiments in which the old and new wordings are administered to random subsets of GSS respondents in a given year; this assesses effects of the altered wording to calibrate its impact on estimated trends.

14. Many core items were drawn from pre-1972 national surveys, permitting trend studies covering longer time frames than the period spanned by the GSS itself. For example, the tolerance items on which Davis focuses were drawn from 1950s surveys (Stouffer 1992), and many questions about race relations studied by Bobo and colleagues came from earlier surveys administered by NORC and other survey organizations.

References

Davis, James A., and Tom W. Smith. 1992. *The NORC General Social Survey: A User's Guide*. Newbury Park, CA: Sage.

Dixon, John, and Clyde Tucker. 2010. "Survey Nonresponse." In *Handbook of Survey Research*, 2nd ed., edited by Peter V. Marsden and James D. Wright, 593–630. Bingley, UK: Emerald.

Hansen, Morris, and William N. Hurwitz. 1946. "The Problem of Non-Response in Sample Surveys." *Journal of the American Statistical Association* 41:517–29.

Harter, Rachel, Stephanie Eckman, Ned English, and Colm O'Muircheartaigh. 2010. "Applied Sampling for Large-Scale Multi-Stage Area Probability Designs." In *Handbook of Survey Research*, 2nd ed., edited by Peter V. Marsden and James D. Wright, 169–97. Bingley, UK: Emerald.

Nakao, Keiko, and Judith Treas. 1994. "Updating Occupational Prestige and Socio-economic Scores: How the New Measures Measure Up." In *Sociological Methodology 1994*, edited by Peter V. Marsden, 1–72. Cambridge, MA: Blackwell.

Pescosolido, Bernice A., John Monahan, Bruce G. Link, Ann Stueve, and Saeko Kikuzawa. 1999. "The Public's View of the Competence, Dangerousness, and Need for Legal Coercion of Persons with Mental Health Problems." *American Journal of Public Health* 89:1339–45.

Rasinski, Kenneth A. 1989. "The Effect of Question Wording on Public Support for Government Spending." *Public Opinion Quarterly* 53:388–94.

Rossi, Peter H., and Steven L. Nock. 1982. *Measuring Social Judgments: The Factorial Survey Approach*. Beverly Hills, CA: Sage.

Shin, Hyon B., and Robert A. Kominski. 2010. "Language Use in the United States, 2007." American Community Survey Report ACS-12, U.S. Census Bureau. http://www.census.gov/hhes/socdemo/language/data/acs/ACS-12.pdf.

Smith, Tom W. 1990. "Classifying Protestant Denominations." *Review of Religious Research* 31:225–45.

———. 2005. "The Laws of Studying Societal Change." *Survey Research* 36 (2): 1–5. Also available as GSS Social Change Report 50, NORC, Chicago.

———. 2006a. "The Subsampling of Non-Respondents on the 2004 GSS." GSS Methodological Report 106, NORC, Chicago.

———. 2006b. "Wording Effects on the National Spending Priority Items across Time, 1984–2006." GSS Methodological Report 107, NORC, Chicago.

———. 2007. "An Evaluation of Spanish Questions on the 2006 General Social Survey." GSS Methodological Report 109, NORC, Chicago.

Smith, Tom W., Peter V. Marsden, and Michael Hout. 2011. *General Social Surveys: Cumulative Codebook: 1972–2010*. Chicago: NORC.

Stouffer, Samuel. 1992. *Communism, Conformity, and Civil Liberties: A Cross-Section of the Nation Speaks Its Mind*. New Brunswick, NJ: Transaction.

Index